Encyclopedia of School Crime and Violence

Encyclopedia of School Crime and Violence

A–N
VOLUME I

Laura L. Finley, Editor

Foreword by Evelyn Ang

 ABC-CLIO

Santa Barbara, California • Denver, Colorado • Oxford, England

Copyright 2011 by Laura L. Finley

All rights reserved. No part of this publication may be reproduced, stored in a retrieval system, or transmitted, in any form or by any means, electronic, mechanical, photocopying, recording, or otherwise, except for the inclusion of brief quotations in a review, without prior permission in writing from the publisher.

Library of Congress Cataloging-in-Publication Data

Encyclopedia of school crime and violence / Laura L. Finley, editor ; foreword by Evelyn Ang.
   v. ; cm.
Includes bibliographical references and index.
   ISBN 978–0–313–36238–5 (hard copy : alk. paper) — ISBN 978–0–313–36239–2 (ebook)
   1. Students–Crimes against–United States–Encyclopedias. 2. School violence–United States–Encyclopedias. I. Finley, Laura L.
HV6250.4.S78E53   2011
371.7′8097303—dc22   2011009812

ISBN: 978–0–313–36238–5
EISBN: 978–0–313–36239–2

15 14 13 12 11   1 2 3 4 5

This book is also available on the World Wide Web as an eBook.
Visit www.abc-clio.com for details.

ABC-CLIO, LLC
130 Cremona Drive, P.O. Box 1911
Santa Barbara, California 93116-1911

This book is printed on acid-free paper ∞

Manufactured in the United States of America

Contents

Alphabetical List of Entries, vii

Topical List of Entries, xiii

Foreword by Evelyn Ang, xvii

Preface, xxiii

Acknowledgments, xxv

Timeline of Significant Events Related to School Crime and Violence, xxvii

The Encyclopedia, 1

Discussion Questions, 547

Extension Activities Related to School and Campus Crime and Violence, 549

Appendix 1: Important Federal Legislation Related to School and Campus Crime and Violence, 551

Appendix 2: Primary Source Documents: Sample Legislation: K–12 Public Schools, 553

Appendix 3: Primary Source Documents: Sample Legislation: Colleges and Universities, 633

Appendix 4: U.S. Supreme Court Cases Related to School and Campus Crime and Violence, 643

Appendix 5: U.S. Supreme Court Decisions Relevant to School Crime and Violence, 647

Recommended Films About School and Campus Crime and Violence, 659

Recommended Resources, 665

Index, *677*

About the Editor and Contributors, 687

Alphabetical List of Entries

A

Abuse and Crime and Violence
ADD/ADHD
Adult Trials for Juveniles
Africa and School Crime and Violence
Alcohol and School Crime and Violence
American Civil Liberties Union (ACLU)
Amnesty International
Anger Management
Anonymous Tip Lines
Arts-Based Programs
Asia and School Crime and Violence
Athletes and Crime and Violence, College
Athletes and Crime and Violence, High School
Athletes and Violence Prevention
Auvinen, Pekka-Eric

B

Bath, Michigan, School Bombing
Baylor College Basketball Murder Case
Beslan School Hostage Crisis
Bias, Len
Big Brothers Big Sisters
Biological Theories
Bishop, Amy
Board of Ed. of Independent School District No. 92 of Pottawatomie County v. Earls
Bosse, Sebastian
Bowling for Columbine
Brazill, Nathaniel
Brewer, Michael
Bullycide
Bullying, College
Bullying, High School
Bullying Laws

C

Canada and School Crime and Violence
Carneal, Michael
Centers for Disease Control and Prevention (CDC)
Central Asia Institute (CAI)
Choice Theories
Clery Act
Columbine High School Massacre
Comprehensive Crime Control Act
Conflict Resolution/Peer Mediation
Conflict Theories
Control Theories

Coon, Asa
Corporal Punishment
Crime and Violence in Private Secondary Schools
Crime Stoppers
Cyber-offenses, College
Cyber-offenses, High School

D

Dann, Laurie
Dating Violence, College
Dating Violence, High School
Davis v. Monroe County Board of Education
Democratic Front for the Liberation of Palestine Attack on Ma'alot School
Dhein, Alaa Abu
Domestic Violence Prevention Enhancements and Leadership Through Alliances (DELTA) Program
Do Something
Dress Codes
Drug Abuse Resistance Education (D.A.R.E.)
Drug Offenses, College
Drug Offenses, High School
Drug Testing
Duke University Lacrosse Team Sexual Assault Case

E

Educational Programs and Training, College
Educational Programs and Training, High School
Elementary Schools and Crime and Violence
Elephant
Emergency Response Plans

European Union and School Crime and Violence
Expect Respect

F

Fear of School Crime and Violence
Federal Bureau of Investigation (FBI)
Fiction and School Crime and Violence
Flores, Robert
Free Speech

G

Gambling
Gang Resistance Education and Training (G.R.E.A.T.)
Gangs and School Crime and Violence
Gender and School Crime and Violence, College
Gender and School Crime and Violence, High School
Gender-Related Theories
Gill, Kimveer
Glen Ridge, New Jersey, Rape Incident
Goss v. Lopez
Gun Control Legislation

H

Hamilton, Thomas
Hamilton Fish Institute
Hate Crimes, College
Hazing, College
Hazing, High School
Hazing Laws
Honor Codes
Houston, Eric
Human Rights Education
Human Rights Watch

I

In loco parentis
Integrated Theories

J

Jeremy
Journals Devoted to School Crime and Violence

K

Kent State National Guard Shootings
King, Lawrence
Kinkel, Kip
Krestchmer, Tim

L

Labeling Theories
La Salle University Sex Scandal and Cover-up
Latin America and School Crime and Violence
Lépine, Marc
Lo, Wayne
Loukaitis, Barry
Lu, Gang

M

Manson, Marilyn
Mental Illness and School Crime and Violence
Mentoring
Metal Detectors
Middle East and School Crime and Violence
Middle Schools and Crime and Violence
Monitoring the Future Survey
Moral Panics and Campus Crime and Violence
Moral Panics and High School Crime and Violence
Movies and School Crime and Violence
Music and School Crime and Violence
Muslims and School Crime and Violence

N

National School Safety Center
National Threat Assessment Center
National Youth Survey
National Youth Violence Prevention Resource Center
Natural Born Killers
New Jersey v. T.L.O.
No Child Left Behind Act
Northern Illinois University Shooting
Northwestern High School Sex Scandal

O

Odighizuwa, Peter
Office of Juvenile Justice and Delinquency Prevention (OJJDP)
Ophelia Project
Owens, Dedrick

P

Parens patriae
Parents and School Crime and Violence
Peace and Justice Studies Association
Peace Education, College
Peace Education, High School
Pennington, Douglas
Police and Surveillance, College
Police and Surveillance, High School
Policies and Campus Violence Laws

Poulin, Robert
Prescription Drugs and School Crime and Violence
Prince, Phoebe
Professor-Perpetrated Crime and Violence
Property Crimes, College
Property Crimes, High School
Public Health Approach
Punitive Responses, College
Purdy, Patrick

R

Race and School Crime and Violence
Ramsey, Evan
Religion and High School Crime and Violence
Resolving Conflict Creatively Program (RCCP)
Restorative Justice
Roberts, Charles
Rural School Violence

S

Saari, Matti
Safe and Drug-Free Schools and Communities Act
Safe Schools/GLSEN
Safford Unified School District #1 v. Redding
Save the Children
School Crime and School Climate, College
School Crime and School Climate, High School
School Crime Victimization Survey
School-to-Prison Pipeline
Search and Seizure, High School
Security on Campus, Inc.
Sexual Assault Crimes, College
Sexual Assault Crimes, High School
Sexual Harassment
Sexual Orientation and School Crime and Violence, College
Sexual Orientation and School Crime and Violence, High School
Social Learning Theories
Social Networking
Social Structure Theories
Solomon, T. J.
South America and School Crime and Violence
Southern Poverty Law Center
Spencer, Brenda
Spur Posse
Steinhäuser, Robert
Stop Bullying Now
Suburban School Violence
Suicide, College
Suicide, High School
Systemic/Structural Violence, College
Systemic/Structural Violence, High School

T

Teacher-Perpetrated Crime and Violence, High School
Technological Responses, High School
Technology and Campus Crime and Violence
Teen Courts
Tinker v. Des Moines School District
Treacy, Wayne

U

United Nations Children's Fund (UNICEF)
U.S. Department of Education
U.S. Department of Justice

V

Vernonia School District 47J v. Acton
Victimless Offenses, College
Victimless Offenses, High School
Video Games
Violent Nonsexual Crimes, College
Violent Nonsexual Crimes, High School
Virginia Tech Massacre

W

Weise, Jeff
Whitman, Charles
Wimberley, Teah
Woodham, Luke
Wurst, Andrew

Y

Youth Activism
Youth Crime Watch of America

Z

Zero-Tolerance Laws

Topical List of Entries

Case Studies

Auvinen, Pekka-Eric
Bath, Michigan, School Bombing
Baylor College Basketball Murder Case
Beslan School Hostage Crisis
Bias, Len
Bishop, Amy
Bosse, Sebastian
Brazill, Nathaniel
Brewer, Michael
Carneal, Michael
Columbine High School Massacre
Coon, Asa
Dann, Laurie
Democratic Front for the Liberation of Palestine Attack on Ma'alot School
Dhein, Alaa Abu
Duke University Lacrosse Team Sexual Assault Case
Flores, Robert
Gill, Kimveer
Glen Ridge, New Jersey, Rape Incident
Hamilton, Thomas
Houston, Eric
Kent State National Guard Shootings
King, Lawrence
Kinkel, Kip
Kretschmer, Tim
La Salle University Sex Scandal and Cover-up
Lépine, Marc
Lo, Wayne
Loukaitis, Barry
Lu, Gang
Northern Illinois University Shooting
Northwestern High School Sex Scandal
Odighizuwa, Peter
Owens, Dedrick
Pennington, Douglas
Poulin, Robert
Prince, Phoebe
Purdy, Patrick
Ramsey, Evan
Roberts, Charles
Saari, Matti
Solomon, T. J.
Spencer, Brenda
Spur Posse
Steinhäuser, Robert
Treacy, Wayne
Virginia Tech Massacre
Weise, Jeff
Whitman, Charles
Wimberley, Teah

Woodham, Luke
Wurst, Andrew

Correlates

Abuse and Crime and Violence
ADD/ADHD
Alcohol and School Crime and Violence
Fear of School Crime and Violence
Free Speech
Mental Illness and School Crime and Violence
Muslims and School Crime and Violence
Parents and School Crime and Violence
Prescription Drugs and School Crime and Violence
School Crime and School Climate, College
School Crime and School Climate, High School
Social Networking
Technology and Campus Crime and Violence
Video Games

Court Cases

Board of Ed. of Independent School District No. 92 of Pottawatomie County v. Earls
Davis v. Monroe County Board of Education
Goss v. Lopez
New Jersey v. T.L.O.
Safford Unified School District #1 v. Redding
Tinker v. Des Moines School District
Vernonia School District 47J v. Acton

Global Comparison

Africa and School Crime and Violence
Asia and School Crime and Violence
Canada and School Crime and Violence
European Union and School Crime and Violence
Latin America and School Crime and Violence
Middle East and School Crime and Violence
South America and School Crime and Violence

Measuring

Monitoring the Future Survey
National Youth Survey
School Crime Victimization Survey

Media

Bowling for Columbine
Elephant
Fiction and School Crime and Violence
Jeremy
Journals Devoted to School Crime and Violence
Manson, Marilyn
Moral Panics and Campus Crime and Violence
Moral Panics and High School Crime and Violence
Movies and School Crime and Violence
Music and School Crime and Violence
Natural Born Killers

Organizations

American Civil Liberties Union (ACLU)
Amnesty International
Big Brothers Big Sisters
Centers for Disease Control and Prevention (CDC)
Central Asia Institute (CAI)
Crime Stoppers
Do Something
Federal Bureau of Investigation (FBI)
Hamilton Fish Institute
Human Rights Watch
National School Safety Center
National Threat Assessment Center
National Youth Violence Prevention Resource Center
Office of Juvenile Justice and Delinquency Prevention (OJJDP)
Ophelia Project
Peace and Justice Studies Association
Safe Schools/GLSEN
Save the Children
Security on Campus, Inc.
Southern Poverty Law Center
Stop Bullying Now
United Nations Children's Fund (UNICEF)
U.S. Department of Education
U.S. Department of Justice
Youth Crime Watch of America

Prevention

Athletes and Violence Prevention
Domestic Violence Prevention Enhancements and Leadership Through Alliances (DELTA) Program
Drug Abuse Resistance Education (D.A.R.E.)
Educational Programs and Training, College
Educational Programs and Training, High School
Expect Respect
Gang Resistance Education and Training (G.R.E.A.T.)
Honor Codes
Human Rights Education
Mentoring
Peace Education, College
Peace Education, High School

Responses

Adult Trials for Juveniles
Anger Management
Anonymous Tip Lines
Arts-Based Programs
Bullying Laws
Clery Act
Comprehensive Crime Control Act
Conflict Resolution/Peer Mediation
Corporal Punishment
Dress Codes
Drug Testing
Emergency Response Plans
Gun Control Legislation
Hazing Laws
In loco parentis
Metal Detectors
No Child Left Behind Act
Parens patriae
Police and Surveillance, College
Police and Surveillance, High School
Policies and Campus Violence Laws
Public Health Approach
Punitive Responses, College
Resolving Conflict Creatively Program (RCCP)

Restorative Justice
Safe and Drug-Free Schools and Communities Act
School-to-Prison Pipeline
Search and Seizure, High School
Technological Responses, High School
Technology and Campus Crime and Violence
Teen Courts
Youth Activism
Zero-Tolerance Laws

Theory

Biological Theories
Choice Theories
Conflict Theories
Control Theories
Gender-Related Theories
Integrated Theories
Labeling Theories
Social Learning Theories
Social Structure Theories

Types of Crime/Violence

Athletes and Crime and Violence, College
Athletes and Crime and Violence, High School
Bullycide
Bullying, College
Bullying, High School
Crime and Violence in Private Secondary Schools
Cyber-offenses, College
Cyber-offenses, High School
Dating Violence, College
Dating Violence, High School
Drug Offenses, College
Drug Offenses, High School
Elementary Schools and Crime and Violence
Gambling
Gangs and School Crime and Violence
Gender and School Crime and Violence, College
Gender and School Crime and Violence, High School
Hate Crimes, College
Hazing, College
Hazing, High School
Middle Schools and Crime and Violence
Professor-Perpetrated Crime and Violence
Property Crimes, College
Property Crimes, High School
Race and School Crime and Violence
Religion and High School Crime and Violence
Rural School Violence
Sexual Assault Crimes, College
Sexual Assault Crimes, High School
Sexual Harassment
Sexual Orientation and School Crime and Violence, College
Sexual Orientation and School Crime and Violence, High School
Suburban School Violence
Suicide, College
Suicide, High School
Systemic/Structural Violence, College
Systemic/Structural Violence, High School
Teacher-Perpetrated Crime and Violence, High School
Victimless Offenses, College
Victimless Offenses, High School
Violent Nonsexual Crimes, College
Violent Nonsexual Crimes, High School

Foreword

After speaking at a teachers' convention a few years ago, I was approached by a man and his son. I guessed the boy was about 12. I had just finished a talk called "Dispute Resolution in Communities and Schools." As a self-proclaimed "mediator," I was director of a community mediation program seeking ways to partner with schools.

"You're a *mediator*?" I heard in the boy's voice a mixture of amazement and amusement. His eyes were wide, "I never *even saw* a grown-up mediator before!" Was he questioning my existence, or his own experience? Then he asserted, "Mediation is for little kids." My immediate response was to say, "Well, no, mediation is for everybody." His father shushed him apologetically, a sheepish look on his face. Like a glimpse of the sun on a cloudy day, the moment and the boy were gone. I regret to this day my disagreeing with him. Perhaps he did not believe me at all, but he did give perhaps a fleeting thought to the notion that adults might mediate their disputes.

Slow as I am, it was almost three weeks before I understood the boy's message. I became aware that his perspective was true: In his world, mediation *was* for "little kids." I supposed that perhaps his school had peer mediation in first or second grade in a simplified form such as the "peace bridge," a script of questions for disputing children. His exposure to age-appropriate conflict resolution may have continued in middle school. Peer mediators selected from their class or grade level receive conflict management training, and as anointed or appointed, go forth to mediate disputes between students. However, this boy's exposure to models in the adult world probably did not include collaboration, inquisitive dialogue, active listening, or respectful exchange of divergent views, values, opinions, or beliefs. As he said, he'd never *even seen* an adult mediator. As much as I wanted to deny it, I needed to listen to what he had said. I thought he was misinformed. I wanted to correct him, to set him on the right path. If I done myself what we teach others to do, I would have truly listened. I would have had the gift of his lesson sooner.

The structured investigation of the phenomenon of school violence seemed to take on heightened urgency following the shooting at Columbine High School. The search for the causes and cures for violence has focused on schools and young people ever since. I wonder why youth violence seems to frighten us so: Is it because we want desperately to believe in the innocence of youth? Or is there something inherently risky and hence scary about the energy and the explosive emotion of adolescence? It is timely to question whether our actions are truly preventive or merely driven by fear. To paraphrase Harriet Lerner, "avoiding the things we fear programs the brain to see the fear as real."

Whenever I visit a school in my city, I am struck by the visual presentation of its facility—heavy black doors with no windows, bars on those windows that may remain, a buzzer at the door, metal detectors at the entry, uniformed security personnel. Perhaps it belabors the obvious to say that the need to examine school violence cannot be neatly compartmentalized separately from the examination of violence in the larger society. This assertion usually leads to debate about media violence, but I believe we generally miss an essential question. Any robust inquiry into how society's violence is linked to school violence must include a critical look at society's messages about *whose* violence is allowed (and whose is not). The bully in the classroom is not always another student. The bully in the classroom may sometimes be the teacher, or a parent, or the principal. Right by force is enacted daily by authority figures. The message is that *some* violence is allowed and yet, as a group, young people cannot engage in this behavior—they must be controlled. Any 12-year-old would naturally be impatient to "grow up" so that he or she could also enter the realm of those who are privileged to act with force in the name of authority—those whose violence is allowed. I leave for others to explain the violent systemic consequences of the No Child Left Behind (NCLB) legislation, or the violence of poverty, racism, or classism. It is enough to say that the inquiry, analysis, and design of interventions cannot be narrowly focused on school and youth violence without consideration of the society in which they are immersed.

An important paradigm shift in this regard began with the work of Deborah Prothrow-Stith in 1991. In her book *Deadly Consequences*, she reframed violence from a matter for criminal law to a public health issue. This shift continues to be supported by evidence that a punitive, punishment-based strategy *alone* does not prevent, and indeed may aggravate, serious violence. A public health framework applies a medical approach, and in this approach violence is viewed as a disease and interventions can be designed to address different levels of prevention.

Using the public health paradigm's framework, violence prevention may be approached with a three-part strategy. For example, a primary prevention strategy might address needs of the general population with curricula for social and emotional intelligence education—that is, development of empathy, forgiveness, and resiliency. Further, a secondary prevention strategy might address the needs of vulnerable individuals, with accommodations being made for those with special needs or those who require grief counseling. Lastly, a tertiary prevention strategy might address the needs of victims and actors of violence with forms of restorative justice, for example. Certainly, the "public health lens" view of violence as disease represents a significant step forward from the strictly punitive approach embodied in violence as crime.

I believe that we continue to mix the paradigms of crime and disease, and that this practice has unintended results. We must be very careful in applying this metaphor by being precise about diagnosing a disease—a disease of *what* exactly? Even if we frame violence as a disease of the community, the temptation is to say that the individual who commits an act of violence is the disease and, therefore, must be excised from society. More incarceration is an answer, but one that produces only short-term results. More saliently, we must grapple with the notion that most of those whom we imprison will return to society eventually. This partial move to a health paradigm returns us to the strategies that delivered us incomplete interventions in the first place.

It is time to consider information from other paradigms as a means to address school crime and violence. African thinkers, including Malidoma and Archbishop Tutu, identify a "lack of *ubuntu*" as a problem of Western society. This indicates a more proper view of violence as a disease of the body of the community; it posits that violence is a sign of improper functioning of the community. Violence is a symptom, not the disease, and every deliberate harmful act is a cry for help.

Human beings are social creatures, with a fundamental need to belong to a community. Such needs are expressed as culture, fellowship, nurturing, learning, belonging, common beliefs, and mutuality. They inform and form us. It is no mistake that punishment often involves separation from loved ones; solitary confinement, isolation from all others, is one of the most severe punishments. Isolation causes stress and pain because it implies that you are not fit to belong with your community: moreover, it embodies rejection.

Writing separately, Kenneth V. Hardy and John Gilligan identified factors that increase individual propensity to do violence. These issues all seem to revolve around losses associated with identity and community. Hardy's aggravating factors are the devaluation of individual, disruption or erosion of community, dehumanization of loss, and suppression leading to rage. Cultural messages about strength and weakness can be misinterpreted, especially in unguided minds. In general, especially in Euro-American Western cultures, being "tough" is equated with being "strong." To show weakness or vulnerability is so abhorrent that it evokes emotions of shame and fear. These serious threats to identity are resisted, such shame hidden by more "toughness."

The risk is that by not recognizing our human need for community, connection, and relationships, well-intentioned interventions will create more problems than they solve. To implement secondary and tertiary interventions, those who are "at risk" or "in need" must first be identified for suitable treatments. The diagnosis leads to the categorization of human beings that, while well intentioned, may have unintended and perhaps detrimental consequences. The labels become incorporated into an individual's Identity and often become self-fulfilling. The unavoidable message is that there is something "different" about you, something "wrong," "bad," "needs fixing." Such messages are damaging and hurtful, especially when they are delivered during the specific stages in a human being's development involving the formation of identity and true self-esteem.

To take the next step, I suggest that the next paradigm shift needs to move from a medical model of public health to a wellness paradigm. It is not enough to prevent disease (prevent violence); our society should be focused on creating health (support human flourishing). We can begin by asking different questions.

Whether framed as the long-term consequences of unacknowledged loss or the death or denial of self through shame, some individuals who suffer traumatic losses, grief, extreme stress, hardships, or poverty never act out violently. The trajectory to violence is not inevitable. Research has identified factors that can act as counter-measures to the proclivity toward violence. Studies examining factors that build resiliency indicate that recovery from loss and psychological healing requires outside assistance, however. Thus the presence of mentoring, strong social support, and prosocial behaviors are essential to change the current trend. Shame is overcome with true self-esteem, which has two aspects: competency and deservedness. True self-esteem is not supported by having things given or done for you—the help that cripples is not really help. A child who makes a mistake needs consistent correction, support, and encouragement, not punishment. Growing up is a complicated and difficult business, requiring structure and discipline. We can begin by overcoming our fears of "going soft" and ignoring complaints that this is "warm and fuzzy." Such demurrals are unwarranted. Offering a genuinely helping hand is actually much harder than sending children to the principal's office, or handcuffing them, or suspending them, or expelling them.

Lately the word "accountability" has come into vogue. I am intrigued by the number of contexts and meanings this word seems to bring to the fore. In it, I hear mixed conceptions about responsibility. If we use "accountability" in its past-oriented view, responsibility is assigned in form of blame with the goal to punish those whom we find at fault. This practice alone does not support the creation of healthy people (supporting human flourishing). If, however, we use "accountability" with a future orientation, responsibility lies with those who may have the power to effect change. In fact, we all have the power to change—ourselves.

Together we may contribute to healing from what was handed to us from the past. With this form of accountability, true progress may be made.

My lesson from the boy at the conference was that to rest social change solely on the backs of children is a recipe for failure. If we would ask a fourth grader to resist striking a classmate over a misspoken word or broken toy, we must be able to demonstrate the same self-discipline in our own words and deeds. It is simply inconsistent (and hence hypocritical) to insist that children find peaceful means to seek redress of their harms, when we adults come to "town hall meetings" in polarized camps and scream at one another. Especially where a child sees adult models in his or her school, community, or home life employing only coercive authority, the conclusion is accurate: Peaceful conflict resolution is in truth for "little kids." The children who learn this lesson will await the day when they can also enforce their wants and needs on others by dint of power. If we will permit some people in some contexts to enact violence on other human beings, the taint of hypocrisy will forever color our messages lecturing nonviolence.

We learn what we live. The difference is that adults presumably know better. It is time we all DO better.

Evelyn Ang

Preface

When I was teaching at a university in Colorado, a student once told me, "You know, Columbine used to be known as the state flower. But now ... " Her observation is instructive. Since the early 1990s, and in particular after the massacre at Columbine High School in 1999, school violence has received a great deal of attention—from media, from lawmakers, from parents, and from school districts. The series of high-profile shootings in schools—perhaps starting when 14-year-old Barry Loukaitis killed a teacher and two students in Moses Lake, Washington in 1996—was indeed troubling. Yet some critics were concerned that this clamor represented a moral panic about school violence. They noted that even during the 1990s, schools remained among the safest places for young people. In fact, some people have complained that the way schools have responded to the threat of school violence is actually more dangerous than the threat posed by students. Additionally, critics have pointed out that, until the shooting at Virginia Tech in 2007, very little attention was focused on college campuses, yet students were at risk here as well.

It is true that certain types of crime and violence in and around school and university campuses occur with regularity. But, instead of the extreme cases involving an armed gunman (and the rare female shooter), the greatest risk actually stems from the more mundane property crime. Additionally, dating violence, race-related offenses, and other forms of harassment are commonplace in educational institutions. Technology has worsened the situation, with rates of cyber-offenses strikingly high, although accurate statistics on this phenomenon are difficult to find. Further, when drug and alcohol use and abuse are included in the picture, we see that not only is crime and violence in and around schools an issue of concern, but one that most people have misunderstood. Many times, stereotypes and misconceptions prevent us from recognizing, and thus appropriately responding to, other forms of crime and violence.

If school crime and violence is a major issue, what is the cause? Are out-of-control kids to blame? The media? Poor parenting? Weak gun control laws?

A drug culture? Or something else entirely? This book is intended to help readers develop an informed opinion about the issue. It provides information about the scope and extent of crime and violence on school and university campuses, including incidents involving shootings as well as property crimes, hate crimes, cyber-offenses, sexual crimes, and more.

Key points made in this book include the following:

- School crime and violence is difficult to measure (readers will learn why).
- Violence and crime occur at all levels of schooling, from kindergarten through college.
- There is no specific "profile" of a perpetrator—even educators are sometimes violent against students.
- Perpetrators have different motives for different types of offenses, and criminological theory can help us understand these rationales.
- Responses to school crime and violence vary, and many have rarely been evaluated.
- There are a great deal of great resources available for youth, parents, educators, and the general reader who wants to know more, get involved, or get help.

The entries in this book are organized alphabetically. A list of entries by topic is included for ease of use as well. Further, readers will find a timeline of significant events related to school and campus crime and violence at the beginning of the book. In addition to the thorough and current entries authored by experts in the field, the book includes a list of recommended books, journals, and websites for further investigation. Finally, discussion questions and activity ideas for teachers are included so that students can extend their understanding of school and campus crime and violence beyond what they read here.

Having taught high school through the Columbine era, and now as a college professor and a community trainer and peace activist, it is my hope that this book will be a useful reference on an essential topic. Even more, I hope that we are able to apply our greater understanding of school and campus crime and violence to better respond to incidents when they occur and to craft more effective prevention programs.

Acknowledgments

In undertaking a multivolume like this, it is essential to surround yourself with helpful people! To that end, my sincere gratitude goes out to all the contributors who worked hard to ensure the entries in this book are informative and up-to-date. Thanks also to those who made suggestions for topics to be included and gave ideas for resources, films, teaching ideas and discussion questions. Each contributor offers a unique perspective based on his or her background, life experience, and world view, which makes this volume exemplary (in my opinion). The contributors to this book represent a variety of scholarly fields and are involved in a number of organizations and activities that lend them expertise about school crime and violence. In particular, I am proud that several of my current and former Barry University and Florida Atlantic University students contributed to this volume.

I would also like to thank Sandy Towers of ABC-CLIO, who worked with me on this project from the start. Originally one book, Sandy helped ensure a contract for an expanded volume, gave me wonderful ideas for the direction of the book, and checked in regularly enough to keep me on task. This is my second project with Sandy and I have found her to be a supportive and thorough editor.

I have edited the book as well as possible. At this point, any errors are mine.

Dedication

As in all things I do, I dedicate this book to my family. My husband, Peter, and my daughter, Anya, who ended up on several "daddy-daughter dates" so that mom had time to work. Anya, I know you believe in peace and will help ensure that this book quickly becomes useful only as a matter of history!

I would also like to dedicate this book to all my students at Barry University, who get to hear pieces of my work all the time (like it or not) and who, unbeknownst to them, inspired several of the entries that are included.

I also dedicate this book to all the amazing people working in schools, organizations, or simply raising children in peaceful ways. In particular, I dedicate this book to my twin sister, Sarah, who is the best teacher I know. She brings humor and humanity to the classroom and is a model for all.

Finally, I hope that this book can in some small way help better the situation for young people in schools and colleges and for the tireless educators working in them. I truly believe that informed discourse about critical topics like school and campus crime and violence can help us move forward with exciting, innovative, and effective policies and practices that make peace, not violence, the norm. Further, I am also committed to helping outside of academia. I am dedicating half of all royalties from this book to No More Tears, a non-profit that provides assistance to victims of domestic and dating violence and their children. As of this writing, No More Tears has rescue forty women and their children, providing them safe housing, food and clothing, and above all, support. It is my pleasure to be able to help this organization, and my good friend Somy Ali, in whatever ways I can.

Timeline of Significant Events Related to School Crime and Violence

May 18, 1927	School board member Andrew Kehoe, 55, kills his wife and sets fire to his farm buildings. Bombs he has planted over the course of several months explode at Bath Consolidated School, killing 45 and injuring 58.
August 1, 1966	Charles Whitman, 25, shoots and kills 14 and wounds 32 others, mostly from an observation tower at the University of Texas at Austin.
February 8, 1968	Policemen kill three and wound 27 unarmed South Carolina State University students who are protesting the segregation of a local bowling alley.
May 4, 1970	Members of the Ohio National Guard fire 67 rounds in just 13 seconds, killing four unarmed Kent State University students who are protesting the expansion of the Vietnam War into Cambodia.
May 14–15, 1970	Police shoot and kill two Jackson State College students who are protesting the Vietnam War. Twelve others are wounded.
May 15, 1974	Three members of the Democratic Front for the Liberation of Palestine shoot and kill 22 Israeli high school students in Ma'alot, Israel.
December 30, 1974	Anthony Barbaro, 18, sets off homemade bombs and firearms at school in Olean, New York. He fires at janitors and responding fire fighters, then commits suicide while awaiting trial for the crime.

May 28, 1975	Michael Slobodian, 16, kills a classmate and an English teacher and wounds 13 others at Brampton Centennial Secondary School in Ontario, Canada. Slobodian commits suicide in a school bathroom.
October 21, 1975	Robert Poulin, 18, shoots and kills one and wounds five others, then commits suicide at St. Pius X High School in Ottawa, Canada.
July 12, 1976	Custodian Edward Charles Allaway, 37, kills two and wounds seven in the library basement at California State University–Fullerton. He is committed to the California state mental hospital system.
May 19, 1978	Honors student John Christian, 13, shoots and kills his teacher in Austin, Texas.
October 15, 1978	In Lanett, Alabama, Robin Robinson, 13, is paddled by school administrators after a disagreement with another student. He returns to the school and shoots the principal.
January 29, 1979	Brenda Spencer, 16, shoots and kills the principal and a janitor, and wounds nine students and adults in San Carlos, California. She uses a sniper rifle she had received for Christmas.
March 19, 1982	Patrick Lazotte kills one and wounds two at Valley High School in Las Vegas, Nevada. Lazotte has been bullied for 12 years.
January 20, 1983	David F. Lawler, a freshman, kills one student when he opens fire in a study hall classroom at Parkway South Junior High School in St. Louis, Missouri. Lawler commits suicide.
January 21, 1985	James Alan Kearby, 14, kills his principal and three students who were bullying him at his junior high school in Goddard, Kansas.
March 2, 1987	Twelve-year-old Nathan Ferris kills the boy who has picked on him and then kills himself at a Missouri school.
February 11, 1988	Jason Harless and Jason McCoy use stolen guns to kill Principal Richard Allen and wound two others at Pinellas Park High School in Pinellas Park, Florida.

May 20, 1988	Laurie Dann, 30, attempts to poison family and friends and then kills one boy and wounds five other students at an elementary school in Winnetka, Illinois. She then takes a family hostage and shoots another man before killing herself.
September 30, 1988	James William Wilson, Jr., 19, shoots and kills one student and wounds 14 elementary school students and a teacher with a .22-caliber pistol in Greenwood, South Carolina.
December 16, 1988	Nicholas Elliott, 16, kills one teacher and wounds another in Virginia Beach, Virginia.
December 6, 1989	Marc Lépine, 25, orders all the men to leave a classroom at the University of Montreal School of Engineering and then kills nine women. Lépine kills five more people outside the classroom, before then killing himself.
September 27, 1990	Curtis Collins shoots one student at El Dorado High School in Las Vegas, Nevada.
November 1, 1991	Gang Lu, 28, shoots and kills four faculty members and one student at the University of Iowa. Another student is wounded before Lu commits suicide.
May 1, 1992	Eric Houston, 20, shoots and kills four students and wounds 10 at his former high school in Olivehurst, California.
August 24, 1992	Dr. Valery I. Frabricant kills four colleagues and wounds a staff member at Concordia University in Montreal, Quebec.
November 20, 1992	Joseph White, 15, shoots another student at Tilden High School in Chicago, Illinois. The shooting is gang related.
December 14, 1992	Wayne Lo, 18, kills one student and one professor and wounds four others at Simon's Rock College of Bard in Massachusetts before surrendering to the police.
January 18, 1993	Gary Scott Pennington, 19, holds a teacher and custodian hostage at his high school in Grayson, Kentucky.
February 22, 1993	Robert Heard, 15, shoots a student who had transferred to Reseda High School in California to flee gang violence.

March 18, 1993	Edward Gillom, 15, kills one student and wounds another at Harlem High School in Harlem, Georgia. He claims to have been bullied.
March 25, 1993	Lawanda Jackson, 19, shoots and kills her ex-boyfriend at Sumner High School in St. Louis, Missouri.
March 26, 1993	Five students get into a fight over the previous night's track meet at Lamar High School in Bryan, Texas. One student is stabbed to death.
April 12, 1993	Karter Reed, 16, stabs and kills one student, whom he thought was someone else, at Dartmouth High School in Dartmouth, Massachusetts.
April 14, 1993	Max Martinez, 17, kills one student who had insulted his girlfriend at Nimitz High School in Irving, Texas.
May 15, 1993	Eric Schmitt, 42, takes 21 students and their teacher hostage at Commandant Charcto Nursery School in Neuilly-sur-Seine, France.
December 1, 1993	Leonard McDowell, 21, shoots and kills an associate principal who had suspended him from school at Wauwatosa West High School in Milwaukee, Wisconsin. McDowell had entered the building in violation of a restraining order sought by a teacher with whom he was obsessed.
April 4, 1994	Flemming Nielsen, 35, shoots and kills two and wounds two others at Aarhus University in Denmark.
April 12, 1994	James Osmanson, 10, shoots and kills a classmate on the playground at Margaret Leary Elementary School in Butte, Montana. Osmanson was aiming at another boy who had been bullying him for years.
May 26, 1994	Clay Shrout, 17, kills his parents and two younger sisters and then takes a class hostage at his high school. Assistant Principal Steve Sorrell convinces Shrout to give up his gun before anyone else is hurt.
November 7, 1994	Keith Ledeger, 37, a former student, kills a custodian and wounds three others at Wickliffe Middle School in Wickliffe, Ohio.

October 12, 1995	Suspended student Toby Sincino, 16, kills three people with a .32-caliber revolver in Blackville, South Carolina.
November 15, 1995	Jamie Rouse, 17, kills a teacher and student and wounds another teacher at Richland High School in Lynnville, Tennessee.
February 2, 1996	In Moses Lake, Washington, Barry Loukaitis, 14, opens fire on a junior high school algebra class, killing two students and one teacher and wounding another student.
March 13, 1996	Thomas Hamilton kills 16 children and one teacher, and wounds 10 others, at Dunblane Primary School in Dunblane, Scotland.
March 25, 1996	Anthony Gene Rutherford, 18; Jonathon Dean Moore, 15; and Joseph Stanley Burris, 15, kill a student they believe planned to tell about their plot to attack the school in Patterson, Missouri.
August 15, 1996	Frederick Martin Davidson, a 36-year-old graduate student, shoots and kills three professors at San Diego State University.
September 17, 1996	Jillian Robbins, 19, kills one student and wounds another at Pennsylvania State University.
February 19, 1997	Evan Ramsey, 16, kills one student and the school principal, and wounds two others, with a shotgun he uses in the high school commons room in Bethel, Alaska.
March 30, 1997	Mohammad Ahman al-Nazari, 48, shoots and kills six and wounds 12 with an illegally obtained assault rifle at Tala'I Private School in Sanaa, Yemen.
October 1, 1997	Luke Woodham, 16, kills his own mother, then shoots two students and wounds seven at his high school in Pearl, Mississippi.
December 1, 1997	Michael Carneal, 14, kills three students and wounds five who were involved in a prayer circle at his high school in West Paducah, Kentucky.
December 15, 1997	Joseph "Colt" Todd, 14, shoots two students whom he said humiliated him in Stamps, Arkansas.

March 9, 1998	Jeffrey Lance Pennick II, 18, kills one student and wounds two at Central Avenue Elementary School in Summit, Washington.
March 24, 1998	Mitchell Johnson, 13, and Andrew Golden, 11, kill one teacher and four students, and wound 10 others, when they shoot at their school from the nearby woods in Jonesboro, Arkansas.
April 24, 1998	Andrew Wurst, 14, kills one teacher and wounds one teacher and two students at a school dance for Parker Middle School in Edinboro, Pennsylvania.
May 21, 1998	Kip Kinkel, 15, kills both his parents, then kills two students and wounds 23 others when he opens fire on his high school cafeteria in Springfield, Oregon.
June 15, 1998	Quinshawn Booker, 14, shoots one teacher and wounds a guidance counselor in the hallway of his high school in Richmond, Virginia.
April 20, 1999	Eric Harris, 18, and Dylan Klebold, 17, shoot and kill 14 students, one teacher, and themselves at Columbine High School in Littleton, Colorado. Twenty-three students and teachers are wounded in the attack.
April 28, 1999	Todd Cameron Smith, 14, shoots and kills one student and wounds another in what is believed to be a Columbine "copycat" attack at W. R. Myers High School in Taber, Alberta, Canada.
May 20, 1999	Thomas "T.J." Solomon, 15, wounds six students with a .22-caliber rifle at his high school in Conyers, Georgia.
November 19, 1999	Victor Cordova, 12, kills one student with a .22-caliber handgun in the lobby of his school in Deming, New Mexico.
December 6, 1999	Seth Trickey, 13, wounds four students when he shoots them with a 9-mm semi-automatic gun at his middle school in Fort Gibson, Oklahoma.
February 29, 2000	Dedrick Owens, 6, finds a loaded gun at his uncle's house and brings it to school, shooting 6-year-old Kayla Rolland at Buell Elementary School in Flint, Michigan.

March 16, 2000	Nathaniel Brazill, 13, kills his teacher with a .25-caliber semi-automatic pistol on the last day of classes in Lake Worth, Florida.
March 5, 2001	Charles Andrew "Andy" Williams, 15, kills two students in the high school bathroom in Santee, California.
March 7, 2001	Elizabeth Catherine Bush, 14, shoots and wounds a female student in the high school cafeteria in Williamsport, Pennsylvania.
March 22, 2001	Jason Hoffman, 18, kills four students and two teachers at his high school in El Cajon, California.
May 7, 2001	Jason Pritchard, 33, cuts and stabs four elementary school students on their playground in Anchorage, Alaska.
June 8, 2001	Mamoru Takuma fatally stabs eight and injures 13 at Ikeda Elementary School in Osaka, Japan.
November 13, 2011	Chris Buschbacher, 17, takes two students and one teacher from his high school hostage in Caro, Michigan. He releases all of them, and then commits suicide.
December 5, 2001	Corey Ramos, 17, stabs and kills his principal in Springfield, Massachusetts.
January 16, 2002	Peter Odighizuwa, 43, a former student, shoots and kills three and wounds three others at Appalachian School of Law in Grundy, Virginia.
March 2, 2002	Mike Placencia, 14, stabs a student who made a racist remark in Cashmere, Washington.
April 26, 2002	Robert Steinhauser, 19, kills 13 teachers, two students, and one police officer at Johann Gutenberg Secondary School in Erfurt, Germany. Steinhauser commits suicide.
April 29, 2002	Dragoslav Petkovic, 17, shoots and kills a teacher and wounds another before he commits suicide in Vlasenica, Bosnia-Herzegovina.
October 28, 2002	Robert Flores, Jr., 41, kills three female nursing professors and then himself at the University of Arizona.
April 14, 2003	Steven Williams and James Tate, kill one student at John McDonogh High School in New Orleans, Louisiana.

April 24, 2003	James Sheets, 14, shoots and kills his middle school principal and then himself in Red Lion, Pennsylvania.
May 9, 2003	Biswanath Halder, a former student, kills one student and wounds a professor and a student at Case Western Reserve University in Cleveland, Ohio.
September 24, 2003	Jason McLaughlin, 15, shoots and kills two students at Rocori High School in Cold Spring, Minnesota.
September 1, 2004	A group of Muslim pro-Chechen rebels take more than 1,200 schoolchildren and adults hostage in Beslan, North Ossetia-Alania. After a three-day standoff, Russian security forces storm the building. A series of explosions, followed by a fire and gunfire exchanges, results in the death of at least 334 hostages, including 186 children.
March 21, 2005	Jeff Weise, 16, kills his grandfather and grandfather's girlfriend before shooting and killing five students, a teacher, a security guard, and then himself at his high school on Red Lake Indian Reservation in Minnesota.
November 8, 2005	Kenny Bartley, 15, kills Assistant Principal Ken Bruce and wounds two other administrators at his high school in Jacksboro, Tennessee.
August 24, 2006	Christopher Williams, 27, shoots and kills his ex-girlfriend's mother. He then attempts to find his ex-girlfriend at the school where she is a teacher. When he cannot locate her, Williams kills one teacher and wounds another. He attempts suicide but is captured instead.
September 13, 2006	Kimveer Gill, 25, shoots 20 people at Dawson College in Montreal, Canada. One victim dies on the spot. Gill commits suicide after being shot in the arm by a police officer.
September 27, 2006	Duane Morrison, 53, takes six girls hostage for hours, molesting them before shooting and killing one girl and then himself, at Platte Canyon High School in Bailey, Colorado.
September 29, 2006	Eric Hainstock, 15, shoots and kills his principal in Cazenovia, Wisconsin.

October 2, 2006	Charles Roberts, 32, ties up and then kills five girls at an Amish school in Nickel Mines, Pennsylvania. Five others were injured before Roberts kills himself.
November 20, 2006	Sebastian Bosse, 18, shoots five people at his former high school in Emsdetten, Germany. When they enter the school, police commandos find Bosse dead.
April 16, 2007	Seung-Hui Cho, a senior, shoots and kills 32 and wounds many others at Virginia Tech College in Blacksburg, Virginia.
September 21, 2007	Loyer Braden, 18, shoots and kills two fellow Delaware State University students.
October 10, 2007	Asa Coon, 14, shoots and kills two students and two teachers, and then commits suicide, at SuccessTech alternative high school in Cleveland, Ohio.
November 7, 2007	Pekka-Eric Auvinen, 18, shoots and kills eight people and then himself at a high school in Tuusula, Finland.
February 8, 2008	Latina Williams, 23, shoots and kills two students, and then commits suicide, at Louisiana Tech College in Baton Rouge, Louisiana.
February 12, 2008	Brandon McInerney, 14, shoots and kills Lawrence King because he was gay at E. O. Green School in Oxnard, California.
February 14, 2008	Steven Kazmierczak, 27, a former student, shoots and kills six people and wounds 18 on the campus of Northern Illinois University.
August 21, 2008	Jamar Siler, 15, shoots and kills a fellow student at Central High School in Knoxville, Tennessee.
September 23, 2008	Matti Juhani Saari, 22, shoots and kills 10 people at the vocational college he attends in Kauhajoki, Finland.
October 26, 2008	Four men (Kawin Brockton, 19; Kelsey Perry, 19; Mario Tony, 20; and Brandon Wade, 20) shoot and kill two University of Central Arkansas students and wound a visitor.

November 13, 2008	Teah Wemberly, 15, shoots and kills friend Amanda Collette at Dillard High School in Ft. Lauderdale, Florida.
March 6, 2008	Alaa Abu Dhein, 26, shoots and kills eight students and wounds 11 at Mercaz Herav Yeshiva, a religious school in Jerusalem, Israel.
March 11, 2009	Tim Kretschmer, 17, a former student, shoots and kills 15 at Albertville Secondary School in Winnenden, Germany.
April 30, 2009	Farda Gadyrov, 29, kills 12 and wounds 13 before killing himself at Azerbaijan State Oil Academy in Azerbaijan.
September 15, 2009	Andy Rodriquez, 17, stabs a classmate to death in Coral Gables, Florida.
September 23, 2009	A 16-year-old student stabs a Special Education teacher in Tyler, Texas. The teacher later dies from the attack. The name of the student was not released due to privacy laws pertaining to special needs students.
October 16, 2009	Trevor Varinecz, 16, is shot and killed by a school resource officer after allegedly stabbing the officer in an altercation in Conway, South Carolina.
January 14, 2010	Phoebe Prince commits suicide after being bullied at South Hadley High School in Hadley, Massachusetts.
February 12, 2010	Biology Professor Amy Bishop kills three faculty members and wounds three employees at the University of Alabama at Huntsville.
February 23, 2010	Bruco Strongeagle Eastwood, 32, allegedly shoots at Middle School students as school lets out in Littleton, Colorado. Two eighth-grade students are injured.
March 9, 2010	Nathaniel Brown, 51, a custodian who had been told he was being fired, kills one coworker and wounds another at Ohio State University.
March 17, 2010	Wayne Treacy, 15, brutally beats and stomps Jose Lou Ratley in Deerfield Beach, Florida. Ratley survives the attack.

April 2010	Xu Yuyuan, 47, stabs 28 children and two adults in an elementary school in China. It is China's fifth attack on schoolchildren in just over a month.
September 2010	A spate of gay teens commit suicide after being bullied by their peers.
October 2010	President Barack Obama, Education Secretary Arne Duncan, and Secretary of State Hilary Clinton speak out against bullying.

A

Abuse and Crime and Violence

Children and youth who have experienced abuse are at risk for subsequent victimization. Additionally, those who have experienced abuse at home are more likely to become perpetrators of violent crime.

A number of forms of child abuse exist, including verbal abuse, physical abuse, sexual abuse, negligence, and maltreatment. Although it is sometimes difficult to clearly differentiate between child abuse and parental discipline, the difference generally lies in societal norms and in long-term impact. Corporal punishment, or spanking, results in immediate pain but does not generally leave red marks or bruising. Abuse violates current conceptions of what is appropriate parental discipline in a given culture.

Child sexual abuse involves an adult utilizing his or her position of power to force or coerce a child into sexual activity. Sexual intercourse is the most severe form of sexual abuse. Sexual exploitation involves allowing, permitting, or encouraging a child to engage in prostitution; or allowing, permitting, encouraging, or engaging in obscene or pornographic photographing, filming, or depiction of a child.

Negligence refers to any act or omission that demonstrates a serious disregard for a child or youth. Negligent behavior results in a clear and present danger to the child's welfare, health, or safety. Failure to provide adequate nutrition, clothing, access to education, and medical care are examples of negligence.

Emotional abuse includes actions or omissions that cause or could cause serious behavioral, cognitive, emotional, or mental disorders.

Although it is difficult to measure child abuse because it is notoriously underreported, data show it is terribly common. More than 3 million incidents of child abuse are reported annually in the United States, which means a report is occurring every 10 seconds. Almost five children die every day as a result of child abuse. More than three out of four are younger than the age of four years. One study combined childhood exposure to all forms of violence (including child abuse, domestic violence, and other forms of community violence) and found that 60% of children in the United States had experienced at least one type of violence.

Child abuse has significant, long-term effects. Abused children are more likely to have difficulties in school, engage in risky substance abuse, and experience depression, suicidal behavior, promiscuity, anger/aggression, anxiety, and post-traumatic stress disorder.

Exposure to domestic violence in the home is also damaging. The United Nations' Secretary General's Study of Violence Against Children in 2006 found a staggering 275 million children worldwide are exposed to violence in the home. Children who experience domestic violence in the home are also more likely to be abused themselves. Both experiences increase the likelihood that they will continue the cycle of abuse as adults. Approximately 30% of abused and neglected children will later abuse their own children.

Children who have been abused are significantly more likely to end up in juvenile detention or prison. Children who experience child abuse and neglect are 59% more likely to be arrested as juveniles, 28% more likely to be arrested as adults, and 30% more likely to commit violent crime. Fourteen percent of all men in prison in the United States were abused as children, and 36% of all women in prison were abused as children.

Exposure to or experience of abuse dramatically increases the individual's risk of engaging in substance abuse. Children who have been sexually abused are 2.5 times more likely to abuse alcohol and 3.8 times more likely develop drug addictions. Nearly two-thirds of the people in treatment for drug abuse report being abused as children.

Several of the infamous school shooters reportedly experienced abuse when they were young. Evan Ramsey, who killed two and wounded two others at his high school in Bethel, Alaska, was said to have been abused by several foster parents. Brenda Spencer, known as the United States' first school shooter, alleged that her father sexually abused her, although the allegations were never substantiated. Asa Coon, who wounded four people at his school in Cleveland, Ohio, in 2007, grew up witnessing domestic violence in the home, which has also been linked to some of the same adverse effects as has child abuse.

Laura L. Finley

Further Reading

Child Maltreatment. (2003). U.S. Department of Health and Human Services. Retrieved from www.acf.hhs.gov/programs/cb/pubs/cm03/chapterthree.htm#types

Langman, P. (2009). Expanding the samples: Five school shooters. Retrieved April 19, 2010, from http://www.schoolshooters.info/expanding-the-sample.pdf

Mignon, S., Larson, C., & Holmes, W. (2002). *Family abuse: Consequences, theories, and responses.* Boston: Allyn & Bacon.

National Child Abuse Statistics. (n.d.). Retrieved from http://www.childhelp.org/pages/statistics

UNICEF. (2006). Behind closed doors: The impact of domestic violence on children. Retrieved April 19, 2010, from http://www.unicef.org/protection/files/BehindClosedDoors.pdf

ADD/ADHD

Attention-deficit disorder (ADD) and attention-deficit/hyperactivity disorder (ADHD) are among the most frequent diagnoses in child and adolescent psychiatry. Diagnosis for these disorders began around 1980. Before that time, they were called different things, such as hyperkinetic disorder. In 1987, the American Psychiatric Association added ADHD to the *Diagnostic and Statistical Manual of Mental Disorders.*

A child or adolescent may be diagnosed with ADD or ADHD if he or she exhibits the following behaviors: attention difficulties/short attention span, motor hyperactivity, restless behavior, impulsivity, temper outbursts, and distractibility. Persons with ADHD or ADD often struggle in educational settings. Many are chronically truant as a result of their disorder. Children and youth with ADD/ADHD often exhibit hostile attributional biases, which refers to the tendency to interpret ambiguous social cues as being hostile. This problem may lead to verbally or physically aggressive behavior, which can then result in suspension or expulsion from school. Because students with ADD/ADHD find it difficult to achieve in a traditional school setting, they may be placed in special education programs.

Many ADD/ADHD-diagnosed children and youth experience comorbidity—that is, the co-occurrence of other disorders. Common comorbid diagnoses or disorders include conduct disorder, learning disabilities, anxiety disorders, Tourette's syndrome or some other type of tic, affective disorders, and personality disorders. Persons with ADD/ADHD are also more likely to have substance abuse problems. All of these factors place them, according to some studies, at high risk for criminal offending.

Critics contend that ADD/ADHD is over-diagnosed. A 2002 study found that as many as 16% of school-aged children in the United States could have ADD/ADHD—a far greater percentage than the previous estimate of 3% to 5%. Some contend that this trend toward diagnosing young people with ADD/ADHD is simply a reflection of a culture of short attention spans. Kids face more stressors today, in particular at schools that engage in high-stakes testing, and critics

Actress Kirstie Alley displays a picture of Raymond Perone, a 10-year-old suicide victim, while testifying in front of the Florida House Education Council in favor of a bill to limit the prescribing of psychotropic drugs such as Ritalin in Tallahassee, Florida, on April 19, 2005. According to Marla Filidei of the Citizens Commission on Human Rights, Raymond committed suicide while experiencing withdrawal from Ritalin. (AP/Wide World Photos)

contend perhaps it is unfair to expect young people to be attentive in these ways. While some go so far as to question whether ADD and ADHD are really disorders at all, many simply assert that the diagnostic process is far too subjective. There is no independent, valid test for ADD/ADHD. As a consequence, it is easy to diagnose a child or adolescent with ADD/ADHD.

Another concern is that, once a person is diagnosed with ADD/ADHD, the primary intervention is the prescription of some psychoactive drug, such as methylphenidate, typically Ritalin or Adderall. These drugs are stimulants much like cocaine, and can have dangerous side effects, including mood swings and loss of appetite. Between 1990 and 1996, prescriptions for methylphenidate increased 500%. The U.S. Drug Enforcement Agency (DEA) noted that, in some locations,

15% to 20% of young people had been prescribed Ritalin, and a *Journal of the American Medical Association* report found prescriptions for preschool-age children had tripled during the 1990s. Between 1990 and 2000, 569 children were hospitalized and 186 died due to taking Ritalin, according to some scholars. A similar trend of overprescribing Ritalin has been documented in the United Kingdom. Between 1995 and 2000, Britain saw a ninefold increase in the number of children being prescribed this drug.

Several infamous school shooters had been taking prescription drugs at the time of their attacks. T. J. Solomon was taking Ritalin when he went on a shooting spree at his Georgia high school, and some evidence suggests Kip Kinkel had taken Ritalin as well.

Laura L. Finley

Further Reading

Barkley, R., & Murphy, L. (1998). *Attention-deficit hyperactivity disorder: A clinical workbook.* New York: Guilford.

Death from Ritalin. (n.d.). Retrieved April 16, 2010, from http://www.ritalindeath.com/ADHD-Truths.htm

Haislip, G. (1996). DEA report: ADD/ADHD statement of Drug Enforcement Administration. Retrieved April 19, 2010, from http://www.add-adhd.org/ritalin.html

Smith, L. (2000, April 25). *Kids on pills*: BBC documentary examines increase in prescription drug use amongst children. *World Socialist website.* Retrieved April 19, 2010, from http://www.wsws.org/articles/2000/apr2000/rit-a25.shtml

Zahn, P. (2002, March 15). The big question: Is ADD overdiagnosed? *CNN.* Retrieved April 16, 2010, from http://transcripts.cnn.com/TRANSCRIPTS/0203/15/ltm.01.html

Adult Trials for Juveniles

In recent years, more juveniles have been tried as adults in criminal courts. What juveniles experience in adult court stands in stark contrast to their experiences in juvenile court. The first juvenile court was created around the turn of the 20th century. It was purposely set up to meet the unique needs of young people. Procedures in the juvenile court differ from those used in the criminal courts. Because of those differences, juveniles are not afforded some of the same legal protections as are adults.

Most laws allowing for juveniles to be tried as adults were passed in the 1990s in response to moral panics about youth and school violence. The case of 11-year-old Nathaniel Abraham in Michigan highlighted this issue.

Although the United States has a separate juvenile court system, there are several ways juveniles can be tried as adults. Judicial waivers, also known as discretionary waivers, allow juvenile court judges to make the decision that a specific individual should be tried in adult court, based on a motion filed by the prosecutor. Judges assess the severity of the incident and decide whether they believe the perpetrator is amenable to rehabilitation before issuing the judicial waiver. In some cases, known as presumptive waivers, judges are required by statute to waive juvenile defendants to adult court unless the juvenile can document that he or she is capable of being rehabilitated. Legislative waivers, also known as statutory exclusion, involve laws that specify when juveniles must be tried as adults. Some legislation specifies particular ages whereby a juvenile must be transferred to adult court or specific offenses that must be waived.

Concurrent jurisdiction allows prosecutors to retain the discretion regarding whether juveniles will be tried in juvenile or adult court. In blended sentencing, juvenile and criminal courts may render sentencing at the same time, requiring an individual to serve, for instance, a short time as a juvenile and then an additional short sentence as an adult.

Between 1994 and 2000, the rates of waivers fluctuated between 6,000 and 12,000 annually. Florida led the nation in the number of youth tried as adults in the 1990s and 2000s. In 2000, 466 youth were incarcerated in Florida state prisons. One-fourth of the youth tried as adults in Florida were mixed into the adult prison population. In 2006, an estimated 200,000 juveniles were tried as adults in the United States, representing an increase of more than 200% since the 1990s.

Critics contend that many of the juveniles who are waived to adult court are not serious, violent offenders. Regardless of the severity of the offense, at some point these juveniles will be released from prison. When they are housed with the most dangerous adult offenders, they may come out of prison even more dangerous than when they entered. Research has shown that juveniles who are held in adult prisons are significantly more likely to experience abuse and are more likely to reoffend than are comparable youth held in juvenile facilities. Moreover, research has not confirmed that trying juveniles as adults helps reduce crime. Finally, research suggests that juveniles do not understand the adult court system well enough to aid in their own defense.

The case of 14-year-old Nathaniel Brazill was one of the first to shed light on the issue of trying as adults juveniles who perpetrated crimes at schools. Teah Wemberly, who was 15 at the time she shot a classmate at Dillard High School in Ft. Lauderdale, Florida, was tried as an adult; she was convicted and sentenced to 25 years in prison. Wayne Treacey, who brutally attacked and almost killed classmate Josie Ratley, was also 15 at the time of his crime; he will be tried as an adult in Florida as well. Three of the boys who attacked 15-year-old Michael Brewer of Deerfield Beach, Florida, were charged as adults.

Laura L. Finley

Further Reading

Hiber, M. (2008). *Should juveniles be tried as adults?* New York: Greenhaven.

Hightower, E. (2008, November 21). Florida teen charged as adult in school shooting death. *World Socialist website.* Retrieved April 20, 2010, from http://www.wsws.org/articles/2008/nov2008/flor-n21.shtml

Marks, A. (2007, March 22). States rethink trying juveniles as adults. *Christian Science Monitor.* Retrieved April 18, 2010, from http://www.csmonitor.com/2007/0322/p03s03-usju.html

PBS Frontline. (n.d.). Does treating kids like adults make a difference? Retrieved April 18, 2010, from http://www.pbs.org/wgbh/pages/frontline/shows/juvenile/stats/kidslikeadults.html

Wright, T. (2010, April 16). Josie Lou's attacker charged as an adult. *NBC Miami.* Retrieved April 20, 2010, from http://www.nbcmiami.com/news/local-beat/Josie-Lous-Attacker-Charged-as-an-Adult-91058499.html

Africa and School Crime and Violence

Existing data indicate that the rate of school violence and crime in Africa has increased in the last two decades, becoming one of the most challenging social problems in that region. School violence is a multifaceted construct that involves both criminal acts and aggression that inhibit development and learning as well as harm the school's climate. Such violence may consist of anything ranging from corporal punishment to bullying, verbal abuse and harassment, and criminal behavior, including assault, gender-based violence, arson, and murder—all of which may occur in classrooms, hallways, school yards, or school bathrooms.

In Africa, physical punishment occurs not only at home, but also at school, a place where children are supposed to be given an education. Most school children in Africa are too familiar with bruises and stinging from whips, canes, and slaps. While school violence is endemic continent-wide, much of the violence remains hidden, because victims are afraid to come forward for fear of repercussions or being stigmatized. In addition, the authoritarian nature of schooling in Africa allows violence to flourish, such as the high levels of sexual aggression demonstrated by boys and teachers' propositioning of girls for sex, both of which are tolerated. Students, teachers, and parents continue to be concerned about school safety. In some countries (such as South Africa), rampant violence against students and school staff is pervasive and disruptive, and impedes the schools' efforts to improve education. Notwithstanding these facts, it is important to remember that school violence is not solely an African dilemma, but rather is widespread throughout most parts of the world.

Students at the Immaculate Conception Junior High School in Kpando, Ghana, join groups such as the Sara club that help to empower young women by reinforcing their focus on education and their goal to stay in school. (Henry Akorsu/USAID)

Corporal punishment is not a new phenomenon in Africa: it has been a method of imparting punishment in schools since the colonial period. Corporal punishment is a method of discipline in which an adult deliberately inflicts pain upon a child in response to his or her unacceptable behavior. According to the United Nations Committee on the Rights of the Child, it breaches a child's fundamental right to be protected from violence and to receive an education. Despite all that is known about its negative effects, corporal punishment continues to be institutionally sanctioned in African schools. As Human Rights Watch (HRW) reported in 1999, the infliction of corporal punishment is often cruel, where teachers cane, slap, and whip students for poor academic performance or to maintain classroom discipline. Severe injuries such as broken bones, knocked-out teeth, and internal bleeding are common occurrences.

Numerous reports have chronicled violations of corporal punishment regulations in Africa, such as the 1999 HRW investigation of corporal punishment in 20 schools in Kenya, which revealed only one school applied corporal punishment according to the regulations. In 2007, HRW reported on severe punishments that were meted out in Kenyan schools, such as having students stand in the hot sun or forcing them to uproot tree stumps.

Shumba (2001) reported incidents of abuse by teachers in Zimbabwe, including sexual, physical and emotional abuse. According to Shumba, out of 246 reported cases of abuse by teachers in secondary schools between 1990 and 1997, 65.6% involved sexual intercourse with students, 1.9% rape or attempted rape, and the remainder other inappropriate teacher conduct.

Other studies found similar results. In Botswana, the Secretary of Education (2007) revealed that 92% of students had been beaten by a teacher—behavior that was approved of by 67% of parents. In a Save the Children (2005) survey of 2,366 children ages 6–18 in Swaziland, 28% reported having been hit with a hand, 59% being beaten with an object, and 28% being humiliated. Most disturbing, Population Communication Africa (2004) found that more than 60% of children were physically abused in Africa, including being slapped in the face, hit with a cane or stick, kicked, punched, or physically bullied. Corporal punishment in South Africa has sometimes resulted in hospitalization or death. For example, in the province of KwaZulu-Natal, a female teacher knocked together the heads of two boys, resulting in the death of one of them. Also, in 2004, a 17-year-old boy died after being beaten by a school principal.

One factor contributing to violence against girls is the lower status afforded to women in African societies. Likewise, violence in African schools has a gender-based dimension; thus schools become breeding grounds for damaging gender practices. Communication Africa (2002) noted that, other than in the home, physical abuse typically takes place at school and that the major perpetrators are teachers and other students. Sexual violence is defined as any sexual act or attempted sexual act using coercion, threats, or physical force. In schools in Africa, it may involve assault, sexual advances, harassment, and forced sex or rape, perpetrated by male students, teachers, or school personnel. Other studies documented cases of female students who left school or skipped classes because a teacher had sexually molested them. Of course, this kind of abuse happens elsewhere in the world too: female students in Papua New Guinea reported that they feared sexual assaults and violence in schools and felt threatened by male teachers.

Rossetti's 2001 survey of 560 students in Botswana found that 67% of students were sexually harassed by teachers, 20% of students asked for sex, and 42% of those who were asked for sex gave in. It is important to point out that violence against girls is not restricted to the classroom or the school yard; rather, it takes place in many locations associated with school, including bathrooms. Most sexual abuse of young children took place in bathrooms, and many children categorized bathrooms as dangerous zones. In her 2007 study, Ruto collected data from groups of 1,279 and 1,206 children, of which two-thirds of the respondents were girls. She discovered that 58 of every 100 children had been sexually harassed, with 29% of the boys and 24% of the girls having been forced into unwanted sex. The main perpetrators were peers, with the home featured as most unsafe place. Omale reported similar behavior in Kenya in 1999, including incidents of rape on the way home from school, as well as teachers having sex with (and impregnating) primary school children. She further cited the infamous St. Kizito incidents in Kenya in which boys went on a rampage through the girls' dormitories, killing 19 girls and raping 71 others. Bunwaree's 1999 study discovered high levels of verbal abuse in schools in Mauritius, while Leach and Machakanja found abuse was prevalent against female teachers in Zimbabwe in their 2000 study.

Akiba et al. studied 37 countries in 2002, noting that violence in schools has more to do with in-school factors than with crime rates from the wider society. Some note, however, that violence is not analyzed within a gendered and sociocultural context, pointing out that the gender of the perpetrators of the crimes often remains unmentioned.

Sexual harassment is common in schools in Africa. It can be verbal, taking the form of teasing, or it can be of a physical nature, such as unwanted touching or sexual contact. It can also be more overtly violent, as in cases where girls are sexually assaulted or raped. Leach and Machakanja's 2000 study in Ghana, Zimbabwe, and Malawi revealed that violence against girls included sexual propositions by older male students and teachers, including the use of sexually explicit language that creates a hostile school environment. Other research reported a prevalence of child abuse in Zimbabwe and found 110 cases (72.4%) of sexual abuse, 38 cases (25%) of physical abuse, 3 cases (2.1%) of hidden curriculum abuse, and one case (0.7%) of emotional abuse during the same period. In refugee camps, such as those in Sierra Leone, Guinea, and Liberia, girls were abused by teachers, including being subjected to the exchange of good grades for sex.

The rise in crimes of a sexual nature has threatened the safety of girls in African schools; consequently, girls who attend upper primary and secondary schools are a small minority. In countries such as Chad, Malawi, and Mozambique, fewer than half of all girls who start school remain there until grade five.

Bullying can take many forms, including physical violence, threats, name calling, persistent teasing, exclusion, tormenting, ridicule, humiliation, or abusive comments. Teacher–student bullying also exists in most schools and takes such forms as verbal abuse, taunts, and assaults. A questionnaire administered to 574 students in grades 8 and 11 at 72 schools in Cape Town and Durban, South Africa, noted that 36.3% of students were involved in bullying behavior, 8.2% were bullies, 19.3% were victims, and 8.7% had been both bully and victim.

In Africa, the widespread failure of educational authorities to address school violence, or to even acknowledge that school violence exists—in particular, in contexts of weak policy compliance, shoddy reports from school principals, and entrenched gender roles—has allowed this problem to flourish unchecked and, therefore, to become institutionalized. Moreover, the existence of gender-based violence in schools is not fully recognized, so it is unlikely that African countries will have dealt with the issue. To fully address the problem of violence in schools, ministries of education must develop policies on school discipline, including clear codes of conduct for teachers that outline procedures for disciplinary measures, sanctions, and prosecution in cases of teacher misconduct. In addition, they must understand and scrutinize the wider cultural norms that shape behavior and attitudes. In doing so, educators will have fulfilled their most basic responsibilities of protecting human rights of the children, including enhancing their moral development. If left unchecked, school violence in Africa will have a negative impact on the education and emotional needs of the children and become an insurmountable barrier to attaining education. Despite these immense challenges, some countries have made efforts to tackle school violence as well as to prohibit corporal punishment.

Njoki-Wa-Kinyatti

Further Reading

Harber, C. (2001). Schooling and violence in South Africa: Creating a safe school. *Intercultural Education, 12*(3), 261–271.

Holan, L., Flisher, A., & Lombard, C. (2007). Bullying, violence, and risk behavior in South African students. *Child Abuse and Neglect, 31,* 161–171.

Leach, F., Mandoga, P., & Machakanja, J. (2000). *Preliminary investigation of the abuse of girls in Zimbabwean junior secondary schools.* London: Department of International Development, Education Division.

Matsoga, J. (2003). *Crime and school violence in Botswana secondary school education: The case of Moeding senior secondary school.* France: LAP Academic Publishing.

Morrell, R. (1998). Gender and education: The place of masculinity in South African schools. *South African Journal of Education, 18*(4), 218–225.

Msani, M. (2007, June). Discipline in a Kwazulu-Natal secondary school: The gendered experience of learners. Retrieved January 31, 2010, from http://146.230.128.84:8080/jspui/bitstream/10413/40/1/Msani%20complete%20thesis.pdf

Ruto, S. J. (2009). Sexual abuse of school age children: Evidence from Kenya. *Journal of International Cooperation in Education, 12*(1), 177–192.

Alcohol and School Crime and Violence

Alcohol is a depressant that affects the brain's chemistry, causing the brain to release dopamine and serotonin. It is the drug most commonly used by people ages 12 to 20. It is also the drug most commonly associated with violence. Alcohol consumption increases the risk of being victimized and of becoming a perpetrator of criminal or violent activity. Additionally, heavy drinking can negatively affect brain development among adolescents, which means it poses a significant risk to the physical, psychological, and social well-being of both juveniles and adults.

Even before a child is born, alcohol consumption can create a propensity toward violence. Prenatal alcohol exposure, which can result in fetal alcohol syndrome or fetal alcohol effects, is associated with a host of behavioral and social problems, including delinquent behavior. The effects of fetal alcohol syndrome are generally experienced throughout the duration of one's life.

Although drinking by persons younger than the age of 21 is illegal in the United States, people aged 12 to 20 years drink 11% of all alcohol consumed in this country. Irresponsible drinking can reduce self-control and the ability to process incoming information. As a consequence, drinkers may not be as adept at assessing risks as nondrinkers, which may make them more prone to engage in dangerous behavior or misread cues suggesting a situation is unsafe. The reduced physical control and inability to recognize warning signs in potentially dangerous situations can make some drinkers easy targets for perpetrators.

Males are more likely than females to be both perpetrators and victims of alcohol-related youth violence. Data from the National Household Survey on Drug Abuse (NHSDA) show that adolescents who drank alcohol in the previous month were significantly more likely to have acted violently in the previous year. The data are even worse for heavy or binge drinkers. Heavy drinkers are most likely to report destroying property and threatening or physically attacking others. The Centers for Disease Control and Prevention (CDC) defines heavy drinking as consuming an average of more than two drinks per day. For women, heavy drinking is typically defined as consuming an average of more than one drink per day. Binge drinking is generally defined as having four to five drinks in a two-hour time period.

According to NHSDA data, heavy drinkers were much more likely than binge or light drinkers to report destroying property and threatening or physically attacking others. Nondrinkers are the least likely to engage in these behaviors. Violence most often occurs in and around bars. In a community sample of 18- to 30-year-olds in the United States, almost 25% of men and 12% of women had experienced violence or aggression in or around a licensed bar during the previous year. However, alcohol-influenced violent incidents occurring in people's homes or dorm rooms are likely under-reported.

Some people use alcohol as a coping mechanism or as a way to self-medicate after experiencing trauma. Data show that approximately 70% of all victims of domestic violence have substance abuse issues, for instance.

Alcohol consumption is associated with the carrying of weapons. Youths who used illegal drugs in the year prior to participating in the NHSDA survey were three times more likely to have carried a handgun than youth who did not use drugs. Binge drinking and heavy alcohol use were also associated with handgun possession, with youth being four and five times more likely, respectively, to have carried a handgun in the past year compared to their nondrinking peers.

Data from countries outside the United States show essentially the same patterns. In Israel, 11- to 16-year-olds who reported both drinking five or more drinks per occasion and having ever been drunk were twice as likely to be perpetrators of bullying, five times as likely to be injured in a fight, and six times as likely to carry weapons. In England and Wales, 18 to 24-year-old males who reported feeling very drunk at least monthly were more than twice as likely to have been involved in a fight in the previous year, and females more than four times as likely, compared to regular but nonbinge drinkers.

Many high school and college students consume alcohol prior to engaging in violent or criminal activity. This behavior is influenced by individual and societal beliefs about the effects of alcohol, which suggest it can increase one's confidence and one's aggression. Alcohol consumption is also more likely in social situations that are related to schools and universities, such as dances, parties, and sporting events. When drinking occurs in crowded and poorly managed venues, the risk of violence increases.

Given that violent crime is costly and is clearly associated with alcohol consumption, politicians, educators, and the general public have a vested interest in reducing under-aged or inappropriate drinking. In the United States, the costs of violent crime related to harmful alcohol use among youth were estimated at $29 billion in 1996. Research has suggested that increasing alcohol prices through higher taxation might reduce the frequency of drinking and, consequently, the chance of heavy alcohol consumption among young people. In the United States, it has been estimated that a mere 10% increase in beer prices would reduce the number of college students involved in violence by 4%.

Additionally, research in the United States has found some evidence that programs that attempt to correct misperceptions about peers' drinking habits are effective. Called social norms campaigns, these programs address the fact that young people typically over-estimate how many of their peers are drinking and how frequently they do it.

Laura L. Finley

Further Reading

Butler Center for Research. (2008). Youth violence and alcohol/drug abuse. Retrieved April 18, 2010, from www.hazelden.org/web/public/document/bcrup_0102.pdf

Centers for Disease Control and Prevention. (2010, April 19). Alcohol and public health. Retrieved April 19, 2010, from http://www.cdc.gov/alcohol/index.htm

The Cool Spot: The Young Teen's Place for Info on Alcohol and Resisting Peer Pressure. (n.d.). Retrieved from http://www.thecoolspot.gov/

World Health Organization. (n.d.). Youth violence and alcohol. Retrieved April 18, 2010, from http://www.who.int/violence_injury_prevention/violence/world_report/factsheets/fs_youth.pdf

American Civil Liberties Union (ACLU)

According to its website, "The ACLU is our nation's guardian of liberty, working daily in courts, legislatures and communities to defend and preserve the individual rights and liberties that the Constitution and laws of the United States guarantee everyone in this country." The nonprofit, nonpartisan ACLU works on numerous civil, political, and human rights issues, including capital punishment, drug law reform, free speech, HIV/AIDS, prisoners' rights, racial justice, reproductive freedom, voting rights, lesbian/gay/bisexual/transgender (LGBT) rights, immigrants' rights, women's rights, and privacy rights. The organization has more than 500,000 members and supporters, with staffed offices in all 50 states as well as Washington, D.C., and Puerto Rico. The ACLU has participated in more U.S. Supreme Court cases than any other private organization, and claims to win more than it loses.

In regard to school crime and violence, the ACLU has often been a leader in protesting unconstitutional practices that are harmful to students. Its members have conducted a thorough examination of corporal punishment and published a report on why it should be prohibited (http://www.aclu.org/human-rights/corporal-punishment-children). The ACLU often backs students in cases where they believe school authorities overstep their bounds or unfairly deny students the freedom of speech and the freedom of the press. For instance, the ACLU became involved when two Indiana high school girls were punished for posting sexually suggestive pictures of themselves on MySpace, an act that had nothing to do with the school. They assisted the plaintiff in contesting unconstitutional school-based strip searches in the case of Savannah Redding, a 15-year-old who was strip-searched based on allegations that she had ibuprofen she had not checked in at the school office. The ACLU also advocates for safe school environments for lesbian, gay, bisexual, transgendered, and questioning (LGBTQ) youth. Zero-tolerance laws, which require students be suspended or expelled for certain violations (typically having weapons or drugs on campus, among other things), have been challenged by a number of groups, but the ACLU has been one of the most active and has long noted these laws' disproportionate impact on racial and ethnic minorities.

At the college level, the ACLU has been active in addressing hate crimes on campus while maintaining support for freedom of speech and academic freedom. It helped address homophobia, for instance, when its members investigated and recommended the reprimand of a Fresno State College health sciences instructor who insulted gays and lesbians and used the Bible in class as justification for those acts. Further, the ACLU has defended students' right to nonviolently protest campus policies.

Persons seeking information about the ACLU's work, needing assistance, or wishing to get involved can find information about local affiliates on the organization's website (www.aclu.org).

Laura L. Finley

Further Reading

ACLU. (n.d.). Retrieved from http://www.aclu.org/

Schmidt, P. (2010, April 2). Fresno City College moves to reprimand instructor who drew ACLU complaint. *Chronicle of Higher Education.* Retrieved April 16, 2010, from http://jobs.chronicle.com/article/Fresno-City-College-Moves-to/64967/

Amnesty International

Founded in 1961, Amnesty International (AI) is a global human rights watchdog and advocacy group with more than 2.8 million members spread across 150 countries. Initially devoted to lobbying to free prisoners of conscience, AI has evolved to focus on numerous human rights abuses. Its current work involves campaigns focusing on the following issues:

- Stopping violence against women
- Defending the rights and dignity of those trapped in poverty
- Abolishing the death penalty
- Opposing torture and combating terror with justice
- Freeing prisoners of conscience
- Protecting the rights of refugees and migrants
- Regulating the global arms trade

AI has worked to address human rights abuses in and around schools across the globe. For instance, it has called attention to sexual abuse of girls in school, the inability of children to safely arrive at school due to violence in the streets, and the school-to-prison pipeline. AI members have advocated for better treatment of lesbian, gay, bisexual, transgendered, and questioning (LGBTQ) youth, who often endure tremendous verbal and physical harassment in schools. Additionally, AI has called attention to the damage caused by corporal punishment in schools.

It notes that the United Nations Convention on the Rights of the Child (CRC) guarantees young people the right to education. Notably, the United States has not ratified the CRC.

Amnesty International USA (AIUSA) works to ensure these and other human rights domestically. AIUSA also provides resources to local and student chapters that wish to advance human rights in their communities. In an effort to reach young people, AIUSA has implemented an extensive Music for Human Rights campaign. Student groups are encouraged to start AI chapters in their schools.

Laura L. Finley

Further Reading

Amnesty International: www.amnesty.org
Amnesty International USA: www.amnestyusa.org
Amnesty International USA's Music for Human Rights Campaign: http://www.musicforhumanrights.org/

Anger Management

Anger is one of the primary risk factors for violent activity, both inside and outside of schools. Students who do not know how to manage their anger are at risk for various forms of aggression, ranging from verbal outbursts to physical violence. Anger management aims to give participants the tools they need to understand their anger and identify anger triggers. It also provides participants with management strategies that can help them reduce the chance that their anger will escalate into violence. These approaches may be taught in a variety of settings—for instance, in a class or as part of a counseling session. Courts often mandate anger management training as part of a criminal sentence or a diversion program. Most colleges and universities offer some type of anger management course, either on a voluntary basis through a counseling or student services center or as a for-credit course. Students who get in trouble on campus may be required to complete an anger management course either on campus or through a local provider.

In these programs participants are taught to take new perspectives, or to see things through the eyes of another. They are given instruction on identifying how they feel when they are angry, and then are taught specific techniques for problem solving. Many anger management programs include specific relation techniques as well. The instruction in such courses is done through lectures, discussion, videos, and role playing.

Studies have found some significant benefits of anger management. One study of anger management training for aggressive elementary school boys found that three years after completion of the program, attendees had increased self-esteem and were less likely to be involved in drugs and alcohol. There was no change in their delinquent behavior, however. Another study of 7- to 13-year-olds who received anger management training in a psychiatric ward found that the youth had significantly increased problem-solving skills one year later. A critical factor is the length of the program. Results are generally not significant for programs that are 6 lessons or shorter. Programs that are 12 sessions or longer, by comparison, have been shown to reduce aggressiveness. Long-term outcomes are increased when "booster sessions" are held one year later or at regular intervals.

Although courts often require domestic or dating violence offenders to complete anger management programs, research has not found that this approach is an effective way to address this specific problem. The failure of such court-mandated training is likely due to the fact that abuse is about offenders seeking to obtain and maintain power and control over victims, not about their inability to control their anger.

A number of anger management resources are available to assist educators in implementing a program. The Partnership Against Violence Network (PAVNET; www.pavnet.org) serves as a clearinghouse for information about anger management and other related topics. George Washington University's Hamilton Fish Institute is another good source of information. The PBS series *In the Mix* has included an episode devoted to anger management. Lesson plans for educators at grade levels 9–12 are available at http://www.pbs.org/inthemix/educators/lessons/schoolviol3/index.html.

Laura L. Finley

Further Reading

Hamilton Fish Institute. (n.d.). Retrieved from http://www.hamfish.org/
Mayo Clinic. (2009, June 25). Anger management tips: 10 ways to tame your temper. Retrieved April 19, 2010, from http://www.mayoclinic.com/health/anger-management/MH00102
Safe and Responsive Schools Project. (2000). Anger management. Retrieved April 19, 2010, from http://www.indiana.edu/~safeschl/AngerManagement.pdf

Anonymous Tip Lines

In 2000, the U.S. Secret Services used its threat assessment model to examine the cases of 41 people who had committed attacks at schools over the previous 26 years. Although they found no specific "profile" of a school shooter, they did find some commonalities among the cases. In particular, most shooters did not just "snap" and begin impulsively shooting. Rather, they had planned their attacks, at least to some degree. More than three-fourths of shooters analyzed held some type of

Despite the "anti-snitch" culture common among teens, police departments across the nation set up anonymous tip lines. In many cases, tippers can even text the information they wish to share with the police and remain anonymous to the public. (iStockPhoto)

grievance related to the school or to students, and in almost all of the cases the individual had told someone about his or her complaint. The confidant was typically a peer—either a friend, a classmate, or a sibling. In only two cases were adults told.

Given that at least one other person was likely aware that something was going to happen in almost all cases of serious violence on school or campus grounds, many assert that anonymous tip lines are among the most important prevention tools for this type of violence. Many tip lines were established after the 1999 massacre at Columbine High School in Littleton, Colorado, for example. Such a vehicle is an easy way for administrators to learn about possible violent activity. At many schools, posters are placed around the building alerting students to what might be deemed suspicious behavior and providing them with a phone number they can call if they see or hear something worrisome.

Some states have established 24-hour tip lines that are operated by police. For instance, the Michigan School Violence hotline is a place where students can report specific threats of imminent harm. Students are told that they will remain anonymous, and are taught to differentiate between when it is appropriate to call the tip line and when more immediate police intervention is needed.

One difficulty is in overcoming the powerful "anti-snitch" culture that often prevails among adolescents. For many youth, it is simply unacceptable to tell adults anything about a peer. Officials hope that the promise of anonymity can assure students that no one will ever know who reported the tip.

Although it is difficult to determine precisely how effective they are, news reports occasionally describe situations that were averted due to tipsters. For instance, a Columbine-like attack was thwarted in December 2009 in Bridgewater, New Jersey, when a student informed school officials about suspicious behavior.

In a number of locations, people are being encouraged to message text their tips to law enforcement or appropriate officials. Baltimore inaugurated its text-message tip line in June 2008. Authorities in Douglas County, Colorado, thwarted a school attack after an anonymous text led them to a student's "kill list." At colleges, campus police are increasingly utilizing tips from text messages to keep order in dorms and at campus events.

Laura L. Finley

Further Reading

Associated Press. (2008, July 30). UR BUSTED: Catching bad guys by txt msgs. Retrieved April 19, 2010, from http://exhibitanewsbaltimore.com/blog/2008/07/30/ur-busted-catching-bad-guys-by-txt-msgs/

Lavoie, D. (2009, November 28). Text-a-Tip programs help police get info from anonymous tipsters in anti-snitching culture. Retrieved April 19, 2010, from http://blog.taragana.com/politics/2009/11/28/text-a-tip-programs-help-police-get-info-from-anonymous-tipsters-in-anti-snitching-culture-2969/

School Violence Hotline. (n.d.). Retrieved from http://www.michigan.gov/safeschools/0,1607,7-181—68589—,00.html

Teppo, G. (2007, April 19). Experts ponder patterns in school shootings. *USA Today*. Retrieved April 19, 2010, from http://www.usatoday.com/news/education/2007-04-18-school-shooters_N.htm

Arts-Based Programs

Involvement in the arts can be tremendously beneficial to both victims and perpetrators of violence. Art therapy or similar programs can help heal those who have been harmed by crime or violence, and arts-based programs can serve a preventive role as well.

Children and youth exposed to various forms of crime, violence, and trauma often find it difficult to articulate their feelings. Arts-based therapy can help them share their emotions and begin healing. Participants may engage in drawing, painting, sculpture, music, drama, and many other art forms. Arts-based therapy is

Collaborative art activity can play an important role in preventing youth violence. (Monkey Business Images/Dreamstime.com)

often used with children who have been exposed to domestic violence in the home, for example. It may occur at the school, where a trained art therapist might hold a session in which she or he examines the child's existing artwork. For adolescents, this technique is commonly used in the treatment of eating disorders.

The Centers for Disease Control and Prevention (CDC) and the *American Psychologist* journal have published reports on "best practices" for youth violence prevention (YVP) Programs. Critical components of school-based YVP programs identified in the reports include interactive student participation; fostering of relationships between students, staff, and families; rewards for positive behaviors; and total school involvement. Prevention programs designed specifically for elementary school children should also include largely group activities, active participation in story-based or narrative learning, opportunities to practice negotiation skills with peers and authority figures, and humor and playfulness.

Arts-based YVP programs fulfill a number of these criteria. Prosocial outcomes of arts-based YVP include increased social well-being, improved motivation and learning, enhanced individual and community development, and reduction in aggression, violence, and crime. The programs that are most successful at reducing crime and violence are generally flexible in their program structure, provide mentorship, offer opportunities for ongoing program involvement, and share links to other community organizations.

Many examples of arts-based YVP can be cited. For example, Urban Improv (UI) is a school-based program that has operated in the Boston Public Schools for 14 years. UI uses structured theater improvisation to assist youth with making difficult decisions, controlling their impulses, and resolving nonviolently. An evaluation of UI found increased prosocial behaviors among its participants. Specifically, UI helped prevent new aggression, and decreased hyperactivity among participants.

Branch Out is an arts-based program created by Molly Foote that focuses on developing interpersonal empathy and open communications among participants. It has been used primarily in the U.S. Northwest and can be integrated into whole-class curricula as well as large- and small-group programs. Creative activities help students learn personal empowerment, social skills, career awareness, diversity appreciation, and community building. Counselors facilitate discussions during and after the activities and can add role playing or other creative activity to enhance students' understanding.

Another example is *Elijah's Kite,* a children's opera that addresses bullying. One evaluation of 104 fourth- and fifth-grade students showed significant increases in knowledge about bullying and reductions in self-reported victimization among those who viewed the opera.

Laura L. Finley

Further Reading

Haner, D., Pepler, D., Cummings, J., & Rubin-Vaughn, A. (2010, March 1). The role of arts-based curricula in bullying prevention: *Elijah's Kite*—A children's opera. *Canadian Journal of School Psychology, 25*(1), 55–69.

Hayes, S., & Foote, M. (2002). Culturally responsive approaches to school violence prevention. *Online Readings in Psychology and Culture.* Retrieved April 17, 2010, from http://orpc.iaccp.org/index.php?option=com_content&view=article&id=104%3Ahayesfoote&catid=35%3Achapter&Itemid=15

Kisiel, C., Blaustein, M., Spinazzola, J., Schmidt, C., Zucker, M., & van der Kolk, B. (2006). Evaluation of a theater-based violence prevention program for elementary school youth. *Journal of School Violence, 5*(2), 19–36.

McArthur, D., & Law, S. A. (1996). *The arts and prosocial impact study: A review of current programs and literature.* Santa Monica, CA: Rand Corporation.

Thornton, T. N., Craft, C. A., Dahlberg, L. L., Lynch, B. S., & Baer, K. (2002). *Best practices of youth violence prevention: A sourcebook for community action.* Atlanta, GA: Centers for Disease Control and Prevention, National Center for Injury Prevention and Control.

Asia and School Crime and Violence

Asia is the world's largest continent, home to 4 billion people residing in 47 different countries. These countries maintain a wide variety of school systems and experience vastly different rates of overall crime in society, making it difficult to generalize about school crime and violence across the continent as a whole. Some of the national school systems in Asia—such as those in South Korea and Japan—are considered to be among the most academically rigorous in the world, while others are held back by poverty and other socioeconomic and political problems.

School crime and violence rates vary throughout Asia. For some countries, the data available about these issues are very limited. The next paragraphs report the findings of just a few of the relevant studies that have been conducted in this area.

In 1994, the Third International Math and Science Study (TIMSS), which aimed to compare rates of student attainment in science and math across many different countries, also surveyed students (in seventh and eighth grades) and teachers about school violence. An analysis of these data reveals that 60% of students in the Philippines said that they had been victims of school violence in the month prior to taking the survey. Slightly more than 30% of students in South Korea, more than 20% of students in Hong Kong and Thailand, and less than 10% of students in Singapore reported such victimization. To put these figures into perspective, more than 25% of students in the United States reported they had been victims of school violence in the previous month.

A different comparative study, which examined representative data from eighth graders, teachers, and principals in U.S. and South Korean schools, found that some measures of school violence were lower in South Korea than in the United States. Although it is important to keep in mind that all cross-national comparative studies have limitations, the findings of both this study and the TIMSS illustrate that, although some Asian countries may have lower rates of school crime or violence than the United States, school crime and violence are still important issues throughout much of the Asian continent.

National statistics seem to support this point. In Japan, although overall crime rates in society have traditionally been very low, the education ministry reported that, in fiscal year 2008, the number of violent acts committed in junior high schools dramatically increased; on the positive side, the number of bullying cases reported at all schooling levels decreased. In the Philippines, a report issued in 2009 by the human rights organization Plan Philippines (affiliated with the global nongovernmental organization Plan International) found that more than 40% of the public school students who were surveyed said that they had been threatened with physical violence at school. (Plan International has also produced publications about school violence in India, Thailand, and numerous other countries around the world. Information about how to obtain these resources is available in the Further Reading section at the end of this article.)

In some Asian nations, concern about school violence has increased in recent years in response to high-profile crimes. For example, although levels of violence in schools are generally reported to be low in India, a number of recent incidents—including two fatal shootings between December 2007 and January 2008—received international media attention and increased Indian awareness of school violence issues. Similarly, several high-profile cases of school violence have raised concerns among Japanese citizens. One particularly infamous case in Japan occurred in 2001, when a mentally ill man stabbed 8 children to death at an elementary school. An eerily similar crime took place in China in 2004, when a mentally ill janitor stabbed 14 students at a kindergarten in Beijing, resulting in one death; this crime and several other incidents of violence in Chinese schools also received some international media attention.

What explains cross-national similarities and differences in rates of school violence? Why do some Asian countries seem to have higher rates of school crime and violence than others, and why do some Asian countries appear to have lower rates of school violence than the United States? Interestingly, the analysis of the 1994 TIMSS data described earlier found that rates of school violence were not related to the overall rates of crime in the countries that took part in the survey. Instead, according to this analysis, rates of school violence were associated with some socioeconomic factors but not others.

Other observers have theorized that different types of instructional methods and school environments could explain contrasting rates of violence. In this vein, one study found that South Korean schools that put students on academic tracking systems had higher rates of school violence than South Korean schools that did not do so.

Finally, some commentators have argued that different rates of school violence could be due to economic modernization. As Asian countries become more industrialized, such commentators claim, young people disassociate themselves from traditional values and immerse themselves in more violent movies and video games; according to this theory, such behavior may raise rates of violence. More cross-national comparative research is needed in the area of school violence to determine whether this and other explanations are correct.

What are Asian countries doing to reduce or prevent school crime and violence? In recent years, awareness of these issues has increased significantly in many countries in Asia, and a number of countries have developed national strategies for monitoring and combating violence. For example, in 2007, China's Ministry of Education declared that it would launch a safety campaign on campuses. In 2005, South Korea's Education Ministry initiated a nationwide plan to combat school violence; in 2010, a second five-year plan was announced, which will include increased use of closed-circuit television (CCTV) to monitor safety in both primary and secondary schools. In 2008, the global human rights organization Plan International launched a campaign to reduce school violence in many countries around the world, including nations in Asia.

The immensity and diversity of Asia makes it impossible to discuss school violence—and measures taken to prevent school violence—in every country in the continent. However, the sources listed in the Further Reading section offer a jumping-off point for readers interested in exploring school crime and violence in Asia in greater depth.

Tiffany Bergin

Further Reading

Akiba, M., & Han, S. (2007). Academic differentiation, school achievement and school violence in the USA and South Korea. *Compare: A Journal of Comparative Education*, *37*(2), 201–219.

Akiba, M., LeTendre, G. K., Baker, D. P., & Goesling, B. (2002). Student victimization: National and school system effects on school violence in 37 nations. *American Educational Research Journal*, *39*(4), 829–853.

Balasegaram, M. (2001, June 8). Violent crime stalks Japan's youth. *BBC News*. Retrieved from http://news.bbc.co.uk/1/hi/world/asia-pacific/1377781.stm

Elementary school text service to go nationwide. (2010, January 14). *The Korea Herald*. Retrieved from http://www.koreaherald.co.kr/NEWKHSITE/data/html_dir/2010/01/14/201001140013.asp

Forney, M. (2004, November 29). China's school killings. *Time*. Retrieved from http://www.time.com/time/magazine/article/0,9171,832294,00.html

Plan International. (2009). Learn without fear: The global campaign to end violence in schools. Retrieved from http://plan-international.org/learnwithoutfear/resources/publications (Plan International's reports about school violence in the Philippines, India, Thailand, and many other countries—which were referenced in this article—can be accessed from this page.)

School violence set record last year. (2009, December 1). *The Japan Times*. Retrieved from http://search.japantimes.co.jp/cgi-bin/nn20091201b5.html

Wax, E. (2008, February 13). India shaken by school violence. *Washington Post*. Retrieved from http://www.washingtonpost.com/wp-dyn/content/article/2008/02/12/AR2008021202694.html

Athletes and Crime and Violence, College

Historically, a scholar's word was considered better than that of a "townsman." Along with scholarly status comes a protective cloak or veil that often affords college intellectuals—the future leaders and professionals of America—impunity from the law and leniency from public officials. In the past, status and respect derived solely from monetary wealth aided law breakers in escaping criminal sanctions for their offenses. Today, a small minority of college students—athletes—are also afforded leniency when they commit criminal violations because of the "star" status derived from being an athlete. This essay provides a historical overview of universities and campus crime, discusses the relevance of the status of athletes, identifies the prevalence of campus violence perpetrated by student-athletes, and explains why some athletes commit crime.

Violence on college campus is not a new phenomenon. Likewise, the sense of "us versus them" and the lack of response by the criminal justice system when scholars commit criminal offenses are well entrenched in our society.

The problem with the criminal justice system not intruding when campus crimes occur dates back to the first university institutions in Europe. Although crime was present in these institutions of higher learning, they remained separated from the rest of society in several ways. In fact, such campuses were originally referred to as sanctuaries. This idea of a campus as a sanctuary had its roots in the violence that was related to the "town versus gown" relationship.

Medieval universities, which were known as *studia generalia*, were institutions characterized by regional significance that drew pupils from beyond their own region. These universities were often at the center of the balance of power between the church and the state. The power of education and its relation to economic and political power were certainly recognized.

Such universities found their origin in the guilds of professors and students who collaborated to protect their rights from those church authorities within their institutions who tried to control their studies and affairs. In fact, the word *university* stems from the Latin *universitas,* which means "consolidation." Prior to the close of the 12th century, the masters in several universities created guilds of medicine, law, theology, and liberal arts because they were vexed at the control exerted by the chancellors who had been given authority over them. The masters wanted control over their own affairs, and they also wanted to issue teaching licenses. They turned to anyone who would help them in their pursuit of autonomy.

During this century, townspeople were often angry at the sense of arrogance students demonstrated because of their privileged status. From this tension, violence ensued. The violence reached its peak at Oxford University on Saint Scholastica's Day in 1354. For three days, the townspeople and the students battled. The university was destroyed and several people died, including two chaplains.

In response to such violent eruptions, the monarchs granted the universities special legal rights and autonomy—including the right of students and faculty to be tried in university courts for any alleged offenses. Thus the tradition of special treatment for college students in courts of law and the criminal justice system dates back to at least the 13th century in Paris and the 14th century at Oxford.

Until recent decades, legal requirements imposed on colleges and universities were virtually absent. Consequently, many universities saw themselves as removed from, and perhaps above, the world of law and lawyers. The tradition of non-intervention by the judicial system and the government can still be seen in the response to campus crime. Student behavior that would have labeled a criminal offense if it happened outside of the university is instead handled from within the walls of academia, generally by the dean of students, who may sanction quick fixes as he or she sees fit. This approach eliminates the criminal stigma for perpetrators, but the outcome may not be well received by victims. Moreover, offenders may not be deterred from reoffending if their behavior is treated so lightly.

Today, status protects a lot of people. On college campuses, the "star" status protects many student-athletes from punitive sanctions when they break the law. Rather than student rebellion and violent demonstrations, which were the more common forms of violence throughout most of academic history, sexual violence is the main issue on college campuses today.

In 2006, Duke University's lacrosse team came to the media's attention after a woman leveled charges of kidnapping and rape at two members of the team. Prior to the scandal, news reports revealed, 15 of the players had court records, generally involving charges of drunken and disorderly conduct.

Although all charges in the Duke case were eventually dropped, sexual assault by athletes remains all too common. One study concluded that while athletes constitute 3.3% of the college population, they perpetrate 19% of all sexual assaults on campus. A study by Dr. Mary P. Koss concluded that male athletes were involved in roughly one-third of all sexual assaults committed on college campuses. This number has held stead, according to the National Coalition Against Violent Athletes. According to a 2005 study, athletes account for less than 2% of the total college student population—but that 2% represents 23% of all sexual assault assailants and perpetrates 14% of the attempted sexual assaults on campuses.

The Benedict-Crosset study was one of the largest and most important on this same topic. It addressed sexual assault at 30 NCAA Division 1 universities in the 1990s. The authors concluded that male student-athletes are responsible for a higher proportion of sexual assaults on Division 1 campuses compared to the rest of the male population.

In the early 2000s, many allegations of inappropriate sexual behavior and rape were made against rugby players at San Diego State; against football players at Penn State, the Naval Academy, the Coast Guard Academy, the University of Oklahoma, and the University of Colorado; and against basketball players at the University of South Dakota. According to the Higher Education Center for Alcohol and Other Drug Abuse and Violence Prevention, gang rapes committed on campuses are most often perpetrated by men who belong to intensive male peer groups who demonstrate rape-supportive behavior and attitudes. One analysis of alleged gang rapes concluded that in 22 of 24 documented cases, the perpetrators were members of either an athletic team or a fraternity. Researchers contend that when such crimes are committed by athletes, society fails to label the act a crime and does not impose harsh sanctions. In fact, many boosters come to the defense of the team they so love. They may deny that a gang rape occurred, instead calling it group sex.

Athletes perpetrate other forms of crime or violence as well. In February 2010, after the starting quarterback at Oregon, Jeremiah Masoli, was accused of stealing laptops, running back LaMichael James was arrested for domestic violence. The athlete faced misdemeanor charges of strangulation, menacing, and assault. James was also arrested in 2008 for disorderly conduct and third-degree battery, but those charges were dismissed. Leniency afforded by status is clearly evident in this case.

The attitude that they are above the law may help explain what prompts athletes to offend. These attitudes may arise because of the special treatment they have been given, often beginning in high school. Additionally, the message sent out to young men in general about being tough, assertive, and aggressive can be detrimental and translate into violence. The "jock culture" and the traditional macho culture in American society have several similarities regarding their underlying values: a sense of entitlement and impunity, bullying, dominance, narcissism, aggression, winning, and being a sexual athlete. These values often lead to violence, rape-supportive attitudes, the devaluation of women, and an us versus them: attitude. From this perspective, anyone who is not a star athlete is flawed and separate from the "heroes."

Sometimes college coaches seem to condone their athletes' violent behavior. For example, the former basketball coach at the University of Maryland, Lefty Driesell, condoned such violence when he called a woman and asked her to drop the rape charges she had brought against one of his athletes. Statements such as the one made by coach Bobby Knight in a 1988 interview—"I think if rape is inevitable, relax and enjoy it"—also send a terrible message to young men in America.

Critics contend that athletes are over-represented as perpetrators not because they actually commit more offenses, but because it is easy to accuse them. They are often very recognizable in their communities. Some note that while athletes are more likely to be accused of sexual offenses, they are not necessarily more likely to be convicted of these crimes. That could mean there is no truth to the charge. Some blame the "groupie" culture that often surrounds high-profile athletes for the frequent charges made against these individuals, asserting that women may throw themselves at these men and then file complaints so as to gain fame or money from out-of-court settlements.

Rebecca Ajo

Further Reading

Benedict, J. (1998). *Athletes and acquaintance rape.* Thousand Oaks, CA: Sage.

Benedict, J. (1999). *Public heroes, private felons: Athletes and crimes against women.* Boston: Northeastern University Press.

Finley, L., & Finley, P. (2006). *The sport industry's war on athletes.* Westport, CT: Praeger.

National Coalition Against Violent Athletes. (n.d.). Retrieved from www.ncava.org

Tarper, J., & Taylor, A. (2006, April 18). Is jock culture a training ground for crime? *ABC News.* Retrieved April 20, 2010, from http://abcnews.go.com/WNT/story?id=1857059&page=1

Athletes and Crime and Violence, High School

Over the years, high school sports have traditionally been seen as a positive factor in students' lives, giving them something to do, keeping them away from delinquency and deviance, teaching them teamwork, instilling in them team spirit and school pride, and providing many with college scholarships. But what of the darker side of sports? What of the associated violence, which may take many forms, and can include many actors, including the players, the cheerleaders, the coaches, the parents, and the fans?

A high school student receives a serious head injury during a football game. Another athlete goes back on the field with a partially healed broken bone and loaded with painkillers. A student suffers a ruptured spleen as a result of an athletic team hazing. Two parents get into fisticuffs at a youth hockey game, and one of them ends up dead. What do we mean by violence and high school athletics? In fact, we mean all of the above, and more.

Some sports, by their very nature, are violent; a certain amount of aggression is allowed, even encouraged. Certain coaching styles may encourage higher levels of aggression. Some high school athletes are rewarded by coaches when they hurt other players, and they may be rewarded again when they receive college scholarships or professional offers to play. Violence on the court or field or rink may be defined as aggressive, dangerous, or excessive unwarranted behaviors that go beyond the bounds of safety and good sportsmanship. Sometimes this violence is intensified because of long-standing team rivalries, rivalries between individual teammates, the desire to win, and the urging of coaches, fans, and parents. One study found that more than 6% of high school sports injuries were caused by illegal actions on the field, particularly in girls' basketball and both boys' and girls' soccer. When sports violence gets out of hand and goes beyond the realm of what is expected, there are restrictions and penalties to punish those who carry it too far.

Students participating in high school sports suffer millions of injuries each year. Two important factors link these injuries to the concept of violence. First, many of these injuries occur in sports that we consider to be violent by nature—football, hockey, rugby, wrestling, and boxing, for example. Second, recurrent injuries are deemed to be more harmful, yet the reality is that many students are encouraged to play before their injuries are completely healed and while loaded up on painkillers to get them through the game. These are unique forms of violence, but violence nonetheless. Recurrent injuries typically involve the head, the ankle, the shoulder, and the knee, and include injuries such as concussions, sprains, strains, and tears. Some injuries may have a permanent effect on the student's lifelong health, just as surely as if they had been brutally mugged on the street.

While a small number of studies differentiate between genders, the majority of research on sports violence has focused on males. Recent research indicates that there is a correlation between males' participation in high school sports and their propensity to engage in fighting, drinking and binge drinking (also correlated with violence), and violence in social settings other than sports. Other studies have found no relationship between sports participation and violent delinquency for either boys or girls; in fact, some researchers have reported that sports can keep young people occupied between the peak hours of juvenile delinquency, from 3:00 P.M. to 6:00 P.M.—that is, after students get out of school, but before their parents arrive home from work. These findings are not necessarily contradictory; one set of studies finds that students who are involved in sports are more likely to get into physical fights than those who are engaged in *other* activities; another set of studies finds athletes are less likely to engage in fighting than students who are not involved in *any* organized activities whatsoever. Some studies have broken down the propensity to fight by the type of sports activity, and found that football players and wrestlers (and even their non-athletic friends) are much more likely to engage in fighting than those playing tennis, basketball, or baseball. Rates of violent and aggressive behaviors among sports participants are similar across rural, suburban, and urban settings.

Some researchers have proposed a direct link between the jocks in the school and the proliferation of school shootings. For example, at Columbine High School, many felt there was a "cult of the athlete," meaning that the coaches and jocks ran the school, not just on the field, but in the halls and any other place where jocks were to be found. It was alleged that student-athletes harassed, humiliated, intimidated, and used violence against the outcasts, such as shooters Eric Harris and Dylan Klebold. In fact, there is a strong pattern of school shooters having been bullied mercilessly (albeit not exclusively by athletes) before they acted.

Another type of violence occurring in high school athletics is hazing. Although there has been widespread publicity about and public outcry against this practice, hazing continues to occur in the schools, and it is very often associated with high school sports teams. Some people believe that hazing today is much more vicious than it was in years past. As a result of hazing, a number of young people have been sexually assaulted, slapped, slugged in the stomach, beaten with hockey sticks or sand-filled bats, dropped on their heads or faces, and piled upon by multiple team members. Youngsters have suffered broken arms, concussions, lacerated/ruptured spleens, broken noses, head injuries, and dental injuries as a result of being hazed. Making the problem even worse is the fact that many times coaches are aware of hazing, but do not intervene to stop it. Some forms of hazing have been comparable to adult criminal activities; consequently, some coaches and players have been charged with criminal offenses, and school authorities have been charged with not reporting instances of child sexual abuse.

Dating violence and sexual assault are among the most prevalent forms of violent crime, in general and specific to athletes. A number of studies have found a correlation between participation in aggressive high school sports and the attitudes of the (male) players toward women. These males have been found to hold more sexist attitudes toward women, and to demonstrate more hostility toward women; they are more likely to use coercion in dating relationships, and are more likely to buy into the rape myths. (Typical rape myths include "no" really means "yes," she was asking for it, and women enjoy being raped.) According to some scholars, success on the field, success with women, and violence are all tools that can raise one's status in the process of male bonding. Of course, although there appears to be a relationship between sports participation and the acceptability of violence in dating, not all athletes are violent in their personal relationships. One scholar, in looking at the relationship between dating violence and sports participation, found that the significant factors were not simply athletic participation or competitiveness, but the need to win or hypercompetitiveness (a "must win" attitude, or the "need to win at any cost").

Sometimes sporting events, particularly evening events, attract unruly crowds, and sometimes students end up dead, as in the case of a California honor student who was shot to death after a high school football game. From Mississippi to Nebraska to Alabama, from football to basketball games (particularly between schools engaged in fierce rivalries), we are seeing everything from after-game brawls to after-game gunshot wounds. Sometimes violence can be attributed to students, at other times to the unruly out-of-school crowds attracted by the game.

Violence does not have to involve the players themselves. It may involve the parents, the coaches, the referees, and the fans. The violence of the parents even has its own name: youth sports rage. In some cases, parental rage has resulted in the death of a coach or another parent, such as the case in Massachusetts where two hockey dads got into a deadly fight—in a bizarre twist, they brawled over the use of violence in the children's hockey game. Youth sports rage has become such a problem that some states, such as New Jersey, are creating or upgrading laws to deal more harshly with parents who become violent in the presence of children at sporting events. While some believe this type of behavior is on the increase, this perception is difficult to confirm; it may be that the media hype associated with the most sensational cases is driving this belief.

One theory that helps to explain violence off the courts is the cultural spillover theory. Simply stated, it suggests that violence by players off the field is the result of society legitimizing violence when it leads to certain socially approved goals or outcomes (such as winning a sporting event)—a modern twist on the old adage, "The end justifies the means." Research indicates that for older players on highly competitive teams, there is indeed a correlation between their sports violence and their violent behavior or their attitude toward violence in certain other settings. Older select league hockey players are more likely to let hockey violence spill over into violence in other sports. By comparison, younger house-league boys are more likely to be involved in domestic violence (although researchers are not certain as to why this is so).

The modeling theory suggests that young children tend to model their attitudes and behaviors on what they see. It is fair to say that young children emulate the behavior of their parents and other close relatives, and that they emulate other role models as well. Professional athletes tend to become role models for young children. The behavior of many professional athletes, both on and off the field, is deplorable, ranging from sexual violence against women, to sponsoring of dog fights, to bar-room brawls, to one former athlete's murder of his wife and her friend. The behavior of the fans, including the child's own relatives, in front of the television or in the stands may also have a deleterious effect on the young child. Children see that in athletics violence is greatly admired and valued, particularly when it leads to a victory. Also, in many cases, the child's games have become so important to the parent, and the parent has such high expectations for performance and the winning of the game, that many children are probably playing much more aggressively than they would if their main objective was to hang out with their friends and have fun. Children may also admire their coaches and look to them as role models, while many coaches, intent on winning, push children into behaviors that inappropriate for their age and incompatible with our societal values.

Other perspectives that help to explain the elevated levels of violence among some athletes include the theory that some young athletes, who because of their "jock identity" tend to belong to the "in-crowd," are greatly admired, believe they are above the law, and are more likely to engage in risk-taking behavior to demonstrate their masculinity. Jock identity is more highly correlated with violence than mere athletic participation. Among the studies that looked at gender, the correlation was higher for males than for females. Another theory is simply that contact sports create positive reactions to violence and/or aggression.

A number of groups have emerged that focus on reducing violence involving and surrounding athletics. Athletes Helping Athletes trains high school athletes in motivational speaking related to violence prevention, among other things. The National Coalition Against Violent Athletes (NCAVA) and Mentors in Violence Prevention (MVP) are two groups that work with athletes and with the public to foster violence prevention through education and outreach programs. MVP encourages young men to become "empowered bystanders" who confront abusers and support victims.

Several other possible solutions have been proposed by a variety of researchers and organizations. Good sportsmanship should be stressed for all players, but especially for youths. Parents, coaches, and children should sign a contract agreeing to maintain civil and non-injurious behaviors on the field and in the stands. Players should not be encouraged to engage in activities designed to "take the other team (or player) out." Fair play and fun should be encouraged. Tougher penalties (such as not being allowed to play for a certain amount of time) could be meted out for on-court misbehavior and violence.

Some believe that youth sports organizations should be licensed, just as day care centers and other organizations are. Background checks should be conducted on coaches. Coaches who believe in nonviolence should be hired and then trained in violence prevention.

Unruly spectators, including parents, could be banned or (as in some places) placed far enough away from the field that they cannot attack a coach or referee or yell inappropriately at the players. Perhaps more violent spectators, and even some overly violent athletes, should be prosecuted in a criminal court.

Finally, with regard to dating violence, mentoring programs could take an athlete-to-athlete approach to speak out against violence and teach athletes about healthy relationships. All of these measures could help emphasize the positive aspects of sports and reduce the some of the associated violence.

Carol Lenhart

Further Reading

Bloom, G., & Smith, M. (1996). Hockey violence: A test of cultural spillover theory. *Sociology of Sport Journal, 13*, 65–77.

Forbes, G., Adams-Curtis, L., Pakalka, A., & White, K. (2006). Dating aggression, sexual coercion, and aggression-supporting attitudes among college men as a function of participation in aggressive high school sports. *Violence Against Women, 12*(5), 441–455.

Gardner, M., Roth, J., & Brooks-Gunn, J. (2009). Sports participation and juvenile delinquency: The role of the peer context among adolescent boys and girls with varied histories of problem behavior. *Developmental Psychology, 45*(2), 341–353.

Kreager, D. (2007). Unnecessary roughness? School sports, peer networks, and male adolescent violence. *American Sociological Review, 72,* 705–725.

Larkin, R. (2007). *Toward a theory of legitimated adolescent violence.* Paper presented at the American Sociological Association Annual Meeting (AN34595204). SocINDEX with Full Text.

Merten, M. (2008). Acceptability of dating violence among late adolescents: The role of sports participation, competitive attitudes, and selected dynamics of relationship violence. *Adolescence, 43*(169), 31–55.

Miller, K., Melnick, M., Barnes, G., Sabo, D., & Farrell, M. (2006). Athletic involvement and adolescent delinquency. *Journal of Youth and Adolescence, 36,* 711–723.

Swenson, D., Yard, E., Fields, S., & Comstock, R. (2009). Patterns of recurrent injuries among U.S. high school athletes, 2005–2008. *American Journal of Sports Medicine, 37*(8), 1586.

Athletes and Violence Prevention

Athletes are over-represented in a number of categories of school crime and violence—in particular, dating/domestic violence and sexual assault. Yet many school and college athletic departments have developed or implemented programs designed to educate students on various types of crime and violence and to help athletes make healthy and safe choices. Additionally, most major sporting leagues have developed some type of program devoted to violence prevention.

The National Collegiate Athletic Association (NCAA) offers numerous resources to assist teams in understanding and preventing hazing. It also makes available a list of speakers who can make presentations focusing on alcohol, tobacco, and other drugs; gambling; sexual assault prevention; and stress management and mental health promotion. Many colleges hire professional speakers to address their athletes and sometimes other groups about specific topics. For example, Mike Domitrz is a speaker whose program "Can I Kiss You?" focuses on healthy relationships. Rape 101: Sexual Assault Prevention for College Athletes is a program designed for college football teams.

Mentors in Violence Prevention (MVP) is one of the most well-known violence prevention programs. MVP is housed at Northeastern University's Center for Sport in Society. It was designed by feminist scholar Jackson Katz to teach student-athletes and student-leaders how to become involved in ending what have often been called "women's issues"—rape, battering, and sexual harassment. The idea is that men and women can both be involved, and that student-athletes and members of other student organizations can take the lead in doing so. MVP trainers are former professional and college athletes.

Instead of assuming that student-athletes and student-leaders are would-be victims or perpetrators, MVP utilizes a bystander approach. These bystanders are then empowered to intervene in safe but helpful ways when they witness abuse and assault. This emphasis is intended to reduce the defensiveness men often feel and the helplessness women often feel when discussing issues of men's violence against women. An independent evaluation that spanned multiple years and utilized mixed messages has found that MVP produces significant changes in regard to students' knowledge about gender violence.

Project Teamwork (PTW) is another program housed at Northeastern University's Center for Sport in Society. PTW was created in 1990 and funded by a three-year grant from Reebok. This six-hour diversity awareness and conflict resolution program is facilitated by former collegiate student-athletes. Multiracial, mixed-gender teams work with middle and high school students to teach them about issues of inequality and discrimination and to provide practical conflict resolution skills. The goal is to empower young people to make positive changes in society.

After completing the six-week PTW curriculum, students form Human Rights Squads. These groups then work together to promote social justice issues in their schools and communities. Once a year, all of the Squads throughout Massachusetts gather at Northeastern University to celebrate their successes.

Coaching Boys into Men (CBIM) is a program designed to help coaches talk to their athletes about respect, integrity, and nonviolence. It is promoted by the Family Violence Prevention Fund and has been adopted by school and youth groups throughout the country.

The National Football League (NFL) has two programs that are designed to help reduce youth violence. NFL Youth Education Towns (YETs) are constructed in Super Bowl host cities. These education and recreational facilities are intended to outlive the actual event and create a positive impact in their communities. The NFL donates $1 million toward YET development during each Super Bowl, focusing on an underserved area of the host city. The Super Bowl host committee finds funds from community groups and corporations to match the NFL's investment, and the NFL requires each host city to establish a 10-year operating and fund-raising plan so that the YETs are a long-term investment. If the Super Bowl is hosted in a city that already has a YET center, the NFL donates the $1 million contribution to that existing center.

Currently, there are 15 YETs in 12 cities: Atlanta, Detroit, Fort Lauderdale, Houston (2), Jacksonville, Los Angeles, Miami, New Orleans, Phoenix, San Diego (2), Tampa (2), and Hawaii. While all of the YET facilities vary to some degree, each provides educational programs, access to physical fitness and personal development programs, recreation opportunities, technology, and many other resources. Further, the NFL partners with the Boys & Girls Clubs of America (B&GCA) to ensure that all centers offer programs and services that effectively meet the needs of youth in the areas of education, technical training, life-skills development, and recreation.

Additionally, the NFL, working with Scholastic, Inc., has created an educational curriculum called One World that emphasizes diversity and acceptance. The 10-week program was created after the terrorist attacks on September 11, 2001. It addresses stereotyping, bigotry, bullying, and racism and can be used in classrooms or afterschool programs.

Major League Baseball (MLB) began a relationship with the Boys & Girls Clubs of America in 1997. B&GCA is a national network of more than 3,700 neighborhood-based facilities annually serving 4.4 million young people, primarily from disadvantaged circumstances, in all 50 states, Puerto Rico, and the Virgin Islands plus domestic and international military bases. Its programs emphasize educational achievement, career exploration, drug and alcohol avoidance, health and fitness, gang and violence prevention, cultural enrichment, leadership development, and community service. Since 1997, MLB and B&GCA have worked together to establish more than 1,000 Reviving Baseball in Inner Cities (RBI) Leagues, which can assist urban youth in resisting crime and violence by offering another prosocial choice. The collaboration has also promoted B&GCA though print, radio, and television public service advertising campaigns. Individual teams and players also work with their local Boys & Girls Clubs to assist young people.

Laura L. Finley

Further Reading

Boys and Girls Clubs of America: Official Charity of MLB: http://mlb.mlb.com/mlb/official_info/community/bgca.jsp
Can I Kiss You?: http://www.canikissyou.com/
Mentors in Violence Prevention: http://www.sportinsociety.org/vpd/mvp.php
NFL Youth Education Towns: https://www.jointheteam.com/programs/program.asp?p=9&c=1
NFL's One World Program Teaches Diversity, Unity: https://www.jointheteam.com/features/?f=34&p=6&c=3
The Program: Coaching Boys Into Men. http://www.coaches-corner.org/the-program/
Project Teamwork: http://www.sportinsociety.org/vpd/ptw.php

Auvinen, Pekka-Eric

On November 7, 2007, in Tuusula, Finland, a city about 30 miles from the country's capital, a school shooting took place at Jokela High School. Pekka-Eric Auvinen, age 18 and a student of the school, killed 6 students, the school nurse, and the principal, and injured at least 10 others; he then killed himself.

Auvinen was described by others as a loner who had suffered from bullying. He described himself as an outcast on his YouTube profile. However, his friends saw him as a normal student who was pretty happy. Auvinen had been on antidepressant medications since the age of 17. The drugs he was taking, however, have been known to cause thoughts of suicide in young adults. Friends said that Auvinen had been changing before the shooting, and they had been seeing a different side to him. When a friend expressed concern to him about his change in behavior, Auvinen claimed he was only joking about comments he would make and drawings of massacres. The friend did not think he would actually do anything.

Police officers walk to the Jokela High School building in Jokela, Finland, on November 8, 2007, one day after a student killed six students, the principal, and the school nurse. (AP/Wide World Photos)

Auvinen was a member of the Helsinki Shooting Club, which recommended that he get a more powerful gun than the one he owned. His application for the weapon was turned down, however, because it was felt to be too strong of a gun for his goal, which he stated was target practice. Auvinen used a .22 caliber pistol during the Jokela school shooting, which he named Catherine. He had no previous record and had no previous incidents at school, unlike some other school shooters.

Auvinen was called "the YouTube Killer," after it was discovered that he had posted approximately 90 videos on the website that were admiring of notorious killers, including Eric Harris and Dylan Klebold (Columbine High School), Hitler and other Nazis, Jack the Ripper, Stalin, Timothy McVeigh, and Jeffrey Dahmer. He also included images of the burning of a cult's compound in Waco, Texas, and other attacks. His user name on YouTube was Sturmgeist89; the word *sturmgeist* in German means "storm spirit." Auvinen changed his user name to this one after his last choice, NaturalSelector89, was taken down by YouTube. One video he posted imitated a video made by Harris and Klebold, the school shooters at Columbine High School.

The most serious video Auvinen posted was titled "Jokela High School Massacre 11/7/07," which chronicled his plans before he carried out the shooting.

In the video, he was shown holding a gun as he claimed that he was a social Darwinist and stated that he would weed out the weak people in society. Auvinen kept saying that he was willing to die for what he believed in, which was changing what he felt to be a messed-up society. In his video foreshadowing what was to come, he also told viewers not to blame anyone except him for what would happen. He said it was not video games, movies, his parents, or anything else that caused him to do what he would do, but instead his own beliefs. He basically said it was him against the world. "Jokela High School Massacre" was the last video Auvinen posted before the shooting. A suicide note written by Auvinen was found after the shooting. In it, he discussed how he hated society and gave his goodbyes to his family.

Many have discussed similarities between this shooting and the one in Columbine High School in the United States. As previously mentioned, Auvinen included Columbine imagery in his YouTube videos. He also used some of the same music in his YouTube postings that Eric Harris, one of the perpetrators of the Columbine massacre, used on his internet. Another similarity was that Auvinen played the video game Doom, which many believe played a large part in motivating the Columbine shootings. Also, all three of these shooters—Auvinen, Harris, and Klebold—had been bullied.

On the day of the shooting, Auvinen killed the headmistress, a nurse, and six students, including five males and one female. Everyone who died that day was shot more than once, some as many as 20 times. According to police, this behavior indicates that Auvinen thought about each shooting, instead of shooting wildly. Also, he targeted his victims' heads and chests. Police said those killed did not move after they were shot, which indicated how deadly even the first shots were. According to officials, the victims most likely could not have been helped even if emergency services came right away, owing to the serious nature of their injuries. Many more students were injured. Although police believe Auvinen was not targeting any students specifically, he did shoot some and chose not to shoot others.

The principal, Helena Kalmi, was killed in an execution-style murder. At first, she ran away from Auvinen, but then for unknown reasons—possibly attempting to stop him—she went back to him. At that point, Auvinen forced her to her knees and shot her seven times, while a number of ninth graders in a classroom watched through the window. Police investigators did not believe the principal was a primary target for Auvinen, although they discovered a disagreement between the two had occurred before the shooting occurred. Auvinen then shot the nurse, who was trying to assist injured students.

In keeping with Auvinen's YouTube profile and videos of changing society, it appeared that Auvinen was trying to start a student revolution during the shooting, as he tried to persuade the other students to destroy the school. However, no students joined him. While he was yelling at them to join him, Auvinen was roaming the school randomly shooting his gun.

The shooting started around 11:40 A.M., and the police were called 3 minutes later. The police came 11 minutes after they were called, although they did not actually go into the school until 3 hours later. By 12:30 P.M., there were approximately 100 police officers surrounding the building. Auvinen used 69 out of the roughly 400 bullets he brought with him. He also tried to set a fire in the school, although it did not work. When police arrived and tried to force him to surrender, he responded by shooting at them. Sometime during this period and in the midst of the commotion caused by students jumping out of windows and trying to escape the shooting, Auvinen shot himself in the head. He did not die at the scene, but rather succumbed to his injury later at the hospital. Sources differ on the length of the shooting incident, citing times varying between 20 and 40 minutes. After Auvinen was found injured, the police continued to scour the building, making sure there were no other shooters.

In the wake of this shooting, Finland considered changing its school security measures. The Finnish government also began considering passing stricter gun laws, as the country has the third highest gun ownership rate among civilians in the world. However, one suggested change—raising the minimum age for gun ownership to 18—would not have made a difference in this incident. The Jokela shooting was very shocking to the Finnish population, although it has a strong tradition of supporting gun ownership. According to a number of sources, school shootings are not very common in Finland. In fact, the shooting by Pekka-Eric Auvinen was only the second school shooting in Finland's history. The only other incident occurred in 1989, when a 14-year-old shot two students at his school. However, there had been other public shootings in Finland, just not in schools. For example, in 1994, a 22-year-old shot 3 people while he was on army leave. In 2002, a 19-year-old killed 7 people and injured 115 with a bomb in a shopping center.

On September 23, 2008, a year after Auvinen's shooting, another school shooting occurred in Kauhajoki, Finland. Ten people were shot and killed by Matti Juhani Saari, who then killed himself. Finnish officials believe Saari knew Auvinen.

Finnish police had to deal with many threats to schools after Auvinen's shooting, which they believe involved people copying that incident. Only two days after the Jokela shooting, threats were made against three different schools on the Internet. One of these was in Tuusula, just like the Jokela shooting; the others were in Maaninka and Kirkkonummi. Three weeks after Auvinen's shooting, the police made a public statement urging people to stop making threats against schools.

After the shooting, people also threatened Auvinen's parents; the police gave them protection. The Jokela school shooting was a case in which there was no one to prosecute, as Auvinen killed himself.

Sharon Thiel

Further Reading

Lieberman, J., & Sachs, B. (2008). *School shootings*. New York: Kensington.

Man kills eight at Finnish school. (2007). *BBC*. Retrieved November 2, 2008, from http://news.bbc.co.uk/

School massacre: Ninth graders saw killing of school principal. (2007). *Helsingin Sanomat*. Retrieved November 15, 2008, from http://www.hs.fi/

School shootings rare in Finland. (2007). *YLE*. Retrieved November 7, 2008, from http://www.yle.fi/news/left/id74423.htm

Sturmgeist89's YouTube rant. (2007). *Herald Sun*. Retrieved November 22, 2008, from http://www.news.com.au/heraldsun

B

Bath, Michigan, School Bombing

The small community of Bath, Michigan, was the scene of the largest school bombings in terms of loss of life in U.S. history. On May 18, 1927, the North Wing of Bath Consolidated School exploded, leading to the deaths of 38 students plus five adults. The final death toll stood at 45 and included the perpetrator and his wife (who was killed before the bombing at the school took place). The perpetrator of this mass murder was school board member Andrew Kehoe, a 55-year-old man who lived in the small community. Although the bombing in Bath resembles many contemporary news stories, the story of this small community and those who lost their lives is not widely known.

In 1927, the Bath Township, located 10 miles northeast of Lansing, was a small agricultural community. There were no street lights in Bath—just one road ran through the middle of town. There was a drug store, a gas station, a small grocery store, and an auto repair/blacksmith shop. There was also the recently built Bath Consolidated School, located in the town's center. In 1922, the citizens of Bath voted to form a consolidated school distinct to serve the school-aged children of Bath and the surrounding areas. As was the case for all public schools in the United States, the township planned to support the school through property taxes levied on property owners. When the newly constructed Bath Consolidated School opened, there were 236 students enrolled from first through 12th grades.

Andrew Kehoe was born in Tecumseh, Michigan, on February 1, 1872. His mother died when Kehoe was very young and his father soon remarried. According to some sources, the relationship between Kehoe and his stepmother was not good. When Kehoe was 14 years of age, his stepmother suffered a horrible accident in their home: While she was attempting to light the family's oil stove, the stove exploded. Kehoe was home at the time of the explosion but reportedly did little to help his stepmother. She later died as a result of the burns she sustained in the explosion. Some believed at the time that Kehoe was involved in the accident.

Kehoe completed high school and later attended Michigan State College in East Lansing, where his interests included electronics and mechanics. He traveled during his early adult years to the Midwest to continue his study of electronics. Eventually he returned to Michigan and married Nellie Price. Kehoe had met Nellie while attending Michigan State College. Once married, the couple bought a 185-acre farm from the estate of one of Nellie's uncles near the township of Bath. They remained there until their deaths in May 1927.

Kehoe was known throughout the area as intelligent, meticulous, and good with machinery and electronics. He was also considered an expert in the use of dynamite and explosives, which were common tools among local farmers for clearing land and stump removal. But there was also a darker side of Andrew Kehoe—he was known for his short temper and the cruel treatment of his farm animals.

Nellie Kehoe contracted tuberculosis, and required many hospitalizations over the years. Her chronic condition was thought to have placed a severe drain on the family finances. Kehoe was publicly critical of the property tax rates assessed by the Bath Consolidated School District and he eventually stopped making his mortgage payments. In an ironic twist, he was elected to the school board in 1924 and served as Treasurer. Throughout this time, Kehoe developed an antagonistic relationship with School Superintendent Emory Huyck, whom he consistently accused of financial mismanagement. While on the school board, Kehoe campaigned for lower taxes, and he blamed the school district for much of his personal financial troubles. Kehoe was an enigma: He was critical of the school district itself, yet he volunteered around the school as an informal mechanic or handyman.

On the morning of May 18, 1927, Kehoe's neighbor, Monty Ellsworth, was planting melons on his farm. He later recalled that at 9:45 A.M., he felt "a tremendous explosion." Ellsworth could not tell where the explosion originated, but his wife was on the second story of their home and could see smoke coming from the east, where the Bath school was located. Monty Ellsworth detected smoke coming from the Kehoe Farm to the west. Suddenly the smoke in the direction of the school cleared, and Mrs. Ellsworth screamed, "My God, the schoolhouse has blown up!" Both Ellsworths ran for the family car and drove as fast as they could to the site that was once the Bath Consolidated School. When they arrived, there were already a dozen or so people on the scene, and the Ellsworths were told that their son, a second-grader, was free from the rubble and evidently unharmed. Immediately Monty Ellsworth began assisting others.

The scene was horrific. The walls of the building had been blown outward, allowing the roof to collapse down into the classrooms, trapping many children. Children both living and dead could be seen in the rubble. It quickly became clear that the rescue effort would require many tools. Ellsworth, along with other townspeople, went back to their homes to gather the necessary items. As he drove back toward his farm, Ellsworth passed Andrew Kehoe driving in the opposite direction, toward the school. Kehoe smiled and gave Ellsworth a big wave.

At that time, no one realized that two bomb blasts had already taken place in Bath that morning: one at the Kehoe farm and one at the school. A third explosion was still to come. Throughout the preceding days, Andrew Kehoe had filled the back seat of his car with metal bits and debris: nails, old pieces of farm machinery, broken tools, and anything else he could find that would act as shrapnel. He then loaded a large amount of dynamite behind the front seat and placed a loaded rifle in the passenger's seat. He drove to the Bath Consolidated School site. When he arrived, he saw Superintendent Huyck and called him over to the car. One eyewitness stated that once Huyck got close to the vehicle, Kehoe fired the rifle into the back seat. The dynamite in the car detonated, causing a third large explosion, instantly killing Kehoe and Huyck, along with Postmaster Glenn O. Smith and Smith's father-in-law. Cleo Claton, a second grader who had survived the school explosion, was hit and killed by flying shrapnel from Kehoe's car. Several others in the crowd of rescuers were injured in this third and final blast.

Those on the scene were now in complete shock. Many did not understand the source of the explosions. O. H. Buck was a foreman for a road crew working in the area. He described the scene: "I began to feel as though the world was coming to an end. I guess I was a bit hazy. Anyway, the next thing I remember I was out on the street."

Hundreds of people worked all day to save children and teachers from the debris of the Bath school building. Volunteers came from surrounding communities, many bringing much needed equipment plus human power. Fire fighters and the Fire Chief of the Lansing Fire Department came to aid the effort, along with members of the Michigan State Police. A triage center was set up in the pharmacy and a temporary morgue in the Town Hall.

Ambulances joined the steady stream of personal vehicles to transport the injured to hospitals in Lansing. Michigan Governor Fred Green arrived in Bath in the afternoon and immediately pitched in to help. As the relief effort went on throughout the day, another 500 pounds of dynamite was found in the school's South Wing—unexploded. The Michigan State Police immediately stopped the recovery effort and disarmed Kehoe's last unexploded device.

In the aftermath of the disaster, along with the discovery of the South Wing unexploded device, a full and complete picture of horrific mass murder began to emerge. Investigators moved to Kehoe's farm to investigate the fires seen by Ellsworth earlier in the day. The next day, investigators combing through the remains of Kehoe's farm discovered the badly burned corpse of Nellie Kehoe. Hospital records showed that she had been released from St. Lawrence Hospital in

Lansing on May 16. The coroner speculated that her death was caused by blunt-force trauma to the head before the fire took place. All of Kehoe's animals were trapped in their pens and stalls and died as a result of the fire. Investigators at the Kehoe farm found a wooden sign on the fence that carried one last message: "Criminals are made, not born." The investigators estimated that the unused materials and farm equipment would have easily paid off Kehoe's mortgage.

Andrew Kehoe devised a merciless act of terror. His actions took the lives of 44 other people, most of whom were children. Somehow the story of the Bath School Bombing has faded from history. The week following the bombing in Bath, another famous Michigander made national headlines: Charles Lindbergh made his historic trans-Atlantic flight on May 20–21, 1927. The Bath School Bombing may not be a well-known story, but it remains the most costly act of school violence in U.S. history.

Karen Lindsey

Further Reading

The Bath School Disaster on Rootsweb: http://freepages.history.rootsweb.ancestry.com/~bauerle/disaster.htm

Bernstein, A. (2009). *Bath massacre: America's first school bombing.* Ann Arbor, MI: University of Michigan Press.

Information about the Bath School Disaster (includes the text of Monty J. Ellsworth's book): http://daggy.name/tbsd/

National Public Radio: Bath School disaster. Retrieved from http://www.npr.org/templates/story/story.php?storyId=103186662

Baylor College Basketball Murder Case

The Baylor college basketball team was already in trouble when perhaps the most tragic of all sports scandals occurred. Under Coach Dave Bliss, the team was under investigation by the National Collegiate Athletic Association (NCAA) for a number of violations when details emerged in October 2003 about Coach Bliss's lurid attempts to cover up under-the-table payments to players.

On June 12, 2003, team member Carlton Dotson shot and killed teammate Patrick Dennehy while the two were firing pistols at a gravel pit. Dotson told no one. A week later, Dennehy's family reported him missing when they were unable to contact him. Dotson virtually turned himself in to authorities in his home state of Maryland, having called them to report that he needed help because he heard voices. He reportedly confessed to killing Dennehy to an FBI agent, but told the agent that he did it in self-defense, claiming Dennehy had tried to kill him at the gravel pit but his gun jammed. Speaking to reporters later, however, Dotson denied that he had confessed. Six weeks after his disappearance but just days after Dotson's arrest, Dennehy's decomposed body was found near the gravel pit outside of Waco, Texas. He had been shot twice in the head.

Dotson was at first ruled incompetent to stand trial and sent to a state mental facility, as he claimed to suffer from hallucinations and paranoia. He thought people were trying to kill him because he was Jesus. Doctors at the facility believed he was faking, however. Just as the trial was about to commence, Dotson pleaded guilty. He was sentenced to 35 years in prison.

Coach Bliss had been making payments to Dennehy to cover his tuition and other expenses, in violation of NCAA regulations. Bliss feared that his blatant disregard for the NCAA rules would be uncovered during the investigation of Dennehy's murder. He concocted the story that Dennehy was really a drug dealer who paid his own tuition through his "work." Unbeknownst to Bliss, Assistant Coach Abar Rouse had taped conversations capturing incriminating information about Bliss's rules violations as well as his plan to cover up those offenses. Bliss was even heard trying to convince another player to go along with his "drug dealer" story.

Bliss was forced to resign on August 8 after admitting that two players were receiving improper payments (totaling more than $30,000) and that he had tried to cover everything up. He was banned from being hired by an NCAA-member team without "just cause," at least until 2015. It was later revealed that Bliss had also made payments to amateur teams with standout players and covered up failed drug tests for players. He did some coaching after he left Baylor, spending one season with the Dakota Wizards of the Continental Basketball Association (CBA) and then a summer in China with a team from Athletes in Action, a ministry that uses sports as a platform. In summer 2009, Bliss moved back to Texas, as his daughter had given birth to his new granddaughter. He claimed he let the competitive world of sports get the best of him.

The NCAA considered shutting down the Baylor basketball program, but reconsidered when Baylor self-imposed sanctions. These included the resignation of Bliss, the loss of scholarships, and a ban on postseason play. The NCAA added to that punishment five years of probation and a ban from playing any nonconference games for one season.

Laura L. Finley

Further Reading

Finley, P., Finley, L., & Fountain, J. (2008). *Sports scandals*. Westport, CT: Praeger.

Jimenez, D. (2009, July 18). Bliss back in Texas again after Baylor basketball scandal. *USA Today*. Retrieved April 22, 2010, from http://www.usatoday.com/sports/college/mensbasketball/2009-07-18-bliss-back-in- texas_N.htm

Lindgren, H. (2002, August 31). The way we live now: 8-31-03; Blood sport. *New York Times Magazine.* Retrieved April 21, 2010, from http://www.nytimes.com/ 2003/08/31/magazine/the-way-we-live-now-8-31-03-blood- sport.html

Beslan School Hostage Crisis

The Russian republic of North Ossetia-Alania is home to many Russian military bases, and a major city there is Beslan (population = approximately 35,000). In early September 2004, a hostage crisis in Beslan resulted in the death of at least 386 children, adults, rescuers and hostage takers in what became known as the Beslan Massacre. This situation originated as a terrorist attack during the Second Chechen War, in which the perpetrators aimed to capture world attention and direct it to the plight of the Chechens. The attackers also expected that it might lead to ethnic violence in the Caucasus and result in spreading conflict throughout the region.

The origins of the hostage crisis lay in the events that had taken place in Chechnya since some Chechens declared independence in 1991 under Dzhokhar Dudayev. This event led to the First Chechen War, as the Russian Federation sought to retain its control over Chechnya, an area rich in oil. The war lasted from 1994 until 1996, when Russian President Boris Yeltsin ordered a ceasefire, leading to a peace treaty in 1997. By this time Chechnya had suffered badly, with at least 35,000 civilians dead, as many as 7,500 Russian soldiers dead, and perhaps as many as 15,000 Chechen separatists killed. Although the fighting had stopped, the region became lawless, with hundreds of kidnappings for ransom, and clashes with the leaders of the increasingly militant Chechen separatists embracing fundamentalist Islam. This instability led to the Second Chechen War, which saw the destruction of much of the rest of Chechnya.

An elderly woman carries a small child past the ruins of the Beslan school just days after the deadly hostage crisis that took the lives of nearly 400 people, mostly young children, in North Ossetia, Russia, in 2004. (AP/Wide World Photos)

Many of the Russian attacks on Chechens were launched from bases in the North Ossetia-Alania. Though most of the fighting took place in Chechnya, some Chechens had launched attacks in Moscow and other places in September 1999. These assaults resulted in the deaths of 300 civilians as apartments were bombed, some of which collapsed. Some of the bombers were arrested and jailed by Russian courts in January 2004. It seemed likely that the Chechens would attack elsewhere, but few expected that the target would be a school.

The school chosen for the attack was Comintern Street S.N.O. Some sources claimed that the Ossetian militia had used this school before the First Chechen War as a site to intern civilians from Ingushetia, a small Russian republic closely connected with Chechnya. Some media reports stated that some of the Ingush civilians were held in the school's gymnasium, which may have also helped influence the choice of the school as a target. Russian government officials have denied claims that some Chechens disguised themselves as repairmen and hid weapons and explosives in the school during the summer holidays.

The Chechens decided to take over the school on September 1, the first day of the Russian school year. This date is known as the "Day of Knowledge" because both new and returning students are accompanied by their parents, and often grandparents and other relatives, in a series of events held at schools to familiarize the entire community with the school curriculum and plans. This practice meant that there would be large numbers of adults at the Beslan school, which normally housed approximately 800 students and 60 teachers and support staff.

The Chechen separatists—men and women—who stormed the building may have arrived in two groups. It was subsequently estimated that as many as 32 participated in the assault. They seized control of the school, firing into the air with machine guns. Some 50 people managed to flee the school, while others hid in various rooms, particularly the boiler room. Armed police and one armed civilian fired at the attackers, killing one of them and wounding two others. Ultimately, the terrorists managed to get between 1,100 and 1,200 hostages—children, adult relatives, and teachers—and herd them into the school gymnasium. There they ordered everyone to speak in Russian only, shooting dead a man who translated the order into Ossetic, the local language. Another student's father was shot dead for refusing to kneel for the attackers, and another was killed when he was found using a mobile telephone; the terrorists had ordered everyone to hand over their telephones. The terrorists also isolated 17 adult males whom they thought might pose a physical threat to them, and shot them all. One of these men was badly injured and survived, and another managed to escape.

By this time, the Russian police and army had surrounded the school, albeit not very effectively. Many local people had arrived at the site and were anxious about relatives held at the school, and some of these newcomers were armed. To stop the authorities from storming the gymnasium, the terrorists put explosive devices around the room and stated that they would kill 50 hostages for each Chechen killed by the authorities. They were also anxious to prevent the police from using gas to subdue the attackers, as they had done in the Moscow Dubrovka Theater in October 2002, and smashed the windows to thwart this tactic. Although the terrorists wanted Alexander Dzasokhov, the president of North Ossetia, to negotiate with them, the Russian Federal Security Service (F.S.B.) refused to let him do so. Consequently, they planned on how to storm the building. By the end of that day the United Nations Security Council, at the request of Russia, demanded the "immediate and unconditional release of all hostages of the terrorist attack."

On the second day of the hostage crisis, the terrorists refused to allow food, water, or medicine to be taken in to the hostages, and would not permit authorities to remove the dead bodies. They attacked the adults and children, while the F.S.B. remained uncertain what to do. The Russian President, Vladimir Putin, made a short statement about the authorities wanting to rescue the hostages, but did not elaborate. By this time, two police headquarters were dealing with the crisis—one that was operating publicly, and another, secret one that was actually making the key decisions.

Ruslan Arushev, a former Soviet Army general and a one-time president of Ingushetia, arrived at the school in the afternoon of the second day. The terrorists released 15 children and 11 nursing mothers to him. Arushev was also given a videotape of the conditions in the gymnasium: The hot weather and the large number of people in the room meant that some people, especially many children, took off some of their clothes. However, without water or food, both children and adults started fainting.

That afternoon terrorists fired grenades at a nearby police car, but the Russian authorities held their fire. It was clear that the government was hoping that the terrorists would tire first. It also seems possible that some of the Chechens were taking drugs to remain alert, resulting in them becoming unpredictable and sometimes hysterically shouting at crying children.

On the third day, a number of local politicians arrived on the scene, a few stating that they were ready to offer themselves as hostages. Aslambek Aslakhanov, an adviser to the Russian president, and a former local police general, managed to get the names of some 700 well-known Russians who were willing to take the places of the children. It was agreed that Aslakhanov would meet with the terrorists at 3 P.M. Two hours before the planned meeting, two ambulances were allowed into the school grounds to remove the dead bodies. However, as they approached the school, an explosion occurred and shooting started, with parts of the gymnasium roof collapsing on the hostages below. Because many of the hostages were so weakened by not having eaten or had any water, many were not able to escape. Later investigations suggested that the explosion was a terrorist bomb that detonated prematurely.

Because the shooting took the authorities by surprise, they were not in a position to return fire immediately. As the terrorists started detonating bombs, the Russian troops stormed the building, with many hostages being killed as they tried to escape. After two hours of shooting, the Russians managed to take control of most of the school compound. One group of terrorists tried to hold out in the basement. Another group of 13 managed to break through the police cordon and enter a nearby building, which was subsequently destroyed by Russian tanks and flamethrowers. One suspected terrorist was lynched by a local crowd, and one was captured alive hiding under a truck. When Putin ordered the borders of North Ossetia closed the following day, rumors circulated that some of the terrorists had escaped.

On September 4, Vladimir Putin appeared at the Beslan hospital where hundreds of people were being treated. It is believed that some 186 children, 148 adult hostages, several members of the security forces, and most of the terrorists were killed—for a total of at least 386 killed. Because of the high death toll, the Russian authorities came in for criticism on a number of fronts. Apart from their unwillingness to negotiate (though the shooting of hostages rendered such discussions very problematic), they did not have sappers or a bomb-disposal group on hand to defuse the bombs in the gymnasium, nor did they arrange for the fire brigade to be close by when the school was stormed. However, their biggest failure was that they did not recognize that many of the adult hostages and most of the children were so weakened, both emotionally and physically, by the 2½ days as hostages that they did not have the energy to escape.

The terrorist aims of inciting a racial war did not succeed, but the event did lead to many members of the Russian public turning on Chechens. In addition, opinion polls revealed that many Russians started to support the death penalty for terrorism. Moreover, as many as one-third of Russians whose opinions were sought wanted all Chechens banned from major cities.

Justin Corfield

Further Reading

Dolnik, A. (2007). *Negotiating the impossible? The Beslan hostage crisis.* London: Royal United Services Institute.

Dunlop, J. (2006). *The 2002 Dubrocka and 2004 Beslan hostage crises: A critique of Russian counter-terrorism.* Stuttgart: Ibidem-Verlag.

Giduck, J. (2006). *Terror at Beslan: A Russian tragedy with lessons for America's schools.* Boulder, CO: Paladin Press.

Lansford, L. (2006). *Beslan: Shattered innocence.* Charleston, SC: BookSurge,

Phillips, T. (2007). *Beslan: The tragedy of School Number 1.* London: Granta Books.

Uschan, M. (2005). *The Beslan school siege and separatist terrorism.* Strongsville, OH: Gareth Stevens Publishing.

Bias, Len

The cocaine overdose of University of Maryland superstar basketball player Len Bias prompted changes not only in the world of collegiate athletics, but in the United States in general. Bias's death at age led to national discussion about drug abuse and motivated the U.S. Congress to enact massive changes in drug policy.

Bias was the undeniable star of the University of Maryland's 1986 basketball team. He was Maryland's all-time leading scorer and a two-time Atlantic Coast Conference Player of the Year. He was also the second-overall draft pick in the 1986–1987 draft, signing with the Boston Celtics as their number one pick.

Bias collapsed in his dormitory room on June 19, 1986, at approximately 6:30 A.M. He and friend Brian Tribble, as well as teammates Terry Long and David Gregg, had been having a "cocaine party" in which "scoops" of cocaine were available to each. Bias had ingested a large amount of the drug and suffered three seizures before the paramedics arrived and pronounced him dead at 8:50 A.M. A subsequent search found nine grams of cocaine in Bias's car. Long and Gregg were kicked off the team for the 1986–1987 season, and the loss of the three players resulted in the team enduring its worst season ever. Charges against Long and Gregg were dropped in exchange for their testimony against Tribble, who was acquitted in June 1987 of having provided Bias with the cocaine.

Immediately, allegations were made against Maryland coach Charles "Lefty" Driesell for tolerating drug use among his players and failing to uphold even the most minimal academic standards. Driesell had previously referred to cocaine as "performance enhancing." Many accused the coach of recruiting athletes who were tremendously gifted athletically but who were very marginal academically. Although he resigned from the head coach position, Driesell went on to take the position of Assistant Athletic Director in charge of fundraising. He later coaches

College basketball star Len Bias poses in his University of Maryland uniform. Bias died from a drug overdose only two days after being drafted by the Boston Celtics. (AP/Wide World Photos)

at James Madison University and Georgia State. He retired in 2003 and was named to the National Collegiate Basketball Hall of Fame in 2007.

The National Basketball Association (NBA) vowed to better investigate the private lives of players who were suspected of drug abuse, a move that was contested by the player's union. At the time, the NBA drug-tested athletes only when it had reason to believe they were using illegal substances. Many called on the league to institute more testing in the wake of Bias's death.

Congress used the Bias case as a high-profile example of why tougher drug laws were needed. Democrats seized the opportunity to best Republicans and "get tough on crime" by enacting mandatory minimum sentences for drug crimes. The Anti-Drug Abuse Act of 1986 required mandatory minimum sentences, ranging from 5 to 10 years, for those found with a specified amount of certain drugs.

Laura L. Finley

Further Reading

Finley, P., Finley, L., & Fountain, J. (2008). *Sports scandals.* Westport, CT: Praeger.

Neff, C., & Selcraig, B. (1986, November 10). One shock wave after another. *Sports Illustrated Vault.* Retrieved April 22, 2010, from http://sportsillustrated.cnn.com/vault/article/magazine/MAG1065459/4/index.htm

Sterling, E. (n.d.). Drug laws and snitching: A primer. *PBS Frontline.* Retrieved April 22, 2010, from http://www.pbs.org/wgbh/pages/frontline/shows/snitch/primer/

Big Brothers Big Sisters

Big Brothers Big Sisters (BBBS) is the oldest and largest youth mentoring organization in the United States. It has provided one-on-one youth services for more than a century for children ages 6 through 18.

BBBS was started in 1904 when New York City court clerk Ernest Coulter noticed an increased number of boys coming through the courtroom. Coulter believed that the guidance of caring adults could help kids stay out of trouble, so he began seeking volunteer mentors. At about the same time, a group called the Ladies of Charity began to assist girls in the New York Children's Court. This organization later became known as Catholic Big Sisters. Both groups worked independently until 1977, when they merged to become Big Brothers Big Sisters of America. The organization now operates in all 50 states and in 12 countries through its global associate, Big Brothers Big Sisters International—Australia,

Bermuda, Bulgaria, Canada, Germany, Ireland, Israel, the Netherlands, New Zealand, Poland, Russia, and South Africa.

Students are carefully matched with a trained adult. Whenever possible, BBBS pairs youth with mentees who are the same sex and same ethnicity. Volunteers are screened and undergo training before they are assigned a youth mentee. Mentors may meet with their mentees in school or in the community, with a commitment to do so at least once per week. These sessions are supposed to be fun, not necessarily academic. Mentors and mentees might get together to play games, walk outside, attend events, share food, or engage in a number of other activities. BBBS treats parents or guardians as partners, ensuring that mentees are positive role models for children but not replacements for family.

Evaluation results have shown BBBS to have a positive impact in the lives of youth. A study conducted in 1992–1993 found that, after spending 18 months with their mentors, young people in the program were:

- 46% less likely to begin using illegal drugs
- 27% less likely to begin using alcohol
- 52% less likely to skip school
- 37% less likely to skip a class
- More confident of their performance in schoolwork
- One-third less likely to hit someone
- Getting along better with their families

In addition to providing information about ways to get involved (as a mentor or a mentee), the history of the organization, and its programs, the BBBS website features specific information on African American, Hispanic, Native American, faith-based, and military mentoring.

Laura L. Finley

Further Reading

Big Brothers Big Sisters: http://www.bbbs.org
Big Brothers Big Sisters International: http://www.bbbsi.org/

Biological Theories

Some researchers maintain that there is a biological basis for crime and violence, theorizing that biological and genetic factors affect the brain and central nervous system in ways that lead to delinquent behavior. Biological theories (sometimes called trait theories or positivism) of crime and violence focus on how a youth's brain and central nervous system respond to the world, and conclude this response is the basis for criminality. To the biological theorist, delinquency is not a youth's choice, but rather a product of biological and genetic factors (or traits) outside the offender's control.

Biological theorists view delinquency as "deviant" or "abnormal." They consider crime to be a product of physical or psychological traits, including intelligence quotients (IQs) and body types. Biological theorists believe that the scientific method can be used to measure the traits of delinquent (abnormal) youths, with such youths being compared to nondelinquent (normal) youths to determine which traits are connected with crime and violence.

Early biological theories focused on the physical features of delinquents, stating that they "looked" different from non-offenders. Cesare Lombroso (1835–1909), an Italian physician, was the first to put forward this theory. He is considered to be the father of criminology. According to Lombroso's theory, which he termed "criminal atavism," delinquents were biologically and mentally less evolved than the average person. While Lombroso was a believer in the theory of evolution, he did not believe that all people were equally evolved. Notably, he viewed delinquents as "throwbacks" to earlier stages in the evolutionary process.

Lombroso's research focused on the measurement of teeth, eyes, ears, jaws, and arms of offenders, and compared these measurements to those in the general population. Often, the larger the features, the more they resembled animal features; thus Lombroso stated that such characteristics were indicative of lesser stages of human evolution. He also researched other features, including purported insensitivity to pain, cruelty, impulsiveness, and tattooing. The more of these features a delinquent exhibited, the more Lombroso thought it likely that the individual was inclined toward criminality. In short, he suggested that criminals were born that way. Lombroso is called the father of criminology because he was the first to apply scientific principles to the study of crime. He carefully measured his subjects of study, recorded his findings, and based his theories on those findings.

Later, English physician Charles Buckman Goring (1870–1919) built on Lombroso's theories. Using scientific methods of measurement and observation, Goring concluded that Lombroso's theory of criminal atavism was incorrect. Goring theorized that delinquency was closely linked to a condition he called "defective intelligence"—an inherited trait passed on from parents. Based on this reasoning, Goring believed that delinquency could best be eliminated by regulating who could have children. People who were deemed to be feeble-minded, were epileptic, or had a history of mental illness or had "defective social instinct" were best prohibited from having children, he suggested.

Researchers who agreed that delinquency was an inherited condition expanded on Goring's work. Richard Louis Dugdale (1841–1883) and Arthur H.

Estabrook traced the family trees of delinquents and criminals in an attempt to determine whether criminality is inherited and delinquency is genetically based. Both of these social scientists studied a particular family who had a crime record going back generations. The Juke family was written about in 1875 by Dugdale (*The Jukes: A Study in Crime, Pauperism, Disease, and Heredity*) and in 1916 by Estabrook (*The Jukes in 1915*). Dugdale found that from the 1700s to the mid-1870s, the Juke family had produced 7 murderers, 60 habitual thieves, approximately 90 other criminals, 50 prostitutes, and 280 paupers. Estabrook, who followed up Dugdale's work 41 years later, identified a further 378 prostitutes, 170 paupers, and 118 other criminals in the Juke family tree.

Other researchers suggested that body type is an indicator of a propensity toward juvenile delinquency and criminality. William H. Sheldon, for example, thought that some body types make youths susceptible to delinquency. Seldon identified four different body types: (1) endomorphs—soft, round, overweight people; (2) mesomorphs—large, athletic, muscular people; (3) ectomorphs—thin, fragile, weak people; and (4) balanced (normal)—not overly fat, thin, or muscular. Sheldon's theory, called "somatotyping," stated that mesomorphs were the most likely to be associated with delinquency and crime because they had the body type inclined to be the most aggressive and violent.

More modern social scientists focused on the biological and genetic make-ups of delinquents, in the belief that crime and violence are genetically inherited, just like hair and eye color or height. In the 1920s, German physician Johannes Lange conducted a study to determine a genetic link to crime. Although his study was criticized for weaknesses in his research methods, Lange reported a strong link between genetics and criminality. Lange's findings were extended in the 1960s through the work of European researchers Karl O. Christiansen and Sarnoff Mednick. In their study of Dutch twins born between the years 1881 and 1910, Christiansen and Mednick found significant statistical support for a link between crime and genes.

In investigations similar to the twin studies, other researchers sought a possible link between delinquency and adoption. In these studies, the criminality of parents was compared to that of their biological children who had been raised by adopted parents. In different adoption studies, researchers David Rowe, Sarnoff Mednick, and Jody Alberts-Corush all showed that delinquency—at least in part—is genetically linked. Recent studies seem to confirm these findings. In 2003, Jeanette Taylor conducted a similar study of teenaged male twins and concluded that violent and criminal traits were linked to genetic factors. It is worth noting that while these studies have produced statistically significant findings, the purported gene–crime link may be nothing more than an individual's genetic trait interacting with certain environmental and social factors that bring out violent or criminal behaviors.

In recent decades, researchers have concentrated on biological theories based on biochemical factors, such as the impact of nutrition on crime and violence. These studies focus on intakes of sugar, food additives, vitamins, and minerals, as well as everyday exposure to minerals such as lead, copper, and zinc. In the 1980s, separate studies by Alexander Schauss and the team of J. Kershner and W. Hawke indicated positive behavioral changes occurred in delinquent youths when they were fed balanced diets. Both sets of researchers found that high-protein, low-carbohydrate, sugarless diets, with adequate vitamins and moderate intake of milk, significantly reduced delinquent behavior. Other experiments conducted in the New York City school system showed that students scored better on national achievement tests when they reduced their sugar intake and eliminated artificial flavors and preservatives from their diets prior to taking the tests.

Other researchers have explored a possible link between delinquency and hormone activity (especially testosterone and serotonin). Many hormone levels peak between the ages of 13 and 19, corresponding with times of high levels of violence and crime in youths' lives. Studies have shown that hormonal changes in teens are linked to delinquency and crime, particularly for teenage boys.

Biological theories of juvenile violence and crime also focus on neurological factors. These theories study the brain and nervous system of delinquent offenders and compare them to the same systems in the average non-offender. As part of this work, researchers measure attention spans, learning ability, cognitive ability, brain waves, and heart rates. These social scientists believe that brain chemistry, as controlled by the endocrine system (glands that secrete hormones into the blood), is the key to understanding delinquent violence and crime.

Some neurological studies of children have pointed to identifiable brain defects as a key cause of violence and aggression. These brain abnormalities, often called minimal brain dysfunction (MBD), are frequently linked to a mother's addiction to drugs or alcohol during pregnancy and result in low birth weight, birth complications, childhood head injuries, or other genetically inherited factors for her child. In separate studies conducted by Stephen Tibbetts and Jean Seguin, brain activity in affected youths showed chemistry that may be linked to violence, aggression, anger, and crime.

Specifically, some researchers are studying the potential relationship between learning disabilities (LD) and delinquency. Young people with learning disabilities have trouble reading, writing, listening, speaking, and organizing their thoughts. Learning disabilities are not associated with vision or hearing problems, motor handicaps, or mental retardation. Studies show that arrested and incarcerated children have higher rates of LD than the general population. In 1976, Charles Murray proposed two explanations for the high rates of LD youth in trouble. The first, which he called the "susceptibility rationale," stated that LD offenders are impulsive, do not learn from experience, and stay engaged in violence or criminal activity despite being punished. The second, which Murray called the "school failure rationale," suggested that LD youths act out violently or criminally because of their frustration at doing poorly in school.

Biological theories of juvenile crime and violence have been criticized on a number of grounds. Often, researchers have used populations of documented youth offenders as samples for their studies, making it difficult to determine whether these offenders are representative of all youth or representative of only offenders who were apprehended. Other criticisms of biological theories suggest that they are politically or socially motivated, harkening back to the eugenics movement of Nazi Germany. Biological theories also often fail to take into consideration social forces, individual factors, social class, and gender issues.

Proponents of biological theories stress that they do not view any biological theory as a generalizable explanation of all youth crime and violence, but simply suggest that biological theories can explain some aspect of delinquent behavior. The core principle of most biological theories is that some youth do have developmental issues that limit their ability to learn and cope with some situations and, as such, place these youths at a disadvantage in society. These developmental issues may be genetic, chemical, or hormonal and may manifest themselves as aggression, violence, or crime.

Eric Bellone

Further Reading

Lombroso-Ferrero, G. (1911). *Criminal man according to the classification of Cesare Lombroso*. Montclair, NJ: Patterson Smith.

Moffitt, T. (1993). Adolescent-limited and life course persistent antisocial behavior: A development taxonomy, *Psychological Review, 100,* 674–701.

Raine, A., Lencz, T., Taylor, K., Hellige, J. B., Bihrle, S., Lacasse, L., et al. (2003). Corpus callosum abnormalities in psychopathic antisocial individuals. *Archives of General Psychiatry, 60*(11), 1134–1142.

Rowe, D. (1995). *The limits of family influence: Genes, experiences and behavior.* New York: Guilford Press.

Seguin, J., Phil, R., Harden, P., Tremblay, R., & Boulerice, B. (1995). Cognitive and neuropsychological characteristics of physically aggressive boys. *Journal of Abnormal Psychology, 104,* 614–624.

Sheldon, W. (1949). *Varieties of delinquent youth*. New York: Harper Bros.

Bishop, Amy

On February 12, 2010, Amy Bishop, age 45, a neurobiology professor at the University of Alabama, Huntsville, shot and wounded three colleagues during a faculty meeting. Apparently Bishop was distraught because she had been informed she would not be granted tenure. Bishop was charged with capital murder and is currently awaiting trial. If convicted, she faces the death penalty.

A promising neurobiologist, Bishop had been awarded grants for her work and was a key player in a biotechnology start-up company. She had helped develop a new approach to treating amyotrophic lateral sclerosis (Lou Gehrig's disease), and a company was in the process of licensing her work for development. She and her husband, a computer engineer with a biology degree, had invented an automated system for incubating cells. Their system was considered to be a vast improvement over the Petri dish. Bishop is also the mother of four children.

In retrospect, Bishop's past suggests that she was troubled despite her many noteworthy accomplishments. Twenty-four years prior to the Alabama incident, Bishop shot and fatally wounded her brother, Seth Bishop, in their home in Braintree, Massachusetts. She was never charged in his death. Interestingly, the police report from the incident had been missing since 1988; after the 2010 shooting, the report was released. In it, Amy Bishop claimed she had been teaching herself to use the family's shotgun after their home had been invaded. She said that she loaded the weapon but was unable to unload it, so she asked her brother for his help. The gun accidentally went off, killing her brother. Bishop said her mother, Judith Bishop, was present during the accident. Judith Bishop confirmed her daughter's account of the event, according to the report.

In 2010, in the wake of the Alabama shootings, Braintree Police Chief Paul Frazier expressed skepticism about Bishop's earlier story, stating that the officer on duty, Ronald Solimini, remembered that Bishop had shot and killed her brother after an argument. She allegedly fired another round from the shotgun into the ceiling as she left the home, with the shotgun in tow. According to Officer Solimini, Bishop also pointed the shotgun at a vehicle in an attempt to get the driver to stop. Another officer, Timothy Murphy, seized the shotgun, and Bishop was arrested and taken to the police station. The booking officer at the time recalls getting a phone call, either from then Police Chief John Polio or from someone on his behalf, asking him to stop the booking. Bishop was then released. Polio, now 87, denied any impropriety.

Seven years later, Bishop was the prime suspect in a 1993 mail bombing attempt involving a Harvard Medical School professor. She was never charged due to a lack of evidence, but colleagues claimed that her motive was similar to the one cited in the 2010 incident—Bishop had received a negative evaluation from the targeted professor. A former coworker at the research lab recalled that Bishop and the professor had a disagreement. She remembers that Bishop was smiling when she described the police questioning she underwent following the discovery of the bomb. Investigators said that they found a novel on her computer that described a scientist who had shot her brother and then sought redemption.

On the day of her 2010 attack, Bishop taught her regular schedule of neuroscience and anatomy courses. She then headed to the third floor of the Shelby

Center for Science and Technology for the faculty meeting. She sat quietly for 30 to 40 minutes, then pulled out a 9-millimeter handgun and began shooting. Either the gun jammed or she ran out of ammunition, prompting Bishop to flee the room, dumping her gun in a second-floor bathroom as she exited the center. Moments later, she was arrested outside the building.

The deceased included G. K. Podila, the department's chairman; Maria Ragland Davis; and Adriel D. Johnson Sr.—all biology professors. Two other biology professors, Luis Rogelio Cruz-Vera and Joseph G. Leahy, as well as a professor's assistant, Stephanie Monticciolo, were injured.

In general, Bishop's colleagues were said to have respected her ability but found her hard to get along with. She had become convinced that the chemical engineering professors were trying to keep biology students from succeeding by making the classes too difficult, and this belief became an obsession. She was considered to be very outspoken, so the fact that she went on a shooting rampage shocked many, who thought she was not the type to bottle up her pain.

Some students also had problems with Bishop's teaching style. They said she simply read from the textbook in class but then tested them on material that she had not covered. Nursing students repeatedly complained about Bishop's teaching methods to Dr. Podila, the department chairman, as well as to the dean. Some even signed a petition to have her removed. At the same time, Bishop was recognized as an advocate for students. She was vocally opposed to a new policy that would require freshmen and sophomores to live on campus, stating that this requirement was too expensive and would affect diversity. The policy was enacted despite her, and others', opposition.

Bishop's husband, James Anderson, has continually expressed his love and support for his wife, although he insists he had no idea what prompted her attack. He did admit the two had visited a shooting range just two weeks before the incident, but stated the family did not own a gun and that he had no idea where she obtained the weapon she used in the attack. Anderson also said that his wife had been fighting the university for more than a year about her tenure status.

Laura L. Finley

Further Reading

Canning, A., McPhee, M., Netter, S., & James, S. (2010, February 15). Alabama shooting suspect's husband: "I'm no psychologist." *ABC News.* Retrieved April 23, 2010, from http://abcnews.go.com/GMA/alabama-university-shooting-suspect-amy-bishops-husband- idea/story?id=9839348&page=1

Dewan, S., & Robbins, L. (2010, February 13). A previous death at the hand of Alabama suspect. *New York Times.* Retrieved April 23, 2010, from http://www.nytimes.com/2010/02/14/us/14alabama.html?pagewanted=1

Sweet, L., Van Sack, J., Fargen, J., & Kantor, I. (2010, February 15). "Oddball" portrait of Amy Bishop emerges. *Boston Herald.* Retrieved April 23, 2010, from http://www.bostonherald.com/news/regional/view.bg?articleid=1232943& format&page=1&list ingType=Loc

Board of Ed. of Independent School District No. 92 of Pottawatomie County v. Earls

On June 27, 2002, the U.S. Supreme Court upheld as constitutional a school-based drug testing program required for participation in any extracurricular activity. The ruling in *Board of Ed. of Independent School District No. 92 of Pottawatomie County v. Earls* came seven years after the Court had upheld school-based drug testing for students involved in extracurricular sports (*Vernonia School District v. Acton*). In *Earls,* the Court held that the random drug testing policy instituted by

The decision of the Independent School District No. 92 of Pottawatomie County to require drug tests from all students participating in any extracurricular activity—even marching band and choir—was upheld by the U.S. Supreme Court. School officials argued that drug-using band members handling heavy equipment posed a safety threat to those around them. (iStockPhoto)

Tecumseh (Oklahoma) School District, which required all middle and high school students to submit to a urinalysis if they wanted to participate in extracurricular activities, was lawful as a means of achieving the school district's goal of preventing and deterring drug use. The Court used a balancing test established in *Vernonia* and, earlier, in *TLO v. New Jersey* to determine that this policy was not overly intrusive.

Lindsay Earls and Daniel James, both 16 at the time, and Lindsay's sister, Lacey, attended Tecumseh High and were tested in 1999 because they were involved in extracurricular activities. Lindsay was in the school choir and marching band as well as on the school's Academic Team and in the National Honor Society. Daniel sought to be on the Academic Team as well. The families filed suit, asserting that the policy was a violation of the students' Fourth Amendment right to privacy. In particular, Lindsay Earls was disturbed that a monitor would stand outside the bathroom, listening while students urinated. She was also concerned that the Academic Team, band, and choir were different from sports or other clubs in that they were part of the school's curriculum and helped fulfill the district's fine arts requirement. Students who refused to submit a sample would receive no credit in those courses.

Once students provided the urine sample, results were released to appropriate school employees but not to law enforcement. If a student tested positive, he or she could agree to enroll in counseling within five days and would then be allowed to continue participating in extracurricular activities as long as the student also agreed to submit to another drug test in two weeks. Students were barred from participating in any activities if they did not agree to those conditions. If the second test was positive, the student was suspended from participation in extracurricular activities for two weeks and had to submit to monthly drug tests as well as complete 14 hours of substance abuse counseling. A third positive test resulted in suspension from all extracurricular activities for the remainder of the school year or for 88 days, depending which was longer.

Oral arguments in the case were very heated. Much debate ensued over whether the drug testing policy was appropriate for students involved in all extracurricular activity, as previously the *Vernonia* decision has considered testing constitutional only when some type of safety concern was involved. The petitioners asserted there was a safety threat, bringing up the silly examples of drug-using band members with heavy equipment. Graham Boyd, the American Civil Liberties Union (ACLU) attorney representing the Earls and James, argued there was no safety threat for students in choir or band. Boyd also asserted that the policy was enacted with no evidence of an actual drug problem in the school; in fact, national data showed that teen drug use was on the decline. Further, discussion focused on whether it was logical to test students who were involved in extracurricular activities when data repeatedly showed that such individuals were the least likely to be using drugs. The Supreme Court Justices also disagreed about the intrusiveness of drug testing. Justice Anthony Kennedy, for example, maintained that drug testing was no more intrusive than requiring students to wear school uniforms.

The Supreme Court eventually ruled 5–4 in support of Tecumseh's drug testing policy. In doing so, the Justices viewed drug testing as an administrative search. As such, it need not be based on probable cause or even reasonable suspicion. Further, the Court held that students who elect to participate in extracurricular activities already have a reduced expectation of privacy. The Court did caution the school to ensure that the results were shared only with appropriate school personnel.

As in the *Vernonia* case, the Court held that drug testing programs can be a deterrent to student drug use. The Justices generally believed drug testing helps students reject peer pressure—although the data seem to tell another story. A 2003 survey involving 76,000 students across the United States found that rates of drug use did not differ significantly between districts with drug testing programs and those without such programs.

Justices David Souter, John Paul Stevens, and Sandra Day O'Connor dissented from the 2002 ruling, as they did in *Vernonia*. Souter was most bothered by the fact that not all of the extracurricular activities were voluntary. Justice Ruth Bader Ginsburg was concerned that the court had backtracked on its decision in *Vernonia,* as the district could provide no specific justification for the policy or any safety threat. She also expressed concern that the decision could deter students from becoming involved in extracurricular activities.

After the decision in 2002, the George W. Bush administration expressed support for greater use of school-based drug testing. Drug czar John Walters repeatedly called such a policy a deterrent, and the Bush administration even made available grant monies for districts wishing to implement drug testing programs. Estimates are that between 18% and 20% of school districts have implemented some type of drug testing program, most often for athletes.

In addition to the concerns noted previously, critics of school-based drug testing note that it is quite expensive to implement. The tests that school districts use are quite vulnerable to cheating; at the same time, they are often not robust enough to provide accurate results. Further, critics assert that these programs assume students to be deviant, a stance that may undermine the trust between educators and students.

Laura L. Finley

Further Reading

Finley, L., & Finley, P. (2004). *Piss off! How drug testing and other privacy violations are alienating America's youth.* Monroe, ME: Common Courage.

Hyman, I., & Snook, P. (1999). *Dangerous schools.* San Francisco, CA: Jossey-Bass.

Kern, J., Gunja, F., Cox, A., Rosenbaum, M., Appel, J., & Verma, A. (2006). Making sense of student drug testing: Why educators are saying no. Retrieved April 8, 2010, from http://www.drugpolicy.org/docUploads/drug_testing_booklet.pdf

Bosse, Sebastian

On November 20, 2006, 18-year-old Sebastian Bosse entered his former high school in northwestern Germany, where he shot five people and set off a series of smoke bombs before police found him dead. Bosse was masked and had pipe bombs and a knife strapped to his body. He had five more pipe bombs in his backpack that explosives experts diffused, and four more were found in his car, which was parked near the school.

A school secretary called the police immediately when Bosse's assault began, and heavily armed officers arrived quickly to begin searching the building. Bosse had retreated to the second floor, and as the officers searched they evacuated the building room by room. Officers fired no shots during the incident. A total of four students ages 12 to 16 and the head caretaker for the school were wounded, although none of the injuries were life-threatening. Twenty-two other individuals, most of them police, were treated for smoke inhalation from the bombs.

The incident brought back memories of another German shooting rampage. In 2002, Robert Steinhauser, who had been expelled from Gutenberg Gymnasium in Erfurt, shot and killed 16 people before committing suicide.

Bosse was described by his peers as a misfit. They said he was obsessed with carrying guns and often played violent video games. Students said he always wore a black hat and coat and kept to himself. Bosse had posted several pictures of himself on his website. In them, he was wearing a military-style uniform and holding a gun. He had also indicated that he planned to do something dangerous and that he was suicidal. He wrote about being treated as a "loser" by teachers and students, saying he intended to seek revenge. Bosse also expressed contempt for police and politicians. He had been caught with a loaded pistol several months prior to the school attack, and was set to go on trial for that offense the next day.

A year later, two students in Cologne, Germany, were accused of plotting a similar assault on their school to commemorate the one-year anniversary of Bosse's attack. The school principal had discovered a website in which one of the students glorified the Columbine (Colorado) attack. One of the suspects, who was 17, committed suicide during a confrontation at the school. The other confessed to the plot.

As of March 2009, Germany was considered second to the United States in terms of the number of deaths from school shootings. This finding renewed calls for stricter gun control laws.

Laura L. Finley

Further Reading

Former student storms school, shooting five people. (2006, November 20). *WHDH News*. Retrieved April 29, 2010, from http://www3.whdh.com/news/articles/world/BO34580/

Paterson, T. (2009, March 15). In Europe's league of school shootings, Germany comes top. *The Independent (UK)*. Retrieved April 30, 2010, from http://www.independent.co.uk/news/world/europe/in-europes-league-of-school-shootings-germany-comes-top-1645387.html

Two students in Germany accused of plotting a school attack. (2007, November 18). *Net News Publisher*. Retrieved April 29, 2010, from http://www.netnewspublisher.com/two-students-in-germany-accused-of-plotting-a-school-attack

Bowling for Columbine

Bowling for Columbine (2002) is the most well-known documentary film to address school violence. Written and directed by filmmaker and author Michael Moore, whose previous work included *Roger & Me* and *The Big One*, *Bowling for Columbine* offers a critique of some of the more commonly held explanations for school violence. In addition to addressing school violence in particular, Moore illustrates that the United States is a culture in which violence is endemic, and shows that easy access to guns makes lethal violence far more common in this country than in other industrialized nations. Approximately 11,000 people die each year in the United States from gun violence—far more than in neighboring Canada, the United Kingdom, or Japan. Moore includes "A Brief History of the United States" and a disturbing montage of actual footage that show how the United States has historically exploited people of color and used violence to maintain its position as a world power.

Bowling for Columbine was the first documentary accepted into the Cannes Film Festival in 46 years, and the Cannes jury unanimously awarded it the 55th Anniversary Prize. Moore won the Academy Award for best documentary in 2003. The film's title comes from a mistaken belief that the Columbine shooters—Eric Harris and Dylan Klebold—attended a school bowling class the morning of the 1999 massacre.

The film features Moore's discussion with an eclectic group of people who comment on violence, both inside and out of schools. Among others, he talks with controversial musician Marilyn Manson, the creators of *South Park,* James Nichols (brother of Oklahoma City bombing accomplice Terry Nichols), and the National Rifle Association's then president Charlton Heston. Manson's music, some of which discusses suicide and seems to condone violence, was considered to be a major influence on the Columbine shooters. The musician offers a unique perspective, in the end asserting that the best way to reduce youth violence is to listen to kids.

Moore also critiques the punitive trend in schools. In one scene he shows an absurd advertisement for a metal detector company that shows a boy unloading multiple high-powered weapons from his pants pockets. Moore uses this imagery to show how some of the responses to school violence, or the fear of it, are simply making others wealthy.

Critics contend that Moore's film is less documentary and more political argument. They note several errors in the film and cite examples of Moore making arguments that are, at best, a stretch. In the beginning of the film, Moore shows a bank in North Carolina that was offering a free gun in exchange for opening an account. Bank employees claim that Moore and his staff misled them and that, in actuality, the guns were shipped to recipients, not handed out on location. Moore also asserts that the violence at Columbine High School was somehow connected to the fact that Littleton, Colorado, is the home of Lockheed Martin, a major weapons manufacturer, which many assert is a weak linkage.

Laura L. Finley

Filmmaker Michael Moore stops for photographs during the 60th Cannes Festival in Cannes, France, on May 20, 2007. (Denis Makarenko/Dreamstime.com)

Further Reading

Bowling for Columbine: http://www.imdb.com/title/tt0310793/, http://www.bowlingforcolumbine.com/

Moore, M. (2002). *Bowling for Columbine* [motion picture]. Alliance Atlantis Communications.

Brazill, Nathaniel

In 2000, there were 15,586 murders committed in the United States. Despite this large number, a single violent incident in Florida ignited a national forum on school violence, guns, and the way the U.S. criminal justice system should deal with juvenile offenders.

On May 26, 2000, the last day of the year at Lake Worth Middle School, seventh grader Nathaniel Brazill was sent home for throwing water balloons. He returned later in the day with a .25-caliber handgun and entered his English Arts class demanding to see two female classmates. When teacher Barry Grunow refused his demand, Brazill shot him in the face and watched him die in front of his classroom door.

Today, Brazill is 20 years old and serving a 28-year prison sentence at the Brevard County Correctional Institution in Florida for a second-degree murder conviction in the shooting death of Grunow. At the time of his crime, Brazill was 13 years and 8 months of age. In Florida, juveniles convicted of second-degree murder receive a sentence ranging from 25 years to life in prison—the same punishment meted out to adults.

Although no one disputes the facts about how Grunow was killed, there is much speculation about what might have motivated Brazill to commit this crime and whether these underlying issues should have been taken into consideration in the criminal disposition of his case. Brazill was raised by his mother, Polly Powell, in a single-parent home. Brazill's biological father, Nathaniel Brazill, Sr., maintained limited contact with Nathaniel. According to court records, Brazill had witnessed his mother being subjected to domestic violence at the hands of her former husbands and boyfriends since he was five years old.

Despite his upbringing, Brazill was an honor student with near-perfect attendance and without any history of violence or discipline. School officials described him as a soft-spoken, bright, and well-liked child. According to the court transcripts of testimony by teachers and classmates, Brazill had often described Grunow as his favorite teacher. In fact, earlier on the day of the shooting, Brazill had asked Grunow to pose in a picture with him. However, according to academic progress reports, the student's grades had been significantly dropping during the school year.

On April 15, 2000, approximately one month before the shooting, Brazill wrote a letter to Grunow explaining that seventh grade had been a very difficult time in his life. He complained of being picked on by classmates and teachers during the school year and suggested that he might commit suicide. Brazill had also confided in friends that he was infatuated with one of his classmates, Dinora Rosales. Rosales was Brazill's first girlfriend, who only six days before the shooting had given Brazill his first kiss. Rosales and fellow classmate Suzy Fleureme had been the two females Brazill had attempted to visit in Grunow's classroom the day of the shooting. According to court testimony, an emotionally upset Brazill had returned to school after being suspended, to say goodbye to Rosales before the beginning of summer break. In fact, on the day of the shooting, Brazill brought a few extra items on the bus with him to school: a card and flowers for Rosales. After the shooting, which was captured on the school's surveillance camera, Brazill ran down the hall, pausing long enough to wave the gun at another teacher before fleeing the school grounds. Within minutes, Brazill flagged down a police cruiser driven by Officer Mike Mahoney, whom he knew from his neighborhood, fell to his knees in the street, and confessed to the shooting.

After his arrest, Florida prosecutor Barry Krischer decided to try the 13-year-old Brazill as an adult, charging him with first-degree murder, which carried a penalty of life in prison, and under certain circumstances, the death penalty. According to the Florida Department of Corrections, at the time of Brazill's arrest, there were 15 inmates who were between the ages 13 or 14 at the time of their crimes and had been convicted of first-degree murder. In the early 1990s, spurred by an alarming rise in juvenile crime, Florida amended its laws to make it easier to try youths as adults. In fact, Florida led the nation in prosecuting juvenile offenders as adults. National data on the number of juvenile cases tried in adult criminal court in the United States do not currently exist, but the Department of Justice reports that the state of Florida grants approximately 5,000 requests annually to try juvenile offenders in adult court.

The state of Florida is not alone in its harsh treatment of young criminals. Over the past decade, 47 states have amended their laws to make it easier to put on trial and punish juveniles as adults. In fact, U.S. jails house nearly 75,000 juveniles who are awaiting trial in adult correctional facilities. As many as 200,000 juvenile offenders are prosecuted each year as adults in the United States. In 2010, the U.S. Supreme Court ruled that juveniles only be sentenced to life in prison without parole for perpetrating homicide.

Juvenile offenders can end up in the adult criminal system under several mechanisms. Transfer and waiver provisions, which are legislated by state law, allow juvenile offenders to be prosecuted in adult courts if they are accused of committing certain crimes. Judicial waiver—the most common of these provisions—allows juvenile court judges the authority to "waive" juvenile court jurisdiction and transfer the case to adult criminal court. Another method, which state prosecutors in Florida used in Brazill's case, is called a prosecutorial waiver. Under this law, prosecutors have the authority to file cases against juvenile offenders in either juvenile or adult court based on the seriousness of the criminal offense. Such provisions are also known as "direct file," "concurrent jurisdiction," or "prosecutorial discretion." Today, 29 states automatically exclude certain crimes (ranging from drug offenses to violent crimes) from juvenile court jurisdiction. Thirty-five states have legal provisions best summarized as "once an adult, always an adult," which mandate that once a juvenile offender has been convicted in adult court, all subsequent offenses, regardless of their severity, will handled through the adult criminal court system.

On May 16, 2001, after 14 hours of deliberations, a West Palm Beach jury convicted Brazill, who was 14 years old at the time, of second-degree murder and aggravated assault. Had he been convicted of the original charge of first-degree murder sought by prosecutors, Brazill would have received a life sentence without the possibility of parole. Instead, he received a 28-year prison sentence and will not be released until his 41st birthday in 2028. On July 28, 2008, his mother died of breast cancer. His father, Nathaniel Sr., has broken off all contact with his son

Tony Gaskew

Further Reading

Campaign for Youth Justice. (2007). Jailing juveniles: The dangers of incarcerating youth in adult jails in America. Retrieved from http://www.campaign foryouthjustice.org//Downloads/NationalReportsArticles/CFYJ-Jailing _Juveniles_Report_2007-11-15.pdf

Coalition of Justice Annual Report. (2005). Childhood on trial: The failure of trying and sentencing youth in adult court. Retrieved from http://www .juvjustice.org/media/fckeditor/Coalition%20for%20Juvenile%20Justice% 202005%20Annual%20Report%20Childhood%20o n%20Trial.pdf

The Disaster Center. (n.d.). Retrieved from http://www.disastercenter.com/crime/ uscrime.htm

Moffatt, G. (2002). *Violent heart: Understanding aggressive individuals.* Westport, CT: Greenwood.

Rochie, T. (2001, July 27). Nate Brazill sentenced to grow up in prison. *Time.com.* Retrieved from http://www.time.com/time/nation/article/0,8599,169246,00 .html

Brewer, Michael

On October 12, 2009, a group of teenaged classmates of Michael Brewer, 15, viciously attacked him, dousing him with rubbing alcohol and setting his body ablaze. Brewer suffered second- and third-degree burns over two-thirds of his body. He survived the attack by jumping into a nearby swimming pool. His screams were captured on a 911 tape. All of the boys attended Deerfield Beach Middle School in Deerfield Beach, Florida. Initially, doctors proclaimed that it would be amazing if Brewer ever emerged from a medically induced coma. For a long time, he was unable to speak and had to use a ventilator to breathe. Miraculously, he was out of the hospital and headed back to school—albeit a different one—just six months after the attack.

The attack came after Brewer had called 911 to report that one of the boys, Matthew Bent, 15, had tried to steal a $500 bicycle. Allegedly, Bent had given Brewer a $40 video game and wanted him to pay for it. Brewer did not pay. Police claim the boys called Brewer "a snitch." Reportedly, Jesus Mendez, age 16, actually set Brewer on fire with a lighter. Denver and Jeremy Jarvis were once friends with Brewer; Denver Jarvis is alleged to have thrown the rubbing alcohol on Brewer. He, Bent, and Mendez have been charged with attempted second-degree murder. All have pleaded not guilty. Jeremy Jarvis, age 13, and Steven Shelton, age 16, are accused of being in the group that surrounded Brewer during the attack at the Limetree Village Apartment Complex. Jeremy Jarvis has expressed remorse for the incident, claiming that it was unplanned and that Brewer was actually a good friend.

Brewer spoke out publicly in April 2010, expressing his eagerness to return to school, but not to Deerfield Beach Middle School, which he called "terrible." While Brewer was still recovering, a classmate, Josie Lou Ratley, was attacked by 15-year-old classmate Wayne Treacey, allegedly over some text messages the two had exchanged. Brewer had visited Ratley in the hospital, encouraging her to think positively so that she, too, could recover. He has scars from the burns but said he is not in pain.

Laura L. Finley

Further Reading

Celizic, M. (2010, April 20). Florida teen set on fire: "This school is terrible." *MSNBC*. Retrieved April 21, 2010, from http://today.msnbc.msn.com/id/36661414/ns/today-today_people/

Miller, C. (2010, April 21). Michael Brewer, boy set on fire, tells happy back-to-school story. *Crimesider*. Retrieved April 21, 2010, from http://www.cbsnews.com/8301-504083_162-20002968-504083.html?utm_source=feedburner&utm_medium=feed&utm_campaign=Feed%3A+CBSNew sHannahsBlog+(Hannah's+Blog%3A+CBSNews.com)

Netter, S., & Clarke, S. (2009, November 25). Michael Brewer talks to police for first time after burn attack; suspect's brother expresses sympathy. *Good Morning America*. Retrieved April 21, 2010, from http://abcnews.go.com/GMA/michael-brewer-talks-police-burn- attack/story?id=9167108&page=1

Olmeda, R. (2009, November 4). Jarvis family apologizes for fiery attack against Deerfield Beach teen. *South Florida Sun Sentinel*. Retrieved April 21, 2010, from http://www.sun- sentinel.com/news/broward/deerfield/fl-burn-suspect-jarvis-parents- bn110409,0,1968462.story

Olmeda, R. (2009, November 25). Jeremy Jarvis says attack on Brewer not planned. *Palm Beach Post*. Retrieved April 21, 2010, from http://www.palmbeachpost.com/news/crime/jeremy-jarvis-says- attack-on-michael-brewer-not-84576.html

Phillips, R. (2009, November 3). Set afire, teen now struggles for survival. *CNN*. Retrieved April 21, 2010, from http://www.cnn.com/2009/CRIME/11/02/teen.burned.recovery/index.html

Bullycide

In 2009, the National Center for Education Statistics reported that almost one in three students between the ages of 13 and 18 had been bullied in school. A survey by the Cyberbullying Research Center found that one in five students ages 10 to 18 had been the victim of cyberbullying, or bullying that occurs through some form of technology such as email, instant messaging, text messages, and social networking sites. Particularly vulnerable are lesbian, gay, bisexual, and transgendered (LGBT) students. A 2009 report by the Gay Lesbian and Straight Education Network

College students attend a candlelight vigil at Rutgers University in memory of freshman Tyler Clementi on October 3, 2010. Clementi committed suicide by jumping off the George Washington Bridge after suffering from bullying by two of his classmates. Bullying prevention programs hope to intervene to help victims see that suicide is not the only way out. (AP/Wide World Photos)

(GLSEN) found that 90% of LGBT students had experienced harassment at school in the previous year.

Students who have been bullied suffer numerous detrimental consequences. They are more likely to skip school and are at greater risk for dropping out. Victims are more likely to be depressed, to use drugs and alcohol, and to engage in violent behavior later in life. Many victims contemplate suicide. In the most severe cases, victims actually take their own lives—a form of suicide called bullycide.

One of the first cases to receive national attention was that of Ryan Halligan of Essex Junction, Vermont. Halligan committed suicide on October 7, 2003, at age 13 after middle school classmates threatened, taunted, and insulted him, both in person and online. On June 29, 2005, Jeffery Johnston of Cape Coral, Florida, committed suicide. Johnston had also been bullied in school and online. On October 9, 2006, 17-year-old Rachael Neblett of Washington, Kentucky, took her own life after being threatened with violence over the Internet. Just eight days later, 13-year-old Megan Meier hung herself after receiving a series of cruel messages on MySpace. A neighbor and the mother of Meier's classmate was later indicted for her role in the bullying.

On August 23, 3008, Alexa Berman, 14, of Brooklyn, Connecticut, hung herself three days before she was to have started high school. On July 3, 2008, Jessie Logan hung herself in her bedroom after her ex-boyfriend sent nude pictures of her to other students at her high school in Cincinnati. In a similar case in September 2009, 13-year-old Hope Witsell of Ruskin, Florida, hung herself after photos of herself topless that she had sent to a boy she liked were distributed to a far wider audience. In October 2009, Tyler Lee Long, who had Asperger's syndrome, hung himself after having endured years of torment at school, much of it before the indifferent eyes of administrators.

Bullycide received a great deal of attention in 2010 due to a spate of well-publicized incidents. On January 14, 2010, 15-year-old Phoebe Prince hung herself after being bullied by classmates in South Hadley, Massachusetts. Nine students were indicted in the case. In September 2010, three teens committed suicide after suffering severe bullying: 15-year-old Billy Lucas of Indiana, 13-year old Asher Brown of Texas, and 13-year-old of California either identified as gay or were perceived to be gay. Tyler Clementi, age 18, a Rutgers University freshman, jumped off the George Washington Bridge in New York after his roommate secretly recorded him with another male student, then broadcast the video online. In October 2010, U.S. President Barack Obama spoke out about bullycides, as did Secretary of State Hillary Clinton.

A multifaceted approach is needed to reduce bullying and to prevent bullycide. Schools must put in place, and enforce, anti-bullying policies. These policies must be inclusive of the variety of forms bullying takes, and should include services for victims as well as training for educators, parents, and students. Bullying often requires the intervention of adults, but because incidents usually occur in front of witnesses, students must be motivated to speak out when they see such events. Additionally, schools must work to create positive climates in which all students feel valued, have a voice, and are empowered to step up when they see or hear someone being mistreated.

Both inside of schools and in the broader culture, experts recommend addressing the continuum of masculinity and femininity. The majority of bullying victims are harassed because they look or act in ways that diverge from traditional notions of masculine or feminine. With greater sensitivity to the many unique humans who constitute society, bullying and other forms of harassment and mistreatment can be reduced. Radio talk show host Dan Savage, joined by many politicians and celebrities, began the It Gets Better Project to help LGBT students see a positive future for themselves. Celebrities filmed a series of short videos discussing life as gay adults and described how to obtain help if needed. Information and videos are available at http://www.itgetsbetterproject.com/. Visitors to the site are encouraged to take a pledge to treat everyone with respect and to stand up to bullying and intolerance. Additionally, teaching young children about peace, justice, and human rights can help them build empathy and understanding.

Laura L. Finley

Further Reading

Chen, S. (2010, October 4). After student's death, a weeklong look into bullying. *CNN.* Retrieved October 28, 2010, from http://www.cnn.com/2010/LIVING/10/04/bullying.special.explainer/index.html?iref=allsearch

Coloroso, B. (2009). *The bully, the bullied, and the bystander: From preschool to high school—how parents and teachers can help break the cycle.* New York: Harper.

High, B. (2007). *Bullycide in America: Moms speak out about the bullying/suicide connection.* Darlington, MD: JBS Publishing. This book is an electronic book available at http://www.bullycide.org/

Ollove, M. (2010, April 28). Bullying and teen suicide: How do we adjust school climate? *Christian Science Monitor.* Retrieved October 28, 2010, from http://www.csmonitor.com/USA/Society/2010/0428/Bullying-and-teen-suicide-How-do-we-adjust-school-climate

Powers, R. (2010, October 22). Obama "shocked and saddened" by gay bullying suicides. *MSNBC.* Retrieved October 27, 2010, from http://www.msnbc.msn.com/id/39800008/ns/us_news-life/

Simmons, R. (2010, October 5). Responding to the bullycides: How we can stand up and honor their memories. *Huffington Post.* Retrieved October 28, 2010, from http://www.huffingtonpost.com/rachel-simmons/responding-to-the-bullyci_b_747806.html

Bullying, College

Bullying is the deliberate and repeated affliction of harm by one individual on another of less physical or social power. The harm often takes place over an extended period of time and can be inflicted physically, verbally, or emotionally. The *victim* of bullying is known as the *target,* while the perpetrator is called the *bully*. While bullying is often associated with early and middle adolescence, bullying may persist into college and the workplace. At colleges and universities, bullying usually occurs either between two students, between a student and a teacher, or between two teachers. More than 60% of college students report having witnessed a peer being bullied by another student, and more than 45% report having seen a student being bullied by a teacher.

The three major forms of bullying are physical bullying, verbal bullying, and emotional bullying. Physical bullying is an example of *direct bullying*, or bullying that outwardly harms the victim. Among college students, physical bullying most often involves shoving, paddling, and other forms of painful physical contact. Physical bullying is relatively common among college men, most often occurs in residence halls or other living quarters, and can be a component of hazing and initiations.

Verbal and emotional bullying are forms of *indirect bullying*, or bullying that does not visibly harm the victim and for which the effects are implicit and delayed. Common examples of verbal bullying among college students include name calling, making threatening remarks, verbal intimidation, use of sexist or homophobic language, gossiping, and other speech acts that cause fear or discomfort. Deliberate attempts to incite fear, intimidation or emotional distress are forms of emotional bullying. Emotional bullying can include intentional social isolation, exclusion from social groups and organizations, and defacing or stealing property.

Emotional bullying is often carried out electronically. *Electronic bullying*, also known as *cyberbullying*, among college students often relies on college-oriented social networking Internet sites, such as www.facebook.com, or on increasingly popular college gossip websites, such as www.juicycampus.com. A cyberbully might publicly share gossip or embarrassing information about another individual, post unflattering pictures or mean comments about the victim, or intentionally exclude others from web-based groups. Unwelcome and harassing emails, instant messages and text messages are other examples of cyberbullying.

Colleges and universities rarely collect bullying statistics. Postsecondary institutions are not required to report incidents of bullying, and no federal agency in the United States compiles data on such occurrences. Several nonrepresentative surveys measuring the frequency of college bullying have been administered, however. Nearly 25% of survey participants reported having been bullied by another student, 19%percent reported having been bullied by a teacher, and 18%

revealed that they had bullied others. There is a strong association between being bullied in high school and being bullied in college. Likewise, there is a strong association between being a bully in high school and being a bully in college.

Hazing is a ritualistic method of initiating a person into a group or organization, often involving harassment, physical abuse, humiliation, or other forms of bullying characterized by an imbalance of power between the target and the initiator. In many cases, existing members of an organization possess power over potential members, who must submit to bullying to gain membership. Hazing rituals may include direct bullying, such as paddling or beating, and/or indirect bullying, such as the performance of degrading and embarrassing tasks. Fraternities, sororities, and athletic teams are examples of college organizations that often engage in hazing.

Sexual harassment, or all forms of unsolicited sexual attention, is a commonplace form of bullying among college students. Sexual harassment can be both direct, such as grabbing or groping of breasts or genitalia, and indirect, such as comments about body parts or the use of sexist or homophobic language. Sexual harassment or sexual violence that occurs within the context of a romantic relationship between students is called *youth dating violence*.

Bullying incidents based on race, ethnicity, color, sex, real or perceived gender identity, real or perceived sexual orientation, native language, national origin, religion, social class or disability are examples of *bias-based bullying*. Sexual minority students, including lesbian, gay, bisexual, and transgendered students, and students from underrepresented racial groups are more likely to report being the victims of biased-based bullying on college campuses than are their peers.

Teacher bullying occurs when a teacher takes advantage of his or her position of authority and subjects a student to repeated public ridicule, degradation, or suggestions of incapability. Teacher bullying is often indirect, and the victim is generally powerless given that the teacher ultimately evaluates the victim's performance in the class. Teacher bullying—particularly bullying based on ideological differences between the student and the teacher—is being reported with increasing frequency at the university level. Bullying by tenured professors toward untenured assistant professors has also been reported.

Chistopher J. Stapel

Further Reading

Chapell, M., Casey, D., De la Cruz, C., Ferrell, J., Forman, J., Lipkin, R., et al. (2004). Bullying in college by students and teachers. *Adolescence, 39*(153), 54–64.

Chapell, M. S., Hasselman, S. L., Kitchin, T., Lomon, S. F., MacIver, K. W., & Sarullo, P. L. (2006). Bullying in elementary school, high school, and college. *Adolescence, 41*(164), 633–648.

Olweus, D. (2004). *Bullying at school: What we know and what we can do.* Cambridge, MA: Blackwell.

Bullying, High School

A Norwegian researcher named Dan Olweus published the first study on bullying, *Aggression in the Schools: Bullies and Whipping Boys*, in 1978. In it, he established the most widely used definition for bullying. Olweus defines bullying as follows:

> A student is being bullied or victimized when he or she is exposed, repeatedly and over time, to negative actions on the part of one or more other students... it is a negative action when someone intentionally inflicts, or attempts to inflict, injury or discomfort on another... Negative actions can be carried out by words (verbally), for instance, by threatening, taunting, teasing, and calling names. It is a negative action when somebody hits, pushes, kicks, pinches or restrains another—by physical contact. It is also possible to carry out negative actions without the use of words or physical contact, such as by making faces or dirty gestures, intentionally excluding someone from a group, or refusing to comply with another person's wishes. (1993, p. 9)

In addition to this basic definition of bullying, researchers who focus their work on secondary schools have identified sexual harassment as a form of bullying. Most recently, bullying behaviors that happen electronically, also known as cyberbullying, have also emerged as prevalent in the lives of many secondary school students.

Bullying has been identified as an international problem. During the years 2001 and 2002, the World Health Organization conducted a comparative study on rates of bullying in Europe and North America among 13-year-olds. The countries with the highest numbers of students who reported engaging in bullying behaviors (two or more times in the past month) were Lithuania (43.6% boys, 29.5% girls), Germany (26.2% boys, 15.8% girls), and Austria (25.7% boys, 14.5% girls). Canada (17.8% boys, 11.6% girls) and the United States (17.9% boys, 11.5 % girls) were in the middle of the pack and ranked 10th and 11th respectively. The countries with the lowest rates were Malta (5.6% boys, 4.2% girls), Czech Republic (5.5% boys, 2.6% girls), and Sweden (5.1% boys, 2.3% girls). The average percentages of all students who reported engaging in bullying in the 35 participating countries were 16.4% of boys and 8.4% of girls.

Researchers have identified a large number of negative effects associated with being the victim of bullying. Students who are victims of bullying often report symptoms of anxiety, depression, stress, hopelessness, and low self-esteem, and are more likely to skip school, have lower grades, and attempt self-harming behaviors and suicide.

Much bullying research focuses on easily observable physical behaviors that tend to be more common among boys. Authors such as Rachel Simmons and Lyn Mikel Brown provide a more in-depth look at the types of covert and relational bullying that happens in girls' social groups; such bullying is quite difficult for researchers to observe and measure but clearly has lasting harmful impacts on the well-being of girls. Neil Duncan has contributed much to this area with his research on "sexual bullying." Duncan has investigated the sexualized element of much of the bullying that goes on in secondary schools. His later works focuses on bullying between girls, including accusations of being a lesbian or heterosexual promiscuity.

Sexual harassment is related to bullying but has some unique factors that distinguish it from other forms of bullying. It is defined as unwanted behaviors that are *sexual* in nature that have negative effects on the target or the *environment*. In one study that examined students' understandings of bullying and sexual harassment, researchers reported that students see sexual harassment as physical contact from a boy to a girl. Nevertheless, much sexual harassment is not physical in nature. As with bullying, it can also take verbal, electronic, and nonverbal forms (e.g., gestures, leers, social exclusion). Gruber and Fineran recently examined the prevalence and impacts of bullying and sexual harassment behaviors and found that more students experienced bullying (52%) than sexual harassment (34%) and that boys and girls experienced similar levels of both bullying (53% versus 51%) and harassment (36% versus 34%). Where they did find a difference was in students who identified as gay, lesbian, bisexual, or questioning their sexual orientation (GLBQ). According to Gruber and Fineran, GLBQ students experienced more bullying (79% versus 50%) and more sexual harassment (71% versus 32%) than non-GLBQ identified students.

The same study also examined the effects of bullying and sexual harassment on the health of students. Gruber and Fineran found that girls and GLBQ students generally have poorer health (self-esteem, mental and physical health, and trauma symptoms) during middle and high school. They concluded that sexual harassment has a more severe impact than bullying on a student's overall health and that schools need to include sexual harassment interventions as a distinct focus in addition to bullying reduction programs.

As noted previously, sexual orientation harassment is a prevalent form of bullying in schools. The earliest published report that began documenting incidents of bullying related to sexual orientation in schools was conducted by the American Association of University Women in 1993. This study addressed issues of sexual harassment in schools, an area that overlaps with much bullying behavior. The

1993 study included a question that asked whether participants had ever been called gay or lesbian in school. When this study was followed up eight years later (2001), researchers found that the one behavior that had increased since the previous study was calling another student gay or lesbian. Boys reported such behavior occurred twice as often, and girls three times as often, as it had a decade earlier, whereas most other forms of harassment had remained constant or decreased.

In research conducted by the Gay, Lesbian, and Straight Education Network (GLSEN), 64% of gay, lesbian, bisexual, and transgendered (GLBT) students reported being verbally bullied at school. In addition, 83% reported that faculty or staff rarely or never intervened when they were present at a time when homophobic remarks were made. A study conducted in California reported the frequency and effects of harassment for gender nonconformity by identifying students who were targeted for being "not as masculine as other boys" or "not as feminine as other girls." This study found that harassment for gender nonconformity was generally related to either actual or perceived sexual orientation: 49% of students who were harassed for their sexual orientation were also harassed for gender nonconformity, whereas 27% of the overall student population reported experiencing harassed for "not being masculine enough" or "not being feminine enough." The most encouraging finding was that in situations where students saw teachers stop negative comments and slurs based on sexual orientation, they reported less name calling and stronger feelings of school safety. These findings demonstrate how effective intervention can alter the experiences of students in schools.

Cyberbullying is defined as "using an electronic medium, such as emails or text messages, to threaten or harm others" (Kosciw & Diaz, 2006, p. 27). Much research has shown strong links between bullying at school and cyberbullying. One online survey in 2008 found that students who were bullies or victims at school were more likely to be involved in cyberbullying as well. In a Canadian study reported in 2006, researchers also found similarities between cyberbullying and schoolyard bullying: Males (22%) were more likely to be cyberbullies than females (12%), and males and females reported being victimized online at similar rates (25% versus25.6%). Cyberbullying is a very difficult phenomenon for educators to address because much of it occurs outside school, yet it has a clear impact on students' experiences at school. This practice differs somewhat from schoolyard bullying in that it can be anonymous and can have broader impacts owing to the widespread dissemination of information through broadcast text messages, posted videos, and webpages. Conversely, these same elements can make cyberbullying easier to prove by documenting the exact nature of the interaction.

Researchers have noted that cyberspace is becoming an increasingly hostile environment, particularly for girls and GLBT youth who are targets for harassment online. According to GLSEN's research, 41% of LGBT students had experienced this type of harassment in the past year. This percentage is four times higher than the national average of 9% reported in a recent large-scale study conducted at the University of New Hampshire. It reflects the higher victimization of GLBT youth in school reported by other studies.

The emergence of new virtual spaces such as discussion boards, blogs, instant messaging programs, and social networking sites such as Friendster, Facebook, and MySpace have created new arenas in which youth can interact—and can bully and harass. The increasing accessibility of these spaces from Internet-connected laptops, personal data assistants (PDAs), portable gaming devices, and cell phones simply multiplies the potential contact points for bullying and harassment. Nevertheless, this factor does not necessarily mean that such bullying falls outside the realm of educators' interventions. The visibility and public forum of Internet interactions can actually provide evidence for investigations as well as a place where teachers and parents can offer support and guidance. This form of online interaction is an important one for educators and researchers to address, as youth behaviors spill out of the schoolyard and into cyberspace.

Elizabeth J. Meyer

Further Reading

Brown, L. M. (2003). *Girlfighting: Betrayal and rejection among girls.* New York: New York University Press.

California Safe Schools Coalition. (2004). *Consequences of harassment based on actual or perceived sexual orientation and gender non-conformity and steps for making schools safer.* Davis, CA: University of California.

Duncan, N. (1999). *Sexual bullying: Gender conflict and pupil culture in secondary schools.* London: Routledge.

Gruber, J. E., & Fineran, S. (2008). Comparing the impact of bullying and sexual harassment victimization on the mental and physical health of adolescents. *Sex Roles, 59,* 1–13.

Harris & Associates. (1993). *Hostile hallways: The AAUW survey on sexual harassment in America's schools.* Washington, DC: American Association of University Women.

Harris Interactive. (2001). *Hostile hallways: Bullying, teasing, and sexual harassment in school.* Washington, DC: American Association of University Women Educational Foundation.

Hinduja, S., & Patchin, J. W. (2008). Cyberbullying: An exploratory analysis of factors related to offending and victimization. *Deviant Behavior, 29*(2), 129–156.

Kosciw, J., & Diaz, E. (2006). *The 2005 national school climate survey: The experiences of lesbian, gay, bisexual and transgender youth in our nation's schools.* New York: Gay, Lesbian and Straight Education Network.

Land, D. (2003). Teasing apart secondary students' conceptualizations of peer teasing, bullying and sexual harassment *School Psychology International, 24*(2), 147–165.

Li, Q. (2006). Cyberbullying in schools: A research of gender differences. *School Psychology International, 27*(2), 157–170.

Meyer, E. (2009). *Gender, bullying, and harassment: Strategies to end sexism and homophobia in schools.* New York: Teachers College Press.

Olweus, D. (1978). *Aggression in the schools: Bullies and whipping boys.* Washington, DC: Hemisphere.

Olweus, D. (1993). *Bullying at school: What we know and what we can do.* Oxford, UK: Blackwell.

Simmons, R. (2002). *Odd girl out: The hidden culture of aggression in girls.* New York: Harcourt.

Wolak, J., Mitchell, K., & Finkelhor, D. (2006). *Online victimization of youth: Five years later.* Durham, NH: Crimes Against Children Research Center, University of New Hampshire.

World Health Organization. (2004). *Health Behaviour in School-aged Children (HBSC) study: international report from the 2001/2002 survey.* Copenhagen, Denmark: Author.

Bullying Laws

As more attention has been focused on school-based bullying, states have moved to enact appropriate legislation that penalizes students who bully and provides assistance to those who have been victimized. By 2003, at least 15 states had passed some type of school anti-bullying law. Some laws also include prevention programming, although precisely what this covers and who is included vary. In July 2009, students involved with the organization Students Against Violence Everywhere (SAVE) testified before U.S. House of Representatives subcommittees on Early Childhood, Elementary and Secondary Education, and Healthy Families and Communities, lobbying for a federal zero-tolerance law for bullying. Democratic Representative Linda Sanchez has sponsored the Safe Kids agenda, which includes several bills related to bullying. She would also like to see federal funds devoted to the creation of anti-harassment groups in schools.

According to Bully Police, a self-proclaimed "watchdog organization," effective anti-bullying laws include 12 essential elements:

1. The word "bully" is used in the text of the bill, law, policy, or statute.
2. The law must clearly prohibit bullying, not address general school safety.

3. Bullying and harassment must be explicitly defined, but there should be no emphasis on delineating who is a victim, as anyone can be the victim of a bully.
4. The legislation should include recommendations on how to make model school policy.
5. All key stakeholders are involved in its creation, including educators at various levels, guidance counselors, administrators, parents, and students.
6. A good law mandates—not just suggests—anti-bullying programs.
7. A timeline is stated for when school policies are required and when they are to be implemented.
8. Legislation must include protection against reprisal, retaliation, or false accusations.
9. Schools must be protected from lawsuits if they have a good policy and follow it.
10. Provisions for counseling for victims should be included.
11. Schools must submit accountability reports and face consequences if they do not implement or follow through with their policy.
12. Cyberbullying must be addressed.

Based on these criteria, the Bully Police assigns letter grades to states in regard to their bullying laws. All states that have no law automatically receive an "F" grade for failing. "D" grades are assigned to states with very poor laws, "C" grades to those with mediocre laws, "B" grades to states with acceptable laws, and "A" grades to those with "near perfect" laws. Delaware, Florida, and Kentucky were recently assigned "A++" grades because their laws both include cyberbullying and provide for counseling for victims.

In Florida, Debbie Johnston pushed for the law, formally called the Jeffrey Johnston Stand Up for All Students Act, after her son, Jeffrey, committed suicide after enduring two years of bullying at school and on the Internet. Another one of the major architects of the Florida law, David Tirella, helped a family win a $4 million verdict against a Tampa area school district that failed to provide adequate protection for a victim of bullying, even after it had been reported to the school principal.

As of August 2008, laws in nine states (California, Illinois, Iowa, Maine, Maryland, Minnesota, New Jersey, Oregon, and Vermont) plus Washington, D.C., prohibited bullying and harassment in schools based on sexual orientation and gender identity. The laws of 25 states do not specifically list protected categories (Alaska, Arizona, Arkansas, Colorado, Connecticut, Delaware, Florida, Georgia, Idaho, Illinois, Indiana, Kentucky, Louisiana, Minnesota, Missouri, New

Hampshire, Ohio, Oklahoma, Oregon, Rhode Island, South Carolina, Tennessee, Texas, Utah, and West Virginia). Oregon, Minnesota, and Illinois are listed twice because, although their anti-bullying statutes do not specifically list protected groups, these groups are covered by the state antidiscrimination laws that cover educational institutions.

Some critics maintain that bullying laws do not work, noting that the United States has spent a lot of money since the 1999 Columbine shooting on ineffective programs and policies. For instance, the website Bullies2buddies argues that anti-bullying legislation tries to legislate morality, which is impossible. Most, however, believe that legislation is one strategy that may assist in preventing bullying and school violence.

Laura L. Finley

Further Reading

Barack, L. (2009, July 20). Congress taking new anti-bulling laws seriously. *School Library Journal.* Retrieved August 16, 2009, from http://www.schoollibraryjournal.com/article/CA6670289.html

Chang, J., Owens, L., & Brady, J. (2008, May 2). Mom's campaign for Florida anti-bully law finally pays off. *ABC News.* Retrieved August 15, 2009 from http://abcnews.go.com/GMA/story?id=4774894&page=1

High, B. (n.d.). Making the grade. Bully Police. Retrieved August 15, 2009, from http://www.bullypolice.org/grade.html

State by state: Anti-bullying laws in the U.S. (2008, August). Family Equality Council. Retrieved August 15, 2009, from http://www.familyequality.org/resources/publications/anti-bullying_withcitations.pdf

State laws related to bullying among children and youth. (n.d/). U.S. Department of Health and Human Services. Retrieved August 15, 2009, from http://stopbullyingnow.hrsa.gov/HHS_PSA/pdfs/SBN_Tip_6.pdf

Why anti-bullying laws are doomed to fail. (2005, November). Bullies2Buddies. Retrieved August 16, 2009, from http://www.bullies2buddies.com/Why-Anti-Bullying-Laws-Are-Doomed-to-Fail

C

Canada and School Crime and Violence

Toronto, Calgary, Ottawa, Montreal, Winnipeg, Vancouver, Victoria, Edmonton, Bowmanville, Brampton, Scarborough, Tabor, and Etobicoke—what do all these places have in common? They have all been the sites of newsworthy incidents of school violence.

> Tabor, 1999: a former student entered a school and shot two students; one died.
> Toronto, 2003: a student was wounded by gunshot fire outside a school for alternate studies.
> Toronto, 2004: one student stabbed another to death at a restaurant during their school lunch break. In an unrelated domestic incident six days later, a teacher was shot in the head in a school parking lot.
> Bowmanville, 2006: a student opened fire in a school with a pellet gun.
> Toronto, 2007: a boy was shot to death in a high school.

And so it goes: Winnipeg, Etobicoke, Scarborough, Calgary—knives and baseball bats, pellet guns, injuries, and sometimes death. Perhaps the title of an academic publication says it best: "School Violence: Not Just in the U.S."

For many years, the Canadian attitude seemed to be that violence and school crime were the products of U.S. culture, and hardly to be found in that country's neighbor to the north. But by the mid-1990s, Canadians were seeing a noticeable uptick in school violence. In fact, one research article, stating that risks for physical aggression were higher for U.S. students than for Canadian students, was careful to point out that the "magnitude of the differences was modest" and that "rates of aggression" were quite similar between the two countries. Other survey results indicated that more than 90% of Canadian adults found school violence to be a major concern. It is fair to say that school violence has now become more of an issue in Canada than it was before.

One study indicated that 46% of Canada's 16- and 17-year-old children were the victims of harassment, verbal aggression, threats, and physical assault at school. Other types of violence found in Canadian schools include violence and verbal abuse against teachers, gang violence, sexual assault and harassment, shootings, stabbings, assault with baseball bats, and, of course, bullying.

A 2002 study reported the frequency of bullying among grade-school children in Calgary, Alberta to be higher than rates found in earlier studies. The research indicated that 27% of students were the victims of both physical and verbal bullying, and 21% and 5%, respectively, were the victims of just verbal bullying or just physical bullying. An earlier study of small-town violent behavior indicated that more than two-thirds of seventh to 12th graders reported being verbally put down or bullied at school.

Bullying can also lead to other types of violence, such as suicide among school-aged children. A 14-year-old girl in Mission, British Columbia (2000), and a 14-year-old boy in Halifax (2002), both of whom committed suicide, left notes alluding to horrendous bullying at the hands of their schoolmates.

Although many believe that violence has escalated in Canadian schools over the years, some debate continues over this issue. One study of self-reported incidents indicated that the number of assaults increased from 1985 to 1999, but then declined in 2001. This study does not specify how many of the assaults occurred in school, although the authors do speculate that part of the decrease could be due to passage of Ontario's Safe School Act in 2000.

Regardless of whether or not violence has actually escalated in the schools, there certainly is a strong *perception* that it is getting worse. In a survey of school students, aged 14 to 18 years old, in British Columbia, Alberta, and Ontario, more than one-third believed that violence had increased in the schools over the previous five years. (Slightly more than 40% believed the rates were the same, and less than one-fourth believed violence had decreased.) The same study looked at the types of violence reported by students. While the most common incidents involved seemingly less serious behavior, such as arguments, name calling, and so forth, other more serious behavior was also reported, albeit at a lower rate. These less frequent but more serious behaviors included fighting and being beaten up, bullying, assaults, physical threats, sexual harassment, and inappropriate touching. Some instances involved as many as six participants. It should be noted that long-term persistent verbal abuse, although categorized as seemingly "less serious," can be quite devastating and detrimental to the victim over a long period of time.

In a cross-national study focusing on the relationship between drug and alcohol use and violence in the United States and Canada, U.S. and Canadian researchers observed that the difference in arrest rates for violent juvenile crime in the two countries has been narrowing in recent years. While U.S. arrest rates for these crimes remain much higher than Canadian rates, Canadian rates have been increasing at a much faster rate over a somewhat similar period of time. In Canada, arrest rates for armed robbery (among juveniles) increased 267% during a six-year period, while U.S. arrest rates for juvenile robbery increased by 57% over a nine-year period. In the United States. juvenile arrest rates for aggravated assault rose 70% over the same period, while Canadian serious juvenile assault rates rose 90%. Previously cannabis use was slightly lower in Canada than in the United States, but now the reverse is true. Moreover, the use of drugs appeared to be more closely tied to violence in the Canadian sample than in the U.S. sample. While violent crime among juveniles in the United States has decreased dramatically since 1995, the reverse seems to be the case in Canada, at least as measured by arrest rates. Another study indicated "remarkably similar rates of physical aggression" among students in Canada and in the United States.

Based on their own data, Canadian researchers observed that Canadian self-reported rates of violence against juveniles greatly exceeded those identified in governmental statistics. More than half of children reported being violently victimized or being the target of unsuccessful victimization during the course of their lifetime. There was a greater likelihood of teenagers being victimized at school than anywhere else. In fact, more than 80% of students said they had been victimized at school one or more times in the previous year; the highest percentage of victimizations were for theft, but more than 42% reported being threatened at school. More than half (56%) of the self-reporters admitted participation in delinquent behavior in the previous year. In fact, more than 45% admitted to participating in some violent activity, such as threatening, punching, kicking, or slapping. Additionally, 28% of self-reporters admitted to having a weapon (knives, bats, clubs, pellet guns, a very small number of guns, and other weapons) in school during the past year. Almost half of those students with weapons at school reported a significant level of victimization (in which they were the victim) while at school. Among those who had weapons at school, close to 59% reported a fairly high level of delinquency as well.

Violence, of course, is not the only type of crime found in the schools. In a study of small-town Canadian students, almost 70% were the victims of theft while at school, almost 47% were threatened, and more than half had something damaged while at school.

In an effort to control school crime, and particularly violence, Canada has implemented a number of measures intended to cut down on the number of incidents. For example, in 2000, Ontario passed the Safe Schools Act. The government implemented safety audits throughout the schools to raise awareness, determine safety and security needs, and initiate various remedies. The Safe Schools Act gave rise to a code of conduct and led to the introduction of a list of unacceptable behaviors that would lead to mandatory expulsion or suspension. A partial list of these behaviors includes threatening serious bodily harm and extensive vandalism (both of which would lead to suspension), as well as weapons possession, causing bodily harm, robbery, and sexual assault (all of which would lead to expulsion). Tighter security measures were instituted in many schools, and every public school was required to implement a bullying prevention program.

In 2007, a new law, referred to as Anastasia's Law (in memory of a student killed in a shootout at Dawson College), was passed. Among other things, it banned firearms in schools, colleges, and daycare facilities, and on school buses in Quebec. The law went into effect in September 2008.

There is one area in which Canada and the United States are very similar: Laws dealing with juvenile offenders have become increasingly harsh and punitive. Canada has also followed the lead of the United States in its implementation of zero-tolerance policies in the schools. Zero tolerance is a philosophy that allows no discretion in dealing with certain types of school misbehavior; in fact, under zero-tolerance policies, suspension and expulsion are the only options for dealing with certain behaviors. Unfortunately, this approach can be used quite inappropriately, as in the cases of the young student who was suspended for bring a squirt gun to school for use in a skit and the 12-year-old student who was suspended for pushing her friend into a snow bank.

While there is some disagreement over whether school crime and violence are increasing in Canada, it is certainly true that there is a perception of higher levels of school violence. It is clear that this problem warrants further research and additional remedies.

Carol Lenhart

Further Reading

Akiba, M., LeTendre, G., Baker, D., & Goseling, B. (2002). Student victimization: National and school system effects on school violence in 37 nations. *American Educational Research Journal, 39*(4), 829–853.

Barwick, M. (2009, April 20). School violence: What you should know, what you can do. *CBC News.* Retrieved April 27, 2010, from http://www.cbc.ca/health/story/2009/04/20/f-barwick-school- violence.html

Canadian Safe School Network: http://www.canadiansafeschools.com/home.htm

Carter, S., & Stewin, L. (1999). School violence in the Canadian context: An overview and model for intervention. *International Journal for the Advancement of Counseling, 21*(4), 267–277.

Carneal, Michael

Michael Carneal, one of the more infamous school shooters in U.S. history, committed a mass shooting at a high school in West Paducah, Kentucky, in 1997. On the morning of December 1, Carneal, then a 14-year-old high school freshman at

Heath High School, killed three of his fellow classmates and injured five others in a deadly shooting spree. The victims had all been holding hands in a Christian prayer circle that was a regular event for some students at the school.

Carneal rode to school in a car driven by his sister and entered Heath High School before classes started, at around 7:45 A.M. He was carrying two shotguns and two rifles wrapped in a large blanket. Carneal also carried a .22-caliber semi-automatic handgun in his backpack. He told several people that the blanket was protecting an art project or theatrical prop he was working on. After making his way into a lobby area where he and fellow Christian students regularly gathered to pray together, Carneal reportedly placed a pair of earplugs in his ears and pulled the handgun from his book bag. He opened fire on students in the prayer circle with the handgun.

Carneal fired a total of 11 rounds, killing three girls and injuring three other girls and two boys. One of the five survivors was left paralyzed from the waist down. She has since visited Carneal in prison and given numerous interviews and speeches about school violence and her traumatic experience during and after the incident.

Initial reports indicated that Carneal stopped firing only when he was tackled or confronted by a fellow student. However, it was later reported that Carneal stopped firing on his own. Carneal knew all of his victims and was friends with several of them. When he stopped shooting, he reportedly placed his pistol on the floor and surrendered to the school principal, Bill Bond. Witnesses said he told student Ben Strong, "Kill me, please. I can't believe I did that."

The West Paducah episode followed the mass school shooting in Pearl, Mississippi, by only two months and contributed to the widespread perception that the United States was in the midst of an epidemic of school violence. Some investigators suspected that other students were in on the plot but backed out of the conspiracy at the last minute. They pointed to the presence of the four long guns wrapped in Carneal's blanket and to the fact that Carneal never used these weapons in his shooting spree. Some suggested that the rifles and shotguns were intended for use by friends of Carneal, who declined to pick them up during Carneal's attack. Intensive questioning of Carneal and his friends and acquaintances, however, led investigators to abandon this theory.

Fellow students reported that Carneal liked to wear black clothing and was thought by some classmates to be a Satanist. Several students came forward after the shooting and reported that Carneal had previously threatened to "shoot up" the school, but noted that they had not taken the threats seriously. Most of Carneal's teachers and fellow students regarded him as typical and well adjusted. He played in the high school band, and his grades were above average. He had never experienced any major disciplinary problems or been arrested. Carneal's father was a respected attorney in the Paducah area.

Carneal's precise motivations are unclear, but an investigation revealed that he was frequently bullied and had been subjected to rumors that he was gay. He was slight of build and physically weaker than other students. In the weeks leading up to the December 1997 shooting, Carneal became fascinated with guns. He reportedly stole a .38-caliber handgun belonging to his parents and attempted to sell it. The handgun ended up in the possession of another student who either stole or bought the gun from Carneal with a promise to pay him. Carneal also stole several more firearms from his own home and from the home of a friend. On Thanksgiving Day 1997, Carneal broke into the garage of a friend and took a Ruger .22-caliber pistol, four .22-caliber rifles, a 30-30 hunting rifle, .22-caliber ammunition, 12-gauge shotgun shells, and a set of earplugs.

After Carneal was taken into custody, prosecutors announced that they would seek to prosecute him as an adult instead of as a juvenile. Carneal's legal team emphasized the fragility of their client's mental health, arguing that he was in the advanced stages of mental illness at the time of the episode. Carneal was examined by several psychologists, including three psychologists retained by the defense team. After several court hearings, a judge pronounced Carneal competent to stand trial as an adult. He ultimately pled no contest, and was sentenced to three concurrent life sentences for the three murders and an additional 120 years in prison for five counts of attempted murder and burglary.

The Carneal slayings also led to a 1999 lawsuit by the parents of the three murdered girls. The parents sued a number of video game makers, including Nintendo, Sega, and Sony Computer Entertainment; two Internet pornography websites; and the distributors of the 1995 movie *The Basketball Diaries*—the claim was that their violent depictions inspired Carneal to commit the mass shooting in 1997. All defendants except Carneal himself were dismissed from the lawsuit after federal courts held that any causal link between the media and Carneal's attacks was unforeseen and speculative. On August 4, 2000, the trial court rendered a judgment against Carneal in the amount of $42 million.

In 2007, when Carneal was 25 years old, he initiated litigation to attempt to reevaluate his sentence. After years of counseling in prison, Carneal claimed he was too mentally ill to plead guilty in 1998. His attorneys argued that new facts had surfaced over the course of Carneal's prison counseling sessions, indicating that Carneal had been suffering from schizophrenia before, during, and after his shooting spree at Heath High School.

Roger I. Roots

Further Reading

Egan, T. (1998, June 14). Where rampages begin: A special report. From adolescent angst to shooting up schools. *New York Times*. Retrieved April 25, 2010, from http://www.nytimes.com/1998/06/14/us/where-rampages-begin-special-report-adolescent- angst-shooting-up-schools.html

Fox, C., Harding, D., Mehta, J., Roth, W., & Newman, K. (2005). *Rampage: The social roots of school shootings.* New York: Basic.

Kimmel, M., & Mahler, M. (2003). Adolescent masculinity, homophobia, and violence: Random school shootings, 1982–2001. *American Behavioral Scientist, 46,* 1439–1458.

Moore, M., Petrie, C., Braga, A., & McLaughlin, B. (Eds.). (2003). *Deadly lessons: Understanding lethal school violence.* Washington, DC: National Academies Press.

Centers for Disease Control and Prevention (CDC)

The Centers for Disease Control and Prevention (CDC) provides a number of resources relevant to school crime and violence in its Youth Violence section. Each year, CDC contributes data to the Department of Education's Indicators of School Crime and Safety. In addition, CDC has collaborated with the Departments of Education and Justice since 1992 to monitor school-associated violent deaths. This agency also sponsors the School Health Policies and Programs Study, which is billed as the largest and most comprehensive of its kind. Every two years, CDC administers the Youth Risk Behavioral Surveillance System, which measures violent behavior, weapon carrying, dating behavior, sexual violence, and suicide among both private and public school students.

In addition to the studies that CDC directly oversees, the organization funds other entities that conduct research relevant to youth and school violence. The University of Illinois at Urbana–Champaign conducts the Bullying and Sexual Violence Project. CDC also funds the Student Health and Safety Survey, and has helped create a tool to assess school environments to see how school designs contribute to fear and violence.

In regard to prevention, CDC funds 10 Academic Centers of Excellence (ACE) on youth violence. Blueprints for Violence Prevention, which has identified 11 model prevention programs, has also received CDC funding. CDC has publicized *Best Practices of Youth Violence Prevention: A Sourcebook for Community Action* and is currently collaborating with four universities on a multisite violence prevention project. The agency has developed a school health assessment tool, the School Health Index (SHI), that assists schools in identifying their strengths and weaknesses and developing action plans to increase student health.

CDC's website (www.cdc.gov) offers information about school violence, including an "Understanding School Violence" fact sheet, data on risk and protective factors, evaluation studies, prevention resources, and additional links.

CDC's Healthy Youth division offers information, resources, and tools relevant to school health and risky behavior on its website (www.cdc.gov/HealthyYouth/). The Violence Prevention division addresses school violence as well as the related issues of child maltreatment, intimate-partner violence, sexual violence, suicide, and more. Featured projects include Choose Respect, about developing healthy dating relationships, and the Rape Prevention and Education (RPE) program, among others. CDC has also produced television programming, including *Break the Silence: Stop the Violence.*

Laura L. Finley

Further Reading
Centers for Disease Control: www.cdc.gov
Healthy Youth Division: http://www.cdc.gov/HealthyYouth/

Central Asia Institute (CAI)

Although quality education is far from assured in the United States and other Western countries, virtually all school-aged children can attend a public school. This is not true in all parts of the world. In India, only 83% of school-aged children are enrolled in primary schools. In Nepal, this rate is 70%, and in Pakistan, just 52%. In Pakistan, 42 million children do not attend school. Fortunately, a number of nonprofit organizations are working to build and staff schools in these regions, including the very successful Central Asia Institute (CAI).

Central Asia Institute is a 501(c)3 nonprofit organization whose mission is to promote and support community-based education, especially for girls, in remote regions of northern Pakistan and Afghanistan. Cofounder and Executive Director Greg Mortenson made a commitment to build a school when he discovered that there was none in the entire town inhabited by the kind and welcoming Balti people whom he met after not-quite summiting K-2, the world's second tallest mountain. Mortenson returned to the United States and attempted to raise funds to build the school. He sold almost everything he owned and sent letters to as many people as possible to solicit support. His first efforts were to little avail, but he finally found a significant funder in Dr. Jean Hoerni. As Mortenson began planning the first school, he realized that construction would be impossible until a bridge was built over the Braldu River. From 1993 to 1996, Mortsenson worked with the Balti people to erect the bridge and then a school in Korphe village. During that time, he realized the importance of empowering the local people and listening to and learning from them. In 1996, Hoerni established CAI, naming Mortenson the director.

The Hushe school in Pakistan is one of more than 100 schools built by the Central Asia Institute to support education for those living in remote areas of Pakistan and Afghanistan. (Central Asia Institute)

As of 2009, CAI had established 130 schools in Pakistan and Afghanistan, reaching more than 51,000 students. Projects are selected to benefit some of the world's most remote areas, where few services are available. CAI schools employ more than 1,200 full or partially supported teachers, and CAI offers teacher training workshops. The organization can build and fully operate a school for $50,000—a remarkable feat.

Mortenson and the board of directors of CAI believe that girls and women are the key to ending the violence in these regions of the world. To that end, CAI has also built and funded women's vocational centers and literacy centers. It has provided training for women's nongovernmental organizations (NGOs), and has established several scholarships for women and girls seeking specialized training. Additionally, CAI has helped provide potable water and sanitation systems in many communities, as well as some basic health care and eye care clinics.

The general public in the United States learned about the amazing work of CAI with the 2006 publication of Mortenson's book about his expeditions, *Three Cups of Tea: One Man's Mission to Promote Peace . . . One School at a Time*. The book has also been adapted for young readers (*Three Cups of Tea: One Man's Journey to Change the World . . . One Child at a Time*). *Listen to the Wind*, a children's book, is told through the voices of Korphe's children. Mortenson's most recent publication, released December 1, 2009, is *Stones into Schools: Promoting Peace with Books, Not Bombs, in Afghanistan and Pakistan.*

CAI is funded by many donors and supporters. People all over the world have contributed small amounts that collectively make a big difference. One innovative fundraising method used is called Pennies for Peace (P4P). Groups simply collect their spare change and send it in. More than 3,000 schools, organizations, and individuals have participated in P4P. A guide is available at this program's website (www.penniesforpeace.org) for educators who wish to teach about the issues addressed here as well as incorporate a P4P service program into their classes. In 2011, a *New York Times* expose' exposed inconsistencies in Mortenson's story about his work. It seems as though he took credit for building schools that were really built by others, and some of the schools he opened were not actually operational.

Laura L. Finley

Further Reading

Central Asia Institute: https://www.ikat.org/
Frontline/World. (n.d.). Extended interview: Mosharraf Zaidi. Retrieved April 24, 2010, http://www.pbs.org/frontlineworld/stories/pakistan901/zaidi.html
Mortenson, G. (2007). *Three cups of tea: One man's mission to promote peace . . . one school at a time.* New York: Penguin.
Mortenson, G. (2009). *Stones into schools: Promoting peace with books, not bombs, in Afghanistan and Pakistan.* New York: Viking.
Pennies for Peace: www.penniesforpeace.org

Choice Theories

Choice theories of crime and violence are based on the assumption that humans can exercise free will and that people make rational decisions. According to this view, delinquents choose to act improperly, just as nondelinquents choose to act properly. These theories suggest that youths choose to behave in certain ways based on personal desires such as revenge, survival, greed, or ethics. Choice theories further assume that based on these desires, youths carefully weigh the costs and benefits (or pleasure and pain) of their actions when making decisions. They assume that most delinquents would not commit crimes if the cost (pain) of such actions were greater than the benefit (pleasure) derived from them. Put another way, criminal behavior becomes more appealing if the rewards outweigh the potential punishments.

More than two centuries ago, philosophers Cesare Beccaria (1738–1794) and Jeremy Bentham (1748–1832) theorized that people make life choices (including crime) in this way. This general theory of crime is known today as the classical school of criminology.

The classical school theory states that, to deter or prevent crime, the cost (pain) of the punishment for the crime must outweigh the benefits (pleasure) of the unlawful gain. Classical criminologists further argue that punishments must be swift, sure, and severe. Punishments must be *swift,* after the person has been proved guilty, to connect in the offender's mind to the crime and the punishment. Punishments must be *sure,* so the offender (and society) can both see and learn from the imposed punishment (i.e., crime does not pay). Finally, punishments must be *severe,* but only severe enough to deter offenders from committing crime; punishments should be more severe for more severe crimes (i.e., let the punishment fit the crime). This classical approach to punishment for crime and violence has been termed "utilitarianism."

The modern counterpart to the classical school of criminology is called "neoclassical" criminology. Under this view, it is assumed that delinquents "choose" crime in a deliberate, rational manner. "Rational choice" theory assumes that delinquents are constantly acquiring and analyzing information, with their "rational" analysis leading them to the conclusion that crime is a lucrative enterprise where the benefits outweigh the risks. An example would be youth gangs selling drugs, where gang members view drugs as illegal but a productive business enterprise. Rational choice theory views both legal and illegal youth behavior as a personal decision, in which the youth evaluates the criminal opportunity, the potential for success, personal values, and the likelihood of getting caught and punished.

In 1992, researcher Felix Padilla studied juvenile delinquents—gang members— selling drugs for profit. Padilla observed that gang members acted much like traditional employers; that is, they offered job skills and security to juveniles in the drug trade, rationalizing that membership would help them achieve business success that would be impossible in the "legitimate" business world. The perception by some youths that an economic ladder does not exist in the legitimate business world is a main driver of delinquency in rational choice theory. Indeed, Padilla noted that the best solution to youth crime would likely be the institution of policies that would prompt would-be offenders to choose legitimate career paths over criminal ones.

A different take on choice theory was offered by sociologist Jack Katz in his 1988 book, *Seductions of Crime.* Katz theorized that youth commit crimes and violence because of the "thrill." According to his argument, delinquents do not need to gain materially from crimes and violence; they must simply get a thrill or rush from them. This theory explains many crimes in which the delinquent does not materially benefit from the act, such as vandalism, graffiti, and the violent defense of meaningless turfs. According to Katz's theory, committing a crime satisfies a delinquent's need to challenge moral boundaries and reject societal expectations. Subsequent studies have supported Katz's "seduction of crime" theory. For example, in 1995, Bill McCarthy updated Katz's research, with similar findings. McCarthy found that delinquents are more likely to be caught up in the thrill of crime or violence if the potential for loss of respect of their peers or the risk of punishment is low.

As an alternative to this view, researchers Lawrence Cohen and Marcus Felson developed the routine activities theory of crime and violence. They argued that structural changes in routine activity patterns can influence crime rates by affecting the convergence in time and space of the three minimal elements of direct-contact predatory violations: (1) motivated offenders, (2) suitable targets, and (3) absence of capable guardians against a violation. Cohen and Felson further argued that the lack of any one of these elements is sufficient to prevent successful completion of a direct-contact predatory crime. Also, the convergence in time and space of suitable targets and the absence of capable guardians may lead to large increases in crime rates without necessarily requiring any increase in the structural conditions that motivate individuals to engage in crime.

The routine activities theory makes no attempt to define a "motivated" offender. Indeed, it assumes that all people are potential offenders and that the structure and organization of daily activities may motivate anyone to become a criminal. The only articulated criteria are that the offender have criminal inclinations and the ability to carry them out. The target must be something of value to the offender or something that gives the offender a thrill or pleasure. A suitable target must also be something the offender is physically capable of acting against in a criminal sense in terms of size or weight; it must be available spatially and temporally as well. "Capable guardians" are not just police or organized security guards in a formal sense, but rather may include anyone or anything capable of guarding a suitable target. Any average person may be a capable guardian for a potential suitable target. Also, a physical or electronic device (i.e., a lock or alarm) may serve as a capable guardian. Routine activities theory holds that the manipulation of one or more of these factors would likely reduce youth crimes and violence.

Prevention of juvenile crime and violence under choice theories can be achieved by making the punishments severe enough that the crime is not worth the act, or by making the crime difficult enough that the gain is not worth the risk. Under choice theories, crime prevention strategies have developed based on two premises: (1) deterrence and (2) situational crime avoidance.

The deterrence concept maintains that the choice to commit delinquent acts can be minimized by the threat of punishment. A core principle of deterrence is that the more certain, swift, and severe a punishment is, the more likely a juvenile will avoid that behavior. While deterrence as a crime prevention theory may make sense, using punishment to deter juveniles is problematic. In the criminal justice system, minors cannot be, and are not, punished like adults. This difference has a major impact on deterrence theory as a viable instrument is controlling youth crime. As a consequence, many critics suggest that trying to deter delinquency with legal punishment is futile.

Situational crime prevention appears more promising as a means for reducing juvenile crime. Its strategies focus on making crime more difficult, so that would-be delinquents find the risk of apprehension and punishment not worth the reward of crime. Situational crime strategies rely on (1) increasing the effort a delinquent must perform to commit a crime, (2) increasing the risks in committing a crime, and/or (3) reducing the rewards. These efforts typically involve "target-hardening techniques" such as installing alarms and installing security cameras, or increasing the number of a location's security guards.

Other strategies involve police "crackdowns" at crime "hotspots." A crackdown is a strategy used by police in which tremendous law enforcement efforts are concentrated on a certain part of a city or a neighborhood. The crackdown focuses on a hotspot—a relatively small part of city or area where a significant portion of police calls originate. The goal of a crackdown is to lower delinquency through an overwhelming show of force.

While the logic of choice theories is difficult to refute, these theories fail to explain irrational youth crimes such as drug abuse, vandalism, and violence. Moreover, these theories do not answer the question of why some youths continually choose to commit crimes even after they have been caught and punished, sometimes severely. Choice theories are valuable is assessing crime patterns and understanding criminal events, but they do not adequately explain why some youths are "motivated" to be delinquent offenders. Other theories covered in this book are more useful in analyzing why some youths are prompted to commit crime and violence while others chose a more law-abiding lifestyle.

Eric Bellone

Further Reading

Beccaria, C. (1977). *On crimes and punishment,* 6th ed. Trans. Henry Paolucci. Indianapolis, IN: Bobbs-Merrill.

Bentham, J. (1967). *A fragment on government and an introduction to the principles of orals and legislation.* Ed. Wilfred Harrison. Oxford, UK: Basil Blackwell.

Katz, J. (1988). *Seductions of crime.* New York: Basic Books.

Padilla, F. (1992). *The gangs as an American enterprise.* New Brunswick, NJ: Rutgers University Press.

Wilson, J. Q. (1985). *Thinking about crime.* New York: Basic Books.

Clery Act

The Jeanne Clery Disclosure of Campus Security Policy and Campus Crime Statistics Act (more simply known as the Clery Act), is a federal law that requires all colleges and universities across the United States to disclose information about crimes occurring on and around their campuses. The Clery Act is named after Jeanne Ann Clery, a Lehigh University student who was tortured, raped, and murdered in her campus residence hall room in April 1986. After the murder of their daughter, Jeanne's parents discovered that Lehigh University had failed to report almost 40 violent crimes that had taken place on or near the campus during the three years before Jeanne's murder. Along with other crime victims and their families, Jeanne's parents testified in front of Congress in an effort to remedy this situation. Their lobbying helped lead to the passage of the Clery Act, which was originally known as the Crime Awareness and Campus Security Act of 1990.

Officially signed into law by President George H. W. Bush in 1990, the Clery Act requires all colleges and universities that participate in federal financial aid programs to abide by the law. Due to this provision, most institutions of higher education, both public and private, are held responsible under the Clery Act. The Clery Act is enforced by the U.S. Department of Education, which has the power to impose different levels of penalties on all institutions found in violation of the Clery Act. Examples of penalties include a $27,500 fine for each violation and suspension from participating in federal student financial aid programs.

The Clery Act has four main requirements. The first is the requirement to submit an annual security report by October 1 of each year. This report must detail crime statistics for the previous three years, security policies, crime prevention programs, and procedures used by the university during an alleged sexual offense case. Institutions must make the report easily accessible to current students, prospective students, and staff. The second requirement of the Clery Act demands that the police or security department of the university keep a crime log of all crimes reported to or witnessed within the past 60 days. Also, information older than 60 days must be made available within two days if requested, and the crime logs must be kept for seven years.

The Clery Act's third requirement calls for the university to issue timely warnings of crimes that threaten the safety of the university community. Policies on timely warnings must be published in the annual security report. Finally, the fourth requirement of the Clery Act states that each institution must keep crime statistics for areas in and around the campus for the previous three years. Institutions must report homicides, aggravated assaults, robberies, arson, burglary, sexual offenses, vehicle thefts, and arrests related to drugs, alcohol, or weapons. These crimes must be reported both in the annual security report and to the U.S. Department of Education.

The Clery Act has been amended a total of three times. In 1992, a requirement that all institutions give victims of sexual assault specified basic rights was added. In 1998, the reporting requirements were expanded and the act was officially named in memory of Jeanne Clery. In 2000, the legislation was amended to require that institutions inform the campus community about Megan's Law and where the information about registered sex offenders living in the campus area can be found.

Since the passage of the Clery Act, significantly more information on crime has been made available to campus communities throughout the United States. Even so, there have been a number of problems with this law. Many institutions are reluctant to publish crime information, as it is akin to a negative marketing campaign for the institution. Universities, not surprisingly, want to advertise their campuses as safe learning environments. Also, it has been reported that the Department of Education has failed to provide adequate direction to institutions on compliance and that many institutions are confused by a lack of clarity in the Clery Act. As a result of these problems, many institutions throughout the years have been in violation of the Clery Act, yet few have been penalized. Significant progress has been made since the Clery Act was passed, but more remains to be done. With a large percentage of serious crimes occurring on campus communities, campus crime remains a persistent problem.

Arthur Holst

Further Reading

Gregory, D. E., & Janosik, S. M. (2002). The Clery Act: How effective is it? Perceptions from the field—The current state of the research and recommendations for improvement. *Stetson Law Review* 32(7), 20–42.

Janosik, S. M., & Plummer, E. (2005). The Clery Act, campus safety and the views of assault victim advocates. *College Student Affairs Journal* 25(3–4), 116–130.

McNeal, L. R. (2006). Clery Act: Road to compliance. *Journal of Personnel Evaluation in Education* 19(1), 105–113.

Wilcox, P., Jordan, C. E., & Pritchard, A. J. (2007). A multidimensional examination of campus safety: Victimization, perceptions of danger, worry about crime, and precautionary behavior among college women in the post-Clery era. *Crime and Delinquency,* 53(2), 219.

Columbine High School Massacre

On April 20, 1999, what is considered one of the worst school shootings in U.S. history occurred at Columbine High School in Jefferson County, Colorado. In this attack, Eric Harris and Dylan Klebold—both students at the school—killed 12 students and a teacher, and injured 23 others, before killing themselves. The Columbine massacre is considered the deadliest school shooting for a U.S. high school, but the fourth-deadliest attack for a school, after the killings at the Bath Consolidated School in 1927, Virginia Tech in 2007, and the University of Texas in 1966.

Eric Harris and Dylan Klebold both had what seemed to be good, stable families. Klebold was going to go to college in the fall, although Harris had been turned down

Columbine High School offers a message of hope on a sign after the infamous shootings at the school. (Bambi L. Dingman/Dreamstime.com)

by a few colleges. Many have debated the causes of the shooting. It has been suggested that Klebold and Harris faced a great deal of bullying in a school that did little about the situation, causing them to become more isolated, angry, and violent. Other students admitted that they teased Klebold and Harris endlessly. They claimed that no one liked the pair, and that they teased them because Klebold and Harris seemed weird (as if they were gay). According to some sources, everyone made fun of the duo to get rid of them or make them act more normal. In the video Harris and Klebold made before the shooting, they said they planned to get back at everyone for the harassment they had faced for so long. Many believed Harris and Klebold planned to get even for their inability to gain acceptance for many different cliques. They plotted against popular people, students who had made fun of them, and students who ignored them.

Klebold and Harris played violent video games such as *Doom,* and some suggest that the pair had become desensitized toward violence through these games, as well as through violent music and movies. Five years after the shooting, a number of psychiatrists and the FBI's main Columbine investigator publicly stated that they believed Klebold had depression and Harris was a clinical psychopath who had control over Klebold. According to these investigators, a major factor in the shooting was that Harris needed to feel he was superior over others. Later, other psychiatrists weighed in against these opinions, suggesting that the diagnoses were not accurate. Critics held that the violent video games Klebold and Harris played, instead of aggravating their anger, helped them release their aggression. According to this view, when the youths were not allowed to play video games as frequently as a form of punishment, they had to instead get their aggression out in the real world.

The school shooting was not the first time Klebold and Harris had gotten in trouble. On January 30, 1998, both were arrested for stealing tools from a van.

They had to take classes and meet with parole officers. Harris also had to go into therapy, which he attended for approximately a year. Both got out of the program early for good behavior. Harris even wrote a letter of apology to the van's owner, and then wrote in his journal later about how he faked it. Harris was also making plans with Klebold to attack the school even while he was in therapy. He was put on Zoloft (an antidepressant) while in therapy, but told the therapist that the medication was giving him suicidal thoughts as well as urges to harm others. The doctor switched him to Luvox, another antidepressant. It was discovered that Harris had this drug in his system when he died. Although these drugs were intended to help Harris, some psychiatrists believe they may have actually led to his violent urges, as these agents have been known to cause depersonalization and increased aggression.

After the attack, officials found journals and videos documenting the plans made by Klebold and Harris. Klebold and Harris had originally planned to bomb the school, shoot any survivors, and then start shooting neighbors and others who came to see what was happening. Harris had created a website that included basics on making bombs and how to cause trouble; the site also documented the mischief he and Klebold had been getting into. It was discovered later that an Investigator with the Jefferson County Sheriff's Office knew about Harris' website two years before the school shooting occurred. The investigator, Michael Guerra, started looking into the website after the parents of another student, Brooks Brown, complained that the site contained threats against their son. Guerra also found threats against many other people at Columbine High School on the site as well as blogs about how Harris hated society. Harris even had a "hit list" on the site, and a list of the guns and bombs he had. Guerra had intended to obtain a search warrant for Harris's home, but never did—it was later discovered that there was not probable cause to obtain one. Members of the Sheriff's Office and other high-ranking officials of the county decided not to mention they had knowledge of this website at the time of the shooting. The documents that stemmed from this knowledge were lost over time, and the officials' previous access to Harris's website was not disclosed until September 24, 2001.

For the shooting, Klebold and Harris bought a rifle and two shotguns from a friend who had purchased the weapons at a gun show. They also collected two 12-gauge shotguns and two 9-mm firearms. They used the Internet to learn how to build their bombs, eventually constructing 99 of them.

On April 20, before they went to the school, Klebold and Harris set a fire bomb in a field near the school to go off at 11:14 A.M. (Mountain Daylight Time). Police speculate that this event was intended to distract emergency vehicles and keep them away from the school. Klebold and Harris arrived at the school at 11:10 A.M. and parked outside the cafeteria. They brought two propane bombs hidden in duffel bags into the cafeteria during the first lunch shift, and left the bags on the floor amidst an array of other students' bags. These bombs were set to go off at 11:17 A.M. After they put the bags down, Klebold and Harris went to their cars to wait for the bombs to explode, planning to shoot students as they ran from the cafeteria.

When the bombs did not go off in the cafeteria, Klebold and Harris had to make an alternate plan. They took their guns and started shooting students who were outside the school, eating lunch and on the staircase outside. They then shot at students in the soccer fields and threw pipe bombs, although none of the shots made their mark and the bombs did not go off. A teacher, Patti Nielson, went to see what was going on and was hit by shrapnel in the shoulder from shots from Harris and Klebold. She ran to the library to warn students to be careful; from there, she called the police. The sheriff arrived at about 11:24 A.M., and shot at Klebold and Harris. Harris shot back and the sheriff made a call for backup.

At that point, Harris and Klebold ran through the school, shooting at anyone who was there and throwing more pipe bombs. The two shooters then made their way to the library, which was considered the worst part of the shooting that day. First they threw two bombs into the cafeteria and one in the library hallway; this time, all of the bombs did explode. Klebold and Harris entered the library at 11:29 A.M., where two teachers, two librarians, and 52 students were taking refuge. Harris and Klebold started yelling at everyone who was hiding to stand up. No one obeyed the command, so the two started shooting anyway. They killed one student, but then saw police evacuating students outside. The pair shot at the police through the windows, and the police shot back. However, the shooters' attention quickly turned back to the students inside the library. They started shooting under computer desks, where students were hiding, injuring and killing more students. Klebold and Harris also walked around the library, knocking down shelves and shooting more students, as well as throwing more bombs.

According to witnesses, Klebold and Harris starting talking to each other about how the shooting was no longer exciting to them. They thought of possibly attacking people with knives, which they supposed might be more fun. Instead of doing so, however, the pair left the library at 11:42 A.M. As soon as they left, some students fled the library and managed to get outside the building, while others hid in the staff break room until about 3:30 P.M., when police found them.

Meanwhile, Klebold and Harris wandered through the school, shooting and throwing bombs as they went. At 12:02 P.M., they went back into the library, which was now empty except for unconscious students on the floor. This is where, at the end of it all, Harris and Klebold killed themselves. Eric Harris, age 18, shot himself in the mouth one time. Dylan Klebold, age 17, died from a single shot to his head.

At 1:09 P.M., the SWAT team went into the school, after the shootings had ended. Team members determined that the school was safe at 4:30 P.M., but later found more explosives, including in Klebold's car; thus the school was not officially declared safe to enter again until 10:00 A.M. the next day. Officials believe the shootings lasted for 45 minutes before Klebold and Harris shot themselves. In total, they killed 12 students and one teacher, and injured 24 others; another three people were injured trying to get out of the school. The casualties of the shooting that day were Cassie Bernall, Matt Kechter, Corey DePooter, Isaiah Schoels, Daniel Rohrbough, Steve Curnow, Lauren Townsend, Kelly Fleming, Kyle Velasquez, Daniel Mauser, John Tomlin, Rachel Scott, and Coach Dave Sanders.

Officials started their investigation at 11:30 A.M. on April 21, while 13 bodies were still in the school. The victims were not taken out of the school to be identified until the late afternoon and early evening that day. During the investigation, officials held a press conference to say they believed other people had helped plan the shooting.

Columbine differed from some school shootings in that afterward, there was no one to take to trial, as Harris and Klebold both killed themselves.

The shooting at Columbine High School opened American society's eyes to many issues related to youth and safety. People began more closely scrutinizing youth violence, gun control laws, high school subcultures, bullying, and the effect of media such as video games, after this shooting occurred. Harris and Klebold also influenced many other school shootings or attempted school shootings, as other students wanted to be like them or wanted to outdo them.

Sharon Thiel

Further Reading

CNN. (2000, May). Report: 12 killed at Columbine in first 16 minutes. Retrieved December 12, 2008, from CNN.com

Fine, M., Weis, L., Pruitt, L., & Burns, A. (2004). *Off white: Readings on power, privilege, and resistance,* 2nd ed. New York: Routledge.

Jefferson County Sheriff's Office. (n.d.). The Columbine report. Retrieved December 14, 2008, from http://web.dailycamera.com/shooting/2000.html

The Rocky Mountain News. (n.d.). Columbine High School shootings. Retrieved December 14, 2008, from http://www.rockymountainnews.com/news/special-reports/columbine/

Comprehensive Crime Control Act

The Comprehensive Crime Control Act was a comprehensive package of crime measures passed by the U.S. Congress and signed into law by President Ronald Reagan on October 12, 1984. Although many important criminal issues, such as capital punishment and habeas corpus, were kept out of the legislation, the Comprehensive Crime Control Act is recognized as one of the largest and most significant reforms of the U.S. criminal justice system. Support for the legislation varied. Many individuals and organizations embraced numerous provisions of the act, yet opposed many others. Given that the act is such a wide-ranging piece of legislation, lawyers and courts have spent many years sorting out all of its details. The act contains 23 chapters, but it is the first 12 chapters that are most important. The legislation, which was submitted as part of Reagan's crime control program, had bipartisan support, but it still took great political pressure to finally get it passed.

The most notable provisions of the Comprehensive Crime Control Act include sections on bail conditions, the insanity defense, sentencing, victims of crime, justice assistance, and drugs and narcotics. The act authorized courts to consider dangerousness when setting bail conditions, and also allowed courts to establish pretrial detention if necessary. If there is reason to believe a person will not return to court as required or that releasing someone on bail would put an individual or community at risk, certain bail conditions and pretrial detention are considered acceptable. Concerning the new insanity defense test, if a defendant can prove with convincing evidence that he or she suffered from a mental disease or defect at the time of the crime, it is accepted that the defendant did not understand the wrongfulness of the activity. Intoxication due to alcohol or drugs does not count during an insanity defense test.

Furthermore, the Comprehensive Crime Control Act established a U.S. Sentencing Commission responsible for collecting information and recommending sentencing guidelines to federal judges. With consent from the Senate, the president is responsible for appointing the seven voting members of the commission; in addition, the U.S. Attorney General is a nonvoting member of this group. If courts do not follow the guidelines created by the Sentencing Commission, they must explain why in writing. The Comprehensive Crime Control Act also created a Crime Victims Fund in the U.S. Treasury. Specific criminal fines are paid into this fund and a certain amount is distributed among the states each year. Much of the funds go to crime victim compensation programs and other assistance programs.

Under the Comprehensive Crime Control Act, the Office of Juvenile Justice and Delinquency Prevention was given an extension to operate, and a missing-children hotline was established. The act also increased many federal penalties for drug and narcotic offenses, while simultaneously reducing some restrictions on compliant manufacturers and distributors of legitimate controlled substances. The act established a National Drug Enforcement Policy Board in the executive branch. This board is controlled by the U.S. Attorney General, who is charged with working with numerous U.S. Cabinet officers who deal with drug enforcement.

The Comprehensive Crime Control Act includes countless other provisions. Some of the more significant ones include the following: clarification of the federal criminal and civil forfeiture laws, improvement in federal statues meant to prevent international money laundering, expansion of emergency wiretapping, strengthening of federal statutes dealing with trademarks, strengthening of the federal labor racketeering law by increasing the maximum period of being disqualified from certain positions from five to 13 years, raising of U.S. attorney salaries, and the creation of federal criminal offenses for misuse and counterfeiting of credit or debit cards.

Arthur Holst

Further Reading

Congress wraps up a crime package. (1984). *ABA Journal, 70*(12), 44–46.
Panter, D. (1985). The changes accomplished by the labor racketeering amendments of the Comprehensive Crime Control Act of 1984. *Labor Law Journal, 36*(10), 744–761.
Purdy, D. (1997). Seeking justice in federal sentencing. *Update on Law-Related Education, 21*(2), 31–35.
Trott, S. (1985). Implementing criminal justice reform. *Public Administration Review, 45,* 795–800.

Conflict Resolution/Peer Mediation

Conflict resolution/peer mediation is a process in which student peer mediators, often recruited from among interested students and trained by trained school staff, use a step-by-step model to help peers negotiate the resolution of conflicts while respecting each disputant's needs. The use of peer mediation as a conflict resolution approach has expanded as schools have increasingly sought to reduce violence, eliminate bullying, and encourage the peaceful resolution of conflicts. The first peer mediation program, *Teaching Students to Be Peacemakers*, dates back to the 1960s and is still widely used. In 1972, another popular conflict resolution curriculum, *Children's Creative Response to Conflict*, was developed to train teachers to teach students about nonviolence. In 2007, Rita Schellenberg, a professional school counselor, developed *Peace Pals*.

Most of the models used in peer mediation curriculum utilize some version of the following six steps:

1. The disputants agree to confidential mediation with a peer mediator.
2. The peer mediator hears the disputants' points of view.
3. The peer mediator helps the disputants focus on their shared interests.

4. The peer mediator works with the disputants to brainstorm win-win options, which are written down on a worksheet.
5. The peer mediator and the disputants evaluate each option.
6. When a resolution is reached, an agreement is created, both disputants sign it in the presence of the mediator, and then all parties shake hands.

Typically, during peer mediation sessions, the peer mediator sits (sometimes at a table) with the two disputants. Most of the conflicts mediated in schools involve verbal and physical fights between students, gossip, name calling, and ongoing disagreements.

Peer mediation among students has many advantages over other conflict resolution approaches. First, it recognizes that only the disputants can resolve their own conflicts, and that they can best determine a suitable resolution. Second, a resolution that is reached by mutual agreement of the disputants is more likely to succeed than a resolution imposed by school authorities. Third, the use of peer mediators makes the process age appropriate. Fourth, peer mediators can help to normalize the use of peer mediation to resolve conflicts among peers, as they understand their peers better than do adults.

Research has identified numerous benefits as accruing from peer mediation programs, particularly among students in the lower grade levels. Schools with effective peer mediation programs report fewer physical fights among students and an overall reduction in disciplinary problems. Peer mediators also benefit from participating in peer mediation, in that they gain peer mediation knowledge and gain self-confidence.

Peer mediation has its critics, however. Some contend that peer mediation does not solve all conflicts and that peer mediators end up addressing only easily resolvable conflicts. Critics also claim that peer mediators and teachers, including those supervising mediators, typically receive inadequate training (a few hours, if that much). Another criticism levied against peer mediation programs is that peer mediators often end up being disliked by their peers, who see them as rule enforcers. For peer mediation to work, mediators must be viewed as impartial, which is not always the case given that mediators are part of peer hierarchies and friendship networks. Most research suggests that such programs produce little to no educational benefit for disputants. Another criticism is that some disputants participate in peer mediation sessions to avoid punishment; thus they may go through the motions and sign an agreement when, in fact, the conflict was not actually resolved. What is more, critics point out, peer mediation is not especially effective with older students, whose conflicts tend to be more complex and serious, and when peers' opinions of them become even more important to students.

Researchers have found numerous impediments to successful implementation of peer mediation programs. Some students are reluctant to participate in peer mediation because they are not informed, or are ill informed, about what peer mediation is and how it works. If they do understand peer mediation, some students do not seek out peer mediators because they do not trust that their privacy will be respected and worry that what they say during peer mediation sessions will not remain confidential. What is more, some students worry that they will be humiliated and embarrassed for either serving as peer mediators or seeking them out, because peer mediation is perceived as "not cool" within their peer world; this concern is especially likely if those involved are less popular students. Also, students may choose to choose to deal with their own problems and may prefer revenge over mediation. Students who are passive may be unwilling to seek out peer mediators to help them resolve a conflict.

Some impediments have to do with school climate and issues related to peer mediation programs. Many teachers do not consistently use conflict resolution and peer mediation strategies; that is, conflicts between school staff and with students may not be resolved using mediation approaches. Lack of ongoing training for teachers and peer mediators has also proved to be a challenge. Fewer students choose to participate in peer mediation when peer mediators are not as diverse as the student population at a school. Students are also likely to dismiss peer mediation if the disciplinary policies at their schools are not aligned with peer mediation principles—that is, if the policies focus on punishment rather than on conflict resolution. When students do not feel respected by teachers, they are less likely to support peer mediation programs. Overcrowding at schools and student concerns about their well-being and safety also make students less likely to seek out mediation. Lack of resources, such as a physical space in which to hold peer mediation sessions, and the lack of district-wide mediation programming limit the effectiveness of peer mediation as well. Another hindrance to the effective implementation of peer mediation programs is the set of social norms that students bring with them from home, the community, and the society at large about violence, aggression, and conflicts.

Given these impediments to effective peer mediation, educators and scholars have made the following suggestions to increase the value of such programs. School districts need to provide teachers—particularly those supervising peer mediators—with the necessary training and time. Peer mediation training should begin in elementary school years. Training should include a better understanding of race, class, gender, sexuality, learning styles, communication skills, and social skills.

Richard Mora

Further Reading

Burrell, N. A., Zirbel, C. S., & Allen, M. (2003). Evaluating peer mediation outcomes in educational settings: A meta-analytic review. *Conflict Resolution Quarterly, 21(1)*, 7–26.

Casella, R. (2000). The benefits of peer mediation in the context of urban conflict and program status. *Urban Education, 35*, 324–355.

Cohen, R. (2005). *Students resolving conflict*. New York: Good Year Books.

Cremin, H. (2007). *Peer mediation: Citizenship and social inclusion in action*. Maidenhead, UK: Open University Press.

Johnson, D. W., & Johnson, R. T. (2001). *Teaching students to be peacemakers: A meta-analysis*. Annual Meeting of Educational Research Association, Seattle, WA.

Jones, T. S. (2004). Conflict resolution education: The field, the findings, and the future. *Conflict Resolution Quarterly, 22*(1–2), 233–267.

Schellenberg, R., Parks-Savage, A., & Rehfuss, M. (2007). Reducing levels of elementary school violence with peer mediation. *Professional School Counseling, 10*(5), 475–481.

Theberge, S. K., & Karan, O. C. (2004). Six factors inhibiting the use of peer mediation in a junior high school. *Professional School Counseling, 7*(4), 283–290.

Conflict Theories

Conflict theories have their roots in radical political movements such as Marxism and anarchism. Since the 1960s, they have also been influenced by the feminist and anti-racist movements as well as post-structuralism and anti-imperialist theories.

Conflict theorists argue that the roots of modern crime problems are linked with those of modern capitalist economies. Capitalist societies, which are founded on a broad division of labor and highly stratified with vast disparities of wealth and poverty, are grounded in often sharp conflicts. As a system based on economic inequality, capitalism has long been characterized by profound struggles over social resources and political decision making. The central conflict occurs between those who own and control property and resources (the bourgeoisie or capital class) and those who have to sell their labor to survive (the proletariat or working class). Extreme differences between "haves" and "have-nots" give rise not only to conflict, but also to sociopolitical institutions that serve to regulate that conflict, typically in ways that secure the success of elites and dominant classes. For conflict theorists, the criminal justice system is a mechanism for enforcement of elite social control and the preservation of economic inequalities to maintain elites' interests.

Conflict theories argue that the state ministers largely to capitalist interests. Agencies of government target not only the underclass for enforcement of policies, but the working class as a whole. Working-class crime is more visible, whether it takes the form of school crime or street crime. In addition, working-class people lack access to the necessary resources to get away with "invisible crimes," such as fraud, tax evasion, insider trading, or influence peddling.

Capitalist ideology even conditions the very ways in which crime is perceived—that is, largely in terms of an ethic of individualism that separates the understanding of social problems from their social structural contexts of inequality and power. Individuals, who are presented abstractly without reference to specific histories and experiences, are blamed for acts and attention is diverted from the socioeconomic structures in which the acts take place and are perceived. Institutions within capitalist societies, such as government, the media, the police, and the courts, tend to individualize highly complex issues and depoliticize the emergence of deviant activities by referring such activities back to "damaged" or deviant individuals who are in need of treatment or punishment. Indeed, for conflict theorists the very notion of "the individual" is a recent modernist notion.

Conflict theories are often contrasted with "consensus theories," which suggest that the basis for society is social consensus—an unspoken general agreement on broad social issues. For conflict theorists, notions of consensus serve to cover up or diminish inequalities and relationships of power that determine, or at least condition, the social opportunities, capacities for decision making, and positive action within people's lives. Consensus suggests that decisions made by powerful and influential members of society—those individuals and groups who have the resources needed to influence social development in a way that benefits their interests—are willfully accepted or agreed to by those lacking power. Where non-elites contest or challenge inequality, their efforts are often met with criminalization, oppression, or repression.

In fact, for conflict theorists, it is not consensus, but rather something more akin to fear or compulsion that drives social action. In this manner, elites are able to assert that their very particular interests are synonymous with the interests of society as a whole, largely because opposition is marginalized or silenced. This construction of particular elite interests as "common interests" is a process that some conflict theorists term "hegemony." Drawn from the writings of Italian Marxist Antonio Gramsci, hegemony refers to the manner in which dominant groups are able to condition non-elites to accept their subordinate status. Media theorist Noam Chomsky modifies this concept to speak of the "manufacture of consent," as elites are able, largely through mass media but also through schools, to secure and maintain the capacity to govern over subordinate groups. For conflict theorists, consensus theories of crime and deviance serve this process of hegemony by deflecting attention away from social structures of inequality and power, which conceivably might be opposed and changed, and toward the failings of individuals, who are targeted for punishment or medicalization.

Conflict theorists prefer to focus on elite deviance, involving acts that are socially, economically, and ecologically harmful, rather than on minor street crimes and the nuisance activities and survival strategies of the poor. They also reject short-term disciplinary approaches administered by the state, such as police, prisons, and punishment. Instead. conflict theorists emphasize restorative justice and reconciliation via community-based processes such as healing circles—a process that brings victims, offenders, and community members together to seek mutual understanding and restore social relations.

Powerful groups are able to mobilize public opinion on behalf of their interests. The law is itself created by economic elites who control the production and distribution of major resources in society, including intellectual and educational resources. Legislators are influenced by powerful segments of society through lobbying groups, political action committees, and campaign contributions.

Dominant groups shape public perceptions of crime and its definition. As a consequence, focus is shifted to "street crimes" and the crimes of working-class youth, such as drug use, petty theft, shoplifting, and minor assault, rather than to corporate crimes or government crimes, which are the crimes committed by elites. Dominant institutions also create "worthy" and "unworthy" victims of crime. Affluent victims receive more press coverage; minority and low-income law breakers are more likely to be publicized as criminals than are corporate leaders, whose crimes may actually be more harmful to individuals, society, and the environment.

Perpetrators of corporate deviance, who profit from unsafe working conditions for their employees, the release of dangerous toxins into the air and water, the sale of faulty products, and fraudulent business practices, among other acts, present ongoing economic, social, and physical threats. Yet those responsible for such activities rarely appear in the media or court records. They receive far less attention than deviant youth, whose actions may be much less harmful. The crimes of major corporations, where they are given attention, are typically dealt with through less visible and less punitive civil procedures rather than criminal trials. Whereas school crime and deviance undertaken by working-class youth become the subjects of moral panics and strict policing and have relatively large amounts of social resources directed toward stopping the offending behavior, corporate crimes receive relatively little media focus, public outcry, or legislative response. Conflict theorists question why it is that the waters are being filled with harmful chemicals, yet attention is directed toward arresting youth for minor drug offenses.

For conflict theorists, authorities should not be assumed to be acting on behalf of society at large, but rather serving their own interests and acting on behalf of other dominant groups. According to this view, rather than being expressions of general will or social contract, laws are methods for a privileged group to oppress or exploit an underprivileged one. Laws against theft, squeegeeing, or squatting prevent a redistribution of social wealth, a point that is highly relevant given that most crimes are actually property crimes.

Conflict theories emphasize that some people and groups wield power and are able to make their definitions of situations stick, whereas others lack this capacity. Thus the definition of deviance is a form of social control exerted typically by more powerful actors over less powerful actors. As part of this process, authorities (the dominant) learn norms and practices of domination, while subordinates (subjects) learn norms and practices of deference.

Conflict theorists do not take rules and regulations as given, but rather view them as part of a sociopolitical process. Labeling of crime and criminals is part of a process of conflict that excludes subordinate actors, particularly poor and working-class youth, from social participation or from power. It can marginalize those who challenge or reject the status quo that leaves them in positions of unequal status.

According to this perspective, the key factor is relative power. Within capitalist societies, the poor have the least power. Thus we might expect them to have the highest rates of criminalization, which is not to say that they exhibit the highest rates of deviance or crime. This understanding helps to explain, for conflict theorists, why poor African American youth are the most criminalized group in North America and are given the most negative attention by the state.

Conflict theorists argue that contemporary criminalization processes work to ensure that those who are brought within the criminal justice system are typically of the lowest socioeconomic standing. Deviants, in a society that demands material accumulation, are those who are not succeeding or who do not accept their diminished status. The poor are more likely to be arrested, formally charged, go to trial, be convicted, and receive harsher sentences. Poor communities are often treated by government and police as though they are enemy territories subjected to sustained and intrusive surveillance.

For conflict theorists, working-class youth within capitalist divisions of labor are socialized, from early ages, to accept subordinate positions within society, including unsatisfactory labor within jobs that offer little satisfaction and few opportunities for personal growth and advancement. Without that socialization, which is a necessary part of the process of hegemony, working-class youth would rebel and pose a challenge to the inequalities of the status quo social relations and their place within them. Numerous studies from within conflict perspectives, including the work of Peter McLaren and Paul Willis, explain how public schools are structured to prepare working-class youth for manual labor. Part of this preparation includes the targeting and punishment of recalcitrant youth who rebel against the bleak prospects that their futures are deemed to hold. Such subcultures become markers for resistance against the apparent gap between the promise of upward mobility and the reality that this is beyond working-class youths' reach.

To quell this rebellion, authorities wield formal rules and laws and informal normal discourses to reintegrate working-class youth within the dominant structures of inequality.

Jeffrey Shantz

Further Reading

Rieman, J. (2006). *The rich get richer and the poor get prison: Ideology, class and criminal justice*. Boston: Allyn and Bacon.

Taylor, I., Walton, P., & Young, J. (1988). *The new criminology: For a social theory of deviance*. London: Routledge.

Willis, P. (1977). *Learning to labour: How working class kids get working class jobs*. Aldershot: Gower.

Control Theories

Control theories are unique in the field of criminology in that they intend to answer a different question than do most other theories. While most criminological theories are intended to explain why criminals offend, control theories seek to identify the reasons why persons refrain from criminal activity. Thus the assumptions are that crime is not innate, and that criminal offenders are not dramatically different from non-offenders. All people are capable of offending, but some never do. For control theorists, the latter population is of most interest. Additionally, some control theories address why offenders stop engaging in criminal activity.

Psychoanalytic theory was an early form of control theory. Developed by Sigmund Freud, psychoanalytic theory proposes that human personalities are made up of three parts: the id, the ego, and the superego. The id comprises our impulses; it must be restrained by other parts of the personality to enable persons to fit into society. The ego offers a sort of check on the impulsive id, in that it brings to the personality realism and organization. The superego fulfills the critical and moral functions. Thus the ego and the superego work together to restrain the id. Freud asserted that the ego and the superego develop through socialization, so that early learning experiences with the family, peers, and school systems help override the id's impulsivity. Freud's ideas are so abstract that they are nearly impossible to test.

Another control theory was developed by Walter Reckless. Reckless called his work containment theory. He asserted that low self-esteem and low self-concept are associated with delinquency. In contrast, high self-esteem help constrain delinquency. Reckless theorized that individuals experience both inner and outer pressures to engage in delinquent acts. By extension, it is the development of both inner and outer pressures that can help an individual resist these forces. High self-esteem, which is developed through positive childhood socialization, is the key inner constraint. Primary groups help provide outer constraints. Some research has found that delinquents' self-esteem is, indeed, considerably lower than that of nondelinquents.

One of the most well known control theories is also one of the most widely used in the field of criminology. Travis Hirschi developed social control theory in 1969. He asserted that the primary mechanism that constrains delinquency is social bonds. Social bonds are composed of four components: attachment, commitment. involvement, and belief. Individuals who do not have these components or who have very weak bonds are prone to delinquency. In contrast, strong social bonds act to thwart delinquency.

Attachment refers to a person's emotional commitment and connection with individuals and groups. According to social control theory. youths who have attachments to individuals and groups will be socialized into norms that promote positive, prosocial behavior. Attachment also involves an individual's sensitivity and ability to empathize with others. Hirschi considered attachment to be the most important social bond, as the individual internalizes these norms. Commitment is the investment in and orientation to reference groups. Because the individual is accepted by these groups, he or she achieves a sense of connection and will be unwilling to risk losing it for sake of committing a delinquent act. Involvement refers to the time an individual spends interacting with prosocial groups and in prosocial activity. Belief is the individual's internalizing of positive social norms and his or her adherence to conformity.

Hirschi's theory is one of the most thoroughly tested in criminology, with some studies finding support for it and others failing to do so. One difficulty arises in operationalizing the four bonds Hirschi described. Researchers have grappled with the best way to define and measure attachment, for instance. Additionally, it is not clear how much attachment, commitment, involvement, and belief a particular individual needs to constrain delinquent activity. Hirschi found that students' attachment to school and school grades was linked to delinquency, although other important variables may exist that were not assessed in his study. In generally, evaluation studies have found control theories to be better at predicting property and drug offenses than violent crime. Critics often point out that specific delinquent groups have all four qualities, but these bonds are directed toward a delinquent lifestyle. For instance, gang members are emotionally committed to one another, are invested in one another, see one another as a reference group, spend a great deal of time interacting with one another, and internalize specific group-based social norms.

In 1990, Hirschi teamed with Michael Gottfredson to develop a different control theory called the general theory of crime (GTC). GTC asserts that it is the coupling of low self-concept with opportunity that leads to delinquency. According to this theory, when they are tempted in a given social environment, individuals lacking a strong self-concept will be unable to resist.

The idea that some of the most violent school and campus shooters lack self-concept and social bonds sounds logical, but does not necessarily hold up upon further investigation. Instead of low self-esteem, many of these individuals seem to have almost narcissistic personalities. Further, while some have unstable home lives and are not involved in school, others do not come from this type of background.

Laura L. Finley

Further Reading

Agnew, R. (1991). A longitudinal test of social control theory and delinquency. *Journal of Research in Crime and Delinquency, 28*(2), 126–156.

Gottfredson, M., & Hirschi, T. (1990). *A general theory of crime.* Stanford, CA: Stanford University Press.

Hirschi, T. (2001). *Causes of delinquency.* Somerset, NJ: Transaction.

Pitarro, M. (2007). School violence and social control theory: An evaluation of the Columbine massacre. *International Journal of Criminal Justice Sciences, 2*(1), 1–12.

Coon, Asa

Asa Coon was just 14 when he snuck into his school, SuccessTech Academy in Cleveland, Ohio, with three knives, two pistols, and two boxes of ammunition tucked into the baggy pockets of his cargo pants. Attacking individuals at the school, Coon wounded two teachers and two students before police arrived. It is believed Coon targeted the teachers, David Kachadourian and Michael Grassie, because they had previously disciplined him. Students described the attacks as random, however. As he saw the swarm of officers coming to get him, Coon shot himself in the head.

Coon's short life had been filled with neglect and abuse. In 1997, at the age of three, Coon lived with his family in Cortland, New York. A caseworker for the Cortland County Social Services Department who was called to visit the home found it to be filthy, with garbage strewn everywhere. Neighbors had reported that Asa's older brothers, Stephen and Daniel, had threatened them with weapons that included rocks, knives, and a fake bomb. The children were removed from the care of their mother, Lori Looney, after the county juvenile court found her guilty of neglect. The boys' father, Thomas Coon, was not involved with the family. Stephen continued to get into trouble regularly and was found guilty of numerous criminal violations, including burglary, felonious assault, and domestic violence.

The family was eventually reunited and moved to Cleveland. In January 2005, at age 11, Asa was arrested for attacking his mother, yelling obscenities at her, and punching her in the left eye. He admitted the crime in juvenile court and was adjudicated to attend six hours per week of counseling, attend an anger management course, and perform community service. Coon did receive one-on-one counseling for five months, until his probation ended. He was unable to attend the anger management course because he was too young to register. At one point, Coon made a suicidal statement to caseworkers and was prescribed medications to treat depression and hyperactivity. Court documents show he was not always compliant. Despite these difficulties, caseworker reports show Coon to be nice and well mannered.

Things seemed to have been going better for Coon when he applied to SuccessTech in the fall of 2007. The school had a great reputation as an alternative to the traditional public schools. It had a graduation rate of 94%—much higher than the district level of 55%. Coon was not treated well by other students, who picked on him because of his stature and his choice of clothing. Coon was short and somewhat chubby and dressed all in black, like a Goth. After his attack, students reported that when they taunted him, Coon would always say, "I'm going to get you," but they did not take him seriously.

Two days before the incident at SuccessTech, Coon's brother Stephen was again arrested, this time for involvement in an armed robbery. That same day, Asa Coon was suspended from school after being involved in a fistfight. It seems these two incidents pushed an already troubled young man over the edge.

When Coon started shooting at the school, the school principal called a "Code Blue" on the intercom, alerting students and staff of the danger. Many hid in closets during Coon's rampage.

Immediately after the attack, critics questioned the school's security. Cleveland Police Chief Michael McGrath said the school sometimes used metal detectors and always had at least one guard near the front door, but students did not have to pass through the detector unless they were going to school district headquarters, which were on the lower level of the building. The district formerly had two other security officers, but they had been transferred to other schools two years earlier due to budget cuts.

Laura L. Finley

Further Reading

Cleveland school shooting: What happened. (2007, October 11). *WKYC Cleveland.* Retrieved April 22, 2010, from http://www.wkyc.com/news/news_article.aspx?storyid=75879&provider=gnews

Maag, C. (2007, October 12). Short but troubled life ended in shooting and suicide. *New York Times.* Retrieved April 22, 2010. from http://www.nytimes.com/2007/10/12/us/12cleveland.html

Police Chief: Teen shoots four, kills self at Cleveland high school. (2007, October 11). *CNN*. Retrieved April 22, 2010, from http://www.cnn.com/2007/US/10/10/cleveland.shooting/index.html

Corporal Punishment

Corporal punishment is the intentional infliction of physical pain with the goal of changing problem behavior. In 1974, the American Psychological Association (APA) passed a formal resolution to ban the practice in schools. The National Coalition to Abolish Corporal Punishment in Schools, which includes the National Center on Child Abuse Prevention, the American Academy of Pediatrics, the American Medical Association, the American Bar Association, the National Education Association, and other high-profile groups, was formed in 1987 with the goal of banning physical punishment of children and youth in school. In 1975, in the *Ingraham v. Wright* case, the U.S. Supreme Court ruled that this practice is not a violation of the Eighth Amendment's prohibition of cruel and unusual punishment.

Twenty-one states have laws permitting corporal punishment of students, although in some of these states individual districts prohibit the practice. A 2008 report by Human Rights Watch and the American Civil Liberties Union found that, in the 2006–2007 school year, more than 200,000 students in U.S. schools had been spanked in the previous school year. In total, 223,190 students were physically punished in schools. Thirteen states use corporal punishment frequently. Mississippi schools used corporal punishment on the greatest percentage of students (7.5%), followed by Arkansas (4.7%) and Alabama (4.5%). Some students are more likely to endure corporal punishment. Although African Americans constituted 17% of the entire student population in 2006–2007, they accounted for 36% of the students who were physically punished—more than twice the rate for white students.

Critics assert that corporal punishment is cruel, and that it is disproportionately meted out against minorities, boys, and special needs students. For instance, the 2008 report found that students with disabilities were paddled more than twice as often as general education students. Students with autism are especially at risk of being punished in this way. Corporal punishment also disrupts learning, as students who are being physically punished are often held up as a spectacle for others to ridicule. Further, it teaches that physical violence is an appropriate way to solve problems. In fact, critics maintain that rather than deterring problem behavior, corporal punishment actually provokes it. The 2008 report cited a correlation with poverty and lack of resources as well, noting that districts and individual teachers lacking other options and stressed by the need to handle overcrowded schools and classes may resort to physical means to keep students in line.

Supporters argue that corporal punishment is quick and cost-effective. They often cite a religious basis for this practice, following the biblical adage "Spare the rod, spoil the child." In its May 4, 2009, issue, *Newsweek* told the story of Principal David Nixon of John C. Calhoun Elementary in Calhoun Hills, South Carolina. Nixon has implemented a discipline program that involves corporal punishment and claims that it is a major reason why the school has dramatically increased its academic performance in recent years. He and other supporters maintain that this policy is better than removing students from classes.

More than just embarrassing, corporal punishment can lead to serious, long-term consequences. The Society for Adolescent Medicine has documented severe muscle injury, extensive blood-clotting, whiplash, and hemorrhaging in students who were subjected to this punishment.

Laura L. Finley

Further Reading

Adelson, E. (2009, May 4). The principal and the paddle. *Newsweek*. Retrieved August 15, 2009, from http://www.newsweek.com/id/195119

Discipline at school. (n.d.). Center for Effective Discipline. Retrieved August 20, 2009, from http://www.stophitting.com/index.php?page=statesbanning

Greydanus, D., Pratt, H., Spates, C., Blake-Dreher, A., Greydanus-Gearhart, M., & Patel, D. (2003, May). Corporal punishment in schools. *Journal of Adolescent Health, 32,* 385–293. Retrieved August 15, 2009, from http://www.adolescenthealth.org/PositionPaper_Corporal_Punishment_in_Schools.pdf

Hyman, I., & Snook, P. (1999). *Dangerous schools.* San Francisco, CA: Jossey-Bass.

More than 200,000 kids spanked at school. (2008, August 20). *CNN*. Retrieved August 15, 2009, from http://www.cnn.com/2008/US/08/20/corporal.punishment/

Stephey, M. (2009, August 12). Corporal punishment in U.S. schools. *Time*. Retrieved August 15, 2009, from http://www.time.com/time/nation/article/0,8599,1915820,00.html

World Corporal Punishment Research: http://www.corpun.com/websch.htm

Crime and Violence in Private Secondary Schools

Private secondary schools are schools that receive no government funding and educate some combination of students between grades 6 and 12. More than 2.5 million students attend private secondary schools in the United States; approximately 80% of those students attend private secondary schools operated by, or affiliated with, a religious organization. Although vast differences exist among private secondary schools, on average these schools tend to have smaller student bodies and lower teacher-to-student ratios than public (government-funded) secondary schools.

Much of the research that has been done on crime and violence in schools has focused on public schools; however, scholars are increasingly studying issues of crime and violence in private schools as well. The 2009 *Indicators of School Crime and Safety* report, compiled by the National Center for Education Statistics and the Bureau of Justice Statistics, contains data from many different sources about levels of school crime and violence in the United States. These sources include surveys of students and teachers in both public and private secondary schools.

How prevalent are crime and violence in private secondary schools? How do rates of crime and violence in private secondary schools compare with rates in public secondary schools? The School Crime Supplement to the 2007 National Crime Victimization Survey, which is described in the *Indicators* report, found that just 1% of private school students between the ages of 12 and 18 said that they had been victims of a crime at school, while 5% of such students at public schools reported this kind of victimization. Similarly, a lower proportion of private school students (2%) than public school students (6%) in this age group said that they were afraid of being attacked or harmed at school. (In this survey, "at school" meant both within school buildings and grounds, as well as on the way to or from school.)

One of the most pronounced differences between public and private secondary schools that this survey uncovered concerned gangs. While only 5% of the students aged 12 to 18 in private schools reported that gangs were active at school, 25% of the students in public schools reported gang activity there. Regarding hate crimes, 6% of private secondary students said that they had been called a hate-based name or word, while 10% of public secondary students made such a report. Approximately 19% of the students surveyed in private schools said they had encountered hate-based graffiti at school, compared to 36% of the students surveyed in public schools. Finally, a separate survey included in the *Indicators of School Crime and Safety* report asked teachers at all school levels (elementary and secondary) about whether they had been victims of crimes at school during the 2007–2008 academic year. Only 3% of private school teachers said that they had been threatened with injury, compared to 8% of public school teachers.

These statistics indicate that, on average, many measures of violence and crime are lower in private secondary schools than in public secondary schools. Has this always been the case? How have rates of crime and violence in public and private secondary schools changed over the past 20 years? The results of the more recent surveys can be put into historical perspective by examining a 1991 report that assessed the results of the 1989 National Crime Victimization Survey. This survey also asked students about their experiences of crime and violence at school. According to the survey, in 1989, 7% of private secondary students said that they had been a victim of a property or violent crime while at school, while 9% of public secondary students reported the same thing. In addition, 13% of private secondary students reported that they feared being attacked at school, while 22% of public secondary students said this. Although differences in methodology make it difficult to directly compare these figures to the current statistics, it seems evident that differences between private and public secondary schools also existed more than 20 years ago.

A few researchers have moved beyond these general statistics and sought to more deeply analyze crime and violence in private secondary schools. Mijanovich and Weitzman (2003), for example, examined data collected in 1998–1999 in the form of interviews with students between the ages of 10 and 18. During these interviews, students were asked whether they had felt unsafe in school yesterday. While 11% of students enrolled in *urban* public schools said they had felt unsafe, only 7% of students enrolled in urban private schools said this. Interestingly, no statistically significant difference was found between the responses of *suburban* private and public school students in regard to this question. The results of this study indicate that there are always many nuances to consider when making broad comparisons.

Why do some private secondary schools have lower rates of crime and violence than some public secondary schools? Observers and researchers have proposed a number of different answers to this question. One such answer focuses on school size. Given that research indicates that overcrowding is associated with higher levels of crime in schools, some private schools may have lower rates of crime because private schools are often smaller than public schools. Another potential explanation is that some private schools are selective—meaning that students must apply for admission, often by taking admissions tests, submitting previous school transcripts, and attending interviews. This process may allow private schools to exclude some students with a history of delinquent behavior. Public secondary schools, in contrast, are not selective. These are just two of the many theories that have been posited to explain differences in some reported crime and violence rates.

Ultimately, although evidence suggests that rates of crime and violence tend to be lower in private secondary schools, the data presented here demonstrate that these issues are present in many private secondary schools as well. More research into the specific features of crime and violence—and ways to prevent crime and violence—in private secondary schools is certainly needed.

Tiffany Bergin

Further Reading

Bastian, L. D., & Taylor, B. M. (1991). *School crime: A National Crime Victimization Survey report*. Washington, DC: U.S. Department of Justice, Bureau of Justice Statistics. Retrieved from http://eric.ed.gov/ERICWebPortal/custom/portlets/recordDetails/detailmini.jsp?_nfpb=true&_&ERICExtSearch

_SearchValue_0=ED339133&ERICExtSearch_SearchType_0=no&accno=ED339133
Broughman, S. P., Swaim, N. L., & Keaton, P. W. (2009). *Characteristics of private schools in the United States: Results from the 2007–08 Private School Universe Survey.* Washington, DC: U.S. Department of Education, National Center for Education Statistics. Retrieved from http://nces.ed.gov/pubs2009/2009313.pdf
Dinkes, R., Kemp, J., Baum, K., & Snyder, T. D. (2009). *Indicators of school crime and safety.* Washington, DC: National Center for Education Statistics and Bureau of Justice Statistics. Retrieved from http://nces.ed.gov/pubs2010/2010012.pdf
Mijanovich, T., & Weitzman, B. C. (2003). Which broken window matter? School, neighborhood and family characteristics associated with youths' feelings of unsafety. *Journal of Urban Health: Bulletin of the New York Academy of Medicine, 80*(3), 400–415.
National Center for Education Statistics (2002). Fast facts: In what ways do public and private schools differ? Retrieved from http://nces.ed.gov/fastfacts/display.asp?id=55

Crime Stoppers

Crime Stoppers is an international organization that uses various media to inform and request that individual citizens report information on unsolved crimes to local law enforcement authorities. The organization was founded by Detective Greg MacAleese, who was trying to solve a murder in Albuquerque, New Mexico. After seeing a story about the crime on a local television station, a caller provided information to police that led to arrests and justice in the case. MacAleese then established Crime Stoppers in Albuquerque as a new tool for law enforcement, which encouraged ordinary citizens to speak up if they witnessed or learned of any type of crime or violence. By allowing citizens to make phone calls anonymously, officials could give assurances for the safety of the caller. Later, free long-distance phone lines and call centers were established to expand the region that accepted tips of possible crime. Area police would then follow up on tips. In some cases, if the tip resulted in a felony arrest, the caller might receive a cash or other reward.

By the 1990s, Crime Stoppers had expanded overseas. Today, Crime Stoppers International and Crime Stoppers U.S.A. have more than 1,100 programs in cities across the globe, including parts of Canada, Great Britain, Northern Ireland, Poland, and Puerto Rico. The mission statement of Crime Stoppers International

Crime Stoppers uses various forms of media, from billboards to the Internet, to spread information about wanted criminals. The idea behind the program is to encourage public involvement so as to keep communities safe. (AP/Wide World Photos)

is "to develop Crime Stoppers as an effective crime-solving organization throughout the world, with the primary objective of the tri-partite organization, Community, Media and Law Enforcement, being Working Together to Solve Crime." The organization behind each Crime Stoppers program establishes targeted goals to reduce crime hotspots. Because the group is a nonprofit organization, some police departments collaborate with it as well as local television and newspaper media to seek information from the public on unsolved crimes by providing phone numbers and assuring anonymity. Crime Stoppers also produces an informational publication, known as *The Caller,* which includes coverage of various crime-related topics as well as training information for program participants.

In terms of solving crime cases, European news reports indicate that Crime Stoppers has been very effective in assisting law enforcement in solving a variety of violent and property crimes. Internationally, the organization has conveyed a strong message that—as a community agency—the public is responsible for reporting crimes and maintaining the neighborhood watch (which is a related program). Major law enforcement organizations support these efforts, including agencies such as the U.S. Marshals Service, the FBI, the Metro Police, and Scotland Yard. Around the globe, tip lines have been extensively advertised, with use of the well-known 1-800-SPEAK-UP number mushrooming after the rash of school shootings in the United States and in other areas with high crime rates.

Crime Stoppers initiated Scholastic Crime Stoppers in-school programs in Boulder, Colorado, in 1983. The focus of the school-based program ranges from middle schools to colleges, and it provides directives and guidance for students who may learn of a crime committed in the school or near it. Although schools are quite safe environments, Scholastic Crime Stoppers encourages anonymous reporting of school crime: thefts, damaging property, threats of violence, drug use or dealing, and weapons. More recently, it has urged reporting of students who indicate they have plans for hurting teachers or students. In addition to establishing hotlines, schools have initiated their own reporting methods, including commercial computer/cell-phone messaging systems called "Talk About It" that are used in hundreds of schools. In addition, other software uses global alert systems for text messaging, and automated emails are a commonplace community and school safety measure used in the United States.

Crime Stoppers has been a solid success in solving crime and deterring violence in communities and schools in many countries.

James Steinberg

Further Reading

Aryani, G., Alsabrook, C., & Garrett, Terry D. (2001). Scholastic Crime Stoppers. *FBI Law Enforcement Bulletin*, 70(9), 1.

Cyber-offenses, College

On July 29, 2008, a student at Georgia Highlands College was charged with hacking into his school's computer system to change grades and steal other students' and professors' passwords. According to police authorities, Christopher Fowler used the login credentials of one of the school's professors to access the school's computer network. He also allegedly hacked the school's VoIP (Voice over Internet Protocol) telephone system. Police investigators determined that Fowler obtained a password from a math professor by setting up a keystroke logger on the professor's computer.

On November 17, 2008, Kentucky law enforcement authorities arrested Sungkook Kim, a college student at the University of the Cumberlands, for allegedly hacking into his fellow students' email accounts and attempting to blackmail them with personal information he obtained in this way. Police investigators were able to determine that Kim pirated another person's wireless router to send the threatening emails and that he had installed spyware on college library computers to capture logon IDs and passwords for students and faculty.

As usage of wireless networks increases in universities (60.1% of public universities, 70% of private research universities, and almost 45% of community colleges have such networks), these types of cyber-offenses have become common occurrences on college campuses across the country. Research on such offenses is conducted by the Campus Computing Project, a top-tier research entity that provides data regarding information technology (IT) on U.S. colleges, and Educational Security Incidents (ESI), an online research repository that collects data on security incidents in higher educational institutions. The number of losses and unauthorized disclosures of data has increased dramatically along with the number of colleges and universities affected, with larger universities becoming bigger targets of cyber-offenses due to their massive output of computer-generated information. The total number of reported cyber-related offenses rose 67.5% to 139 incidents in 2007, affecting 112 college campuses across the country—a 72.3% jump from 2006. Physical theft of computers is also on the rise. Incidents of stolen computers were reported by 17.1% of college campuses, an increase from 13.5% in 2005.

The most common types of cyber-related offenses at college campuses tend to involve the release of information to unknown or unauthorized individuals, specifically from university IT personnel, with hacker-related offenses declining in the last several years. In fact, university employees are responsible for 47% of these types of cyber-related incidents, outnumbering outside hacker-style breaches by about 2 to 1. Although 2006–07 data shows that cyber-offenses involving social networking sites such as Facebook continue to increase annually (13%), network security is considered to be one of the greatest challenges facing college campuses across the United States. Personal information data, including names, addresses, birth dates, and Social Security numbers, from students and faculty members alike are the target of many of the breaches. More than 1 million numbers were disclosed, stolen, or lost in 103 separate cyber-related incidents on college campuses in 2007, according to the ESI. The largest increase came in disclosures of "educational" data, such as grades, which were involved in 30 cyber-related incidents in 2007 compared to only one in 2006.

To combat cyber-related offenses, legislation such as the Cyber Crime Act of 2007 and the Former Vice President Protection Act of 2008 has been enacted. The provisions of the Cyber Crime Act criminalize any threat to damage a computer network or disclose confidential information illegally obtained from a network; criminalize online conduct that causes damage to a large number of computers; prohibit the creation of a botnet, which a criminal could use to attack online businesses and other computer networks; permit law enforcement to seize computer equipment and other property used to perpetrate computer crimes; and authorize the U.S. Sentencing Commission to update its guidelines to reflect the severity of Internet crimes.

College campuses across the United States have also begun increasing their own cyber-security efforts in an effort to protect their networks from virtual threats. More than 44% of college campuses have a plan for network disaster recovery, according to the Campus Computing Project. Sixty-three percent of institutions had assessed their campus IT security risk in 2005, compared to 58% last year. Almost 60% have a plan for responding to hackers or data losses to the campus network infrastructure. In fact, 82.9% of college campuses have policies that discourage or discipline students who illegally download music and 29.1% use blocking technology of some kind.

Tony Gaskew

Further Reading

Campus Computing Project. (n.d.). Retrieved from http://www.campuscomputing.net/

Educational Security Incidents. (2007). Retrieved from http://www.adamdodge.com/esi/year_review_2007

Guess, A. (2008). Data breaches hit more campuses. Retrieved from http://www.insidehighered.com/news/2008/02/12/breach

How ready are IT managers for a crisis. (2007). Retrieved from http://www.insidehighered.com/news/2007/10/24/computing

Cyber-offenses, High School

In the 1990s, when the Internet first gained a public face, it belonged to adults. In most cases, a home had only one computer that all family members shared, with adults being the primary users. In recent years, however, with the introduction of a wide variety of new products linking to the web and the vast collection of social networking groups that exist online, a new group has come to rule the Internet—teenagers.

Many parents are worried by the idea of predators creeping around on the Internet hunting for their teens. The reality is that they have far more to worry about when it comes to cyber-offenses and their children. Rather than focusing on how strangers may be interacting with teenagers on the Internet, adults perhaps should be more concerned with how teens are interacting with one another on the web.

Adults may be surprised to learn that the threat of predators online is exaggerated and misunderstood. For the vast majority of youths who have contact with a stranger on the Internet, the contact with that individual occurs because the teen sought out the interaction, at least in the beginning. Most teenagers know, without any doubt, not to give out personal contact information to strangers over the web. According to *Frontline* producer Rachel Dretzin, who filmed *Growing Up Online,* a documentary that follows teens through their experiences with the Internet, she and her crew had trouble contacting teens online while doing their research for the film. "Most kids we approached were suspicious and loath to respond to requests for an interview over the phone. We tried everything—links to our Web site, offers to send copies of films we had made—but kids are conditioned not to talk to strangers online. It was oddly reassuring," Dretzin said in an interview with *Frontline.*

With networking sites such as Facebook, MySpace, and YouTube, teenagers today spend far more time expressing themselves and learning about one another than ever before. The availability of Internet access on cell phones makes it possible for teens to always be connected. Electronic hangouts have simply replaced real ones, physical friendships have been reduced to buddy lists and "top friends" on social networking sites and instant messengers, and face-to-face conversations and confrontations barely exist with the availability of text messaging and email. Without the burden of actually having to see the people whom they are speaking and interacting with, teenagers are far more open in these new electronic environments and relationships. It is simply easier for them to present themselves in a riskier light on the web than it is in the physical world.

According to John Grohol, an expert in online psychology issues, "The online disinhibition effect, the phenomenon that prompts people to say and do things in cyberspace that they wouldn't ordinarily say in the real world, is strongly at work here." Grohol notes that almost one-fourth of teens have admitted that technology causes them to be more forward than they normally would be. A study done on Grohol's website, PsychCentral.com, shows that one in five teens is likely to use a cell phone and online technology to send sexually explicit pictures of himself or herself to others. What may seem more surprising is that most teens admit to knowing that this type of behavior is likely to result in serious consequences, but they choose to participate in such risky interactions anyway. Teenagers are aware of the ease with which someone is able to save photographs on a cell phone and computer, and then share those images with others, as a majority of them who have received sexual photographs have already done so. Also, while teenagers understand that these actions can end in horribly embarrassing situations, such as damaged reputations around school, they do not seem to be thinking about the more serious consequences that can occur later in life, such as these explicit photographs surfacing at a college or professional job interview.

The practice of sending sexually explicit images through text messaging and emailing has become so popular that the act has earned its own name—"sexting." This offense can result in far more than just embarrassment, and even more than the loss of a prospective job or position at a college: Sexting can end in charges of child pornography. It is illegal under federal and state child-pornography laws to create explicit photos of a minor, possess them, or distribute them. These laws were originally drafted to address adult abuse of minors, but they do not exempt minors, even if the photos they are creating and distributing are of themselves. Thus teenagers may find themselves in extremely bad situations after taking part in sexting, even though it might seem to be normal behavior among their peer group.

Decades ago, a child's home served as a safe haven from bullying and the vicious gossip that exists in schools. Today, with the Internet so widely available in homes, problems at school often follow teenagers into their homes, to their bedrooms, living rooms, and family offices. Because teens are always in contact, so are the rumors, and so are the bullies or people starting the rumors. Cyberbullying is perhaps the most common danger that teenagers face on the Internet.

Reports from a 2008 study published in *The Journal of School Health* show that 75% of teens have been bullied online, but only 10% have reported the problem to their parents or other adults. Cyberbullying can involve taunting messages; threatening emails; the posting of embarrassing photos or videos on social networking sites such as MySpace, Facebook, and YouTube; or harassing text messages. Bullying on the Internet is extremely similar to the bullying that goes on in schools. For the aggressor, however, it is much easier to attack someone anonymously, or from behind a computer screen, than it is to attack someone in person. This anonymity also allows the faceless aggressor to be more cruel, and the victim to be left more confused and without any kind of certainty of the attacker's identify.

According to the *Journal of Adolescent Health*, even if "the majority of kids who are harassed online aren't physically bothered in person, the cyber-bully still takes a heavy emotional toll on her victims. Kids who are tormented online are more likely to get a detention or be suspended, skip school and experience emotional distress." In recent years, this emotional distress has even led some teenagers to commit suicide. Many parents and other adults continue to perceive bullying as something that involves only physical contact, which makes it more difficult for them to recognize the psychological bullying that is happening virtually. While suicide represents the most severe outcome of the decline in health and mental wellness that may occur when dealing with teens and Internet offenses, several notable studies have shown that teenagers are greatly affected in other ways, too. An article entitled "Texting Until Their Thumbs Hurt," which appeared in *The New York Times,* states that in 2008, teenagers received approximately 2,272 text messages per month, on average 80 messages per day. According to physicians, this nonstop communication is leading teenagers to anxiety, distraction in school, stress injuries, sleep deprivation, and failing grades.

The World Wide Web has allowed teenagers to realize a new kind of independence. Teens who have early curfews and strict parents have the ability to stay out all night in virtual hangout spots, and those who have lenient parents can find infinite freedom online. The dangers of the Internet seem to revolve around poor choices, not predators or lunatics who prey on innocent teen users. Because teenagers are the new rulers of the web, it is up to them to make smarter decisions about how they portray and treat themselves, and how they portray and treat others.

Sheena Vega

Further Reading

Dretzin, R. (Writer); Maggio, J., & Dretzin, R. (Directors). (2008). *Growing up online. Frontline.* Public Broadcasting System.

Grohol, J. M. (2009, January 6). Teens, sex, and technology. *World of Psychology*, 1-1. Retrieved July 30, 2009, from http://psychcentral.com/blog/archives/2009/01/06/teens-sex-and-technology/

Parker-Pope, T. (2007, November 27). More teens victimized by cyber-bullies. *New York Times*, 1-1. Retrieved July 30, 2009, from http://well.blogs.nytimes.com/2007/11/27/more-teens-victimized-by-cyber-bullies/

D

Dann, Laurie

On May 20, 1988, Laurie Dann (born Laurie Wasserman) shot and killed one boy and wounded five other children at Hubbard Woods Elementary School in Highland Park, Illinois. Prior to the attacks, she had mailed and delivered food and drink laced with arsenic (which she had stolen from a lab) to family, friends, and even acquaintances she had not seen for some time. Immediately after the shootings, Dann took a family hostage and shot one man before shooting and killing herself.

Dann grew up in Glencoe, an affluent suburb of Chicago. She was the daughter of an accountant and his homemaker wife. By all accounts, Dann had a relatively normal childhood. She was described as a shy, withdrawn, but attractive girl. By high school, she had dated a number of males, although none seriously. Despite her poor grades, she graduated and began attending Drake University in Des Moines, Iowa. After improving her grades, she transferred to the University of Arizona, where she was studying to become a teacher. It was there that she began dating a pre-med student. Although the relationship was fairly serious, Dann grew tired of her boyfriend's possessiveness and incessant demands. To leave the situation, she moved back to her parents' home and transferred to Northwestern University. She eventually dropped out of college.

In the spring of 1982, Laurie met Russell Dann. He was an executive in a successful insurance brokering firm, and the two were fast in love. They married that September. Early on, things did not go well. Laurie began exhibiting very strange behaviors—leaving trash around the house, for instance, and she appeared to have obsessive–compulsive disorder. She saw a psychiatrist for a short time.

Three years after marrying, Laurie and Russell Dann separated. Laurie claimed that Russell had been violent and abusive during the marriage, and in the month following their separation, the police were called to investigate a number of incidents involving the two. In April 1986, Laurie accused Russell of breaking into her parents' home, where she was living, and vandalizing it. Shortly thereafter, she purchased a Smith & Wesson 357-magnum handgun. Laurie continued to do odd things and make strange accusations. She accused her former boyfriend of raping her when he refused to believe her claim that she had his child. In September 1986, Russell Dann reported being stabbed with an ice pick while he slept. He thought it was likely Laurie, but did not actually see her. Police refused to charge her, suspecting that Russell had inflicted the wound himself. Laurie was arrested once for making harassing calls to Russell's sister, but the charges were later dropped due to lack of evidence. Laurie accused Russell of having raped her and of planting an incendiary device in her home. Despite having failed two polygraphs, no charge were filed against Russell.

It had become clear that Laurie had some mental problems. She began seeing another psychiatrist for obsessive–compulsive disorder. According to this psychiatrist, while she needed professional help, Dann was neither suicidal or homicidal. Her behavior continued to be odd, however, and seemed to be deteriorating. In November 1987, Dann moved to Madison, Wisconsin, where she was under the constant observation of a psychiatrist. She had previously been prescribed clomipramine, a new drug for treatment of obsessive–compulsive disorder, and the new psychiatrist both increased its dosage and added a prescription of lithium to help address Dann's phobias.

At the end of December 1987, Dann purchased a .22 semi-automatic Beretta. She abruptly stopped seeing her psychiatrist in March 1988, and began making plans for her attacks. She stole library books about poison and some arsenic from a lab. Dann also shoplifted clothes and wigs and was arrested for theft once. Both her psychiatrist and her father tried to persuade her to enter the hospital as an inpatient, but she refused. She continued making threatening calls and, because at least one of the threats crossed state lines, the FBI got involved in the investigation.

Leading up to May 20, 1988, Dann prepared rice-cereal snacks and juice boxes poisoned with the arsenic she had stolen and diluted. She mailed these items to several individuals, including her psychiatrist and Russell Dann. She delivered snacks and juice "samples" to others, including friends in fraternities at Northwestern University. No one became seriously ill, however, because the arsenic was quite diluted and because the smell tipped the recipients off that the food and drinks were tainted.

Dann then went to the home of the Rushes, a family for whom she had previously done some babysitting. She promised to take the two youngest Rushe children on an outing, but instead took them to Ravinia Elementary school, where her former sister-in-law's two sons were enrolled. Dann left the two children in the car and entered the school, where she tried to detonate a fire bomb. The small fire was quickly extinguished. Dann left and drove to a local daycare center, which she tried to enter with a can of gasoline. She was stopped at the entrance.

Next, Dann took the Rushe children back to their home and offered them some poisoned milk, but they spat it out. She then lured them to the basement and used gasoline to set the house on fire, trapping the two boys and their mother downstairs The Rushe family managed to escape.

At that point, Dann drove to nearby Hubbard Woods Elementary School and wandered into a classroom, then left. Outside the classroom she found a boy and, after pushing him into the restroom, shot him with one of the three guns she had brought. Another gun jammed as she tried to fire at two other boys in the restroom, so she threw it into the sink and left. Dann then went back into the classroom she had previously entered and demanded that all of the children move to the corner. The teacher tried to disarm her, and did manage to unload the Beretta. Dann pulled a .32-caliber handgun from her waistband, however, and shot at several students, killing eight-year-old Nicholas Corwin and wounding four others before she fled.

Dann was unable to leave the area in her car due to a funeral procession, so she started running. She ran through the woods with her two remaining guns and entered the home of the Andrew family. Mrs. Andrews and her 20-year-old son, Philip, were home, and Dann told them that she had been raped and had shot the rapist. The pair believed her and tried to convince her to call the police, but she refused. Apparently they did call Dann's mother, who knew nothing about what was happening and could not come to get her because she did not have a car. Shortly thereafter, Mr. Andrew arrived home and insisted that Dann give up the gun. Again, they called Mrs. Wasserman. When Dann spoke to her mother, Mrs. Andrew left the house and called the police. Dann shot Philip Andrews in the chest when she saw the officers arrive, although he managed to escape and was rescued by police and ambulance. Dann knew the house was surrounded, so she went upstairs to a bedroom. At approximately 7:00 P.M., an assault team entered the house. Police found Dann dead in the bedroom, having shot herself in the mouth.

Although some of the victims sustained very serious wounds, all except Nicholas Corwin (the lone fatality) recovered. All of the children at the school (Hubbard Wood Elementary), especially those who were wounded, received special counseling. Many in the community went on to lobby for gun control. Philip Andrew ended up becoming executive director of the Illinois Council Against Handgun Violence. The Wassermans were criticized for refusing to be interviewed by police initially, as well as for not allowing access to their daughter's medical records (they were eventually obtained through a court order).

Some have blamed Dann's behavior on the drug she was taking for her obsessive–compulsive disorder, which at the time was not approved for this indication. Others consider this case to be a clear-cut example of mental illness. In any event, this school shooting case is unique in two aspects: Dann's bizarre behavior and the fact that she was female.

Laura L. Finley

Further Reading

Eggington, J. (1991). *Day of fury: The story of the tragic shootings that forever changed the village of Winnetka.* New York: William Morrow.

Kaplan, J., Papajohn, G., & Zorn, E. (1991). *Murder of innocence: The tragic life and final rampage of Laurie Dann, the schoolhouse killer.* New York: Warner Books.

Dating Violence, College

Dating violence has been defined as the use or threat of physical, sexual, verbal abuse, or stalking within a dating relationship. This term is meant to encompass any form of violence that occurs in a relationship from an initial date to cohabitation. Dating violence occurs in both heterosexual and same-sex relationships. Although perpetrators of dating violence are often men, women also participate in various forms of partner abuse.

Research has indicated that violence in dating relationships among university and college students is extremely common and, in fact, is on the rise. For example, in 2002, Leonard, Quigley, and Collins reported that approximately 30% to 40% of both male and female college students had experienced some form of abuse in their intimate relationships. Although some argue that violence in college dating relationships is often less sustained than in adult relationships, it is clear that violence in intimate relationships between college students is a widespread issue.

Rates of dating violence are difficult to determine with any precision. This difficulty stems from the extremely low numbers of incidents of dating violence that are reported to police. Many individuals who experience dating violence keep quiet about their experiences because of embarrassment, self-blame, and fear. It has also been suggested that the general lack of understanding of the nature of dating violence creates some confusion around the labeling of abuse. As a result of this ambiguity, many incidents of intimate-partner abuse go unreported because they are not recognized as dating violence, but rather are perceived as noncriminal acts.

In addition to these issues, some scholars have argued that because various forms of dating violence are often studied in isolation, it is difficult to formulate an overall estimate of the prevalence of dating violence. White and Koss estimated in 1991 that one in five to one in three college women experience physical violence in their dating relationships. In 2000, Fisher, Cullen, and Turner stated that one in three college women experience sexual assault by their male partners. These findings illustrate the prevalence of specific forms of partner abuse. Few researchers, other than those identified earlier in this article, have aggregated these results to estimate broader rates of dating violence on university and college campuses. Despite these many difficulties in calculating specific rates of dating violence, it is generally understood that dating violence on university and college campuses is extremely prevalent.

Forms of dating violence can be separated into two broader categories of abuse: physical violence and sexual violence. Physical violence encompasses any form of physical intimidation or harm, including emotional and psychological harm. Although both men and women are perpetrators of physical abuse, as much research has demonstrated, women are most commonly the victims of physical dating violence. While physical violence can exist in isolation, it is often accompanied by various forms of sexual violence.

Sexual violence can be defined as a nonconsensual violation of an individual's sexual integrity. It can take the form of sexual harassment and/or sexual abuse. Other terms are often used in the place of "sexual violence," such as "sexual assault" and "rape." The term "sexual assault" is used within the legal system to define all attacks that are of a sexual nature, ranging from inappropriate touching to aggravated assault. Rape, a specific form of sexual assault, is defined as nonconsensual sexual intercourse. Within the majority of academic literature, however, the term "sexual violence" is used, as it captures a range of experiences and levels of violence.

Historically, acts of sexual violence were not seen as forms of aggression. Instead, they were considered to be types of seduction. Rape from this perspective was seen as sex. The shift toward seeing nonconsensual sexual acts as violent was pivotal in sexual violence becoming a recognized concern within the criminal justice system and for academic research.

Despite the widespread misunderstanding that perpetrators of sexual violence are most often strangers to the victim, sexual violence has been shown to occur most commonly between acquaintances, friends, spouses, and family members. As a result of this knowledge, the term "date rape" has been coined to highlight rape that occurs between individuals who are dating.

Much academic debate persists regarding the proper language to refer to those who have experienced physical or sexual dating violence. Within the legal system, the term "victim" is always employed. However, within rape crisis and domestic violence centers, as well as in the majority of academic literature, the term "survivor" is most common. Among those who have experienced forms of dating violence, the use of "victim" versus "survivor" is often contingent on the way in which an individual understands his or her own experience. While some individuals who are targets of dating violence label themselves as victims or survivors, others struggle to see their experience as a form of abuse and choose not label themselves as either.

Researchers have found that college women and men who experience dating violence often suffer from various levels of post-traumatic stress disorder, increased substance abuse, lowered self-esteem, and forms of cognitive impairment. Dating violence has been shown to negatively affect the scholastic performance of university and college students who experience it. Abuse in dating relationships has also been illustrated to have harmful effects on other individuals besides the victim. In particular, friends and family members who are informed about the violence may experience severe distress.

Many scholars have studied the causes of dating violence. Much of this research has focused specifically on the roots of male-perpetrated dating violence. Several scholars have suggested that participation in aggressive sports, beliefs in male dominance, and hostility toward women are all connected to aggressive male behavior within college dating relationships. Male sexual aggression, more specifically, has been discussed by some researchers as being the result of traditional notions of gender roles and a belief in male authority and control. Some researchers have argued that, in addition to these factors, the predominance of media highlighting sexual and sometimes violent imagery of women as well as the prevalent media representations of male aggression and female sexuality contribute to sexual violence within dating relationships.

To date, little academic research has been directed toward female-perpetrated dating violence. However, within the work that does exist, scholars have suggested that substance abuse, childhood victimization, and relationship conflict all contribute to increased rates of female dating violence.

Andrea Quinlan

Further Reading

Domitrz, M. (2003). *May I kiss you: A candid look at dating, communication, respect and sexual assault awareness.* Greenfield, WI: Awareness Publications.

Harned, M. (2005). Understanding women's labeling of unwanted sexual experiences with dating partners: A qualitative analysis. *Violence Against Women, 11*(3), 374–413.

Katz, J. (2006). *The macho paradox: Why some men hurt women and how all men can help.* Naperville, IL: Sourcebooks.

Mahlstedt, D., & Welsh, L. (2005). Perceived causes of physical assault in heterosexual dating relationships. *Violence Against Women, 11*(4), 447–472.

Dating Violence, High School

The Centers for Disease Control and Prevention (CDC) defines dating violence as physical, sexual, or psychological violence within a dating relationship. It is a type of intimate-partner violence (IPV). In the United States, an estimated 5.3 million IPV incidents occur each year, and approximately 1,300 people die as a result of domestic violence.

Rates of dating violence in high school are nearly as high as adult IPV rates. In a 2001 study, 20% of female high school students reported that they had been physically or sexually abused by a dating partner. Another study in 2005 found that one-third of reporting teens knew a friend or peer who had been hit, punched, kicked, slapped, choked, or punched by a dating partner. Approximately one-fourth reported being coerced or forced into performing sex acts they were not comfortable with. Abuse is not always physical, however, More than one-fourth of respondents in the 2005 survey reported experiencing verbal abuse from a dating partner.

Dating violence tends to start out very subtly, and teenagers often mistake their partner's attention and jealousy for love. Ultimately, abuse is about power and control. It involves one party seeking to obtain and maintain power and control over the other. Early warning signs, then, tend to focus on controlling actions. For instance, teen abusers may try to control what their partner wears, who he or she sees, and where he or she goes.

Unlike in adult domestic violence, studies tend to show that boys are almost as likely to be victimized in their high school relationships as girls, although the abuse tends to take different forms. Whereas girls are more likely to suffer from physical and sexual abuse, male victims endure verbal and emotional abuse as well as threats and harm to their property.

As with domestic violence, the risk of serious injury often increases when victims attempt to end the relationship. In a Liz Claiborne–sponsored survey conducted in 2005, almost 20% of teenage girls who had been in a relationship reported that their boyfriend had threatened violence or self-harm when they mentioned a breakup.

Technology can be a useful tool for abusers. An abuser may purchase a phone for his or her victim and then demand that it be answered whenever the abuser makes contact or require the victim to show who she or he called or received calls from. Many teen victims report receiving threats from their dating partner via phone or text message. Abusers may also use social networking sites such as MySpace and Facebook to control their victims. Some make threats via these sites, or post embarrassing information.

Victims of domestic or dating violence are not just at risk for injury and death. The effects of enduring abuse can be lasting, sometimes even lifelong. Victims of dating violence are more likely to engage in risky sexual behavior, unhealthy dieting behaviors, substance use, and suicidal ideation or attempts. Dating violence victimization has also been found to increase the risk of involvement in abusive adult relationships.

Many victims have a difficult time leaving their abusers. Often, they feel stigma and shame; as a consequence, they may tell no one about the abuse. Teen victims are especially likely to keep their abuse a secret. A 2002 study found that only 7%

of female high school students said they would call the police if they were subjected to dating violence. Teens are most likely to report such abuse to a friend, who may not be equipped to offer the necessary help. Sometimes teens feel as though they can help their abusers, so they stay in the relationship for that reason. Often, teens have never been taught what a healthy relationship is and, having little life experience with relationships, do not realize the danger they are in.

All 50 states plus the District of Columbia have laws prohibiting domestic violence and many of the behaviors associated with dating violence, such as sexual assault and stalking. Some states do not use the language "dating violence," however. Victims of dating violence can obtain protective orders from their abusers in 39 states plus the District of Columbia, although specific requirements for these court orders vary. In Florida, for instance, victims must have been in the relationship for at least six months and must have a parent or guardian with them when they apply. These limitations often pose a difficulty for teen victims.

In many cases, dating violence occurs at schools. Abusers may make threatening remarks in school, may stalk their victims, and may spread rumors. In a few sad cases, abusers have seriously injured or killed their victims in or around schools.

Some states have enacted legislation requiring students and staff to receive education about dating violence Both Texas and Rhode Island have this type of law, for example, and both pieces of legislation were passed after a female was killed at the hands of an abusive partner. Texas now mandates awareness education for students and parents, while Rhode Island has incorporated dating violence into the curriculum for all students in grades 7 through 12. Schools can help in other ways, too. Counselors can help identify warning signs and discuss dating violence and healthy relationships with students. Guest speakers should be brought in to discuss these issues as well. Having posters and literature around can also help teens see that they are not alone and find appropriate phone numbers and websites where additional information is available.

Laura L. Finley

Further Reading

Associated Press. (2008, October 5). R.I. schools must teach about dating violence. *MSNBC*. Retrieved April 29, 2010, from http://www.msnbc.msn.com/id/27035312/

Black, M., Noonan, R., & Legg, M. (2006, May 19). Physical dating violence among high school students: United States, 2003. *Morbidity and Mortality Weekly*. Retrieved April 28, 2010, from http://www.cdc.gov/mmwr/preview/mmwrhtml/mm5519a3.htm

Burleigh, N. (2007, September 10). A high school student's nightmare: Dating violence. *People*. Retrieved April 29, 2010, from http://www.people.com/people/archive/article/0,,20060228,00.html

National Teen Dating Abuse Hotline: www.loveisrespect.org
Teen Dating Violence Fact Sheet: http://www.ncvc.org/ncvc/AGP.Net/
  Components/documentViewer/Download.aspxnz?DocumentID=38057

Davis v. Monroe County Board of Education

On May 24, 1999, the U.S. Supreme Court ruled that school districts can be held legally liable in cases of student-on-student sexual harassment, but only when the district was "deliberately indifferent to sexual harassment, of which they had actual knowledge, and that the harassment was so severe, pervasive, and objectively offensive that it can be said to deprive the victims of access to the educational opportunities or benefits provided by the school."

LaShonda Davis, a fifth-grade student, had endured a prolonged pattern of sexual harassment from a classmate, G. F., at Hubbard Elementary School in Monroe County, Georgia. The harassment began in December 1992, when the boy attempted to touch LaShonda's breasts and genital area. He also made vulgar comments to her, saying, "I want to get in bed with you" and "I want to feel your boobs." The boy continued this behavior in January 1993, and LaShonda reported it to both her classroom teacher and her mother, Aurelia Davis. LaShonda's mother contacted the school administration. Other than the reports being passed along to Principal Bill Querry, no further action was taken by the school.

The boy's conduct allegedly continued for several months. In early February, G. F. purportedly placed a doorstop in his pants and proceeded to act in a sexually suggestive manner toward LaShonda during physical education class. LaShonda reported the incident to her physical education teacher, Whit Maples. Approximately one week later, G. F. again engaged in harassing behavior, this time while under the supervision of another

The attorney for LaShonda Davis, Verna Williams, addresses reporters during the Supreme Court case, *Davis v. Monroe County Board of Education,* in Washington, D.C., on January 12, 1999. (AP/Wide World Photos)

classroom teacher, Joyce Pippin. Once more LaShonda allegedly reported the incident to the teacher, and again Aurelia Davis contacted the teacher to follow up.

According to Aurelia Davis, G. F. again harassed LaShonda during physical education class in early March; in turn, LaShonda reported the incident to both Maples and Pippen. In mid-April 1993, G. F. allegedly rubbed his body against LaShonda in the school hallway in what LaShonda considered a sexually suggestive manner, and LaShonda again reported the matter.

The string of incidents finally ended in mid-May, when G. F. was charged with, and pleaded guilty to, sexual battery for his repeated misconduct. LaShonda suffered emotionally during the months of harassment. She was unable to concentrate in class, and her formerly high grades fell dramatically. In April 1993, her father discovered that she had written a suicide note. LaShonda also expressed concern that G. F. would eventually sexually assault her.

During the litigation of the suit filed by the Davis family, it became obvious that LaShonda was not G. F.'s only victim: He was also harassing other girls in class. At one point, LaShonda and several other victims attempted to speak with Principal Querry about the abuse, but a teacher allegedly blocked them from doing so. Aurelia Davis claimed that, despite repeated conversations with teachers and the principal, no action was ever taken to end the abuse. At one point, Principal Querry even asked Aurelia why LaShonda was the only one complaining. No effort was made to separate G. F. and LaShonda, and it was only after she had been reporting harassment for more than three months that she was finally allowed to change her classroom seat so she was no longer sat next to G. F. Aurelia Davis also claimed that at the time of these incidents, the Monroe County School Board had not instructed personnel on how to respond to sexual harassment and had no specific policy on the issue.

The Court's ruling was only a partial victory for victims of school-based sexual harassment. While the decision established that it is a school's responsibility to respond when alerted that sexual harassment is occurring, it did not require schools to take preventive measures to keep such abuse from happening. Given that sexual harassment occurs with great frequency, it is imperative that schools go beyond what the Court required to ensure a safe educational climate for all. In a previous decision—1992's *Franklin v. Gwinett County Public Schools*—the Supreme Court also held that a district receiving federal funding can be held liable for abuse involving a faculty member and a student.

Laura L. Finley

Further Reading

Davis, *as next friend of LaShonda* D. *v.* Monroe County Board of Education *et al.* Retrieved April 25, 2010, from http://caselaw.lp.findlaw.com/scripts/getcase.pl?court=US&vol=000&invol=97-843

DeMitchell, T. (2000, April). Peer sexual harassment: More than teasing. *International Journal of Educational Reform, 9*(2), 180–185.

Sexual harassment at school: Know your rights. (2010). Equal Rights Advocates. Retrieved April 25, 2010, from http://www.equalrights.org/publications/kyr/shschool.asp

Webb, D., Hunnicutt, K., & Metha, A. (1997). What schools can do to combat student-to-student sexual harassment. *NASSP Bulletin, 81*(585), 72–79.

Democratic Front for the Liberation of Palestine Attack on Ma'alot School

In a region notorious for its history of wars and terrorist attacks, perhaps one of the most shocking incidents involved the attack on a group of schoolchildren on May 15, 1974. That day began with a school trip celebrating Israel's independence day, during which 105 religious school students from Safed went for a hike in the country's western Galilee region. After a long day of trekking, the students went to the Netiv Meir School in the area known as Ma'alot, where they laid down and slept. The group members awoke to find they were being attacked by three terrorists from the Democratic Front for the Liberation of Palestine (DFLP). At the conclusion of the events, 25 victims were dead and more than 50 were injured.

The origin of this incident can be said to be rooted in the creation of the State of Israel, which inspired a sharply negative reaction from many of the new country's Arab residents and neighbors. In 1948, in the weeks and months leading up to the date when the Jewish state was slated to become independent, Arab leaders both within and outside the territory coaxed the Arab residents within the borders of the future state to leave, thereby creating an open battlefield in which militant Arab groups promised to destroy the nascent country. Many Arab residents complied with this request, traveling to Lebanon, Transjordan, and Syria to await the Arab victory and the fulfillment of promises to give them the property and land of the vanquished Jews.

At the end of what would be called the "War of Independence," Israel survived, following an armistice. For their part, the Arabs who left their homes were forced by the aforementioned host countries to remain in refugee camps, denied both citizenship and the right to permanently settle there. Over time, a number of radical terrorist groups would arise from these camps, with most eventually cooperating to form the umbrella group called the Palestine Liberation Organization (PLO), whose charter calls for an "armed struggle" to conquer and destroy the State of Israel. The two largest factions within the PLO during its first decades were Fatah, led by Yasser Arafat, and the Popular Front for the Liberation of Palestine (PFLP), a Marxist–Leninist group led by Lebanon-born Christian named Dr. George Habash.

In 1969, a group of people in the PFLP led by Nayef Hawatmeh, a Jordanian Arab from a Malachite Catholic family, broke away to form a new terrorist faction called the Democratic Front for the Liberation of Palestine. A decade earlier, Hawatmeh had participated in a coup attempt that sought to overthrow the government of Lebanon. After that failed action, he traveled to Iraq, where he was imprisoned for his anti-government activities. Hawatmeh would eventually participate in revolutionary and terrorist activities across the Middle East before returning to the fold by joining the PFLP and then creating his own power base. Eventually, the DFLP began to engage in terrorist activities. For example, the group sought to overthrow the regime of King Hussein of Jordan. That failed effort ended with the deaths of many DFLP members (as well as members of Fatah and the PFLP), the destruction of the DFLP office in Amman by Jordanian tanks, and a shift in the group's strategy from the destabilization of moderate Arab leaders to attacks focusing on Israel.

The DFLP's planning of the attack on the Netiv Meir School was both meticulous and sinister. The target was a group of schoolchildren who would be sleeping at the targeted location—a school that otherwise would be empty. as its facilities consisted of only classrooms and no dormitories. The students were participating in a program called "Gadna," which stresses good citizenship, physical training, and endurance. Even today, this popular one week program is undertaken by most Israeli students.

The team of three terrorists infiltrated Israel's northern border from their base in Lebanon. En route to their target, their first victims were two Arab Christian women who were being driven home in a van driven by a Druze. One woman was shot and died instantly; the wounded driver succeeded in continuing to drive the vehicle to safety, where the other woman died from her gunshot wounds. The terrorists then knocked on several homes' doors until one was answered by Yosef and Fortuna Cohen. Fortuna was seven months' pregnant. The Cohens were shot dead, as was their four-year-old son Eliahu. Their five-year-old daughter Miriam was also shot, but survived. Unhurt was the Cohens' 16-month-old deaf-mute son Yitzchak. Leaving the Cohens' home, the terrorists asked a sanitation worker, Yaakov Kadosh, for directions; they then severely beat and shot Kadosh, assuming that they had taken his life, too.

Before dawn, the terrorists entered the three-story concrete-constructed school and immediately took charge of the sleeping hostages. Screaming in Arabic and Hebrew, the terrorists demanded that everyone follow their orders or be killed. Seventeen students, the driver, and two army escorts managed to escape by climbing out the windows during the commotion. Several hours later, the terrorists, who set up explosives amidst the captive schoolchildren, released Narkiss Mordecai, a medic escort. She was given letters addressed to the French and Romanian ambassadors, instructing them to act as intermediaries between the terrorists and the Israeli authorities. The letters also demanded the release of 23 Arab terrorists and three people of other nationalities held in Israeli prisons. Among the latter were Kozo Okamoto, a Japanese Red Army commando who had taken part in the Lod Airport Massacre, a bloody event in which Okamoto and two partners opened fire with automatic machine guns in Israel's (now Ben Gurion) international airport, murdering 25 people and wounding 70 more victims. The attack was a joint operation between the PFLP and the Japanese Red Army, the latter a leftist terrorist group that declared its goals as overthrowing the Japanese monarchy and overthrowing the world.

The terrorists' note declared that the school building was rigged with explosives, and stated that the Israeli government had until 6 P.M. (local time) to comply with the demands or the hostages would be executed. During the hours of that day, the Israeli Parliament, under the leadership of Prime Minister Golda Meir, held heated debates about the complex situation, including the difficulties of arranging the release of convicted terrorists within such a limited time span as the looming deadline approached. Public statements were made asserting the willingness to comply with the demands, although political pundits and analysts still debate their authenticity.

Most importantly, the terrorists made it clear that they would not hesitate to carry out the massacre at the appointed time if their code word were not communicated back to them by their freed comrades upon their release and subsequent arrival in either Damascus, Syria, or Nicosia, Cyprus. After that, the terrorists' note continued, the terrorists would release half the hostages and would fly with the other half to an unnamed Arab country, where they promised to then release the rest of the schoolchildren. The Israeli Cabinet agreed that this arrangement would never be accepted, although this information was not disclosed to either the public or the terrorists.

As Israeli soldiers were put into place around the outer perimeter of the school, Minister of Defense Moshe Dayan personally came to Ma'alot to oversee the operation, accompanied by Army Chief of Staff Motta Gur. The initial negotiator was Victor Cohen, the head of negotiations from Israel's General Security Services (equivalent to the FBI). Cohen had also been the negotiator with the Black September terrorists when they captured 11 members of the Israeli Olympic team in Munich, West Germany, during the Summer Olympics in 1972.

Beginning at 9 A.M., the leader of the terrorist team began to appear at the window of the school with five students, firing his gun wildly and sometimes throwing live grenades, as he continuously threatened to begin killing hostages. One local man on leave from the army was killed by a stray bullet during these tirades. As the day wore on, Dayan became more convinced that only a military rescue operation could succeed in saving the hostages, as the terrorists continued to reiterate their threats of a massacre. Even so, the Israeli Cabinet continued to plan for the possibility that an alternative might exist in which the students could be released in exchange for the freeing of prisoners, as Prime Minister Meir refused to abandon this possibility.

In the afternoon, the top three terrorists on the list were transported from prison to the Ma'alot area in preparation for an attempted compromise. It was proposed that the French ambassador would approach the school to engage the terrorists in a face-to-face negotiation. The terrorists rejected this proposal, however, stating that anyone who approached the school without the code word would be shot on sight.

At 5:40 P.M., the Israeli Defense Forces stormed the school. The terrorists opened fire with their Russian-manufactured AK-47s, spraying the captive schoolchildren with bullets and exploding at least one grenade in a classroom full of students before the three members of the DFLP were killed. The military operation was far from flawless, as some confusion ensued during the operation when Israeli soldiers entered the school from various entrances and windows, creating some amount of chaos before the mission was completed.

Today, Netiv Meir School is still open as a school for religious schoolgirls. A memorial in its library commemorates the fallen students and their escorts who died there.

Len Lubitz

Further Reading

Dolnik, A., & Fitzgerald, K. (2008). *Negotiating hostage crises with the new terrorists*. Westport, CT: Praeger.

Pedahzur, A. (2009). *The Israeli Secret Services and the struggle against terrorism*. New York: Columbia University Press.

Statement to the Knesset by Prime Minister Meir. (1974, May 20). Retrieved from http://www.mfa.gov.il/MFA/Foreign+Relations/Israels+Foreign+Relations+since+1947/1947-1974/28+Statement+to+the+Knesset+by+Prime+Minister+Meir.htm?DisplayMode=print

Dhein, Alaa Abu

On March 6, 2008, Alaa Abu Dhein, 26, entered the Mercaz Harav yeshiva, a religious school in Jerusalem, Israel. Armed with an AK-47 and several magazines, the Palestinian Dhein reportedly fired as many as 500 to 600 rounds, killing eight students and wounding 1 others. An Israel Defense Force officer, David Shapira, then shot Dhein.

Alaa Abu Dhein was from the Arab neighborhood of Jabel Mukaber in eastern Jerusalem. He reportedly worked as a driver at the yeshiva. Dhein did not leave a letter or other statement of his motive, but his sister, Iman Abu Dhaim, said he had been obsessed with the violence in Gaza. Only days before his attack, 126 Palestinians militants were killed by Israeli forces in multiple days of fighting. That attack had represented the Israeli response to rocket fire from a Palestinian terrorist group on Gaza. Dhein likely selected the yeshiva for his attack because it is identified with the Jewish settlements in the West Bank.

Before it became clear that Dhein had acted alone, several groups claimed responsibility for the attack. One group calling itself the Galilee Liberators Brigades—The Martyrs of Imad Mughniyeh claimed on Hezbollah (television) station Al-Manar that it was responsible for the attack. Group members stated that the assault was intended as retaliation for the assassination of Imad Mughniveh. Another group, Hamas, praised the attack, but did not claim responsibility for it, although the Reuters news agency did receive an anonymous call implicating Hamas.

Israel's Prime Minister Ehud Olmert denounced the attack and praised the good work of the yeshiva. Olmert also condemned groups like Hamas for celebrating the attack with parades in Gaza. Thousands in Israel mourned the deaths of those killed.

A major concern in the wake of this event was the possibility that the attack would incite even more retaliatory violence. News reports suggested that some alumni of the yeshiva were planning an attack against a mosque in Jerusalem's Temple Mount, although these threats were found to be baseless. However, Israel's Education Minister Yuli Tamir was forced to leave early from her condolence visit to the yeshiva when she was kicked in the back, spat at, and verbally attacked by a group of youths demonstrating outside the facility. The next morning, Yuli Tamir threatened to cut off funding for the yeshiva. The yeshiva members also told Ehud Olmert that he was not welcome.

Other groups acknowledged the sorrow of the incident. The Israel Football Association held a moment of silence before the football matches that weekend, although some supporters of the Arab team Bnei Sakhnin booed.

Less than 10 days later, on March 17, hundreds of people attacked Arab homes in Dhein's former neighborhood. For three hours, the activists chanted, "Revenge, revenge"; vandalized property; and clashed with the police. Despite a heavy police blockade at the entrance to Jebl Mukaber and a massive deployment of security forces in the area, the marchers managed to enter the village, stone residents' homes, and damage several cars belonging to villagers.

Mahmoud Abbas, President of the Palestinian National Authority, condemned the violence as well. *Al-Hayat al-Jadida,* the Palestinian National Authority newspaper, put a picture of the gunman on the front of the paper and called him a martyr.

In a poll taken two weeks after Dhein's assault, 84% of Palestinians supported the attack on the Mercaz Harav yeshiva.

Laura L. Finley

Further Reading

Frenkel, S. (2008, March 7). Jerusalem buries student massacre victims. *Times Online*. Retrieved April 25, 2010, from http://www.timesonline.co.uk/tol/news/world/middle_east/article3502365.ece

Israel Ministry of Foreign Affairs. (2008, March 6). Terror shooting at Mercaz Harav Kook yeshiva in Jerusalem. Retrieved April 25, 2010, from http://www.mfa.gov.il/MFA/Terrorism-+Obstacle+to+Peace/Palestinian+terror+since+2000/Terror+shooting+at+Mercaz+Harav+Yeshiv a+in+Jerusalem+6-Mar-2008.htm

Domestic Violence Prevention Enhancements and Leadership Through Alliances (DELTA) Program

The Domestic Violence Prevention Enhancements and Leadership Through Alliances (DELTA) program was established and is run by the Centers for Disease Control and Prevention (CDC). It emerged from the Family Violence Prevention Services Act (FVPSA), which authorizes CDC to distribute federal funds to support coordinated community responses (CCRs) that address domestic and dating violence, or what is collectively known as intimate-partner violence (IPV). A CCR is an organized, community collaborative that seeks to respond to and prevent IPV in a community. CCR members generally include community organizations, victim services, law enforcement, prosecutors, health professionals, faith leaders, and educators. Historically, these organizations have focused on providing services to victims, holding perpetrators accountable, and reducing the number of recurring assaults. In 2002, CDC established the DELTA program to focus on primary prevention—that is, stopping IPV before it can occur.

Currently, CDC funds 14 state-level domestic violence coalitions. These groups provide prevention-focused training, technical assistance, and financial support to local CCRs. The CCRs, in turn, develop their own strategies for primary prevention so that they are community specific. Funded state-level coalitions are found in Alaska, California, Delaware, Florida, Kansas, Michigan, Montana, North Carolina, North Dakota, New York, Ohio, Rhode Island, Virginia, and Wisconsin.

The DELTA program helps meet an important need, in that domestic and dating violence are among the most prevalent crimes. It is estimated that one-third of all women in the United States will experience some form of domestic violence, and one in three adolescent girls will experience verbal, emotional, or physical abuse in a dating relationship. The CDC, through the DELTA program, recognizes these shocking rates and has helped fund programs that address the interconnected issues of community poverty, violence, and inequalities.

Although not all states receive DELTA funding at this time, CDC has partnered with the Robert Wood Johnson Foundation to help provide resources to the 36 remaining states that have not established state-level coalitions. State and community leaders in these states receive training and materials on primary prevention strategies they can implement when funding becomes available.

Laura L. Finley

Further Reading

Centers for Disease Control and Prevention. (n.d.). The DELTA program: Preventing intimate partner violence in the United States. Retrieved April 23, 2010, from http://www.cdc.gov/violenceprevention/pdf/DELTA_AAG-a.pdf

National Coalition Against Domestic Violence: www.ncadv.org

Teens. (2010). Family Violence Prevention Fund. Retrieved April 24, 2010, from http://www.endabuse.org/section/programs/teens

Do Something

Do Something.org is a website that has a wealth of information on anything that could possibly interest an American teenager. Its content includes information about celebrity teen stars, volunteer opportunities, human rights movements, daily news bulletins, and much more. Just as the name suggests, Do Something urges teenagers to be active participants in the world. In addition, the organization lends a voice to various causes around the country and in the community.

Do Something challenges youth to act on the problems that face society as a whole, such as action and planning for schools to become more environmentally friendly, helping the homeless by donating used jeans, or sending letters, cards, or emails to support the troops overseas. It empowers youth to take action in a fun and interactive way. This website provides numerous ideas for action, ranging from something as simple as sending an email to something as complex as dedicating more extensive amounts of time and energy to larger projects of the teen's choice. Whatever someone may choose to do, Do Something is a great resource to use to fulfill any community service requirements a student might need to graduate.

"What's your thing?" is a tab on Do Something's home page that lists 1 different areas of interest. There are three choices relating to schools: Discrimination, Education, and Violence and Bullying. For example, if someone is most interested in school violence, clicking on this link brings up a new page that lists options related to child abuse, cyberbullying, dating violence, gang violence, gun control, hate crimes, school violence, and violence against women. The Do Something website puts a wealth of knowledge about multiple subjects at the user's fingertips in an instant. If the user selects school violence as an area of interest, for example, one statistic that would appear is the following: "In the same year, students ages 12–18 were the victims of about 628,200 violent crimes at school, including rape, aggravated assault, and robbery." Do Something also gives students the tools they need to help put an end to bullying and harassment in schools. This is accomplished by not putting the student in harm's way, but rather helping other students to not become a victim.

Probably one of the coolest things someone can do is to create his or her own Do Something Club. All that is needed is five friends who want to Do Something positive in their community or school. Groups complete a simple online application, and they have the flexibility to fix the problems that they see in and outside of a school environment with their own creativity. Do Something even provides grant money to support student projects. Do Something offers students a way to fulfill Mahatma Gandhi's famous quote, "Be the change that you want to see in the world."

Natasha Abdin

Further Reading

Do Something: www.dosomething.org

Dress Codes

Many school districts have enacted dress codes in the belief that they will help increase student self-esteem, enhance school unity, increase attendance and reduce dropout rates, and reduce violence—in particular, violence related to gang activity. The types of dress codes established by schools vary widely, running the gamut from simple prohibitions on specific logos or inappropriate slogans to the more extreme uniform policy. Many dress codes or uniform policies were enacted after President Bill Clinton encouraged them in his 1996 State of the Union speech. Approximately 14% of public schools required students to wear uniforms in the 2005–2006 academic year. Although parents often support these policies, research does not necessarily show that they achieve the desired result. Court rulings on this issue are also mixed, with courts siding with educators when there is a safety or sexual component involved, and siding with students who are expressing legitimate political views.

Jane E. Workman and Beth Winfrey-Freeburg of Southern Illinois University found that gang-related headwear was the number one target of dress codes and uniform requirements, cited in 89% of the more than 80 school policies they

Children in uniform leave school at the end of the day. Although the evidence supporting the increased academic benefit from this policy is not solid, many people believe that school uniforms are good for the learning environment. (Monkey Business Images/Dreamstime.com)

reviewed in 2006. Because gangs can be highly creative in adopting signs and colors, some dress codes are minutely detailed. For instance, some school districts prohibit "do rags" or handkerchiefs, as they have been used for gangs to identify members. Likewise, some schools have prohibited the wearing of anything red or blue, as they are typical gang colors. Complying with these rules can be difficult for both students and parents, who have to be aware of the specific requirements. Such policies are also problematic for the educators who must enforce them.

A different problem is related to sexually provocative clothing. One notable trend in school policies is banning of clothing that shows the "three B's": breasts, bellies, or bottoms. The attire of female students in particular is often heavily influenced by popular culture, which repeatedly shows images of barely clad women.

Parents tend to favor school dress codes. The most frequent argument they make in support of these policies is that such rules make it easier to get students ready for school and out the door. Parents also believe that dress codes help reduce other social issues in schools, as it makes it more difficult to detect which students have more money than others and thus lessens peer pressure. Some teachers believe that such policies help create an academic climate more conducive to learning, as students are less likely to be distracted by the inappropriate clothing of others.

All dress code policies must meet the standard set in the U.S. Supreme Court's ruling in the 1969 case *Tinker v. Des Moines,* which allows students free expression as long as it does not create a "material or substantial disruption." Of course, it can be very difficult to determine precisely what constitutes a material or substantial disruption. Judges usually side with administrators if a student's clothing sends a violent or discriminatory message or if it advocates drug use. In contrast, if the clothing has a clear political message, the decision usually goes the other way. The American Civil Liberties Union (ACLU) often argues on behalf of students in these cases.

Long Beach Unified School District reported seeing a marked reduction in school disciplinary problems and violence after it instituted a mandatory school-uniform policy. Critics contend that other changes occurring in the school district could have been responsible for the reduction in violence and disciplinary problems noted in the California district. Other districts have not experienced this type of reduction, instead seeing an increase in students suspended due to dress code violations.

A study of a nationally representative sample of eighth graders found that students who attended schools with uniform requirements did not differ from other students in attendance, attitudes toward school, or behavior problems. The biggest problem is that few of the studies used control groups and appropriate independent measures to ensure that the dress code or uniform policy was the cause of any change they noticed.

Laura L. Finley

Further Reading

Hudson, D. (2010, January 11). Clothing, dress codes and uniforms. *First Amendment Center.* Retrieved April 26, 2010, from http://www.firstamendment center.org/speech/studentexpression/topic.aspx?topic=clothing_dress_codes _uniforms

Johnson, A. (2008, October 18). Students, parents bare claws over dress codes. *MSNBC.* Retrieved April 26, 2010, from http://www.msnbc.msn.com/id/ 26875980/

Peterson, R. (2008). Fact sheet #6: Student uniforms. *Consortium to Prevent School Violence.* Retrieved April 26, 2010, from http://www.prevent schoolviolence.org/resources_assets/CPSV%20Fact%20Sheet-6- Student%20 Uniforms.pdf

Raby, R. (2010). "Tank tops are OK but I don't want to see her thong": Girls' engagements with secondary school dress codes. *Youth and Society, 41,* 333–356.

Zirkel, P. (2000). Dress codes. *NASSP Bulletin, 84,* 78–82.

Drug Abuse Resistance Education (D.A.R.E.)

The Drug Abuse Resistance Education (D.A.R.E.) program was founded in Los Angeles in 1983. In this program, a trained police officer leads a series of classroom lessons for children in kindergarten through 12th grade about the dangers of illicit drugs, ways to resist peer pressure, and strategies to live a drug-free life. D.A.R.E. has been implemented in 43 countries and in 75% of the schools in the United States, reaching millions of school children each year.

D.A.R.E. officers are selected based on their background. Those who have interest in and experience with young people are then provided 80 hours of specialized training that covers topics such as child development, classroom management, and teaching strategies. Officers then receive an additional 40 hours of training about the D.A.R.E. curriculum.

D.A.R.E. has been held up as an example of community policing, in that officers are interacting in a proactive way with citizens. The U.S. Department of Justice has stated that among other things, D.A.R.E. helps communities by humanizing the police to young people, opening the lines of communication, and facilitating dialogue between schools, parents, and police.

The D.A.R.E. website provides information for children, parents and caregivers, and officers about various drugs and their effects. Additionally, it provides information about D.A.R.E.-sponsored events. Further, the website describes the nonprofit organization D.A.R.E. America, which provides officer training and resources to communities to augment the basic D.A.R.E. program.

Although D.A.R.E. has been widely adopted and is beloved by educators and police alike, research has not necessarily supported the contention that it is an effective means to prevent drug use. The U.S. General Accounting Office (GAO) released a report in 2003 that assessed the findings from six long-term evaluations of D.A.R.E. The report concluded that D.A.R.E. graduates were no less likely to report drug use than were nongraduates. Two studies found that D.A.R.E.-graduate students held stronger negative attitudes about drugs in the short term, but that the effect faded over time. The biggest criticism directed at D.A.R.E. is that the program has made drug abuse seem more common than it actually is. Faced with growing criticism, D.A.R.E. officials announced the program was being revamped in 2001. The new program uses a social norms approach, focusing on altering students' perceptions of how many students use drugs. This strategy stands in contrast to the previous "Just say no" approach.

Laura L. Finley

Further Reading

D.A.R.E.: www.dare.com

DARE admits failure. (n.d.). *Common Sense for Drug Policy.* Retrieved May 1, 2010, from http://www.csdp.org/news/news/darerevised.htm

Zernike, K. (2001, February 15). DARE drug-resistance campaign, called ineffective, is being retooled. *Common Sense for Drug Policy*. Retrieved May 1, 2010, from http://www.mapinc.org/newscsdp/v01/n277/a07.html

Drug Offenses, College

The frequency of drug abuse on college campuses is alarming. An appalling 43.5% of college freshmen reported having become heavy drinkers in their first year of college in 2004 alone. An estimated 1,700 college students die from alcohol-related activities each year. On an annual basis, 19% of college students report having had a serious altercation with an intoxicated person, 19.5% report having been the victims of unwanted sexual advancements from an intoxicated person, 8.7% reporting having been physically assaulted by an intoxicated person, and 1% report having been raped by intoxicated students. These statistics represent only some of the detrimental effects of alcohol on college campuses across the United States. Unfortunately, alcohol is just one of many substances that college students are abusing.

According to Joseph Califano, President of Columbia University's National Center on Addiction and Substance Abuse (CASA), the group's 2007 study concluded that nearly one-fourth of all full-time college students have a substance abuse problem meeting the medical criteria for addiction. Researchers with the Office of National Drug Control Policy suggest that these drug addictions reflect the "gateway drug theory" in action. Gateway drugs consist of alcohol, tobacco, and marijuana. According to the theory, use of these "gateway" drugs encourages experimenters to try more dangerous drugs, both illegal and prescription. CASA's findings that 50% of college students both binge drink and take part in using and abusing illegal and prescription drugs seem to support the theory.

In response to these findings, CASA released a statement emphasizing the urgency of the problem. Its study concluded that alcohol and drug abuse occur at higher rates on college campuses than they do among members of the general public. In response, agencies that deal with the effects of drug abuse, whether they are governmental, collegial, or social agencies, have all called for more concerted efforts on college campuses to prevent and reduce drug abuse.

Drug abuse is defined as a habit of using drugs to change one's mood, emotional state, or state of consciousness. Prescription drug abuse is defined as the use of a prescription drug by someone other than the patient for whom it is prescribed or at a dosage that is inconsistent with the prescribed amount. It follows, then, that illegal drug abuse is the habitual use of illegal drugs to alter one's state.

While no age, race, or gender is immune to falling into dependency on drugs and alcohol, some patterns within the realms of race and age do exist. According to a study by CASA, Caucasian students are more likely to abuse drugs and alcohol. When asked why students turn to drugs, CASA's Califano replied that most do so as a means of relaxing and coping with stress.

The most commonly abused substance by far is alcohol. Almost half of all full-time college students (approximately 5.4 million people) binge drink at least once per month. Binge drinking is generally defined as consuming four or more drinks in an hour.

In a 2007 study conducted by the Department of Health and Human Services, young adults between the ages of 18 and 25 were found to have increased their use of prescription drugs since 2006. College students, according to the U.S. Department of Education's Higher Learning Center, use prescription drugs for a number of reasons. Some say these drugs help them concentrate when they are rushing to write papers or cramming for tests. Many use them as self-medications to treat their anxiety or depression. Others use such drugs to boost their performance in the athletic arena. Because they are prescribed drugs, many college students feel that prescription drugs are a safe way to stimulate their brains to work at maximum capacity.

Use of both prescription drugs and marijuana by college students has increased since the mid-1990s. In 2005, 4% of the nation's college students admitted to smoking marijuana at least 20 days in a month's time. The most commonly abused prescription drugs are types of opioids, central nervous system (CNS) depressants, and stimulants.

Opioids—which include such drugs as Oxycontin, Darvon, Vicodin, Dilaudid, Demerol, and Lomotil—are prescribed to treat pain. In 2005, 3.1% of students admitted to abusing painkillers. CNS drugs are used for the treatment of anxiety and sleep disorders; they include Nembutal, Valium, and Xanax. Stimulants are used to treat conditions such as narcolepsy, attention-deficit/hyperactivity disorder (ADHD), and obesity. Stimulant drugs include Dexedrin and Ritalin. While the drugs listed here are not the only drugs used to treat these conditions, they are the most commonly abused prescription drugs on campuses.

Although students may feel safe when taking these opioids and CNS drugs, long-term use of these agents carries a high risk of becoming physically dependent and addicted to them. Individuals who abuse stimulants are at risk of developing paranoia, dangerously high body temperatures, and irregular heartbeats.

A host of myths have sprung up surrounding the use of illegal drugs. For example, many students believe that marijuana is a virtually safe drug. In reality, marijuana can be harmful in both the short and long term. Short-term effects of marijuana include memory loss, distorted perception, trouble with thinking and problem solving, and anxiety. This drug can also cause neurological changes like those associated with cocaine, heroin, and alcohol use, and can produce an addicting reaction. Long-term marijuana use increases the person's likelihood of developing a drug dependency (not necessarily to marijuana) and increases the chances of risky sexual activity, poor job performance, cognitive lung deficits, and lung damage. Experts say marijuana interferes with memory and attention span. Some recent studies have suggested that this drug has an association with schizophrenia as well. The clearest indicator that marijuana may be an addicting drug is the fact that some heavy users have experienced withdrawal symptoms when they stopped using the drug for a sufficient amount of time.

There is no "safe" drug to be addicted to. While some researchers have found that drug abuse rates have decreased slightly in recent years, all researchers agree that preventing drug use and helping those who have already developed an addiction is essential. According to Califano, two-thirds of U.S. school officials and administrators do not see drug abuse as either a priority or their responsibility to address, making intervention and prevention difficult. The attack on drug abuse must come from three angles—parents, school administrators, and, in the case of prescription drugs, physicians.

According to CASA, three-fourths of students who abuse alcohol and drugs in college actually began abusing them before they entered college. The statistics on the abuse of drugs between the ages of 12 and 18 could fill a few essays by themselves. To prevent this problem, parents must get involved with their children's lives. Moreover, when 43.5% of college freshmen are becoming heavy drinkers, it becomes quite evident that it is time for school administrators across the board to intervene. Whether that means setting up peer groups to help addicts and educate students, making sure sufficient information goes to students warning them of these dangers, or increasing security to decrease on-campus incidents of drug abuse, these officials must take action. As far as prescription drugs are concerned, the National Institute on Drug Abuse suggests that physicians should screen for drug abuse during routine examinations. They can also note any increases in the number or frequency of requests for medication, as such behavior is suggestive of a potential problem.

No single organization, administrator, parent, physician, or student can stamp out the abuse of drugs on a grand scale, but each can make at least some impact on the problem. If all parties work together, they can help significantly reduce drug abuse on the college campus.

Angelica Jones

Further Reading

Califano, J. A. (2008, June 18). Chairman's statement: Accompanying statement of Joseph A. Califano, Jr. on non-medical marijuana III: Rite of passage or Russian roulette? National Center on Addiction and Substance Abuse. Retrieved January 13, 2009, from http://www.casacolumbia.org/absolutenm/templates/ChairmanStatements.aspx?articleid=528&zoneid=31

Colihan, K. (2008, September 4). Who uses and abuses drugs and alcohol? U.S. government survey shows patterns of illicit drug, alcohol, and tobacco use. *WebMD*. Retrieved January 13, 2009, from http://www.webmd.com/mental-health/news/20080904/who-uses-and-abuses-drugs-and-alcohol

De Jong, P. W., & Ross, P. V. (2008, March). *Alcohol and other drugs among first year students*. Newton, MA: InfoFacts Resources: The Higher Education Center for Alcohol and Other Drug Abuse and Violence Prevention.

Drug abuse. (2009). *Medical Dictionary*. Retrieved January 13, 2009, from http://medical-dictionary.thefreedictionary.com/Illegal+drug+abuse

Leinwand, D. (2007, March 15). College drug use, binge drinking rise. *USA Today*. Retrieved March 8, 2011 from http://www.usatoday.com/news/nation/2007-03-15-college-drug-use_N.htm

NIDA InfoFacts: Prescription and over-the-counter medications. (2008, August). National Institute on Drug Abuse. Retrieved January 20, 2009, from http://www.nida.nih.gov/infofacts/PainMed.html

Office of National Drug Control Policy. (2008). Marijuana use has many harmful effects. In N. Merino, *Opposing views: Gateway drugs* (pp. 57–66). Detroit, MI: Greenhaven Press.

Prescription medications. (2008, April 23). National Institute on Drug Abuse. Retrieved January 13, 2009, from http://www.nida.nih.gov/drugpages/prescription.html

Drug Offenses, High School

Broadly defined, a "drug" is any nonfood substance that in some way alters the physical or psychological processes of the body. As to the legality and availability of drugs, there is enormous variation in the regulation of the manufacture and sale of these substances. Some drugs, such as aspirin and caffeine, are readily available and may be legally purchased by anyone. In addition, some readily available household items, such as glue, paint, and aerosol spray cans, emit fumes that have intoxicating effects when inhaled and, therefore, may be considered to fit the definition of drugs. Some drugs, such as alcohol and nicotine, are readily available but may only be legally purchased or used by adults. Some drugs, such as codeine and Valium, are strictly regulated by the government and may be administered only with the authorization of a physician. Finally, some drugs, such as heroin and LSD, are considered to have no legitimate uses and are completely proscribed by law. With respect to marijuana, there is an ongoing debate as to whether it may be legally used. Although a few states (e.g., California) have enacted laws that allow marijuana to be prescribed by physicians, the federal government does not recognize marijuana as having any legitimate medical uses and considers the cultivation, possession, trafficking, and use of marijuana to be criminal acts.

In general, the term "drug offenses" refers to any offense involving the illegal use of a drug. To provide a few examples, the possession or consumption of alcohol by anyone younger than the age of 21 could be considered a drug offense. The possession or use of a controlled substance such as Ritalin, Librium, Xanax, or Demerol without a doctor's prescription may be considered a drug offense. Likewise, the manufacture, distribution, possession, or use of any prohibited drug such as heroin, PCP, or LSD could be considered a drug offense. In addition, the possession or use of an antibiotic (a drug designed to eliminate harmful bacteria) such as penicillin or amoxicillin without a doctor's prescription could be considered a drug offense, but criminal justice agencies typically focus their efforts on controlling the illegal use of psychoactive drugs (drugs that alter a person's consciousness) such as marijuana.

The majority of controlled and illegal psychoactive substances such as alcohol, marijuana, and heroin produce pleasurable effects in the user by affecting neurotransmitters such as serotonin and dopamine. The effects of such substances vary widely. For example, whereas heroin generates an intensely pleasurable rush accompanied by hours of drowsiness, methamphetamine produces high levels of energy and an increase in attention capacity.

Although government agencies at all levels—federal, state, and local—have long utilized a number of tactics designed to eliminate adolescent drug use and keep illegal drugs out of U.S. schools, the reality is that a variety of illegal drugs are readily available in high schools throughout the nation and that a substantial portion of school-age youths use illegal drugs. Analyses of data from the 2005 Youth Risk Behavior Survey show that more than one-third of high school students (38.1%) had used marijuana at least once in their lifetime when they responded to the survey, more than one in 10 high school students (12.4%) had sniffed glue or inhaled some other substance to get high at least once in their lifetime, almost one in 10 high school students (7.6%) had used cocaine at least once in their lifetime, and one-fourth of high school students (25%) had been offered, sold, or given a drug while at school. Similarly, analyses of data from the 2007 Monitoring the Future survey show that more than one-third of all 12th graders responding to this survey (36%) had used some illicit substance. In fact, analyses of Monitoring the Future data indicate that illicit drug use is higher among 12th graders than any other demographic group, including college students and young adults. Among the variety of illicit substances available in U.S. schools, marijuana is by far the most commonly used. Research suggests that school-age youths are more likely to use marijuana than any other illicit drug, including cocaine, hallucinogens, or methamphetamines.

The good news is that research also shows that although the use of illicit substances remains a problem among secondary school students, illicit teen drug use has significantly decreased in the past decade. Whereas a substantial increase in illicit drug use among teenagers occurred during the early to mid-1990s, by the end of the 1990s the rates of illicit drug use had begun to decline. For example, between 1992 and 1997 the rates of marijuana use among high school students nearly doubled, but since then marijuana use among teens has decreased, as has the use of numerous other illicit drugs such as cocaine and LSD. Although the use of ecstasy increased among high school students during the late 1990s and very early 2000s, since 2002 there has been a reduction in the use of this drug by such students.

Although teen drug use and the availability of drugs at school may have decreased, drugs continue to pose a threat in the schools. As noted earlier, research conducted by federal agencies indicates that roughly one out of every four students in the United States has either bought, been given, or been offered drugs while at school. The widespread availability and use of drugs by high school students negatively affect the school environment and the learning process. While under the influence of psychoactive substances such as alcohol, amphetamines, marijuana, and ecstasy, students may be unable to concentrate on their studies and may disrupt teachers and other students. Additionally, early experimentation with alcohol and illicit drugs increases the likelihood that a youth will drop out of school and may lead to long-term problems with substance abuse and addiction.

Ben Brown

Further Reading

Centers for Disease Control and Prevention. (2008, April 11). *Trends in the prevalence of marijuana, cocaine, and other illegal drug use. National YRBS: 1991–2007*. Atlanta, GA: Centers for Disease Control and Prevention, Division of Adolescent and School Health, National Center for Chronic Disease Prevention and Health Promotion.

Dinkes, R., Cataldi, E. F., Lin-Kelly, W., & Snyder, T. D. (2007, December). *Indicators of school crime and safety: 2007* (NCES 2008-021/NCJ 219553). Washington, DC: U.S. Department of Education, Institute of Education Sciences, National Center for Education Statistics, & U.S. Department of Justice, Office of Justice Programs, Bureau of Justice Statistics.

Johnston, L. D., O'Malley, P. M., Bachman, J. G., & Schulenberg, J. E. (2008). *Monitoring the Future national survey results on drug use, 1975–2007: Volume I. Secondary school students* (NIH Publication No. 08-6418A). Bethesda, MD: National Institute on Drug Abuse.

National Institute on Drug Abuse. (2002). *Methamphetamine abuse and addiction*. Bethesda, MD: U.S. Department of Health and Human Services, National Institutes of Health, National Institute on Drug Abuse.

National Institute on Drug Abuse. (2005). *Heroin and drug addiction*. Bethesda, MD: U.S. Department of Health and Human Services, National Institutes of Health, National Institute on Drug Abuse.

Drug Testing

Drug testing has become a relatively popular means of addressing student drug use. Before it was introduced in the school environment, such testing was used in the military, in the workplace, and in college and Olympic competitions to see if athletes were using prohibited substances. At the college level, drug testing is generally reserved for persons involved in athletics and is conducted by the National College Athletic Association (NCAA). Proponents of this practice maintain that drug testing is a deterrent to drug use, that it is used to identify those in need of help, and that it ensures a safe and fair educational climate and/or athletic field. Critics assert that research does not support the purported deterrent effect.

Vials from the National Center for Drug Free Sport contain samples that tested positive for drugs. The National Center for Drug Free Sport is the NCAA's official drug testing laboratory. (AP/Wide World Photos)

Further, such tests are vulnerable to cheating, not very reliable in their results, cost too much, and are invasive of students' privacy rights.

The U.S. Supreme Court first ruled on the constitutionality of school-based drug testing in 1995 in *Vernonia School District 47J v. Acton.* In that case, the justices held that drug testing of student athletes was constitutional. The Court considered this practice a useful means to address student drug use and did not find it to be overly intrusive. This decision was an outgrowth of the "special need" standard for schools developed in the Court's ruling in *TLO v. New Jersey* in 1985, which stated that schools must balance students' rights with their special need to protect the educational climate.

In 2002, the Supreme Court decided the case of *Board of Education v. Earls.* In *Earls,* the Court held that drug testing of public school students engaged in all extracurricular activities was constitutional. Hence the *Earls* decision represented a significant expansion of the rights afforded school districts in regard to drug testing students. Prior to the *Earls* case, approximately 7% of public school districts employed drug testing (5% for student athletes, with an additional 2% for students engaged in extracurricular activities). Estimates are that 18% to 20% of school districts employed some type of drug testing in 2010, a dramatic increase. Notably, the George W. Bush administration advocated greater use of drug testing, even arguing that schools should randomly test their entire student body. Some schools have enacted such programs, so it is likely the courts will again hear a case on student drug testing.

Drug testing is not an inexpensive proposition. The cost of an individual test ranges between $25 and $60. These tests are not necessarily robust, and they are not always able to detect use when it has occurred. Conversely, they might detect use when it has not occurred (a false positive).

The largest national study of the impact of school-based drug testing, which involved 76,000 students across the United States, found that drug use was just as prevalent in schools with testing as in those without such a policy. Another study found that athletes in schools with testing actually held more positive attitudes toward drug use than those in comparable schools without testing.

Cheating on drug tests is quite easy. Students can take substances to mask their use, substitute someone else's urine, or tamper with the tests. It is easy to purchase products designed to cheat drug tests, as many are available at local nutrition stores or online.

Although the courts have not found drug testing to be a violation of students' Fourth Amendment rights, critics maintain that they are indeed intrusive. Students may be embarrassed in the process of procuring a urine sample and in some cases have even been asked to urinate in front of monitors to ensure they are not cheating.

The NCAA uses more robust tests for student athletes. This organization randomly draws the names of student athletes to be tested. It also ensures that test results are sent to accredited labs and analyzed by experts, helping reduce the room for error.

Laura L. Finley

Further Reading

Beger, R. (2003). The "worst of both worlds": School security and the disappearing Fourth Amendment rights of students. *Criminal Justice Review, 28,* 336–354.

Finley, L., & Finley, P. (2003). *Piss off! How drug testing and other privacy violations are alienating America's youth.* Monroe, ME: Common Courage.

Goldberg, L. et al. (2003). Drug testing athletes to prevent substance abuse: Background and pilot study results of the SATURN (Student Athletes Testing Using Random Notification) study. *Journal of Adolescent Health, 32,* 16–25.

Hughes, T. (2005). Public student drug testing and the special needs doctrine in *Board of Education v. Earls:* "Just getting tougher." *Criminal Justice Policy Review, 16(3),* 3–17.

Duke University Lacrosse Team Sexual Assault Case

On March 13, 2006, members of the Duke University lacrosse team held a drunken party at the home of the team's three captains. They decided to hire some strippers for the party; indeed, the team was known around the area for having wild parties. The two African American women who arrived were not quite what the largely white squad had expected, and reports indicate that the players berated and insulted the women, who had thought they were performing for a bachelor party involving older men. The women reportedly left the party, but then one returned at the request of a player, who apologized for his teammates' behavior. She told police that after she returned, she was dragged into the bathroom by three men, who brutally beat and raped her for approximately 30 minutes.

The university and police kept the story quiet for the first two weeks after the incident, fearing outrage and a negative spotlight on the university's highly touted team. By March 24, however, reports about the incident had leaked out, prompting outrage by many. The following day, demonstrators held a silent vigil near the lacrosse field, where the Blue Devils were scheduled to play the Georgetown Hoyas. Duke ended up canceling the game and, eventually, the entire lacrosse season. Duke's coach, Mike Presler, resigned. The case had ignited a powder keg, as it prompted discussions of race (white men assaulting a black woman), social class and privilege, and athletes' receipt of preferential versus harassing treatment.

Later that spring, three of the lacrosse players—Colin Finnerty, Reade Seligman, and David Evans—were indicted on charges of rape, sexual assault,

Mike Nifong is escorted by supporters to Durham County Detention Center after being sentenced to one day in jail for contempt of court for his involvement in the Duke University Lacrosse court case in Durham, North Carolina, on September 7, 2007. The courts found Nifong's actions and involvement in the trial to be dishonest and pursued for reasons of self-interest. (AP/Wide World Photos)

and kidnapping by Michael B. Nifong, the district attorney of Durham County, North Carolina. The indictments came after DNA tests were run on 47 members of the team. One player was African American; because the woman did not implicate a black man, he was not asked to submit to the testing. All of the DNA tests were negative.

Fifteen months later, on April 11, 2007, North Carolina Attorney General Roy Cooper announced that all charges had been dropped. Nifong was removed from his post as district attorney amid scathing criticism of his handling of the case, and was eventually disbarred. It seems that Nifong was seeking reelection at the time of the incident and thought prosecuting this case would assist him in his bid.

All 33 lacrosse players were all given an extra year of athletic eligibility by the National Collegiate Athletic Association (NCAA). Finnerty moved on the Loyola College in Maryland and played for their lacrosse team. Seligman transferred to Brown University, and Evans graduated from Duke. In June 2007, the three reached a settlement for an undisclosed amount; the settlement specifies that they cannot sue Duke University. In February 2010, the woman who accused the players was charged with attempted murder, arson, and several other counts after a fight with her boyfriend.

Laura L. Finley

Further Reading

Associated Press. (2010, February 18). Woman in Duke lacrosse case is arrested. *New York Times.* Retrieved April 30, 2010, from http://www.nytimes.com/2010/02/19/sports/ncaabasketball/19duke.html

Duke lacrosse sexual assault case. (2007, June 20). *New York Times.* Retrieved April 30, 2010, from http://topics.nytimes.com/topics/reference/timestopics/organizations/d/duke_university/duke_lacrosse_sexual_assault_case/index.html

Finley, P., Finley, L., & Fountain, J. (2008). *Sports scandals.* Westport, CT: Praeger.

Leonard, D. (2007). Innocent until proven innocent: In defense of Duke lacrosse and white power (and against menacing black student-athletes, a black stripper, activists, and the Jewish media). *Journal of Sport and Social Issues, 31,* 25–44.

Looking back at the Duke lacrosse case. (n.d.). Retrieved April 30, 2010, from http://news.duke.edu/lacrosseincident/

E

Educational Programs and Training, College

The shootings at Jonesboro, Columbine, Virginia Tech, and other high schools and universities have shaken Americans' basic belief that students and staff are safe while at school. While the Clery Act of 1990 (formerly the Student Right to Know and Campus Security Act) requires schools to inform all students and staff of safety risks, it really addresses only ways that schools approach crimes that have already occurred. A more prevention-based tactic that schools have explored in response to the public's growing concern for the safety of the country's schools is an increase in training and educational programming. With the more current goal of ensuring that students and staff feel safe in colleges and universities, college staffs have the added task of providing safety information and preventive strategies. These programs address the issue of alcohol consumption, which can contribute to acts of violence; address the prevention of sexual violence; and strengthen campus housing staff to better prevent violence by providing alterative social outlets and to effectively handle crimes once they do occur.

Problems surrounding alcohol consumption on college campuses range from underage drinking to drinking and driving to sexual violence. Many of these problems result from binge drinking, which is defined as drinking four alcoholic beverages in a single session for women, and five drinks in a single session for men. Given that more than 40% of college students report binge drinking, these problems are at the forefront of collegiate staff efforts to lower campus crime rates. One way to do so is to target groups known to abuse substances at higher rates than even general college students. Students involved in Greek life (i.e., fraternities and sororities) tend to binge drink, drink to intoxication, and drink to the point of blacking out, and use marijuana at higher levels than students not involved in such organizations. By investing in programs aimed at fraternity/sorority students, and at the campus population at large, university staff can begin to address problems associated with student drinking.

One such program that staff can use to help minimize alcohol-related violence is *Alcohol 101*, which is aimed at first-year college students who are either commuting or living on campus. It is carried out in different universities in a variety of ways, from required online reading and quizzes to presentations and discussions. One study examining the effectiveness of various alcohol prevention programs aimed at college freshman found that, when it is made voluntary, this program is accessed by students more often when resident assistants (RAs) seek them out specifically. Information is shared in a one-on-one setting. While this is a less effective way to provide Alcohol 101 to students on a mass scale, including students who do not live on campus, students who learn about the program in this way take part in it at higher rates than students who hear about the program in other ways. Getting specific information on steps to take with a person who blacked out from drinking, prevention of excessive drinking, and ways to reduce the risks of drunk driving, sexual violence, and other situations that can be associated with binge drinking, as well as provision of alternative social activities, is important in preventing school violence and related problems. Alcohol 101 programs reach students early enough to help them develop healthier relationships with alcohol, their new peers, and the campus.

Violence within relationships—here referring to violence within any type of romantic relationship—is a problem consistently plaguing college campuses. Nevertheless, it is not as widely discussed or addressed as general underage and binge drinking prevention, or sexual health, including birth control availability, condom use, and sexually transmitted diseases. One program worked to address this issue after the campus counseling center reported an increase in dating violence cases. This program aimed to show how gender stereotypes heighten the likelihood of relationship violence, examine different forms of relationship violence, provide ways to avoid relationship violence, and increase the collective social interest in this issue, encouraging people to take responsibility for this social problem.

Sexual violence, specifically rape, was addressed by one college in a prevention program targeting first-year college students. An experiment done on this program divided students into two groups. The experimental group received a more interactive program including a presentation and an interactive activity; the control group received only a presentation. The results showed that the students who gained the most knowledge were those who participated in the interactive activity and listened to a presentation. This and other types of programs addressing rape lessen society's tendency to stay relatively quiet on the subject. The college that ran the previously described experiment reported that the most important issue in preventing rape was clarifying what consent is. This knowledge could help a victim see that the perpetrator has committed a crime and realize that the victim may be able to prevent this person from victimizing other individuals by going to the hospital soon and being tested with a rape kit. It could also prevent perpetrators from going through with such a crime, by showing them the potential legal consequences they could face if convicted.

From relationship violence to sexual assault, a broad spectrum of school violence along these lines needs to be addressed. One study examined the use of interdisciplinary task forces that bring together students and staff members from various student organizations, academic departments, and other groups on campus to study which measures are already addressing these issues and what can be repaired or added. One specific task force worked to improve campus policies, protocols, and services available to victims; develop more innovative prevention strategies; and provide faculty and staff training. The unified structure and pooled resources, power, and perspectives increased the university's ability to achieve these goals. Such goals are made more specific when they are applied to the specific gaps in the existing programs, training, and services.

Because so many students live on campus at some point in their college careers, resident hall staff members—many of whom are students themselves—are generally the first people to handle violent situations. *Counselor-in-residence* programs bring counselors generally housed in offices in health and human services centers to the residence halls and resident staff. They work to lower the high caseloads with which counseling centers often must cope, helping RAs and other staff to handle more minor problems themselves. They provide these individuals with the training needed to handle various situations, helping them develop the skills and empathetic attitude necessary to assist residents in crisis. Counselors who are part of these programs will be working primarily with residence life staff. The undergraduate student RAs and higher-level graduate student supervisors are the clients, receiving group and individual training so that they can better deal with a variety of issues, including violent incidents. By providing resident hall staff with licensed counselors, such programs ensure that particularly high-risk situations can be immediately handled by a professional, and they lighten the counseling center's general caseload by engaging student staff to help with more minor issues.

Coping with the many types of violence that college campuses must deal with calls for consistently effective programming. Such programs help prevent violence by working to reduce risky behaviors such as doing drugs or drinking to excess that increase the likelihood of violence. They bring students and staff together, pooling valuable resources to fund and carry out more innovative programs that will appeal to more students. With so many people living and working in such a small area, there is an ongoing need to diffuse stress and stay vigilant for potentially violent situations. The more focus that is put on increasing positive programs aimed at preventing campus violence, the safer that students and staff will be. Every program has the potential to save a life, prevent an injury, and open a mind.

Meghan McHaney

Further Reading

Alcohol 101 Plus: http://www.alcohol101plus.org/home.html

Can I Kiss You?: http://www.canikissyou.com/

Rawls, D., Johnson, D., & Bartels, E. (2004). The counselor-in-residence program: Reconfiguring support services for a new millennium. *Journal of College Counseling, 7*(2), 162–170.

Educational Programs and Training, High School

It has taken several decades of research and worldwide media coverage of unspeakable cruelty, suicide, and homicide in school to bring school officials, law enforcement, school counselors, students, and parents together in a global effort to combat violence in secondary schools. In the United States, the recent spate of school shooting incidents in the nation's high schools—for example, at Pearl High School in Kentucky (1997), at Columbine High School in Colorado (1999), and at Santana High School in California (2001)—has prompted teachers, school officials, and policymakers to address the issue of school violence more directly. According to the Wellesley Center for Women, although the incidence of serious violence in schools (e.g., homicide, weapon carrying, fighting) has declined by 4% since the 1990s, students' reports of "less serious" (e.g., bullying, taunting) and less recognized forms of violence (e.g., date rapes) have increased in high schools across America. One study, for example, found a major decline in fighting and weapon carrying among U.S. high school students between 1991 and 1997. In contrast, another study found that between 1994 and 1999, school-associated violent death rates increased. Despite a recent decline in homicide rates in U.S. schools, homicide continues to claim the lives of many adolescents in high school. Moreover, "less known" types of violence, such as sexual harassment and dating violence, remain major problems among high school students and have serious consequences. Clearly, violence is a pervasive problem in U.S. high schools that calls for school-based interventions and preventive measures.

The recent concern over violence and homicide schools has led many high schools to adopt "zero-tolerance" policies in regard to dangerous and threatening behaviors. Much debate has surrounded the zero tolerance approach, which was adopted by many schools in the wake of the Columbine High School shootings.

Although it was designed to prevent and deter violence and misconduct in school so as to ensure safety and order, several researchers and politicians have questioned the punitive nature (i.e., suspension, expulsion, and arrest) of such measures.

In conjunction with school-related policies such as zero tolerance, education and training programs for bullying and violence prevention and intervention programs have also been adopted in several high schools. According to the U.S. Secret Service, approximately 71% of all high-profile school shooters have been victimized by their peers and classmates in school, with these actions ultimately leading to the school attacks. Bullying has been found to be a major issue in the development and behavior of American children and teenagers. Many school-based bullying and violence prevention programs, such as the Olweus Bullying Prevention Program (OBPP), have taken a "whole-school" approach by targeting not just the individuals involved (i.e., victims, perpetrators), but the entire school. The premise behind the "whole-school" approach is that everyone (i.e., students, teachers, school administrators, parents, and—most recently—community leaders) has a hand in preventing violence in school. OBPP, for example, provides education and training for students, teachers, school officials, and parents concerning bullying victimization and ways to prevent or intervene when students are bullied or harassed by their peers or classmates. Other bullying prevention programs include SafePlace, an expansion of Expect Respect Program, which is also based on a multilevel, multicomponent, school-based prevention program similar to OBPP. Components of SafePlace include classroom curriculum, staff training, policy development, parent education, and support services. Although these programs are not necessarily designed exclusively for high school students, they have proved effective for youths of various ages, including high school students.

Recognizing the serious consequences of dating violence in high school, many high schools have also implemented dating violence prevention programs in recent years. Fantastic Four Guidance Department, for example, has recently initiated a dating violence program in an effort to increase awareness among high school students, parents, and school staff members of dating violence and to create a positive school climate that will promote healthy intimate relationships among teenagers. This program provides educational seminars, outreach and referral services, and resource information. Dating violence awareness programs for teenagers have also been implemented in several high schools nationwide. The Utah Department of Health, for example, established a Teen Dating Violence Awareness and Prevention Week to raise awareness of the problems and consequences of dating violence. This effort not only raises awareness of dating violence, but also provides education on healthy intimate-partner relationships. Other dating violence education and training programs include the Teen Dating Violence Program, which has been facilitated by the Needham Youth Commission in collaboration with Needham High School in Massachusetts. This seminar provides all high school students with a forum in which to raise awareness and increase understanding of teen dating violence.

The serious consequences of violence in U.S. high schools, such as mental/emotional problems, suicide, and shootings, have led many school districts to adopt prevention and intervention programs that are designed to ensure a safe learning environment for high school students. Many of these programs, which adopt a multilevel education and training approach for students, teachers, parents, and school staff members, have been recognized to be highly effective in decreasing violence and promoting prosocial behavior among adolescents. Because school violence (i.e., bullying, fighting, dating violence) is a phenomenon that is influenced by complex relationships between the individual, family, peers, school, and community, it is necessary to initiate education and training programs that address multiple systems and are ecologically based. After all, it takes a village to prevent school violence.

Jun Sung Hong

Further Reading

Anderson, M., Kaufman, J., Simon, T. R., Barrios, L., Paulozzi, L., Ryan, G., et al. (2001). School-associated violent deaths in the United States, 1994–1999. *Journal of American Medical Association, 286*(21), 2695–2072.

Brener, N. D., Simon, T. R., Krug, E. G., & Lowry, R. (1999). Recent trends in violence-related behaviors among high school students in the United States. *Journal of the American Medical Association, 281*(5), 440–446.

City of Needham. (n.d.). Teen dating violence seminars. Retrieved June 12, 2009, from http://www.needhamma.gov/index.aspx?NID=147

Dahlberg, L. L. (1998). Youth violence in the United States: Major trends, risk factors, and prevention approaches. *American Journal of Preventative Medicine, 14*(4), 259–272.

Espelage, D. L., & Holt, M. K. (2007). Dating violence & sexual harassment across the bully–victim continuum among middle and high school students. *Journal of Youth & Adolescence, 36*, 799–811.

Espelage, D. L., & Swearer, S. M. (2003). Research on school bullying and victimization: What have we learned and where do we go from here? *School Psychology Review, 32*(3), 365–383.

Garbarino, J. (2004). Forward. In D. L. Espelage & S. M. Swearer (Eds.), *Bullying in American schools: A social–ecological perspective on prevention and intervention* (pp. xi–xiii). Mahwah, NJ: Lawrence Erlbaum Associates.

Limber, S. P. (2004). Implementation of the Olweus Bullying Prevention Program in American schools: Lessons learned from the field. In D. L. Espelage & S. M. Swearer (Eds.), *Bullying in American schools: A social–ecological perspective on prevention and intervention* (pp. 351–363). Mahwah, NJ: Lawrence Erlbaum Associates.

Utah Department of Health. (n.d.). Teen dating violence awareness and prevention week. Retrieved June 12, 2009, from http://www.health.utah.gov/vipp/dating%20violence/awarenessweek.html

Whitaker, D. J., Rosenbluth, B., Valle, L. A., & Sanchez, E. (2004). Expect respect: A school-based intervention to promote awareness and effective responses to bullying and sexual harassment. In D. L. Espelage & S. M. Swearer (Eds.), *Bullying in American schools: A social–ecological perspective on prevention and intervention* (pp. 327–350). Mahwah, NJ: Lawrence Erlbaum Associates.

Elementary Schools and Crime and Violence

The percentage of students being victimized at U.S. schools has declined in recent years. Specifically, between 1995 and 2001, the percentage of students who reported being victims of crime at school decreased from 10% to 6%. These numbers included decreases in both theft (from 7% to 4%) and violent victimization (from 3% to 2%). In fact, children appear to be safer at school than in their homes. However, school crime figures in California show that while rates of vandalism and other offenses dropped among elementary school students during that same period, "crimes against persons," such as assault, nearly doubled. While the U.S. Department of Education keeps figures on school violence, most of these data do not specify the age of the child responsible. Overall, federal figures show that violence against teachers has dropped—in the 1999–2000 school year, 9% of elementary school teachers were threatened by a student, down from 12% in 1993–1994.

As a reaction to highly publicized violent acts on school campuses, zero-tolerance policies have been enacted in many school districts in an effort to create safer learning environments. Such policies may be contributing to the declining rates of school violence, but they have also resulted in younger and younger students being suspended, expelled, and incarcerated for behavioral issues. Some critics suggest that younger students are not actually becoming more violent, but rather that schools are simply focusing on and issuing harsher responses to disruptive behavior beginning as early as kindergarten. Some educators blame these behavioral issues on everything from rising rates of mild disabilities to violent video games to a bad economy, and some point to an increase in firearm ownership in the home. Federal figures also show that of the 3,523 children who were expelled in the 1998–1999 school year for bringing a gun to school, one in 10 was a student in elementary school. As a result of zero-tolerance policies, children as young as five years old have been arrested and sent to detention facilities for "offenses" ranging from throwing temper tantrums, to having scissors in their backpacks, to bringing a knife to cut a birthday cake to school. Boys are five times as likely to be incarcerated as girls, with children of color and poor children being at highest risk for arrest and detention. Experts urge parents to remember that fewer than 1% of all homicides among school-age children happen on school grounds or on the way to and from school, and they note that the vast majority of students will never experience violence at school.

Many schools have chosen to institute anger management, peer mediation, and impulse response interventions to directly address social and behavioral skill deficits in elementary-school-age children that can cause in behavioral issues in the classroom and have taken other precautions to keep students safe. Some have focused on keeping weapons out by conducting random locker and bag checks, limiting entry and exit points at the school, and keeping the entryways under teacher supervision. Other schools use metal detectors to look for weapons. Intervention programs have also been expanded to include a greater awareness of problems such as bullying and discrimination.

Doreen Maller

Further Reading

Indicators of school crime and safety 2003. (2004). Retrieved February 26, 2010, from http://nces.ed.gov/pubs2004/crime03/7.asp?nav=2

Managing anger at the childcare center and school. (2005). Retrieved February 26, 2010, from http://actagainstviolence.apa.org/anger/atschool.html

School violence and the news. (n.d.). Retrieved February 28, 2010, from Kidshealth.org

Southern Poverty Law Center launches school to prison reform project to help at-risk children get special education services, avoid incarceration. (2007, September 11). Retrieved February 26, 2010, from http://www.splcenter.org/get-informed/news/splc-launches-school-to-prison- reform-project-to-help-at-risk-children-get-special

Elephant

Director Gus Van Sant's 2003 film *Elephant* was the winner of three awards at the 2003 Cannes Film Festival. The film was nominated for six other awards and won two titles. *Elephant* is a fictional story that depicts seemingly ordinary high school students Alex and Eric, who calmly plan and carry out a mass execution at their high school in suburban Portland. The boys are shown calmly watching Nazi films and ordering firearms over the Internet. They intricately plan the details of their attack, planting bombs throughout the school, just as Eric Harris and Dylan Klebold did during the Columbine High School massacre in 1999.

Throughout the film, Alex and Eric are shown being bullied by jocks. On the day of the attack, they warn a classmate, John, who attempts to stop others from entering the building but to no avail. Unlike the Columbine shooting, the film ends with no resolution, rather than with the boys committing suicide. Except for the scenes of bullying and a shot in the shower in which the boys share a kiss (suggesting they were suffering from identity issues), Van Sant offers no specific explanation for the shooting. Like the idea of blindfolded people feeling an elephant, the film shows a variety of perspectives on the lives of so-called average teens.

Some critics noted that Red Lake, Minnesota, school shooter Jeff Weise was a big fan of the film and asserted that it had influenced him in his decision to engage in a shooting rampage at his school.

Laura L. Finley

Further Reading

Elephant: http://www.imdb.com/title/tt0363589/

Emergency Response Plans

According to the U.S. Department of Education's National Center for Education Statistics, there were more than 4,000 two- and four-year public and private institutions of higher education in the United States in 2006. More than 15 million students attend these institutions, and they employ several million faculty and staff members. These organizations are charged with not only providing education to students, but also ensuring those students' safety and general welfare while on campus. Each college or university must develop policies, procedures, and strategies to ensure its campus is safe and to respond in a timely and efficient manner when incidents occur. The rash of campus shootings since 2000 has drawn renewed attention to the issue of safety at these institutions. Most campuses have convened committees or task forces to examine existing policies and practices and to consider enhancements where necessary. In particular, many have created special emergency response teams that plan, implement, and review crisis management activities.

Higher education institutions face unique challenges when thinking about safety on their campuses. First, many college and university campuses sprawl over large geographic areas. Some have satellite or regional locations as well, and many now host medical centers, sports complexes, research facilities, performing arts venues, and even businesses, in addition to classrooms, offices, and student residence

166 | Emergency Response Plans

College campuses such as Purdue University, pictured here, pose unique challenges when developing an emergency response plan. Considerations for the distance between buildings and the constantly varying student population need to be made. (Purdue News Service, Photos by Dave Umberger)

halls. Each of these buildings may pose its own set of challenges and require a different safety plan. Further, the campus population changes daily, so it is difficult to monitor access and to create procedures that keep the campus safe without infringing too much on the college or university experience. Additionally, campuses do not operate on a traditional business or school schedule. Classes may run at night and on weekends, events may be planned at all hours, and students who reside on campus are free to roam around whenever they want. Even when classes are not in session, students from other states or countries may still live on campus.

Unlike corporations or even public schools, institutions of higher education tend to be governed in complex and democratic ways. Although this can be good in some respects, it may make decision making more difficult and lengthy than in a more hierarchical structure. While inclusion of all important stakeholders is recommended, it is imperative that colleges and universities develop a clean authority structure when it comes to emergency management. This effort must be accompanied by a communication plan that can disseminate information to faculty, staff, students, and guests in a timely and accurate fashion.

Given that most college students are at least 18 years and thus are older than the legal age of majority, they are expected to be able to make their own decisions.

Campuses thus face the challenge of requiring adults to follow policies that may be necessary for safety purposes but may not be pleasing to students. K–12 schools, with their generally minor student populations, do not typically have to deal with this dilemma.

The best emergency management plans emanate from the college or university president, chancellor, or provost. These individuals have the power and authority to devote the necessary resources to emergency management. This high-level support is especially important for financial reasons, as college and universities must make decisions within specific fiscal parameters that not all personnel or students are privy to. It is not recommended that these high-level officials dictate the plan without seeking input, but rather that they take the lead in creating an emergency management plan and team.

To be truly effective, an emergency management plan must focus on collaboration and partnerships, both on campus and in the larger community. All relevant departments must be involved in the planning process, and external partners such as law enforcement, fire department personnel, emergency medical services, media, and local social services must be included.

Although the threat of a campus shooter has received the most attention in recent years, experts recommend that institutions of higher education create "all hazards" plans instead of preparing for a specific type of threat. An all-hazards plan allows development of capacities and capabilities to respond to a variety of emergencies and natural disasters, including inclement weather, natural disasters, biological hazards, violence, and terrorism.

Each portion of the emergency plan should specifically address how to care for vulnerable populations, such as those with language barriers or disabilities. Thus each campus must create a plan that is unique and specific to its size, geographic setting, number and type of buildings, composition of student body, and other factors. Simply importing another school's plan will not be effective.

Ideally, all faculty, staff, and support personnel will receive routine multiple-hazard training that allows them to become familiar with the protocols and procedures of the emergency plan. Community partners should be included in the training as well, so that every potential responder is amply prepared. Role-playing exercises can enhance the experience and lead to needed discussion and adjustments.

A key component of campus emergency planning is dissemination of the necessary information to relevant parties. Campuses must create a communication plan that allows them to share critical emergency information with students, such as where to go if a natural disaster occurs and how to evacuate campus if needed. General emergency management information can be displayed on university websites and on posters on campus as well as incorporated into student and faculty handbooks.

The Federal Emergency Management Agency (FEMA) has developed a four-phase framework for planning and implementing an emergency management plan.

The four phases identified are prevention–mitigation, preparedness, response, and recovery.

Prevention focuses on decreasing the likelihood of a crisis. Mitigation refers to actions taken to eliminate or reduce loss of life or property damage during a crisis. To prevent and mitigate crises, campuses must identify all hazards that could potentially cause a problem. This effort might begin with a review of campus and community data, assessing the vulnerability of the surroundings and the facilities as well as analyzing recent crime data and inclement weather probabilities. If there are no existing reviews of this nature, it is recommended that campuses conduct them. The U.S. Department of Education's Office of Safe and Drug-Free Schools has developed assessment tools and information for applying the Crime Prevention Through Environmental Design (CPTED) program, which involves assessing the ability to see what is occurring in a particular location, restricting who enters or exits, and maintaining respect for property.

Ensuring a healthy campus climate can help prevent emergencies as well. To further this goal, campuses can sponsor activities that allow students to develop healthy relationships and a sense of connectedness to the school.

The preparedness phase focuses on designing strategies, processes, and protocols to prepare the college or university for potential emergencies. It includes development of campus collaborations and contracting with community partners to provide services. Plans should be coordinated with state and local entities' plans, thereby ensuring that no duplication occurs. Further, preparedness strategies include assigning appropriate personnel and delineating responsibilities. The creation of a Continuity of Operations Plan (COOP) and a Business Continuity Plan (BCP) for all campus operations functions is recommended as part of the preparedness phase as well. The COOP ensures that the campus can maintain essential functions such as housing, food service, and transportation when an emergency occurs. The BCP addresses administrative functions such as payroll and communications, enabling them to continue in an emergency. Additionally, preparedness involves establishing a reunification program in the event students or staff become separated from loved ones during an emergency. It also involves the development of mental health counseling services for persons who are traumatized.

During the response phase, campuses enact their plans to contain and resolve an emergency. An emergency operations center should have been identified and should serve as a central command center during the incident. Decision makers then move forward based on information gleaned from other members of the emergency management team. Ideally, colleges and universities will have readily available a copy of the emergency plan and procedures, communication equipment and phone directories, relevant blueprints and maps, a list of personnel and contact information, building security information, backup power and lighting, and emergency supplies.

In the recovery phase, campuses assist students, staff, faculty, and the campus community as a whole return to full functioning. Necessary steps will include assessing physical damage to the campus and contracting for repair, utilizing the COOP and BCP to ensure needed services return to operational status as soon as possible, and restoring the learning environment. Although classes may need to be cancelled for a short time, a good emergency plan can help ensure the amount of time off is minimal. Finally, all those affected by the incident should receive appropriate counseling and services.

In addition to the resources provided by the federal government, many private companies specialize in campus and school safety. For example, National School Safety and Security Services helps schools establish crisis plans that are specific to their unique challenges. It also conducts training for personnel on emergency planning and carries out drills to ensure plans are enacted efficiently. In addition, National School Safety and Security Services helps schools enhance their communication capabilities and work with relevant community providers.

Laura L. Finley

Further Reading

Crisis response and violence prevention resources. (n.d.). National Mental Health and Education Center. Retrieved from http://www.naspcenter.org/safe_schools/safeschools.htm

FEMA emergency management guide for business and industry. (n.d.). Retrieved from http://www.fema.gov/business/guide/toc.shtm

National School Safety and Security Services: http://www.schoolsecurity.org/resources/crisis.html

Readiness and Emergency Management for Schools Technical Assistance Center: http://rems.ed.gov/

Security on Campus, Inc.: www.securityoncampus.org

Trump, K. (2000). *Classroom killers? Hallway hostages? How schools can prevent and manage school crises.* New York: Corwin.

U.S. Department of Education, Office of Safe Schools. (2009). Action guide for emergency management at institutions of higher education. Retrieved April 30, 2010, from http://www2.ed.gov/admins/lead/safety/emergencyplan/remsactionguide.pdf

European Union and School Crime and Violence

School crime, bullying, and violence are major concerns and pose an increasing challenge for European Union (EU) authorities. School violence encompasses a range of actions and threats, including verbal, physical, sexual and psychological violence; social exclusion; violence relating to property; violence relating to theft; threat; insults; and rumor spreading.

Considering that violence is culturally and historically determined, a 1999 report indicated that the diversity of European cultures made it difficult to define school violence in a uniform manner and to make valid comparisons between different countries' rates of school violence. Hence, it was difficult to ascertain whether school violence was on the increase in this region. Therefore, to develop a better understanding of school violence in Europe, and to devise more effective prevention and intervention mechanisms, there is a need to accept a multiplicity of definitions of school violence and to accommodate a range of cultural perspectives.

Reported incidence of school violence varies widely across EU member states. In Denmark, approximately 7% of pupils became victims of violence at least once during the previous month, according to the 1999 survey. Countries such as Switzerland, Belgium, Sweden, and Norway reported a 15% rate of violence among pupils, while Ireland and Spain were among countries reporting rates of violence in schools ranging from 15% to 30%. At the other end of the scale, 65% and 75% of pupils in Romania and Hungary, respectively, reported being victims of school violence.

An important and interesting result from the Trends in International Mathematics and Science Study (TIMMS), which included survey data from 37 countries, highlighted the fact that school violence rates were not related to general crime rates. TIMMS data indicated that rates of violence in school were related to certain social indicators such as absolute deprivation and age distribution, but did not reflect other indicators such as income inequality or social integration. Furthermore, school violence rates were related to school-system variables and the effect of these variables was independent of social variables.

Overall, EU data and reports on school bullying indicate that:

- School violence is an international phenomenon and not limited to one country.
- Bullying is a major component of school violence throughout Europe, yet bullying is not a well-understood phenomenon in this region.
- For victims, occurrence of bullying decreases as the age of pupils increases; for offenders, rates of bullying among boys show a marked increase with age, and are relatively stable for girls.
- Verbal bullying is the most frequent type of bullying.
- Boys are more often victims of physical harassment and bullying, whereas girls are more often victims of social exclusion.
- At least 5% of pupils in primary and secondary schools are bullied weekly or more often.

- Bullying by means of cell phones is increasing in Europe, where at least 15% of pupils using mobile phones experience bullying.
- Overall, various forms of bullying seem to be increasing, including school bullying, cell phone bullying, and cyberbullying.

EU countries have initiated a number of projects and programs to address the problem of school violence and its various forms. In fact, subsequent to the Council of Europe meeting in Brussels, Belgium, on September 22, 1997, and following the publication of the Council of Ministers' conclusions on safety in schools, which called on the European Commission and its member states to enhance communication and cooperation so as to address problems and questions in relation to school safety and violence, the European Commission launched a two-year (1998–2000) "Violence in Schools" initiative that aimed to support a range of actions and interventions in order to prevent and tackle violence. These actions and interventions included a series of pilot projects and networks, in-service training, and the exchange of information and best practices approaches.

This initiative was followed by one of the most significant projects funded by the European Commission in relation to tackling school violence—namely, the "Connect" project. This program, which was subtitled "Tackling Violence in Schools on a European-Wide Basis," produced country reports in 2001 that aimed to provide a cross-sectional view of school violence in the 15 EU member states and Iceland and Norway. It highlighted important challenges in tackling school violence in the region, including the lack of comparable data in different European countries. In particular, the project's findings included the following points:

- Differences in the way violence was defined in various European states did not allow valid comparison between member states, or cumulative data aggregation at the European level.
- Large differences were noted between officially reported and/or documented cases of violence and data obtained from self-report questionnaires and victim surveys.
- The nature of data from different member states (e.g., structured interviews, victim surveys, self-report questionnaires, teachers' reports) and an overall lack of systematic data hampered analysis of the problem.
- A range of specific measures and targeted programs had been implemented, including individual work with at-risk pupils in some of the member states, such as Austria, Finland, Germany, Portugal, Spain, and Sweden.

- A number of countries (e.g., Belgium, Finland, France, Germany, Ireland, Luxemburg, Sweden, and the United Kingdom) had established legal frameworks and requirements to prevent violence and bullying in school premises. However, without appropriate combination with other initiatives, such policies could prove ineffective.
- A number of other initiatives had been launched to that point, including "preventive approaches to promote pupil responsibility and a positive school climate," security measures (e.g., help lines, use of alarm bracelets, and video surveillance), whole-school approaches, and teacher training.
- Overall, there was a lack of systematic evaluation of the various initiatives addressing school violence.

Following this project, the Council of Europe sponsored similar themes in a broader initiative (2002–2004), entitled "Response to Violence in Everyday Life in a Democratic Society." However, in their final declaration at a conference in Strasbourg (December 2–4, 2002), Council members stated that several tragic incidents at schools in Dunblane, Scotland; Erfurt, Germany; Barcelona, Spain; and Paris, France, had received extensive media coverage and had become widely known through media reporting; they noted that in reality the extent of such problems was much more limited and such incidents were relatively rare and rather isolated. The Council concluded that although it was important not to exaggerate the dimension of the problem, these tragic events were reflective of an increasing number of low-level violent incidents in schools and communities. Furthermore, the Council declaration pointed out that circumstances differed significantly between and within the context of different member states (in terms of the forms, contexts, and causes of school violence); thus there was a general need to devise and implement local and interinstitutional strategies to raise awareness, help prevention, and provide response to incidents of violence.

In 2005, the Council of Europe launched an action program entitled "Children and Violence," whose main objective was to assist with the identification and implementation of consistent policies to combat youth and school crime and violence. This project was integrated within the larger Council of Europe program "Building a Europe for and with Children," which itself was a three-year program with two important stands—namely, promoting children's rights and protecting them from all forms of violence. This initiative came in response to the Council's mandate to guarantee an integrated approach to promoting children's rights and well-being. The key concepts and central methodologies in this program were transversality, an integrated approach, partnerships, and communication. In fulfilling its objectives, the program relied on both the Council of Europe and its relevant institutions as well as outside partners to achieve sustainable change.

The program's strategy was subsequently reassessed and adopted for the years 2009–2011 by the Council of Ministers in November 2008.

Claudia Megele

Further Reading

Building a Europe for and with Children: http://www.coe.int/t/transversalprojects/children/default_en.asp

Moore, K., Jones, N., & Broadbent, E. (2008). *School violence in OECD countries*. United Kingdom: Plan Limited.

Ruxton, S. (2005). *What about us? Children's rights in the European Union.* Belgium: European Children's Network.

Siegel, L., & Welsh, B. (2008). *Juvenile delinquency: Theory, practice and law.* Florence, Kentucky: Wadsworth.

Smith, P. K. (Ed.). (2003). *Violence in schools: The response in Europe*. London: Routledge Falmer.

Violence in Schools Training Action (VISTA): http://www.vista-europe.org/index.php

Expect Respect

Expect Respect is a school-based program that focuses on preventing teen dating violence and educating young people about healthy relationships. It was created for schools in Austin, Texas, where it has been used since 1989. This curriculum, which is appropriate for middle and high school students, has also been used by domestic violence centers and schools throughout the United States.

The Expect Respect program includes several components—school-wide prevention activities, youth leadership training, and support groups for at-risk youth. Support group participants are youths who have experienced abuse in the home or in dating relationships. Groups include only members of the same gender, and they run for 24 sessions and are delivered during the school day. Evaluations have found that the support groups offer an emotionally safe and supportive environment for their members, and participants report that they produce changes in attitudes and beliefs, knowledge, self-awareness, and skills in developing healthy relationships. Girls who participate in the groups also report a decrease in insecurity and an increase in their ability to identify unhealthy behaviors by dating partners. In addition, high-risk youth—those who have experienced physical or sexual violence (as perpetrators or victims) in the three months prior to the program—have shown significant decreases in emotional abuse perpetration, emotional abuse victimization, and physical/sexual violence perpetration following completion of the Expect Respect curriculum.

Expect Respect includes three youth leadership programs: the SafeTeens leadership training for middle and high school students, the Heroes leadership training for elementary school students, and the Changing Lives Youth Theater Program for high school students. In an evaluation of youths who participated in one of these programs, 89% reported increased understanding of abusive and healthy relationships; 88% reported increased knowledge of how to help themselves and others; and 82% reported increased willingness to help others.

School-wide plans include faculty training, teacher-led classroom lessons, parent seminars, display of materials throughout the campus, screening of videos and public service announcements, and projects and activities initiated by a team made of both youths and adults on each campus. Students in schools that have implemented these programs express less support for abuse and better understanding of healthy relationships, and more ability to identify abusive behaviors.

Laura L. Finley

Further Reading

Ball, B. (2008, October). Expect Respect program evaluation: Executive summary. Retrieved April 26, 2010, from http://www.safeplace.org/Document.Doc?id=52

Love Is Not Abuse: http://www.loveisnotabuse.com/web/guest/home

National Teen Dating Violence Hotline: http://www.loveisrespect.org/

Whitaker, D. J., Rosenbluth, B., Valle, L. A., & Sanchez, E. (2004). Expect Respect: A school-based intervention to promote awareness and effective responses to bullying and sexual harassment. In D. L. Espelage & S. M. Swearer (Eds.), *Bullying in American schools: A social–ecological perspective on prevention and intervention* (pp. 327–350). Mahwah, NJ: Lawrence Erlbaum Associates.

F

Fear of School Crime and Violence

Although rates of school violence have decreased, the number of U.S. teenagers who skip school for fear of being hurt has steadily increased. According to the Centers for Disease Control and Prevention (CDC), which surveyed 10,000 public and private high school students across the nation, 5.4% of high school students skipped at least one day of school in 2003 because of safety concerns. That proportion was up 1% from 1993. Yet the same survey found an almost 9%decrease in the number of students saying they had been in a fight the previous school year and an almost 6% reduction in the number of students who reported carrying a weapon on school grounds. Media attention to major shootings like the Columbine High School massacre of 1999 scared many students into believing this type of incident could happen anywhere at any time. The media often describe somewhat isolated or rare incidents as trends, which may result in people overestimating the likelihood that a similar event could occur again. Misplaced fear not only affects students' attendance, but also shapes school policies that are intended to keep students safe. These policies, such as zero-tolerance programs, metal detector searches, and school police officers, may or may not help keep the school. Research is clear on one point, however: They are likely to increase students' fear, as implementing these policies tells students that something horrible is likely to happen that necessitates such an extreme response.

In essence, school violence has become a *moral panic*. Stanley Cohen coined this term to describe the reaction of media, politicians, and agents of social control (such as police) to youth deviance may or may not help secure the school. His initial work examined the Mods and Rockers, two groups of deviant youth in England. Cohen found these groups were labeled as threats and consequently were treated as such. Jock Young's 1971 book *The Drugtakers* drew additional attention to the media's role in constructing deviant identities.

Cohen identified five stages of a moral panic. First, someone or something is defined as a threat to society's values and interests. Second, the threat is depicted by media and repeated in easily identifiable ways. Third, public concern about the so-called problem builds, until fourth, there is some type of response from authorities or opinion makers. Fifth, the panic either results in social change or recedes.

It is easy to apply Cohen's five stages to the case of school violence. The 1980s and 1990s were a time period in which adolescents were largely viewed as problems. Even criminologists had warned of the emergence of a dangerous generation of "superpredators," who were far more violent than any group of juveniles to precede them. Despite the continued decline of actual youth violence in the 1990s, news reports continued to focus on these "ticking time bombs." For instance, Ann Curry introduced a child psychologist on her *Today show* and asked about the "trend" of students shooting one another. Vincent Schiraldi, the director of the Justice Policy Institute, then reminded viewers that three times as many people were struck by lightning as were killed in school shootings that year. Other national figures such as Katie Couric emphasized that youth today were out of control, echoing the theme that schools were a site, and students the cause, of a major social problem. The official response was to implement a series of punitive and technological strategies aimed at reining in the supposedly out-of-control youth. Thus districts invested in surveillance cameras and metal detectors and hired school police officers. At the White House conference on School Safety, President Bill Clinton proposed spending $12 million for Project SERV (School Emergency Response to Violence), to be modeled after the FEMA response to violence. Clinton also set aside $65 million to hire 2,000 community and school police officers and $25 million for districts to develop safety plans. The Safe and Gun Free Schools Act was passed in 1994, before most of the high-profile shootings occurred. It requires districts receiving federal funds to establish specific penalties for students found with weapons on campus. By the later 1990s, districts had used this act to justify the implementation of zero-tolerance policies for numerous offenses, some going well beyond weapons. In most cases, students found violating a zero-tolerance provision face mandatory suspension or expulsion. Although this reaction might be appropriate in some of the most serious cases, zero-tolerance policies have been found to disproportionately affect students of color who have not perpetrated any act of violence.

College campuses have responded in similar ways, albeit a bit later and less punitively. Since 1990, five federal laws and many state laws have been created to increase security on university campuses. These measures include the Clery Act—legislation requiring the reporting of school crime. As in the case of secondary schools, the results of these laws have been mixed. The idea is that parents and students have a right to know whether a given campus is safe, but the increased focus on crime may unwittingly heighten students' fear of victimization. Experts recommend that campus officials gauge students' fear of crime and violence so they can develop appropriate security measures, then create awareness campaigns that address the most concerning offenses.

In both secondary schools and colleges, the moral panic about extreme forms of violence often leads people to fear the wrong thing. That is, while the chance of being shot in a school on a college campus is fairly low, the chance that someone's property will be stolen or a person will become the victim of an abusive relationship is much greater. If media attention and school or campus policies focus exclusively on the worst-case scenario, they may be doing students a tremendous disservice. By far, the most common campus crime, year after year, is burglary. Almost all school or campus shooters were "insiders," or persons who belonged on the grounds. Yet many school districts and some colleges responded to fear of intruders by investing in ID badges or other forms of identification for students and staff. This might not be a tremendously costly measure, but it also may not be useful. A more helpful response is for a school to develop an emergency management and communication plan and to host awareness events and trainings so that students and staff can identify real threats and be equipped to respond to them, if necessary.

Laura L. Finley

Further Reading

Bedenbaugh, C. (2003). *Measuring fear of crime on campus: A study of an urban university.* Thesis retrieved from http://etd.lsu.edu/docs/available/etd-0704103-080530/unrestricted/Bedenbaugh_thesis.pdf

Cohen, S. (1973). *Folk devils and moral panics.* St. Albins: Paladin.

Cosgrove-Mather, B. (2004, July 29). Report: Teens fear school violence. Retrieved April 29, 2010, from http://www.cbsnews.com/stories/2004/07/29/national/main632972.shtml

Fox, J., & Savage, J. (2009). Mass murder goes to college: An examination of changes on college campuses after Virginia Tech. *American Behavioral Scientist, 52,* 1465–1485.

Hemphill, B., & LaBanc, B. (2010). *Enough is enough: A student affairs perspective and response to a campus shooting.* New York: Stylus.

Killingbeck, D. (2001). The role of television news in the construction of school violence as a "moral panic." *Journal of Criminal Justice and Popular Culture, 8*(3). Retrieved from http://www.albany.edu/scj/jcjpc/vol8is3/killingbeck.html

Lindle, J. (2008, January). School safety: Real or imagined fear? *Educational Policy, 22*(1), 28–44.

Paludi, M. (2008). *Understanding and preventing campus violence.* Westport, CT: Praeger.

Young, J. (1971). *The drugtakers: The social meaning of drug use.* London: McGibben and Kee.

Federal Bureau of Investigation (FBI)

The Bureau of Investigation of the U.S. Department of Justice was developed in 1908. In 1935, this agency became the Federal Bureau of Investigation (FBI). Apart from undertaking intelligence operations, the FBI investigates different kinds of federal crime. Given that campuses have become the scenes of brutal killings, assaults, and violence in recent years, as part of its mandate the FBI is taking this problem very seriously and joining in investigations of criminal cases affecting schools. The FBI, through its different agencies, is analyzing the problem as well as suggesting methods to prevent unbridled school crimes. The spate of killings and escalating violence in places of learning has put the investigating agency on alert.

As early as 1953, the FBI had become involved in investigating campus crimes. In that year, FBI agents successfully solved the case of the Greenlease kidnapping, in which a six-year-old student at the French Institute of Notre Dame De Sion in Kansas City, Missouri, was kidnapped and murdered. The culprits were caught soon afterward and executed for the crime.

FBI special agent Michael Tabman briefs Minneapolis media about the investigation into the Red Lake High School shooting as attorney Tom Heffelfinger listens on April 18, 2005. (AP/Wide World Photos)

More than 45 years later, after the Columbine High School massacre in Littleton, Colorado, on April 20, 1999, the Investigative and Prosecutive Graphic Unit of the FBI took a leading role in documenting the crime. By using high-tech methods, investigators were able to reconstruct the sequence of events and movements of particular persons during the incident. The FBI's data were a great help in the investigation, as the agency is equipped to do things that local police cannot. The FBI also conducted an in-depth study of school shootings after the tragedy at Columbine. It pointed to factors such as troubled relationships, frustration, selfish behavior, a sense of alienation, violent video games, easy access to weapons, and a sense of revenge as some of the primary reasons for the perceived escalation of school violence. In June 1999, the FBI held a special conference where a threat assessment perspective was emphasized rather than profiling of the potential school shooter.

The FBI was involved with the Red Lake shooting spree in March 2005, as it occurred on an Indian reservation. In this case, a 17-year-old student indiscriminately fired shots in his school, resulting in the deaths of 14 students and a teacher.

In the last several years, the FBI has published special reports and held conferences aimed at enabling all sorts of educational institutions to tackle violence on their campuses more effectively. In the wake of Virginia Tech massacre of April 16, 2007, the FBI again began an in-depth study, this time focusing on the unique issues faced by college campuses.

The FBI cannot completely eliminate school violence, but the agency has taken specific steps to counteract the horrendous social evil associated with these crimes. With 56 field offices dotted around the United States, the FBI is endeavoring to tackle the problem on a wide scale.

Patit Paban Mishra

Further Reading

Balcavage, D., & Schlesinger, A. (Eds.). (2000). *Federal Bureau of Investigation*. New York: Chelsea House.

Benedek, E. P., & Cornell, D. G. (Eds.). (1989). *Juvenile homicide*. Washington, DC: American Psychiatric Press.

FBI cases. (n.d.). Retrieved March 2, 2009, from http://www.fbi.gov/hq/lab/org/cases99.htm

FBI history: Famous cases. (n.d.). Retrieved March 6, 2009, from http://www.fbi.gov/libref/historic/famcases/greenlease/greenleasenew.htm

Finley, L. (2007). *Encyclopedia of juvenile violence*. Westport, CT: Greenwood Press.

Jeffreys-Jones, R. (2007). *The FBI: A history*. New Haven, CT: Yale University Press.

O'Toole, M. (1999). The school shooter: A threat assessment perspective. Retrieved March 1, 2009, from www.fbi.gov/publications/school/school2.pdf

Reebel, P. (Ed.). (2002). *Federal Bureau of Investigation: Current issues and background.* New York: Nova Science Publishers.

U.S. Department of Justice. (2007). Crime in schools and colleges. Retrieved March 2, 2009, from www.fbi.gov/ucr/schoolviolence/2007/schoolviolence.pdf

Fiction and School Crime and Violence

Since the 19th century, writers have set large numbers of their stories in schools; these works are meant mainly for a school-age audience, although some are intended for older readers. The traditional form featured an account of bullying, where the bullied student, usually a boy, eventually triumphs. Charles Dickens's *Nicholas Nickleby* (1838–1839), for example, recounts boys being bullied in the fictional school Dotheboys Hall run by the vicious Wackford Squeers. Bullying—

Nicholas astonished Mr. Squeers and family in Charles Dickens' book *Nicholas Nickleby*. (Dickens, Charles. *Nicholas Nickleby*, 1839)

this time by older fellow students—is also the central theme of Richard Hughes' famous book *Tom Brown's Schooldays* (1857). Set at Rugby School in England, which Hughes attended from 1834 until 1842, the book became so popular that it has been in print ever since its original publication. A sequel, *Tom Brown at Oxford* (1861), was also successful, and a series of "Flashman" books by George MacDonald Fraser were based on the later life of the leading bully in the story, Harry Flashman, and his cowardly actions around the British Empire. Since *Tom Brown's Schooldays*, many books have used schools as their primary setting, with a number of them centering on the themes of bullying, theft, and murder.

Incidents of bullying, especially in boys' boarding schools, pervade many novels that focus on school days, just as they often do in autobiographies. Some of the most well-known accounts are by Roald Dahl in both his autobiographical *Boy* (1984) and his short story "Galloping Foxley" (1960). Other books such as Rudyard Kipling's *Stalky & Co* (1899) and Nicholas Drayson's *Confessing a Murder* (2003), about a student at school with Charles Darwin, include in-school bullying scenes and then follow the victimized student into later life. The violence in many of these fictional boarding schools, however, is nowhere near the treatment meted out to inmates in juvenile detention centers and youth custody centers. The latter literature includes such works as Steven Slater's *Approved School Boy* (1967) set in Dorset, England, and Lorenzo Carcaterra's *Sleepers* (1995), set in New York State; both of these books are partially autobiographical in nature. Damon Galgut's *A Sinless Season* (1982), set in South Africa, covers bullying by other inmates and staff in detail. William Golding's *Lord of the Flies* (1954) goes even further in describing the lives of boys stranded on an island with no adults.

The proliferation of books for school-age children has led to many books that focus on children solving crimes in school settings. Terence Rattigan's play *The Winslow Boy* (1961), which is often performed in schools, focuses on the Archer-Shee case that rocked British politics in 1908–1911, in which a father sought to clear the name of his son who was expelled for theft. Other popular children's stories involving crimes include Anthony Buckeridge's *Rex Milligan's Busy Term* (1953), in which a boy from a London grammar school uses information from his history teacher to prevent a greedy developer from illegally taking over the school. Stories set in boarding schools offer an easier environment for writers, as they typically include a limited number of characters and suspects. One example of this genre is Buckeridge's *Jennings Follows a Clue* (1951), which is set in an English preparatory school. Richmal Crompton's character "William," is regularly involved in trying to solve mysteries and crimes, with some 40 books devoted to his career.

Erich Kästner's *Emil and the Detectives* (1929), set in Berlin in the 1920s, describes a boy tracking down the pickpocket who stole some money from him (and who turns out to be a wanted bank robber). Paul Berna's *Le Cheval sans tête*

(1955; published in English as *A Hundred Million Francs* in 1957) involves a group of schoolchildren in Paris becoming involved in the hunt for a major bank robber. Maurice G. Woodward's *The Mystery of Lodge School* (1987) has as its setting a remote British boarding school where a mysterious series of events follow the arrival of a new German master. Murders also occur on a regular basis in Hogwarts, the school attended by J. K. Rowling's Harry Potter. Mention should also be made of Charlie Higson's *SilverFin* (2005) and subsequent books about the young James Bond at Britain's Eton College. In addition, child spies dealing with murders and other cases appear in the Alex Rider stories of Anthony Horowitz, starting with *Stormbreaker* (2000), and in the Alpha Force series by Chris Ryan.

A number of historical crime novels have centered on events in schools or around schoolchildren. Caroline Lawrence's "Bread and Circuses," a short story set in Rome during the reign of the Emperor Titus, has school children deciding to solve the mystery surrounding bread stolen from a baker. In *The Owls of Gloucester* (2000), the 10th in the Domesday Book series by Edward Marston (pseudonym for Keith Miles), set in about 1085, two boys serving as novice monks at Gloucester Cathedral uncover the body of a monk who was one of their teachers. Cynthia Harnett's *The Load of Unicorn* (1959) focuses on the life of a boy at St. Paul's Cathedral School, London, in the early 1480s, and features scriveners trying to keep paper from William Caxton to prevent him from printing books that would cause them to lose business. Michael Clynes (pseudonym for Paul Doherty), in his Sir Roger Shallot murder/mystery journals set during the reign of Henry VIII, features Benjamin Daunbey, the nephew of Cardinal Wolsey, as a schoolmaster. In all of these works, however, the central issue in the story is historical, not the school.

Ashley Gardner sets his *The Sudbury School Murders* (2005) in Regency England, with the importance of the honor of the school being an initial theme until it is overwhelmed by money-making schemes devised by a wealthy student. Set n Australia, Jackie French's *Tom Appleby: Convict Boy* (2004) covers the life of a fictional child convict in Australia in the 1790s, and Gary Disher's *Moondyne Kate* (2001) has a schoolboy involved with bushrangers in mid-19th-century Australia.

There are also some crime stories whereby schoolteachers become involved in crime. Ernest Raymond's *We, the Accused* (1935), made into a film in 1980, is about a teacher who tries to shorten the life of his ill wife and finds himself trying to escape from the police.

The vulnerability of schoolchildren to being kidnapped also features in many stories, such as Frank Richards's *Lord Billy Bunter* (1956); Jerrard Tickell's *Whither do You Wander* (1959); and Arden Winch's *Blood Money* (1981), which was turned into a television series by the British Broadcasting Corporation. The crime writer Ellis Peters (pseudonym for Edith Pargeter) wrote *City of Gold and Sorrows* (1973), which involves the disappearance (and murder) of an inquisitive teenage boy on a school history excursion to the site of a Roman villa. Kingsley Amis's *The Riverside Villas Murder* (1973) has a London schoolboy inadvertently solving the mystery over a murder of a local man.

Another genre consists of murder stories written for adults but focusing on schools. R. C. Woodthorpe's *The Public School Murder* (1932) covers the murder of an English public school headmaster; James Hilton's *Murder at School: A Detective Fantasia* (1935) has two brothers attending the same school and having separate accidental deaths; and the mystery in Josephine Bell's *Death at Half-Term* (1939) surrounds a murder in an English preparatory school during a performance of *Twelfth Night*. Edmund Crispin's *Love Lies Bleeding* (1948) is set in a public school near Stratford-upon-Avon and describes the murders of two schoolmasters as an unknown person seeks to get his hands on the manuscript of a long-lost Shakespearean play. Evidence quickly points to a member of the school staff, and the crime is solved by an Oxford University professor at the school for speech day, who aids (and then takes over from) the police investigation. Key elements of this novel include the "regular" habits of several schoolmasters and the length of time taken to write school reports. The great British writer of spy fiction, John Le Carré (pseudonym for David Cornwell), in *Murder of Quality* (1962) also sets a murder in a school context, but this time highlights a student who may, or may not, have cheated in an examination. The spy George Smiley is involved in solving the mystery. Michael Gilbert's *The Night of the Twelfth* (1976) focuses on a teacher and the disappearance of children near a school, and Robert Barnard's *School for Murder* (1983) places a murder in a British preparatory school. Howard Shaw's *Pageant of Death* (2000) has a murder carried out during the performance of a school's 500th-anniversary pageant.

The intrusion of war into school life leads to new criminal offenses that affect civilians. In R. F. Delderfield's *To Serve Them All My Days* (1972), a student who refuses conscription and becomes a conscientious objector appears in the story, albeit briefly. Ian Serraillier's *The Silver Sword* (1956) follows the life of a boy in German-occupied Warsaw, and Danish writer Anne Holm's *David* (1963, published in English as *I Am David* in 1965) covers the experiences of a Jewish boy in Nazi Europe.

A number of well-known films have also addressed war's effects on schools and the lives of children, with the committing of war crimes as a backdrop. The French film *Fiesta* (1995) explores the life of a Spanish schoolboy leaving school for the Spanish Civil War, and *Au revoir les enfants* (1987) deals with the hiding of a Jewish boy in a Carmelite boarding school during the German occupation of France. Bryce Courtney's *The Power of One* (1989), set in South Africa during the 1940s, focuses on the introduction of apartheid, and Robin Brown's *When the Wood Became the Trees* (1965) relates the growing up of a white schoolboy during a state of emergency and killings in Rhodesia.

Series of revenge killings are rarely a theme in popular fiction, although Agatha Christie does cover this possibility in *Nemesis* (1976), when a former headmistress takes a coach tour with the friends of a former female student with whom a wrongly convicted young man had fallen in love many years earlier. Gavin Newman (pseudonym for Guy N. Smith), in *The Hangman* (1994), has an evil young man seeking revenge on all who wronged him, including his former headmaster who had punished him too many times.

The range and variety of these stories illustrate how the nature of crime and the clear interest in crime writing have led to many books set around schools, teachers, and students. As a genre, it has attracted many well-known writers, most of whom are famous for other books, as well as a number of schoolteachers and former schoolteachers such as Buckeridge, Doherty, and Woodward.

Justin Corfield

Further Reading

Fitzpatrick, R. (1990). *Bullies, beaks and flannelled fools: An annotated bibliography of boys' school fiction 1742–1990.* London: privately published.

Gathorne-Hardy, J. (1977). *The old school tie: The phenomenon of the English public school.* New York: Viking Press.

Flores, Robert

At approximately 8:30 A.M. on October 28, 2002, Robert Stewart Flores, Jr., entered the College of Nursing at the University of Arizona armed with a Norinco .45-caliber semi-automatic pistol, a Glock .40-caliber semi-automatic pistol, a Smith and Wesson .357-caliber revolver, a Colt .357 semi-automatic revolver, a Czech 9-mm semi-automatic pistol, and approximately 250 rounds of ammunition. Flores then shot to death three nursing professors before taking his own life. Flores had a valid "concealed carry" permit. The requirements for obtaining such a permit in Arizona included the successful completion of a 16-hour safety training course and a successful background check conducted by the Federal Bureau of Investigation.

Flores was born in 1961 in Los Angeles, California. He had two older sisters and a younger brother. His parents were divorced, and Flores labeled them as "marginal at best." Flores described his father as distant and lacking in any parenting skills, and his mother as an enabler who lacked self-confidence. Flores enlisted in the Army at age 19 and did a tour in the Gulf War. He separated from the service in 1992. At the time of the shootings, Flores was divorced and had two children ages 15 and 10.

Flores attended nursing school in San Angelo, Texas. He graduated with a degree in practical nursing and worked as a licensed practical nurse (LPN). Eventually, he enrolled in the College of Nursing at the University of Arizona. Flores indicated that he believed his relationship with the College of Nursing faculty was contentious from the very beginning. He felt slighted when the College of Nursing would not give him transfer credit for nursing classes he had completed in his practical nursing program. Flores also suggested that the faculty viewed registered nurses who held associate degrees as not being "professional" and that they viewed LPNs as not being "real nurses."

Flores had several confrontations with faculty during his two years at the University of Arizona. He was given a written reprimand by a clinical supervisor for improperly administering medications without direct supervision. In addition, he was given written reprimands for several minor rules violations during his clinical rotation. Flores viewed these confrontations as the reason he failed some classes and the reason he a failed clinical rotation.

The descriptions of Flores's relationships with fellow students and coworkers differ. Faculty members, including the victims, expressed concern with his potential to act out. Flores was described by students as being aggressive, mean, and having anger issues. In contrast, coworkers at the Veterans Administration hospital where Flores worked as an LPN described him as being very nice, intelligent, and soft spoken.

At 8:37 A.M. on the morning of Flores's attack, the first 911 call was received. Officers from the University of Arizona Police Department (UAPD) responded. At 8:40 A.M., 10 officers from the Tucson Police Department (TPD) also responded. Officers for the UAPD and the TPD were over-represented on the campus at the time of this shooting because both departments had responded to an unrelated student disturbance at the McHale Center ticket office. Officers from both departments had been trained in this type of emergency deployment, but officers had not been cross-trained. While officers were deploying, hundreds of students, faculty, and staff were exiting the building where Flores was shooting. Officers had to scan the crowd for a suspect as they entered the building and progressed to the fourth floor, where the initial shootings were reported to have occurred.

At 8:43 A.M., the police chiefs from both UAPD and TPD responded and set up a command center. Thirty-three additional TPD officers reported to the scene as well. Officers conducted a building search. At 8:52 A.M., two victims and the suspect were located in a classroom on the fourth floor. At 10:23 A.M., the third victim was located in her office on the second floor.

Flores had sent a "communication from the dead" to the *Arizona Star* prior to the events of October 28, 2002. This document explained the events in his life that precipitated the shootings. In his missive, Flores described himself as depressed. He indicated that he was falling behind in his bills, his child support, and his student loan responsibilities, and he was failing in his studies. Flores blamed the failures in his recent adult life on the faculty and staff of the College of Nursing at the University of Arizona. He summarized the events of October 28 as a "reckoning"—a settling of accounts.

Dennis Bulen

Further Reading

Buchik, N. (2002, October 30). 2 slain profs feared Flores. *Arizona Daily Wildcat Online*. Retrieved November 10, 2008, from http://www.wc.arizona.edu/papers/96/47/01_1.html

Flores, R. S. (2002, October 30). Communication from the dead. *Arizona Daily Wildcat Online*. Retrieved November 10, 2008, from http://www.wc.arizona.edu/papers/96/47/01_1.html

Zdziarski, E., Zdziarski, E. II, Dunke, N., & Rollo, M. (2007). *Campus crisis management: A comprehensive guide to planning, prevention, response, and recovery*. Hoboken, New Jersey: Wiley.

Free Speech

How much and which types of free speech and expression rights students in public schools and colleges have has been an issue of much contention, both publicly and in the courts. Generally, parents and administrators are cautious about allowing students to have the same free speech and expression rights as adults, suggesting that full freedom would lead to chaos and a hazardous educational climate. Civil liberties advocates, however, assert that students are citizens of the United States and, therefore, are deserving—with few limitations—of the same basic rights as adult citizens.

The U.S. Supreme Court heard the first school free speech case during the Vietnam War era. In 1969, the Court set a precedent with its ruling in the case *Tinker v. Des Moines Independent Community School District.* In this case, John Tinker (age 15), MaryBeth Tinker (age 13), and Christopher Eckhardt (age 16) wore black armbands to school as a means of protesting U.S. involvement in the war. Their action was in violation of a recently adopted school district policy prohibiting armbands. The students were sent home from school. Their families then filed suit, alleging the district's policy infringed on the students' free speech rights. The Supreme Court ruled in favor of the students, and issued the now famous line that students and teachers do not "shed their constitutional rights to free expression at the schoolhouse gate." Justice Abe Fortas expressed concern that schools were becoming too totalitarian. Many school officials were upset with this decision, which they saw as inviting problems and perhaps even violence.

The Supreme Court heard another important free speech case in 1986. In this case, Matthew Fraser gave a speech at an official school assembly nominating his friend for high school student council. The speech was full of sexually provocative double entendres, in which Fraser compared his friend to a penis. Approximately 600 students, some as young as age 14, attended the assembly, and many began hooting, making gestures simulating masturbation and sexual intercourse. The following day, the principal suspended Fraser for violating the district's rules on obscene or profane language and gestures. Fraser was given a hearing, per the Supreme Court's decision in *Goss v. Lopez,* and his two-day suspension was affirmed. The Supreme Court ruled in favor of the school, maintaining that students can learn only in a disciplined atmosphere. Because the event in question was a school-sponsored assembly, the school was allowed to limit Fraser's right to free speech. In this ruling, the Court drew on previous decisions [i.e., *Ginsberg v. New York* (1968), *Board of Education v. Pico* (1982)] to determine that the state had a legitimate interest in protecting students from sexually explicit, vulgar, offensive, or violent speech.

In 2007, the Court heard what was called the "most significant student free-speech conflict." Although, like *Tinker,* the 2007 case addressed protest speech, the protest led by Joseph Frederick was far different than that mounted by the Tinkers and Eckhardt. Frederick unleashed a 14-foot banner with the phrase "Bong Hits 4 Jesus" during an Olympic torch event in Juneau, Alaska, on January 24, 2002. According to reports, Frederick's aim was to get under the skin of his principal, Deborah Morse, and to get on television. Frederick had an ongoing feud with Morse, who had previously called the police when he refused to move from a commons area where he was reading and who reprimanded him when he refused to stand for the Pledge of Allegiance.

Morse saw the banner at the event, which was not held on school property, and confiscated it. She also suspended Frederick for 10 days. Frederick and his family filed suit, with the support of the American Civil Liberties Union (ACLU) and a host of other organizations, both liberal and conservative. The school district was represented by Kenneth W. Starr, who had become famous for his investigation of former President Bill Clinton. The district maintained that Frederick's banner encouraged marijuana use, which was obviously prohibited by school rules. Frederick maintained he was not trying to advocate drug use or even a particular message at all. Rather, he was trying to test the district's adherence to a student's right to free speech. The school district even admitted that Frederick's banner created no real disturbance at the torch event. School administrators disagreed, however, that the event was school sponsored. They claimed it was school sanctioned, given that the entire student body had been released to attend and that the school's cheerleaders and band performed at the event. The Supreme Court ruled in 2007 that Frederick's action were unprotected speech.

The ACLU regularly represents students involved in free speech challenges. For instance, in 2002, the group negotiated with a Massachusetts school district to end the punishment for a student who had held up a protest sign at a school talent show. It has supported students who were suspended for taking part in the *Vagina Monologues* play, and a student who sang a song about God at a school talent show, among other issues.

At the college level, one of the most recent issues to emerge regarding free speech has been the controversy over policies intended to limit racially or sexually offensive speech. For instance, the University of Michigan developed its policy on discrimination and discriminatory harassment in 1988 after several incidents of racial harassment on campus. Someone had distributed a flyer around Ann Arbor declaring "open season" on "saucer lips, porch monkeys, and jigaboos"—racially offensive terms for African Americans. A campus radio station allowed the broadcast of a racially offensive joke, and a Ku Klux Klan uniform was displayed outside a dorm window. The University of Michigan policy prohibited behavior that "stigmatizes or victimizes an individual on the basis of race, ethnicity, religion, sex, sexual orientation, creed, national origin, ancestry, age, marital status, handicap, or Vietnam-veteran status, and/or . . . that creates an intimidating, hostile, or demeaning environment for educational pursuits." A graduate student challenged this policy, arguing that it limited his right to discuss controversial theories abut biological differences. The courts agreed with this student, striking down the university's policy as overly broad.

Although schools and campuses are concerned that provocative speech can incite violence, they also worry that too many limitations might prompt revolts. More likely, however, is the prospect that excessive limitations on speech will lead to apathy. Recent research has demonstrated that few students are knowledgeable about their First Amendment rights. Critics maintain that this lack of awareness arises because school districts fail to teach students about these important issues and, even more, because they do not practice them. The consequences are disastrous, say critics, because students who do not know about or think about their rights will become adults who do not question inappropriate and unconstitutional limitations on the First Amendment.

Laura L. Finley

Further Reading

ACLU free expression. (n.d.). Retrieved from http://www.aclu.org/studentsrights/expression/index.html

Barnes, R. (2007, March 13). Justices to hear landmark free-speech case. *Washington Post*. Retrieved August 15, 2009, from http://www.washingtonpost.com/wp-dyn/content/article/2007/03/12/AR2007031201699.html

Dautrich, K., & Yalof, D. (2008). *The future of the First Amendment: The digital media, civic education, and free expression rights in America's high schools.* Lanham, MD: Rowman & Littlefield.

Hudson, D. (2009, April 22). Hate speech and campus speech codes. First Amendment Center. Retrieved August 27, 2009, from http://www.firstamendmentcenter.org/speech/pubcollege/topic.aspx?topic=campus_speech_codes

McMasters, P. (2005, June 5). When school grounds become free-speech battlegrounds. First Amendment Center. Retrieved August 15, 2009, from http://www.firstamendmentcenter.org/commentary.aspx?id=15390

G

Gambling

Young people are increasingly getting involved with gambling, especially males. Many are even developing gambling addictions. Research presented at the 106th Annual Convention of the American Psychological Association showed that between 5% and 8% of American and Canadian youth had serious gambling problems, compared to 1% to 3% of adults. The same research suggested that addictions to gambling may be worse than addictions to alcohol, smoking, and drugs. Antisocial behavior and frequent use of alcohol are also associated with increased gambling activity.

One of the largest studies of youth gambling, conducted by Dr. Randy Stinchfield and colleagues at the University of Minnesota, surveyed 122,700 sixth-, ninth-, and 12th-grade students in 1992 and then followed up with 75,900 of them in 1995. This study found that gambling behavior was relatively stable over the three-year period. The only change was in gamblers' preferences, which shifted from a preference for informal games to legal games, which corresponded with the students' increasing ages. Those who were heavier gamblers at the beginning of the study continued to be the heaviest gamblers during the follow-up period. Most of the students in the study had gambled at least once during the previous year, with rates far higher for boys (80%) than for girls (50%). Twenty percent of boys gambled weekly or more, while only 5% of girls gambled that frequently. Older students generally gambled more than younger ones.

Another study of 21,297 eighth- through 12th-grade students in 79 public and private schools in Vermont found that 53% of students had gambled in the previous year. Seven percent reported problems they attributed to their gambling. Males were again more likely to gamble. A host of negative behaviors were associated with gambling, including use of alcohol and illegal drugs, smoking cigarettes, not using a seat belt, driving under the influence of alcohol or drugs, being threatened, being in a fight, carrying a weapon, and engaging in risky sexual activity. Although one of the primary motivations to gamble is the hope of winning, sometimes youth gamble for other reasons.

Stinchfield and his colleagues concluded that some of the prevention efforts designed to curb adolescent drug use could also be helpful in curtailing or reducing youth gambling. The Vermont researchers suggested that medical and mental health professionals should include gambling in their assessments of youth.

Many college students are also involved in gambling. A 2005 study measuring rates of gambling among college student-athletes found that 24% claimed to have never gambled, but another 15% had a gambling problem. A review of college student handbooks found that gambling was infrequently included as a topic in these documents; only 22% of the 119 college handbooks reviewed contained policies on gambling. A 2003 study of college students' gambling found similar associations with negative behaviors as those found with adolescents. Compared with nongamblers, gamblers were more likely to binge on alcohol, use marijuana, smoke cigarettes, use illicit drugs, and engage in unprotected sex after drinking.

Online gaming has exploded in recent years, likely fueled by television coverage of poker tournaments and easy access to the Internet. This form of gambling is particularly popular with college students, who often play Black Jack or Texas Hold 'Em online. A study by the Annenberg Public Policy Center found a 20% increase in gambling rates from the same month a year earlier, with 57% of young men reporting that they gamble at least once per month. Experts suggest as many as half a million students could be addicted to gambling. They caution that few colleges are prepared to identify and help those students, given that many colleges see it as a harmless extracurricular activity.

Historically, many athletes and coaches have gotten in trouble for gambling on games in which they are involved. How frequently this problem occurs is difficult to measure, as data often emerge only after some type of scandal. A 2003 study by the National Collegiate Athletic Association (NCAA) found 63.4% of males reported some type of gambling, and that student-athletes were most frequently involved with gambling in the form of playing cards or board games for money, betting on games of personal skill, lottery tickets, slot or electronic poker machines, sports cards, football polls, or parlays.

In January 1951, the *New York Journal-American* reported on widespread point shaving in college basketball. Point shaving occurs when a player or group of players attempt to fix a game or match so that a particular team does not cover the published point spread, which helps those who have bet on the other team. In one scandal, Junius Kellogg of Manhattan College was offered $1,000 to shave points. Kellogg told his coach, who told the university president. The police got involved, telling Kellogg to take the offer so they could arrest the perpetrator, Henry Poppe, a former standout at Manhattan. A month after the Manhattan

College scandal, three players from the City College of New York were arrested for throwing games during the 1950–1951 season; only days later, three players from Long Island University were arrested for the same offense. Other point-fixing scandals in college basketball occurred in 1961, at Boston College in 1978–1979, and at Tulane College in 1985 with the indictment of eight players. One of the biggest football point shaving scandals involved Northwestern University in 1994. Other college gambling scandals in the 1990s involved the University of Maine, the University of Rhode Island, and Bryant College. In 1996, Boston College suspended 13 football players for gambling on college and professional sports, in violation of NCAA rules.

Laura L. Finley

Further Reading

Christianson, E. (2004, May 12). NCAA study finds sports wagering a problem among student-athletes. *National Collegiate Athletic Association.* Retrieved May 2, 2010, from http://www.ncaa.org/wps/portal/ncaahome?WCM _GLOBAL_CONTEXT=/ncaa/NCAA/Media+and+Events/Press+Room/News +Release+Archive/2004/Research/NCAA+study+finds+sports+wage ring+a +problem+among+student+athletes

Finley, P., Finley, L., & Fountain, J. (2008). *Sports scandals.* Westport, CT: Praeger.

Gambling takes hold of college students. (2006, March 10). *ABC News.* Retrieved May 2, 2010 from http://abcnews.go.com/WNT/story?id=1710705&page=1

Kerber, C. (2005). Problem and pathological gambling among college students. *Annual of Clinical Psychiatry, 17*(4), 243–247.

Labrie, R., Shaffer, H., LaPlante, D., & Wechslet, H. (2003). Correlates of college student gambling in the United States. *American College Health, 52*(2), 53–62.

Pathological gambling more prevalent among youths than adults, study finds. (1998, August 20). Retrieved April 29, 1010, from http://www.sciencedaily .com/releases/1998/08/980820075118.htm

Proimos, J., DuRant, R., Pierce, J., & Goodman, E. (1998, August). Gambling and other risk behaviors among 8th- to 12th-grade students. *Pediatrics, 102*(2), 23.

Shaffer, H., Donato, A., Labrie, R., Kidman, R., & LaPlante, D. (2005). The epidemiology of college alcohol and gambling policies. *Harm Reduction Journal, 2*(1).

Gang Resistance Education and Training (G.R.E.A.T.)

Gang Resistance Education and Training (G.R.E.A.T.) is a school-based program designed to prevent youth violence and delinquency—in particular, membership in gangs. Trained law enforcement officers provide instruction in public school classrooms. They also work with community youth organizations such as the Boys and Girls Clubs of America and the National Association of Police Athletic Leagues. Not only does this program help educate young people, but the collaborations forged in its delivery build important community relationships. Since the program it was created 1991, more than 10,000 law enforcement officers have been certified as G.R.E.A.T. instructors and more than 5 million students have graduated from G.R.E.A.T.

The G.R.E.A.T. programs include a 13-session middle school curriculum, an elementary school curriculum, a summer program, and training for families. Lessons focus on providing life skills to students to help them avoid using delinquent behavior and violence to solve problems. All G.R.E.A.T. instructors are sworn law enforcement officers who receive additional training on the G.R.E.A.T. curriculum at one of four regional training centers.

The G.R.E.A.T. umbrella covers a continuum of components for students and their families. Specifically, the elementary program, which consists of six 30- to 45-minute lessons, focuses on building positive bonds between students and law enforcement. Lessons cover bullying, discussing the role of offenders, victims, and bystanders; ways to communicate; strategies for cooling down when you feel angry; appreciating differences; and identification of adults who can help when needed. This elementary school program is typically implemented in the fourth or fifth grade.

The middle school program is designed for sixth or seventh graders and focuses more specifically on gang prevention. Students learn facts and fiction about gangs and violence and discover what they can do to help. They also discuss verbal and nonverbal communication, empathy, resisting peer pressure, and other social skills.

The G.R.E.A.T. summer program is flexible but is really intended to help reduce the boredom that leads many youth into trouble when they are out of school. Students might take field trips and participate in other outdoor activities or games in addition to receiving information about gangs, violence, and positive conflict resolution.

The family program takes place in six sessions. It is designed to help parents and guardians identify warning signs of youth crime and violence and resist participation in gangs or other deviant or criminal behavior.

The G.R.E.A.T. program was developed in 1991 by the U.S. Bureau of Alcohol, Tobacco, Firearms and Explosives (ATF) and the Phoenix Police Department (PPD). It was originally an eight-lesson middle school curriculum, but in early 1992, the Federal Law Enforcement Training Center (FLETC) joined the ATF and PPD to expand the program. The first G.R.E.A.T. officer training was held in 1992. By 1998, the La Crosse, Wisconsin, Police Department; the Orange County, Florida, Sheriff's Office; the Philadelphia, Pennsylvania, Police Department; and the Portland, Oregon, Police Bureau were all providing assistance.

In 1995, a five-year longitudinal evaluation of the G.R.E.A.T. program was launched. Results showed that students who completed the training had lower levels of victimization, more negative views about gangs, and more favorable attitudes about police. Researchers also found a reduction in risk-seeking behaviors, and increased association with peers involved in prosocial activities.

G.R.E.A.T. underwent an extensive program and curriculum review in 1999–2000. The review led to the addition of lessons, from eight to 13, and included more active learning. In 2001, the new curriculum was piloted in 14 cities nationwide and implemented nationally beginning in 2003.

Laura L. Finley

Further Reading

Esbensen, F., & Osgood, D. (1997). National evaluation of G.R.E.A.T. *National Institute of Justice Research Brief.* Retrieved May 4, 2010, from http://www.ncjrs.gov/txtfiles/167264.txt

Gang Resistance Education and Training: http://www.great-online.org/Default.Aspx

Gangs and School Crime and Violence

In the 1970s, only 19 states in the United States reported gangs and gang violence to be issues faced by criminal justice personnel. By 1995, however, all states as well as the District of Columbia reported gangs and gang violence to be problems. Roughly 4,000 cities, towns, villages, and counties now report ongoing problems with gangs. California, Illinois, Texas, and Florida are home to the largest numbers of gangs and gang members. This essay discusses the reasons why individuals join gangs, the pervasiveness of gangs and gang violence in the community and in schools, and prevention and intervention programs aimed at curbing the number of gangs, the number of gang members, and the rate of gang-related violence.

Before moving forward, it is important to establish a definition of a gang. Different jurisdictions have different definitions for gangs, and historically researchers have had trouble defining gangs due to the differences in the types of gangs and their activities. Additionally, every jurisdiction's gang problem is unique from the rest. Such a lack of consensus means that law enforcement agencies, as well as criminologists and sociologists, must select their own criteria for defining a gang.

Although the definition of a gang may vary depending on the particular jurisdiction or law agency, the following criteria are generally used to define a gang: (1) the group has a formal organizational structure, (2) the group has a leader as well as a hierarchy, (3) the group is identified with a specific territory, (4) the group's members have consistent interaction, and (5) the members participate in deviant and criminal offenses. This essay uses the definition of a gang or a youth gang, as defined by the National Youth Gang Center, is "a group of youth or young adults in your jurisdiction that you or other responsible persons in your agency or community are willing to identify as a gang." Motorcycle gangs, hate groups, prison gangs, and gangs consisting solely of adults are excluded from this definition.

Young people join gangs for a variety of reasons: to find a sense of belonging, security, respect, entertainment, peer influence, status, acceptance, and monetary success.

Although gangs date back hundreds of years, in the 1960s heightened concern in reference to violent crime in the United States began to come to the surface. In the 1970s, although not yet causing much alarm, gang violence and membership continued to rise. By the 1980s, more police officials, criminologists, and politicians began to focus on the illegal activities of gangs. In the 1990s, gang violence peaked and reached alarming levels. During this decade, gang activity was viewed as widespread, threatening, and on the rise. It was in this environment that gang officers were assigned and gang units were born. Moreover, research into gangs began, gang programs were created and implemented, and the U.S. Department of Justice created the National Youth Gang Center.

According to data gathered by a law enforcement survey, in 1991 there were roughly 4,881 gangs in the United States with an estimated 249,324 members. In 1994, more than 90% of the nation's largest cities reported youth gang problems, an increase of 40% since 1983. In 1999, 66% of large cities, 47% of suburban counties, and 27% of small cities reported active youth gangs.

According to the Violence Prevention Institute, 100% of cities with a population of 250,000 or more reported gang activity in 2001. That same year, 85% of cities with a population between 100,000 and 229,440 reported gang activity. Moreover, 65% of cities with a population between 50,000 and 99,999 reported gang activity, 44% of cities with populations of 25,000 to 49,999 reported such activity, and 20% of cities with populations of 2,500 to 24,995 reported gang activity in 2001.

In addition, 35% of suburban cities and 11% of rural cities reported gang activity in 2001. Also noteworthy is the fact that 56% of cities with populations larger than 100,000 reported either an increase or no change regarding numbers of gang members in 2001. A year later, in 2002, the Youth Gang Survey estimated that there were 732,000 gang members in the United States, a 5% increase over the number tallied in the previous year.

The mid-1990s until the early 2000s saw a slight decline in gang violence. In 2007, however, one-third of jurisdictions—the highest proportion since the 1990s—experienced gang problems. Within the areas surveyed, 86% of law enforcement agencies in larger cities, 50% of agencies in suburban counties, 35% of agencies in small cities, and 15% of agencies in rural counties reported gang problems.

Overall, roughly 3,550 jurisdictions served by city and county law enforcement agencies experienced gang problems in 2007. In that same year, there were a total of 788,000 gang members and 27,000 gangs in the United States.

These statistics convey the sense that gang violence is a serious issue in communities throughout the United States. Research suggests that teens and young adults who belong to a gang are far more likely to commit violent or serious offenses. For example, a survey in Denver concluded that while only 14% of teens were active gang members, that small percentage was responsible for committing 89% of the violent crimes in the city. Across the United States, crime trends indicate that the number of violent acts committed by youth gang members is increasing. The explanation for this rise of violence by youth gang members is simple: guns.

Beginning in the 20th century, rather than using a knife or fists as weapons, gang members began to use revolvers, semi-automatic weapons, and other powerful guns to commit violent acts. With the larger number of gangs, more fearless members, and ever deadlier weapons, gang violence began to soar, particularly in the 1990s. For example, in 1994, Chicago and Los Angeles alone accounted for more than 1,000 gang homicides. While gang homicides decreased in the vast majority of large cities between 1995 and 2000, homicides considered to be gang related increased by 50% between 1999 and 2002.

A 1998 study comparing gang and non-gang criminal behavior produced the following findings:

- 30.4% of gang members and 14.3% of non-gang members shoplifted
- 44% of gang members and 4.1% of non-gang members committed auto theft
- 51.1% of gang members and 14.3% of non-gang members committed other forms of theft
- 72.3% of gang members and 16.3% of non-gang members assaulted rivals
- 29.8% of gang members and 10.2% of non-gang members bribed police officials
- 40.4% of gang members and 2% of non-gang members committed drive-by shootings
- 15.2% of gang members and 0% of non-gang members in this sample carried out a homicide

According to the Violence Prevention Institute, 69% of cities with populations larger than 100,000 reported gang-related homicides in 2001. In that same year, 59% of all homicides in Los Angeles and 53% of homicides in Chicago were gang related. In Los Angeles and Chicago combined, there were a total of 698 gang-related homicides. In comparison, in 130 other cities with populations greater than

100,000 that were experiencing gang problems, there were a total of 637 such homicides.

In August 2005, there were 160 reported gang-related robberies and 59 attempted gang-related homicides in Los Angeles alone. Research indicates that in 2007, one in five of the largest cities reported an increase in gang homicides and about two in five reported an increase in other violent offenses by gang members.

In addition to being connected to violent crimes in the community, youth gang activity is correlated with serious crime problems in elementary, middle, and high schools in the United States. In schools attended by gang members, students have roughly double the likelihood of violent victimization of students in non-gang-populated schools. According to the Youth Gang Survey, among the respondents reporting gang activity in 2000, 95% identified activity within one or more high schools in their jurisdictions. Furthermore, a startling 91% reported gang activity within one or more middle schools in their jurisdictions. Moreover, According to an NCVS (National Crime Victimization Survey) sample of 10,000 students ages 12 to19, 26% of 12-year-olds, 34% of 13-year-olds, and 41% of 14- to19-year-olds reported gang presence in or around their school.

In a different study, 45% of a student sample reported being threatened or shot at on the way to or from school. In the School Crime Supplement to the NCVS, one-third of youths surveyed reported a gang presence in their schools in 2005. The majority of these gangs seen in schools are involved in one or more of the following types of criminal offenses: selling drugs, carrying guns, and violence. Additionally, compared with previous years, higher percentages of students reported knowing a student who brought a gun to school when gangs were present at school (25%) than when gangs were not present (8%).

In another sample of 1,279 schools in the United States in 2001, 7.6% of male secondary students and 3.8% of female secondary students reported belonging to a gang in the previous 12 months. Approximately 28% of gang-involved boys reported being threatened with a gun or knife that school year. Additionally, 5% of boys who were not affiliated with a gang reported being threatened with a weapon. For girls, those numbers were 18% and 2%, respectively.

Researchers have found that 40.4% of gang members, compared to 10.2% of non-gang members, bring a gun to school; 19.1% of gang members, compared to 8.2% of non-gang members, sell drugs in school. In addition, the National Youth Violence Prevention Resource Center reports substantial drug availability when gangs are present in schools.

Rebecca Ajo

Further Reading

Curry, D., & Decker, H. (2003). *Confronting gangs: Crime and community.* Los Angeles: Roxbury.

Dudley, W., & Gerdes, L. (eds.) (2005). *Gangs: Opposing viewpoints.* Farmington Hills, MI: Greenhaven Press.
Klein, M. (2006). *Street gang patterns and policies.* New York: Oxford.
Klein, M., Maxson, C., & Miller, J. (2001). *The modern gang reader,* 2nd ed. Los Angeles: Roxbury.
National Gang Center: http://www.iir.com/NYGC/
Shelden, R., Tracy, S., & Brown, W. (2004). *Youth gangs in American society,* 3rd ed. Belmont, CA: Wadsworth.
Worth, R. (2002). *Gangs and crime.* Philadelphia, PA: Chelsea House.
Youth gangs and violence. (2008, January 4). National Youth Violence Prevention Resource Center. Retrieved May 5, 2010, from http://www.safeyouth.org/scripts/faq/youthgang.asp

Gender and School Crime and Violence, College

Campus crime in general, and gender-based violence in particular, attracted considerable attention during the 1990s. This attention has continued into the 21st century. One of the highest-profile crimes involved the on-campus rape and murder of Jeanne Clery, a 19-year-old freshman who was killed in her dormitory at Lehigh University in 1986. Following Clery's murder, public persistence along with leadership by the Clery family demanded action on a national level. The federal response included several laws initially formulated in 1990 as the Student Right-to-Know Campus Security Act. The 1990 act was amended first in 1992 and again in 1998, and was renamed the Jeanne Clery Disclosure of Campus Security Policy and Campus Crime Statistics Act. Subsequent amendments in 2000 and 2008 added provisions for registered sex offender notification and campus emergency response. Moreover, in 1999, the Department of Justice awarded $8.1 million to 21 campuses to combat sexual assault, domestic violence, and stalking.

Colleges and universities are supposed to be safe places for personal and social growth and maturation, but violence on college campuses is commonplace. Sexual assault is a crime primarily against women and youth, and its occurrence on college campuses is not declining; crimes such as rape, assault, sexual harassment, stalking, and even murder are prevalent at such sites. Like domestic violence, gender violence that occurs on college campuses is largely hidden and often overlooked; thus these crimes are allowed to occur in secrecy and go under-reported, under-prosecuted, and under-punished.

According to the National Crime Survey, prior to 1987 sexually violent crimes, such as sexual assault, were infrequent and the rarest of violent offenses. Several studies have since identified the prevalence of gender crimes on college campuses—for example, the Department of Justice estimated that a woman has between one in four and one in five chance of being raped during her college years. The U.S. House of Representatives survey from 1987 discovered that 38% of college women had either been raped or were victims of felony sexual assaults. Ten years later, the National Sexual Victimization of College Women Survey (published in 2000) involving 4,446 women attending two- or four-year colleges reported victimization rates of 35.3 per 1,000 among college women in 1996–1997; of these assaults, 12.8% were completed rapes, 35% were attempted rapes, and 22.9% were threatened date rapes. Thus a college with 10,000 female students could expect to see more than 350 rapes per academic year—a finding with serious policy implications for college administrators.

A female college student demonstrates the use of a campus emergency call box. In an attempt to decrease the likelihood of a violent attack, various security measures are in place on college campuses nationwide. (iStockPhoto)

Although much national attention has focused on the use of drugs to facilitate a rape, alcohol continues to play a crucial role in many college crimes. Several studies have linked excessive alcohol consumption with sexual assault: Fisher et al. (2000) discovered that from half to three-fourths of sexual assaults on college campuses involved alcohol consumption by the victim, the perpetrator, or both. Abbey et al. (1996) reported that more than half of 1,600 women had experienced some form of sexual assault; of these assaults, 95% involved alcohol consumption by the man, the woman, or both. Koss and Dinero (1989) and Miller and Marshall (1987) noted similar findings in both of their studies. Miller and Marshall found that 60% of women who engaged in sexual intercourse had been using alcohol or other drugs, while Koss and Dinero listed alcohol use as one of four primary predictors associated with college women's chances of being raped. In interviews conducted by Kanin (1985), more than half of college date rapists felt their status would have been enhanced if they forced sex on the woman they drank with, while three-fourths reported getting a date high to have sex with her. Mailman, Riggs, and

Turco's 1990 survey of campus males and females about unwanted sexual experiences revealed that 3.2% of females were victims of unwanted attempted intercourse, and 11.5% experienced unwanted completed intercourse during their college years; for both men and women who reported attempted unwanted sexual experiences, more than half admitted alcohol was a factor. Furthermore, alcohol use was cited by the perpetrators in 55% of the sexual assault incidents and by women in 39% of unwanted sexual encounters. Moreover, 60% of college women who acquired sexually transmitted diseases, including HIV/AIDS, had been drinking at the time of their infection.

Other empirical studies suggest a strong association between alcohol consumption and sexual aggression on campus. A 1987 study of 635 college men and women that explored sexual aggression in dating discovered that 77.6% of women experienced sexual aggression and 14% unwanted intercourse; in comparison, 57.3% of men reported involvement in sexual aggression, and 7.1% reported unwanted sexual intercourse. Muehlenhard and Linton's 1987 study reported similar findings, including heavy alcohol use as a major factor for both sexual aggression and rape. In this research, among men who acknowledged committing sexual assaults on dates, 55% reported being intoxicated at the time while 29% were mildly high.

Dating violence is comprised of controlling, abusive, and aggressive behavior, and can include verbal, emotionel, physical, or sexual abuse, or a combination of these forms. According to Schwartz et al. (2006), dating violence is a major problem on college campuses that requires preventive interventions. Research studies have continued linked dating with gender violence: Edward H. Thompson found one in three college students has experienced or been an initiator of violence in a dating relationship in his 1991 research; Kerry E. Hannan and Barry Burkhart reported in 1993 that 25% of college men surveyed admitted to slapping, pushing, or restraining a female partner; the National Center for Victims of Crime revealed in 2006 that 32% of college students reported dating violence by a previous partner and 21% by a current partner; and Schwartz et al. discovered in 2006 that more than one-fifth of the undergraduate dating population was physically abused by their dating partners. Koss's 1985 survey about date rape at 32 colleges discovered that most of the rapes occurred on campus, and 84% of women knew their assailants before the attack. However, only 27% of victims knew that their sexual assault fell within the legal definition of rape; 16% thought what happened to them was a crime; 11% did not think a crime was committed; and a disturbing 46% believed they were victims of serious miscommunication. Additionally, one in 12 men admitted committing acts that met the legal definition of rape or attempted rape.

Sexual violence has a serious negative impact on the academic performance of the collegiate victim. For example, when sexual crimes occur, victims may drop out of school or at least stop attending for an extended period of time. In a study by Frintner and Rubinson in 1993, 37.1% of the women who experienced sexual assault reported a decrease in grade-point average after the incident. Ten other women reduced their course load, while three others suspended their studies.

According to the American College Health Association, stalking is also a concern within college communities. Stalking is the willful, repeated, and malicious following, harassing, or threatening of another person. Elizabeth Musatine and Richard Tewsbury's 1999 study of women attending nine institutions of higher education reported that 10% of female students said they had been stalked in the previous six months. According to Fisher et al. (2000), the most common forms of stalking behaviors reported by victims were being telephoned (77.7 %), the offender waiting outside or inside (47.9%), being watched from afar (44 %), being followed (42 %), being sent letters (30.7 %), and being emailed (24.7 %). Almost two-thirds of the sample admitted being stalked at least two to six times per week, while 13.1% reported having been stalked since the school year began. Victims also stated that the stalker either threatened or attempted to harm them in 15.3% of the incidents; in 10.3% of the incidents, the stalker forced or attempted sexual contact. The researchers noted that many women do not characterize their victimizations as a crime for several reasons: they are embarrassed; they do not understand the legal definition of rape; they are unwilling to accuse someone they know of being a rapist; or they blame themselves. Furthermore, many college administrators simply ignore the relatively high prevalence of stalking on their campuses.

Women have experienced violence throughout the history of higher education, but the murder of Annie Le in September 2009 at Yale University served as a recent reminder of how violent some institutions of higher education have become. Several other women have been murdered on campuses nationwide in the last few years as well: Katherine Rosen was stabbed to death at the University of California in Los Angeles (2009); a female student was killed at Northern Illinois University (2008); a 22-year-old female was murdered at Eastern Michigan University (December 2006); a second-year female student at the University of California at Berkeley was raped and murdered (2004); Susannah Chase was beaten and left to die in December 1997 at the University of Colorado in Boulder—and the list goes on.

While gender-based violence is endemic on college campuses, college administrators typically do not respond to sexual crimes, thus distorting crime statistics. These startling statistics of gender violence on campuses should serve as a wake-up call for higher education administrators. The unremitting prevalence of sexual assault against college women indicates a need for careful reflection by institutions of higher education regarding their policies related to deterrence of sexual violence on campus. Recognizing that a problem exists is the first step toward solving gender violence in higher education institutions. Examining institutional policies that are designed to protect college students from crimes may then lead to improved effectiveness in combating campus violence. Additionally, campus policies against sexual assault must be enforced and reflect a zero-tolerance response toward sexual assault against women. Moreover, campus-wide efforts to fight violence should target the entire academic community. It is important that women on campus become aware of violent crimes, take precautionary measures to prevent assaults, learn how to characterize their victimizations by understanding the legal definitions of sexual crimes, and learn the procedures to follow in such cases. Finally, efforts must be directed toward making sure that the response to, and prevention of, sexual assault is victim-centered.

Njoki-Wa-Kinyatti

Further Reading

Abbey, A., Ross, L., Ross, D., & McAuslan, P. (1996). Alcohol and dating risk factors for sexual assault among women. *Psychology of Women Quarterly, 20,* 147–169.

Fisher, B., Cullen, F., & Turner, M. (2000). The sexual victimization of college women. National Criminal Justice Resource Center. Retrieved January 21, 2010, from http://www.ncjrs.gov/pdffiles1/nij/182369.pdf

Koss, M., & Dinero, T. (1989). Discriminant of risk factors for sexual victimization among a national sample of college women. *Journal of Counseling and Clinical Psychology, 57*(2), 242–250.

Koss, M., Gidycz C., & Wisnicwski, N. (1987). The scope of rape: Incidence and prevalence of sexual aggression and victimization in a national sample of higher education students. *Journal of Counseling Clinical Psychology, 55,* 162–170.

Muehlenhard, C., & Linton, M. (1987). Date rape and sexual aggression in dating situations: Incidence and risk factors. *Journal of Counseling Psychology, 34,* 186–196.

Pezza, P., & Bellotti, A. (1995). The nature of the problem and its frequency. *Educational Psychology Review, 7*(1), 93–102.

Schwartz, J., Griffin, L., Russell, M., & Frontaura-Du, S. (2006, Spring). Prevention of dating violence on college campuses: An innovative program. *Journal of College Counseling, 9*(1), 90–96.

Gender and School Crime and Violence, High School

The issue of crime and violence in high schools cannot be fully appreciated apart from gender considerations. Gender is a significant factor in power constructs, especially among young people. Behavior among students both reflects the gender relations of adults in the current generation and shapes the gender relations of the next generation of adults. Furthermore, school crime and violence has special relevance to girls in many regions of the world. The World Health Organization (WHO) reported in 2001, "For many young women, the most common place where sexual coercion and harassment are experienced is in school." This article explores the impacts of gender-based violence in schools and efforts to combat this violence in schools both in the United States and abroad.

"Gender" refers not to biologically determined sexuality but rather to socially constructed notions about what it means to be male or female. The United Nations (UN) has defined violence against women as any act of gender-based violence that results in, or is likely to result in, physical, sexual, or psychological harm or suffering to women, including threats of such acts, coercion, or arbitrary deprivation of liberty, whether occurring in public or private life. While women are by no means the only victims of gender-based violence in schools, they are the primary victims, especially in schools outside the United States. Primarily female victimization is considered here. The alternative to gender-based violence in schools would be "gender safety," a term that refers to freedom from fear of gender-based violence physically, sexually, or socially throughout school premises, as well as equal opportunities for males and females to learn and acquire skills both in the classroom and in extracurricular activities.

Gender-based violence, as with any form of violence, stems from power conflicts. In American society, the notion that women should be quiet, passive, nurturing, and sexually naive is still very prevalent. Conversely, men are expected to be aggressive, competitive, and, often, sexually violent. In the United States, it is estimated that a woman is murdered by her spouse every 6 hours, physically assaulted every 15 seconds, and raped every 6 minutes. While these statistics may seem staggering at first, surveys of U.S. high school students reveal that more than half of those surveyed believed "that a woman dressed seductively and walking alone at night is asking to be raped." Furthermore, more than 20% believed that if a child older than the age of 12 suffered incest, the child could be responsible for the crime, and 20% believed there were circumstances in which men had the right to engage in sexual behavior with nonconsenting females.

Other studies suggest that such sexist perspectives on the part of students are not merely found in schools as one facet of society, but rather that schools serve as breeding grounds for gender inequity, hierarchies of domination and subordination, and gender-based violence that are experienced in broader society. Schools play both active and passive roles in furthering gender-based violence. Gender-based violence is actively promoted through inequitable treatment by teachers of males and females in the classroom, with studies revealing that males are much more likely to be called upon in class, to be held to high academic standards, and to be engaged in teacher–student dialogue than female students. Gender-based violence is passively promoted through a lack of response to sexual harassment and violent incidents among students. Studies have found that the majority of gender-based violence in American schools is perpetrated by peers, usually male against female.

Although females are most often the victims of violent incidents in schools, they are not the only products of a sexist and violence-based culture. Adolescence is a time of great peer pressure, as young people are learning their roles, socially and sexually in the larger world, and they are eager to fit in and find their place. Girls learn—through powerful media messaging and observation of gendered interactions at home and at school—that they are to be quiet, be submissive, and accept any abuse they experience because they probably deserve it. Conversely, boys are taught through these same venues to assert themselves, to speak up, and to dominate through their sexuality. The result is that boys and girls engage in a sort of role play, with each living up to the standards they feel have been set for them. For this trend to be reversed, schools, as one of the primary social institutions for shaping young people, need to stop their active and passive promotion of gender-based violence, and instead offer young people an alternative way of relating—one involving mutual respect, gender equity, and nonviolent conflict resolution.

Several initiatives to help reverse the prevalence of gender-based violence in schools are currently in use. A conference in Massachusetts titled "Sexual Assault and Adolescents: A Hidden Epidemic" brought together educators and public health officials to discuss four aspects of gender and school violence:

1. Violence limits options and robs individuals of the freedom to develop their full potential.
2. Violence tends to occur in cycles, resulting in a perpetuation of violence.
3. Violence is pervasive in society, and modeled as a solution to conflict.
4. Boys in the United States are acculturated to exercise power over others, and one of the ways this bias is demonstrated through sexual violence.

Solutions for these widespread social phenomena were discussed at the conference, and it was acknowledged that young women must be encouraged to know their own rights, protect themselves, and to have their self-esteem fostered in a school setting. Likewise, young men need to be challenged that what they have been taught are appropriate male behaviors, such as domination, entitlement, and objectification of women, are neither equitable nor appropriate; instead, they should be given a model of respect and equity toward others.

As bleak as the scenario of gender-based violence may seem in the United States, conditions abroad are in many cases far worse. The Deputy Director of the United Nations High Commissioner for Refugees (UNHCR) in Kenya was reported as saying, "How can a parent want to educate his daughters when learning institutions have become places and sites of rape and HIV/AIDS infection?" In many parts of the world, young women have only recently been granted the right to even attend school. But the battle does not end with getting young women into schools. In regions of sub-Saharan Africa and East Asia, in particular, although women are now allowed to attend school, they still face many obstacles. Many young women fear for their safety in school, as sexual assault from teachers and students is common. Such assaults have resulted in the spread of sexually transmitted diseases (STDs), especially HIV/AIDS. According to Human Rights Watch (2001), "Left unchecked, sexual violence in schools has a negative impact on the educational and emotional needs of girls and acts as a barrier to attaining education . . . Rape and other forms of sexual violence place girls at risk of contracting the HIV/AIDS virus [which has in turn] taken its toll on the educational system and disrupted education . . . especially for girls."

Furthermore, gender equity is far from fully realized in many of these regions. Many young women must exchange sexual favors with "sugar daddies" to obtain assistance with their schoolwork or school costs. A sixth-grade student in Zimbabwe reported that her teacher had proposed to her: "He told me that he loved me and I yelled at him. After that in class he tried to hit me or send me out of class for no apparent reason. The memory makes me cry every time I think about it." In the country of Botswana, where 10 free years of schooling is provided, 11% of girls say that they have considered dropping out of school due to sexual harassment from their teachers.

For those girls who stay in school, educational achievement may still prove challenging. Sexist perspectives that disempower women and give disproportionate control to men are still widely held. Many teachers focus on the boys in the classroom to the detriment of the girls. Even in classrooms where the teacher is equitable, the curriculum conveys messages of disempowerment to women.

Unfortunately, many victims of gender-based violence in schools choose not to report these crimes, as there are no real structures for redress. A teacher reported for perpetrating or allowing sexual violence in his classroom may be warned or transferred to a different school, but the scale of the situation calls for much greater measures to be taken. For instance, teachers need to be trained in gender equity and appropriate teacher–student interactions and equipped with curriculum that promotes an environment of mutual respect and equitable gender relationships. Furthermore, a system of redress, which provides not only support for victims but also standard repercussions for perpetrators, needs to be implemented.

Fortunately, several such efforts toward greater gender equity and decreased gender-based violence in schools are being executed. For example, the Story Teller Group in South Africa consists of teams of teachers and students who create comics about issues of gender equity and violence as they affect young people in school. An all-girl team and an all-boy team each produce a comic depicting their perspective. The two perspectives are then brought together and disseminated in theaters for the purpose of sparking discussions about gender equity. Also in South Africa, a nonprofit organization called DramAidE has collaborated with the University of Natal in an effort called "Mobilizing Young Men to Care," which helps young men envision alternative forms of "masculinity," and teaches respect and self-control; the same group has also worked with young girls, teaching them that they have a choice over what happens with their own bodies. In India, nongovernmental organizations are implementing Better Life Option programs, which seek to give boys aged 10 to 19 factual information about sexuality, masturbation, menstruation, and reproductive and sexual health, along with counseling and guidance in life skills and career planning.

Megan Barnes

Further Reading

Caterina, M. (1992). Conference on sexual violence and adolescents highlights need for treatment and intervention. Retrieved February 1, 2007, from http://www2.edc.org/WomensEquity/pubs/digests/digest-gbviolence.html

Clark, S. (2001). What social workers should know about gender-based violence and the health of adolescent girls. *National Association of Social Workers, 1*(2).

Leach, F., &Mitchell, C. (2006). *Combating gender violence in and around schools*. Sterling, VA: Trentham Books.

Robbin, D. J. (1992). Educating against gender-based violence. Retrieved February 1, 2010, from http://www2.edc.org/WomensEquity/pubs/digests/digest-gbviolence.html

Wellesley Center for Research on Women. (2003). Unsafe schools: A literature review of school-related gender-based violence in developing countries. Retrieved February 1, 2010, from http://www.wcwonline.org

Gender-Related Theories

Criminology has historically been an androcentric, or male-focused and male-centered, field. Early criminologists basically ignored female crime. Those who did discuss this issue considered it to be part of females' pathology or hysterical nature, as psychologist Sigmund Freud suggested. A theory is based on some type of data, which may be collected from actual subjects (in surveys, in interviews, or by other means) or through secondary sources (e.g., analysis of court records, historical documents). Historically, criminologists studied only men or analyzed data only from men in developing their theories.

Social disorganization theory posits that certain neighborhoods are more prone to delinquency and crime because they are disorganized or chaotic. Rapid change, as suggested by Emile Durkheim, can create this disorganization. The disorganization then leads to the breakdown of social controls that would otherwise serve to constrain crime. Although other criticism has been directed at this theory, scholars today note that all the data on which it is based came from studying male delinquency rates.

Similarly, Edwin Sutherland focused on male case studies to formulate his differential association theory. Sutherland's theory, which generally posits that crime, like other behavior, is learned, is one of the most influential in criminology. The same gender bias applies to Travis Hirschi's social bond theory, which is considered the most cited criminological theory. This theory describes which factors constrain or prevent crime, as opposed to which factors influence it. Hirschi posited that persons with strong social bonds would be less likely to offend. He articulated four qualities of social bonds: attachment, commitment, involvement, and belief.

In the 1970s, with the rise of the women's movement, criminologists began to pay more attention to gender as a factor in crime. In 1975, Rita Simon offered what has been called the liberation hypothesis. Simon asserted that, as women earned greater participation in the workplace, they would become more involved in certain types of crime. They would commit largely white-collar offenses, according to Simon. That same year, Freda Adler cited tremendous increases in the number of female arrests for property crimes—proof, she said, that women's liberation was indeed leading to more and different types of female crime. Critics contended, however, that her data might have been misconstrued. Given the relatively small number of female arrests, any increase looked dramatic. Further, crime rates increased in this time period for males as well. Additionally, critics argued that the increase might have been the result of increased police attention, not actual incidence.

The idea of female-oriented crime received new attention in the 1990s, as scholars, politicians, and pundits noted increases in female arrest rates. This time, female arrests for violent crime were up as well. Deborah Prothrow-Stith argued that because the United States is a culture that equates violence with power, women may resort to violence to obtain what they still lack.

Several theories were developed in the 1980s and 1990s that specifically addressed female crime. In particular, John Hagan's power-control theory sought to explain why rates of crime and violence are higher for males than for females. Power-control theory maintains that criminal behavior is influenced by family structure, which mirrors the wider patriarchal social structure. Most families in the United States are still patriarchal, in that they are characterized by fairly strict gender role division. Patriarchal families exert less control over boys than over girls, allowing boys to have more freedom and take more risks. In egalitarian families, which have become more common, Hagan speculated that delinquency rates would be closer for male and female members.

Some sources have pointed to sex-based hormones as the primary reason why males perpetrate more violent crime than females. Most studies have focused on male testosterone as a causative factor. Animal studies have repeatedly found those animals with less testosterone are calmer than those animals with more testosterone. Testosterone may predispose someone to react aggressively when challenged or threatened. Thus it is not just the hormone, but also the environment that matters when it comes to violence.

Outside the field of criminology, some social critics have called for greater attention to be paid to the fact that virtually all school shooters have been males. For instance, Jackson Katz has been a leader in arguing that male gender socialization contributes to violence in all its forms, but in particular to violence against women. He points out that popular culture and sports encourage males to be tough, aggressive, and powerful to be considered "masculine." In this milieu, violence against women and aggressive homophobia are regularly depicted as if they are laughing matters.

In many of the school rampages, the shooters' masculinity had been threatened, sometimes publicly. In a study of 28 random school shooters, all were found to have "overconformed" to a hyperviolent definition of power and masculinity. Sociologist Michael Kimmel has authored a number of books that make the connection between gender roles, patriarchy, and violence. Canadian shooter Marc Lépine stated that his reason for killing 14 women and wounding 14 more at l'École Polytechnique in Montreal in 1989 was because he felt women had been given preferential treatment.

Laura L. Finley

Further Reading

Brickman, J. (1992). Feminist lives, feminist deaths: The relationship of the Montreal massacre to dissociation, incest, and violence against women. *Canadian Psychology, 33*(2), 128–143.

Garbarino, J. (1998). *Lost boys*. New York: Free Press.

Katz, J. (2006, October 11). Coverage of the "school shootings" avoids the central issue. Common Dreams. Retrieved May 4, 2010, from http://www.commondreams.org/views06/1011-36.htm

Katz, J. (2006). *The macho paradox: Why some men hurt women and how all men can help*. Naperville, IL: Sourcebooks.

Kellner, D. (2008). *Guys and guns amok: Domestic terrorism and school shootings from the Oklahoma City bombing to the Virginia Tech massacre*. New York: Paradigm.

Kimmel, M., & Mahler, M. (2003). Adolescent masculinity, homophobia, and violence. *American Behavioral Scientist, 46*(10), 1439–1458.

Klein, J., & Chancer, L. S. (2000). Masculinity matters: The omission of gender from high-profile school violence cases. In S. U. Spina (Ed.), *Smoke and mirrors: The hidden content of violence in schools and society.* Lanham, MD: Rowman & Littlefield, 129-162.

Newman, K., Fox, C., Roth, W., & Mehta, J. (2005). *Rampage: The social roots of school shootings.* New York: Basic.

School shootings the result of crisis of masculinity, gun culture, professor argues. (2008, February 18). *Science Daily.* Retrieved May 4, 2010, from http://www.sciencedaily.com/releases/2008/02/080217133643.htm

Tonso, K. (2009). Violent masculinities as tropes for school shooters. *American Behavioral Scientist, 52*(9), 1266–1285.

Gill, Kimveer

At 12:30 P.M. on September 13, 2006, 25-year-old Kimveer Gill began unloading weapons from his car outside the campus of Dawson College in Montreal, Quebec. Gill was dressed all in black and wearing a trench coat. He briefly held a passerby hostage and made him carry a bag of weapons and ammunition, then began shooting outside the de Maisonneuve Boulevard entrance to the campus. Next, Gill proceeded to the atrium by the cafeteria on the main floor, where he readied himself in the corner next to a microwave oven. After firing a shot into the floor and then into the cafeteria, Gill demanded that all the students lie down on the floor. He continued shooting at them until police officers arrived, which was within three minutes of being called. At that point, Gill briefly took two more people hostage. He was shot in the arm by one of the officers, and then shot himself in the head. Officers tried to resuscitate him to no avail. In all, Gill killed one person, 18-year-old Anastasia De Sousa, and injured 19 others before he killed himself. Officers found a short suicide note on Gill's body.

Once people heard about the attack, nearby businesses went into lockdown. Two shopping centers adjacent to the campus were evacuated, as was the Pepsi Forum entertainment center, which housed an AMC Theater. Many evacuees fled to nearby Concordia University, which provided shelter, food, water, blankets, and phones. The university also put together a crisis counseling team to work with those who had been traumatized. Other students were unable or too scared to leave the campus and hid until they were escorted out by police with dogs nearly three hours later. Cell phone networks were jammed because so many people were trying to use them at the same time.

Gill lived with his parents in Fabreville, north of Montreal. A search of Gill's home found an apology note as well as a letter praising the Columbine High

School shooters, Dylan Klebold and Eric Harris. Investigations also revealed that Gill had obtained all of the weapons he used (a Beretta Cx4 Storm Carbine, a Glock 9-mm handgun, and a Norinco HP0-1 shotgun) legally. The young man was extremely interested in video games, and he regularly posted on the site VampireFreaks.com under the name fatality666. Gill's posts were scary, commenting on how "everything sucks" and displaying his "homicidal" mood. He was also a fan of the heavy metal band Megadeth, and had mentioned their song "A Tout Le Monde" on his blog the day of the shooting. When Megadeth performed in Montreal later that year, members of the group announced at the concert their horror over the shootings and stated that any linkage between them and Gill was unwanted. Gill had also posted several photographs of himself with various weapons, and claimed to be obsessed with guns. He described guns as "the great equalizer." Gill was also a member of a local gun club.

Former classmates at Rosemere High School called Gill a loner. After high school, he had enlisted in the Canadian Forces Leadership and Recruit School, but was deemed unsuitable for service and discharged a month later. He developed depression in the wake of this event, to which Gill responded by collecting firearms and spending hours at the shooting range. After the shooting, Gill's parents, who were both in ill health, expressed their sympathy for the victims and their families but asked for privacy amid the media onslaught.

Around the world, the shooting evoked images of the Columbine shootings. In Canada, however, comparisons were more often made with Marc Lépine's 1989 massacre of 14 women at Montreal's l'École Polytechnique. Canadian Prime Minister Stephen Harper called Gill's attack a "cowardly and senseless act of violence." Two years later, a study by the Fernand Seguin Research Centre of Louis H. Lafontaine Hospital and McGill University Health Centre documented severe post-traumatic stress symptoms among the Dawson College community. Most students who received psychological services after the shooting rated them as satisfactory, but some groups such as college support staff and cafeteria workers felt overlooked. The gunman who shot Gill in the arm, Denis Cote, was praised for his quick response, as were the other four officers who arrived on the scene.

Laura L. Finley

Further Reading

Authier, P., & Larouche-Smart, M. (2006, September 17). Killer's family sorry for deadly shooting. *Canada West*. Retrieved August 24, 2009, from http://www2.canada.com/topics/news/features/dawsonshooting/story.html?id=3fdeeb60-ae01-48dd-ac5c-04dd3442df72

College shooter Gill obsessed with guns. (2006, September 15). *CBC News Canada.* Retrieved August 24, 2009, from http://www.cbc.ca/canada/montreal/story/2006/09/15/aftermath-shooting.html

Kimveer Gill: Canada's angel of death. (n.d.). *Investigation Discovery.* Retrieved August 24, 2009, from http://investigation.discovery.com/investigation/internet-cases/gill/kimveer-gill.html

Montreal gunman calls himself "angel of death." (2006, September 14). *CBC News Canada.* Retrieved August 24, 2009, from http://www.cbc.ca/canada/story/2006/09/14/gunman-shooting.html

The Montreal killer was a death-obsessed Goth. (2006, September 14). *Toronto Daily News.* Retrieved August 24, 2009, from http://www.torontodailynews.com/index.php/WorldNews/2006091420montreal-gunman

A study reveals the extent of the psychological impact following the tragedy on September 13, 2006. (2009, June 29). Dawson College. Retrieved August 24, 2009, from http://www.dawsoncollege.qc.ca/?676A8D5C-8835-4C47-BB13-D0F4A59E9C8F&extendedview=1&extendedres=F1098DC2-3C1B-4B7F-94E0-AB8C15536F1E&parameters=modView:detail%7Centry:70728596-ED24-414B-A2DA-88F94DBACF95

Swift police action praised in Dawson College shooting. (2007, September 12). *CBC News Canada.* Retrieved August 24, 2009, from http://www.cbc.ca/canada/montreal/story/2007/09/12/mtl-dawsonshooting0912.html

Glen Ridge, New Jersey, Rape Incident

On March 1, 1989, a group of teenage males, including several student-athletes, lured a mentally disabled 17-year-old girl into the basement of the home of two of the athletes and raped her. One of the boys, Christopher Archer, brought the girl, whose IQ was 64, from the park where she had been playing basketball to the basement where twins Kyle and Kevin Scherzer lived. Archer had promised the girl a date with his brother, Paul, if she went with him. When they arrived, Paul Archer, the Scherzer twins, Richard Corcoran, Peter Quigley, and Bryant Grober commanded the girl to masturbate and then perform various sex acts on them. They sexually assaulted her with a broomstick and a baseball bat, and then threatened to tell her mother if she told anyone. Given the girl's mental capacity, said to be that of an eight-year-old, she did not reveal the incident for several days.

The boys, however, bragged about what they had done, and rumors began to circulate around the community. Eventually, the girl told her swimming coach at the special school she attended. The police were notified and officers questioned her as well as the boys she implicated. On May 24, 1989, the Scherzer twins, Peter

Quigly, and the Archer brothers were arrested and charged with several crimes each. Richard Corcoran was arrested a few months later.

As the boys awaited trial, the affluent town of Glen Ridge tried to make sense of what had happened. Many blamed the girl, claiming she was promiscuous and had previously exhibited inappropriate sexual behavior. Some students at Glen Ridge High School defended their classmates and athletic idols, and one even tried to trick the girl into admitting she had consented to the sex acts in the basement. Yet others defended the girl and pointed out that several of the accused had histories of violent and deviant behavior but had been allowed to act with relative impunity because of their status as jocks.

Christopher Archer and Peter Quigley accepted plea bargains and agreed to work with the prosecution to testify against the others. The defense tried to paint a picture of the boys as being wholesome and the girl as a sexual deviant during the five-month trial. The prosecution introduced evidence of rape trauma syndrome, the first time such evidence had been allowed in a New Jersey court. The jury deliberated for 12 days before finding the defendants guilty of various charges. Christopher Archer and the Scherzer twins were sentenced to serve at a juvenile detention facility. Richard Corcoran was never tried and actually won a $200,000 settlement against the Essex County prosecutor's office for malicious prosecution. The Associated Press reported in 2005 that he had shot his wife and another man and then killed himself at Fort Bragg, North Carolina, where he was a Special Forces soldier.

Laura L. Finley

Further Reading

Associated Press. (2005, February 7). Man from Glen ridge rape case kills self in bloodbath. *New York Daily News.* Retrieved March 9, 2011 from http://www.democraticunderground.com/discuss/duboard.php?az=view_all&address=104x3072655

Atkinson, A. (Ed.). (2009). *Battleground sports, volume 2.* Westport, CT: Greenwood.

Finley, L. (Ed.). (2007). *Encyclopedia of juvenile violence.* Westport, CT: Greenwood.

Finley, P., Finley, L., & Fountain, J. (2008). *Sports scandals.* Westport, CT: Praeger.

Laufer, P. (1994). *A question of consent: Innocence and complicity in Glen Ridge rape case.* San Francisco, CA: Mercury House.

Lefkowitz, B. (1997). *Our guys.* New York: Vintage.

Goss v. Lopez

In *Goss v. Lopez*, 419 U.S. 565 (1975), the U.S. Supreme Court held that a school must conduct a hearing before subjecting a student to suspension. Failure to hold such a hearing constitutes a due process violation under the Fourteenth Amendment. The Fourteenth Amendment guarantees due process and equal protection with respect to the laws of the state.

In the *Goss* case, nine named students, including Dwight Lopez, were suspended from school for 10 days for destroying school property. At the time, Ohio law allowed schools to suspend students without a hearing. Lopez testified that at least 75 other students were suspended on the same day. The events in question transpired at Marion-Franklin High School, where several students were actively engaged in protests against the Vietnam War. The school had been consumed by a general state of unrest in February to March of 1971. Tyrone Washington, another of the defendants, was accused of demonstrating in the school auditorium while a class was in session and refusing to leave when asked. As he was escorted from the auditorium, Rudolph Sutton physically attacked a police officer. All of the other named defendants were suspended for similar conduct.

No student was given a hearing to determine the facts of the incident. The students and parents were invited to attend a conference subsequent to the suspension to discuss the students' futures.

The appeal to the United States District Court for the Southern District of Ohio was initiated by the Columbus, Ohio, Public School System (CPSS), which was seeking to overturn the judgment in favor of the plaintiffs made by the lower court. CPSS lost its appeal, with the U.S. Supreme Court asserting that because Ohio had declared education to be a right, it could not deny this right to citizens without due process of law. The Supreme Court's decision largely echoed the reasoning of the District Court, which had established public education as a property interest requiring due process protection.

The Supreme Court went to great care not to overly burden school administrators with precise rules for the handling of suspensions. Its ruling applied to short suspensions, less than 10 days according to Ohio law, suggesting that more procedural safeguards might be necessary for longer suspensions. The Court also suggested that its decision would not place any more burden on school administrators than a fair-minded administrator would already assume to prevent unfair suspensions.

The majority opinion was written by Justice Byron White, with Justices William O. Douglas, Potter Stewart, William Brennan, and Thurgood Marshall joining the opinion. The dissent was written by Justice Lewis Powell and joined by Chief Justice Warren Burger and Justices William Rehnquist and Harry

Blackmun. The decision split along tradition liberal/conservative lines. Interestingly, long-time conservative Justice Harry Blackmun, who sided with the conservative faction in *Goss*, would go on to become the leading liberal on the Supreme Court.

Nick Sciullo

Further Reading

Goss v. Lopez: http://www.oyez.org/cases/1970-1979/1974/1974_73_898

Gun Control Legislation

In 1791, the United States Constitution was ratified. The Second Amendment of the Constitution states, "A well regulated Militia, being necessary to the security of a free State, the right of the people to keep and bear Arms, shall not be infringed." This amendment has since been debated in the courts and legislatures.

Over the years, the U.S. Congress has enacted a variety of legislation for the purpose of regulating the sales and possession of firearms. In 1934, Congress passed the National Firearms Act, which established strict registration requirements and placed a transfer tax on machine guns and short-barreled long guns. Four years later, in 1938, Congress enacted the Federal Firearms Act, which provided for the licensing of all manufacturers and dealers in the interstate commerce of firearms. Criminals were banned from either receiving or sending firearms in interstate or foreign commerce. Stolen firearms and those with obliterated serial numbers were barred from such commerce. In 1968, Congress passed the Gun Control Act, which prohibited mail-order sales and interstate sales of firearms by licensed dealers. This legislation also added convicted felons, persons who had been found mentally incompetent, and drug users to the list of persons banned from possessing firearms. Furthermore, it prohibited transfers of firearms to minors, limited access to "new" assault weapons, and set forth penalties and licensing requirements for manufacturers, importers, and dealers.

In 1996, the Lautenberg Amendment amended the Gun Control Act of 1968. This legislation expanded the group of persons banned from possessing firearms to include persons who had ever been convicted of a misdemeanor crime of domestic violence, including those whose convictions had occurred prior the 1996 enactment of the Lautenberg Amendment. In effect, the amendment made domestic violence a felony for anyone convicted of this crime. It also added individuals under a domestic restraining order to the class of persons prohibited from owning or possessing a firearm.

White House press secretary James Brady was shot in the head during the failed assassination attempt directed at President Ronald Reagan on March 30, 1981. Brady's efforts resulted in the passage of the Brady Handgun Violence Prevention Act of 1993. (Ronald Reagan Presidential Library)

In 1994, Congress passed the Brady Handgun Violence Prevention Act. It established a national waiting period of five business days for handgun purchases from a licensed dealer. This bill further required local authorities to conduct background checks on handgun purchasers. In 1997, the U.S. Supreme Court, in *Printz v. United States* (1997), ruled that the provision compelling state and local law enforcement officials to perform the background checks mandated by federal law was unconstitutional. The Court determined that this provision violated both the concept of federalism and the concept of the unitary executive. Justice Antonin Scalia opined that the Framers designed the Constitution to allow federal regulation of the people, not the federal regulation of the states. The Court also offered an alternative basis for striking down the provision, stating that it violated the constitutional separation of powers by robbing the president of his power to execute the laws; that is, the law contradicted the unitary executive theory. The Court did allow for state and local law enforcement officials to conduct the background checks if they so chose, and many continued to do so under appropriate state law.

Individual states have addressed the issue of citizens carrying concealed weapons, primarily handguns. "Concealed carry" is the legal authorization for private citizens to carry a handgun or other weapons in public in a concealed manner, either on the person or in close proximity to the person. As of February 2008, 48 U.S. states allowed some form of concealed carry. In 39 concealed-carry states, issuing officials may not arbitrarily deny a concealed-carry application, a practice known as "shall issue." Nine states have "may issue" or "discretionary issue" laws requiring the applicant to demonstrate a specific need for concealed carry. These "may issue" states range from "shall issue" in practice, such as Alabama, Connecticut, and Iowa; to "at the whim of local officials," such as New York,

Massachusetts, and California (where rural officials more liberally issue permits but urban officials seldom do); to "almost non-issue," in states such as Maryland and New Jersey; to "never-issue" Hawaii, where, although state law allows for the issuance of permits, officials choose not to issue them under any circumstances. As of July 2008, Wisconsin, Illinois, and Washington, D.C., had no provision for legal concealed-carry.

In 2004, Congress enacted the Law Enforcement Officers Safety Act. This legislation allows the "qualified law enforcement officer" and the "qualified retired law enforcement officer" to carry a concealed firearm in any jurisdiction in the United States. This law is subject to few state or local law exceptions (18 U.S.C.926).

In 2008, the U.S. Supreme Court ruled on a District of Columbia law that banned handgun possession by simultaneously making it a crime to carry an unregistered firearm and prohibiting the registration of handguns. The law further provided that no person could carry an unlicensed handgun, but authorized the police chief to issue a one-year license. In addition, the District law required residents to keep lawfully owned firearms unloaded and dissembled or bound by a trigger lock or similar device. The Supreme Court held that the District's ban on handgun possession in the home violated the Second Amendment, as did its prohibition against rendering any lawful firearm in the home operable for the purpose of immediate self-defense.

In 1990, Congress enacted the Gun Free School Zones Act (18 U.S.C. §, 922). This act made it a federal offense "for any individual knowingly to possess a firearm at a place that the individual knows, or has reasonable cause to believe, is a school zone." In 1995, the Supreme Court ruled on the constitutionality of this legislation. In the *United States v. Lopes* (1995), the Court held that the Act was an unconstitutional exercise of Congress's Commerce Clause power.

In 1994, Congress enacted the Gun-Free Schools Act (20 U.S.C.§ 8921). This act required that each state receiving federal funds for its schools pass a state law requiring local schools to expel from school for a period of not less than one year any student who is determined to have brought a weapon to a school.

In 2008, the state of Ohio passed legislation referred to as the Castle Doctrine (SB 184). A provision in this legislation allowed persons to convey firearms on school property if that person (1) is carrying a valid concealed handgun license, (2) is the driver or passenger in the vehicle in the school zone while immediately in the process of picking up or dropping off a child, and (3) is not in violation of the "improperly handling firearms in a motor vehicle" code.

The recent shooting incidents on college campuses have spawned a movement to permit those students, faculty, and staff who are licensed to do so, to carry a concealed firearm on campus. Georgia House Bill 915, also known as the "Second Amendment Protection Act of 2008," allows permit holders to carry a concealed weapon on college campuses. Colorado State University is one of the few campuses where students are permitted to carry concealed weapons provided they possess a concealed weapon permit. Its policy allows students with a permit to carry their handgun most places on campus, including classrooms but not residence halls. Arizona Senator Karen Johnson sponsored an amendment to Arizona's concealed carry legislation that would allow persons with valid permits to carry a concealed weapon on college campuses (SB 1214).

Since the ratification of the Constitution of the United States in 1791, the right of an individual to possess a firearm has routinely been addressed by legislative action and judicial ruling. While the Supreme Court ruled in *District of Columbia v. Heller* that a ban on handgun possession violated the Second Amendment, it left many issues unsettled. Further attempts by the legislature and the judiciary to define the rights of the individual within the guidelines of the Second Amendment will be forthcoming.

Dennis Bulen

Further Reading

Brady Handgun Violence Prevention Act of 1983, Pub.L. 103-159, 107 Stat. 1536.
Concealed Weapons, School Grounds, Arizona SB 1214 (2008).
District of Columbia v. Heller, 554 U. S. (2008).
Federal Firearms Act, ch. 850, 52 Stat. 1259 (1938).
Georgia HB 915, 08 LC 28 3829 (2008).
Gun Control Act of 1968, 18 U.S.C. § 924 (c), (1970), amended 1996: http://www.gunlawnews.org/GCA-68.html
Gun Free School Zone Act of 1990, 18 U.S.C. § 922(q)(1)(A) (1988 ed., Supp. V).
Gun-Free Schools Act of 1994, 20 U.S.C., ch 70 § 8921 (1994).
National Firearms Act, ch. 757, 48 Stat, 1236 (1934).
Ohio SB 184, 127th General Assembly (2008) (enacted).
Printz v. United States, 521 U.S. 898 (1997).
Right to carry. (2008). National Rifle Association of America, Institute for Legislative Action.
United States v. Lopez 514 U.S. 549 (1995).

H

Hamilton, Thomas

Thomas Hamilton was a Scottish school shooter who committed the deadliest mass homicide in the recent history of the United Kingdom. On March 13, 1996, Thomas Watt Hamilton, an unemployed 43-year-old former shopkeeper and Boy Scout leader, entered the Dunblane Primary School in the north-central Scottish town of Dunblane and murdered 16 children and one adult before committing suicide.

Hamilton first cut the telephone lines to the Dunblane School at an outside pole and then entered the school through a door adjacent to the gymnasium. He was wearing four holsters carrying two 9-mm Browning HP pistols and two Smith & Wesson .357-Magnum revolvers. He also carried 743 rounds of ammunition and was wearing ear protection on his head. After gaining entry to the school, Hamilton began shooting at the first teachers and students he saw in a corridor. He then walked into the gymnasium and opened fire on a class of five- and six-year-olds. The children were sitting on the gym floor in a play circle, and many died instantly with gunshot wounds to the head. Others fled in several directions. Fifteen children and one teacher, Gwen Mayor, were killed. At least one child played dead and was not shot.

Hamilton then exited the gymnasium and went outside to a playground. He fired numerous bullets into the outer wall of a mobile classroom in which other students were gathered for class. A teacher in the mobile classroom had directed her students to hide under their tables, so Hamilton's bullets struck only walls, bookshelves, and equipment. For unknown reasons, Hamilton returned to the gymnasium and fired his last shot into his own mouth, killing himself instantly. An investigation later concluded that Hamilton fired a total of 109 bullets in all.

Speculation circulated that Hamilton was motivated by shame or humiliation stemming from police inquiries into his suspicious behavior toward young boys at youth clubs he operated. Complaints had been made for several years that Hamilton had a perverse obsession with children, especially young boys. His summer camp business, which he operated in the early 1990s, catered to young Scottish boys in the area and often subjected the boys to rough exercises and militaristic regimentation. Hamilton was said to require the boys to engage in rigorous exercise with their shirts off, and he often photographed them. Letters by Hamilton before the Dunblane massacre indicated that rumors about him had caused the failure of his shop business in 1993.

Hamilton had never married and lived a relatively reclusive personal life. Although Hamilton had a clean arrest record, he was well known to police agencies in central Scotland. Central Scotland's Child Protection Unit had investigated complaints that Hamilton had committed assault, obstruction of justice, and multiple violations of the Scottish Children and Young Persons Act at his Loch Lomond summer camp, although no action was taken and no formal charges were filed. Less than two years before the Dunblane massacre, Hamilton had been confronted by police in Edinburgh, Scotland, after he was found with his trousers down in a "compromising position" with a young man.

In the aftermath of the Dunblane killings, numerous political leaders and British celebrities visited the site. A funeral for the victims was broadcast live throughout Great Britain and was watched by a high percentage of the population. The Dunblane Primary School gymnasium was demolished shortly after the massacre and replaced by a small garden with a simple plaque bearing the names of the victims. A larger memorial garden was created at the town's cemetery, where most of the murdered victims were buried.

Within six weeks after the shooting, an anti-gun petition with 705,000 signatures was delivered to the British Parliament. In 1997, a series of restrictive gun laws banned private ownership of handguns in the United Kingdom. These gun laws make England one of the world's most highly regulated nations in the world with regard to handguns. Even some of Great Britain's Olympic handgun shooting athletes must now train in Switzerland and other countries.

These historic political changes left many people asking whether the Dunblane massacre was exploited for political gain by politicians and gun control advocates. Conspiracy theorists have repeatedly suggested that Thomas Hamilton was a member of British Intelligence agencies, that the shooting was a freemason plot, or that he belonged to one of the Northern Ireland terrorist organizations. Such conspiracy theories have been fueled by the secretive nature of the investigations that followed the massacre. For example, the results of the Cullen Inquiry into the episode were only partially published, with a 100-year restriction placed on some of its findings.

Roger I. Roots

Further Reading

Bell, R. (n.d.). The Dunblane massacre. *TruTV.* Retrieved May 2, 2010, from http://www.trutv.com/library/crime/notorious_murders/mass/dunblane_massacre/index.html

Hodgson, M. (2008, June 5). Murray describes fight to cope with trauma of Dunblane School killings. *The Guardian (UK).* Retrieved May 2, 2010, from http://www.guardian.co.uk/sport/2008/jun/05/tennis.scotland

Lieberman, J. (2008). *School shootings: What every parent and educator needs to know to protect our children.* Yucca Valley, CA: Citadel.

Massacre in Dunblane school gym. (n.d.). *BBC.* Retrieved May 2, 2010, from http://news.bbc.co.uk/onthisday/hi/dates/stories/march/13/newsid_2543000/2543277.stm

Uttley, S. (2006). *Dunblane unburied* London: Book Publishing World.

Hamilton Fish Institute

The Hamilton Fish Institute on School and Community Violence is located at George Washington University in Washington, D.C., and housed in the Graduate School of Education and Human Development there. The Institute was established in 1997 through aid from the Office of Juvenile Justice and Delinquency Prevention, Office of Justice Programs, and the U.S. Department of Justice. It was named after U.S. Senator Hamilton Fish, Jr., of New York (1926–1996). As a senator from the state of New York from 1969 until 1996, Fish was a participant in the group that framed both the mission and the intellectual foundation of the Institute.

The Hamilton Fish Institute fulfills its mission by working with seven other institutions and projects around the United States. Since 2001, it has worked with the Boston Trauma Center, which offers counseling to children and their families in the eastern part of Massachusetts. Since 1997, Atlanta's Morehouse School of Medicine's Violence Prevention Coalition Project has been studying school violence in African American–dominated middle schools in Georgia. Eastern Kentucky University began working on its Violence Prevention Project with the Fish Institute in 1999; this project concentrates on rural high schools. Also in 1999, Syracuse University in New York State started a Violence Prevention Project to study urban school violence in the Syracuse City School District. In 1997, the University of Oregon started its Institute on Violence and Destructive Behaviors, which works with the Hamilton Fish Institute to "study the conditions, developmental processes, and risk-protective factors that are related to the prevention of violence, school failure, delinquency and other destructive outcomes among at-risk children and adolescents." Recently the Institute on Violence and Destructive Behaviors has been focusing on the study of teenage girls.

Two additional members of the consortium working with the Hamilton Fish Institute are the Stafford County schools in Fredericksburg, Virginia, and a research team at the University of Wisconsin–Milwaukee. Since 1999, the Stafford County schools have been looking at problems in both rural and suburban Virginia. The University of Wisconsin–Milwaukee and its research team joined the Hamilton Fish Institute in 2001. In collaboration with both the Milwaukee Public Schools and the Milwaukee Police Department, and with the Hamilton Fish Institute, they have created a Violence Prevention Curriculum for Adolescents that is being implemented and assessed in Milwaukee.

The Hamilton Fish Institute has also created, along with the Northwest Regional Educational Laboratory, 12 guidebooks in two series—*Creating Safer Schools and Communities* and *Providing Quality Youth Mentoring in Schools and Communities*—that are offered free to the public on the institute's website (www.hamfish.org). Besides developing these publications, the Institute has created programs for various schools on ways to deal with violence on campus. For example, it has successfully run programs for universities that train resident advisors in dormitories how to deal with either violent students or potentially violent students.

Scott Sheidlower

Further Reading

About the institute: About our name. (2007). Washington, DC: George Washington University, Hamilton Fish institute. Retrieved December 14, 2008, from http://www.hamfish.org/

George Washington University, Washington, DC: Hamilton Fish institute [Home page]. (2007). Retrieved December 13, 2008, from http://www.hamfish.org/

Publications: School safety and mentoring guides. (2007). Washington, DC: George Washington University, Hamilton Fish institute. Retrieved December 14, 2008, from http://www.hamfish.org/

Hate Crimes, College

Hate crimes have been defined as criminal incidents that are specifically motivated by bias. They range from threats to physical assault to vandalism and other property crimes. Experts say hate crimes differ from other crimes in that they are almost always perpetrated by young, white men as random, spontaneous acts against strangers; they are far more likely to result in excessive violence; and they generally involve more than one offender. Many perpetrators are "thrill seekers" who are looking for fun and peer validation. Others are more reactive, offending based on some perceived injustice connected to the targeted individual or group. Contrary to what many believe, and what is presented in popular films such as *Higher Learning*, most hate crimes are not committed by members of organized hate groups like the Ku Klux Klan or Aryan Nation.

Examples of college-based hate crimes in recent years include the drawing of racial epithets on students' dorm-room doors and in restrooms, burning of swastikas, parties where fraternities and other groups dress up and stage mock lynchings and "border control" actions, threatening emails to minority faculty members and letters to interracial couples, vandalism of worship centers, physical assaults, and more. College students are most likely to be victimized by other college students.

One difficulty in measuring hate crimes is that definitions and laws vary tremendously. In addition, the federal government began tracking hate crimes, through the Hate Crimes Statistics Act, only in 1990. In some states, gender and sexual orientation are included in the definition of such crimes, while in others they are not. Campuses may also be reluctant to label an offense as a hate crime, because doing so may reflect negatively on the school. Police are not always well trained in investigating hate crimes, especially those working on campuses. Further, if police are investigating a hate crime on campus, they may not report it to campus authorities. As a consequence, the incident may not be reported as a campus-based hate crime.

Additionally, many victims do not report hate crimes. A study by the National Institute Against Prejudice and Violence (NIAPV) found nonreporting rates between 80% and 94%. Students say they do not report incidents because they do not perceive them as being serious, they do not believe school officials would or could do anything, and they are worried about retaliation. Studies of gay and lesbian victims have found they are particularly unlikely to report hate incidents because of fear of additional attacks. Given these multiple issues with current statistics, Howard Clery III, Executive Director of Security on Campus, Inc., argues that it would be safe to quadruple the number of incidents found in law enforcement or campus-based reports.

One of the first studies of hate crimes on college campuses was conducted by the Federal Bureau of Investigations (FBI) in 1998. This study included 450 higher education institutions in 40 different states. Of the 450 institutions surveyed, 222 (49%) reported a hate crime on campus in 1998, with a total of 241 incidents occurring on campuses that year. The most common motivation for hate crimes cited in the FBI report was racial prejudice, followed by anti-Semitism, bias against sexual orientation, and "other" biases. The International Association of College Law Enforcement Administrators (IACLEA) also conducted a study in 1998, surveying 411 campuses in the United States. In this study, 88 of the 411 campuses reported a hate crime incident, with these campuses averaging 3.8 hate crimes in that year.

The Southern Poverty Law Center (SPLC), a leader in studying hate crimes and pursuing legal action against hate groups, suggests that hate crime rates are actually far higher. Its researchers assert that more than half a million college students are the targets of bias-motivated slurs or physical assault each year, and state that an incident occurs each day on college campuses. A major factor in this widespread prevalence is the tolerance for biased speech on college campuses. SPLC maintains that students on campuses hear racist, homophobic, sexist, or other biased-speech every minute. No campus is immune to the problem, with small and large, urban and rural, public and private colleges all experiencing hate crimes.

Similarly, Baltimore's The Prejudice Institute, which has studied campus-based "ethno-violence" for almost two decades, estimates that between 850,000 and 1 million students are targeted by hate crimes each year. Ethno-violence includes racial and ethnically motivated name calling, emails, phone calls, verbal aggression, and other forms of psychological and physical incidents. The NIAPV estimates that 20% to 25% of minority students are the targets of ethno-violence each year.

Some sources have argued that the problem of campus hate crime has been exaggerated. They cite examples where students have made false claims as a means of getting attention, such as when a group of African American students hung a black doll from a tree and then blamed the mock lynching on white students.

In the 1980s and 1990s, in response to increasing verbal and physical incidents, campuses began establishing discrimination and harassment policies. These policies came under scrutiny, however, as impinging on free expression and as overly broad. The U.S. Supreme Court invalidated some of these policies in *Doe v. University of Michigan* in 1989 and other cases. The Court did decide, in *Wisconsin v. Mitchell* in 1993, that states have the right to enact hate crime statutes that specify enhanced penalties for such offenses. These laws might provide a model for campus codes that authorize penalty enhancements for bias-motivated incidents

Experts have identified a number of factors that contribute to hate crimes, including lack of knowledge, the influence of peer groups, group rivalry, increased presence of minorities on campuses, and inadequate legal protection. In its guide titled "10 Ways to Fight Hate on Campus," Teaching Tolerance provides recommendations for student organizing against these factors, including meetings, vigils, marches, making ribbons, buttons, or other gear; offering support for victimized individuals and groups; and pledging unity. Students are encouraged to speak out and to condemn biased acts. Administrators are encouraged to develop clear codes of conduct for all persons on campus as well as protocols for handling hate crime incidents, to promote civil discourse, to respond swiftly when an incident occurs, and to offer courses and other programs that foster dialogue about rights, responsibilities, diversity, and other related topics.

Laura L. Finley

Further Reading

Downey, J., & Stage, F. (1999, Jan/Feb). Hate crimes and violence on college and university campuses. *Journal of College Student Development.* Retrieved August 22, 2009, from http://findarticles.com/p/articles/mi_qa3752/is_199901/ai_n8840639/

Hate crimes on campus: The problem and efforts to confront Ii. (2001, October). U.S. Department of Justice Office of Justice Programs. Retrieved August 22, 2009, from http://www.ncjrs.gov/pdffiles1/bja/187249.pdf

Sanders, J. (1998, September 14). Hoax crimes. *National Review.* Retrieved August 22, 2009, from http://findarticles.com/p/articles/mi_m1282/is_n17_v50/ai_21129275/

10 ways to fight hate on campus. (n.d.). Teaching Tolerance. Retrieved August 22, 2009, from http://www.tolerance.org/campus/

Tompkins, R. (N.d.). Briefing paper: Hate crimes on the college campus. School Violence Resource Center. Retrieved August 15, 2009, from http://www.arsafeschools.com/Files/Hate%20CrimesBP.doc

Willoughby, B. (2003, June 13). Hate on campus. Teaching Tolerance. Retrieved August 15, 2009, from http://www.tolerance.org/news/article_tol.jsp?id=780

Hazing, College

While definitions of hazing can vary, they typically include two main elements: (1) the initiation of new members of a particular group by more senior members and (2) activities that result in physical, psychological, and/or emotional harm. Hazing is a form of power exerted by senior members of a group over new members wishing to gain acceptance. This practice may also be referred to as initiations, initiation rites, and initiation rituals. Reports indicate that more than 80% of high school and college students experience some form of hazing in the United States. In an attempt to curb harmful initiation activities, 43 states have implemented legal statutes against hazing. Each of these states has its own distinct statutes that have variable definitions of hazing and different penalties for engaging in activities associated with hazing.

Activities involving hazing are difficult to police, as they often occur in private with few official reports ever being made. The secrecy of these acts also makes it difficult to gauge just how prevalent the problem is in colleges in the United

Fraternities, sororities, and school clubs set up booths during freshman week outside the University of Toronto. Although hazing among high school and college organizations can be fun, some forms can be dangerous to initiates. (iStockPhoto)

States. When reports are made, it is generally because the activities went beyond humiliation and psychological harm, and caused serious physical harm, even death. Reports indicate that at least 75 students have been killed, accidentally or otherwise, during acts of hazing in the United States. Hazing is difficult to stop because of its cyclical nature. New members of a particular group eventually become senior members, and they often duplicate the harm they received by hazing new members.

Hazing has a long history on college campuses in the United States. It is believed to have been started by fraternal organizations hundreds of years ago. Members of the Freemasons structured their organization in the form of lodges, which were also termed "rites." When new members went through an initiation process to join these lodges, they went through a passage into the rite. The Freemasons secret society formed a model for other secret societies and college fraternities. The first college fraternity in the United States was Phi Beta Kappa, founded in 1776. Since its establishment, college fraternities have flourished across the United States.

Hazing on college campuses typically occurs in three groups: fraternities, athletic teams, and religious organizations. More generally, hazing is common within the U.S. military. Hazing is not limited to these specific groups, as it can occur whenever new members attempt to join a group, such as in marching bands, social clubs, multicultural organizations, dormitories, and work settings. Fraternities often use hazing to decide who to initiate into their group. This practice is part of a selection process that is often rooted in the unique traditions of the particular fraternity. Such traditions are passed on from year to year and are difficult to stop regardless of the threat of legal sanction. In contrast, on athletic teams, hazing often occurs when new members, termed rookies, have already made a team. Hazing activities might be limited to the preseason, or they might persist throughout the entire duration of the season against first-year athletes. Although hazing is most common on team sports, it also occurs in individual-based sports such as tennis.

Hazing can take on many forms, with varying degrees of severity. Three main types of hazing can be distinguished: subtle, psychological, and violent. These categories are not mutually exclusive, however, as a particular act might encompass all three. Examples of subtle hazing could include deprivation of privileges, being forced to do meaningless tasks, social isolation, gossip, and name calling. The severity of these cases is typically minimal, although individuals can be emotionally harmed by such behaviors. Psychological hazing may include threats, verbal abuse, being forced to dress in opposite-gender clothing, sleep deprivation, and being forced to harass others. Violent hazing, the most severe form, sometimes results in criminal penalty or academic reprimand in many colleges. Violent hazing can include forced alcohol or drug consumption, ingestion of vile substances such as gasoline, public nudity, being forced to commit an illegal act, sexual prodding, and kidnapping. Violent hazing can result in serious harm, even death.

Institutional responses to hazing vary by state and by severity of the offense. In some instances, legal action is taken when police file charges against the individuals who perpetrated the hazing. This crime may be charged as a felony carrying the possibility of jail time in some states, or as a misdemeanor offense in other states. Each state, apart from a few, has its own legal statutes pertaining to hazing. The seven states that have not passed such legislation are Alaska, Hawaii, Michigan, Montana, New Mexico, South Dakota, and Wyoming. This does not mean that individuals who engage in hazing activities in these states are immune from civil and criminal liability; rather, it indicates that these states do not have laws that specifically address hazing.

Institutional responses to hazing might also be handled by the administration of the particular college where the activities took place. Most colleges and universities in the United States have a policy that strictly forbids hazing; however, many have provisions that do not bar athletic teams from engaging in such activities as long as they do not produce serious harm. Likewise, many state laws do not forbid hazing in college fraternities and on athletic teams. Disciplinary actions by school officials in instances of hazing can involve anything from a verbal reprimand to expulsion from the college or university.

Many theories exist as to why hazing occurs and the purpose that it serves. One theory suggests that it is used as a tool of solidarity to unite new members through the shared secrecy of the hazing activities. Another theory is that individuals feel more attached to a particular group if they had to work hard or endure pain to gain entrance into the group. Others propose that hazing is the result of a cycle of violence, whereby individuals haze others as payback for the harm that was perpetrated against them. Hazing has also been perceived as an exercise of power stemming from the inherent hierarchies present in the structure of groups; it can be explained as a power struggle for dominance and control within a group.

Other sources suggest that hazing exists and persists because groups are not provided with other viable options for initiating members into a group.

Curtis Fogel

Further Reading

Guynn, K. L., & Aquila, F. D. (2005). *Hazing in high schools: Causes and consequences.* Bloomington, IN: Phi Delta Kappa Educational Foundation.

Johnson, J., & Holman, M. (Eds.). (2004). *Making the team: The inside world of sport initiations and hazing.* Toronto: Canadian Scholar's Press.

Nuwer, H. (2001). *Wrongs of passage: Fraternities, sororities, hazing and binge drinking.* Bloomington, IN: Indiana University Press.

Nuwer, H. (2004). *The hazing reader.* Bloomington, IN: Indiana University Press.

Hazing, High School

Hazing is the process of initiating new recruits into a particular group by way of some challenge or request. These challenges or requests are intended to humiliate or degrade the new recruit. Hazing might include physical or emotional degradation, such as being denied privileges, being forced to perform menial tasks, being called names, and even being coerced or forced into performing of sex acts. Sometimes it involves one night of activity; in other cases, it may last for weeks. Many times, new recruits agree to participate because they want to be included in the group. Their consent, however, does not make the hazing acceptable. The military, fraternities and sororities, and athletic teams are all known to haze new members. However, it is not just these groups that haze individuals, in particular at the high school level.

Many dismiss hazing as trivial and even amusing, but it can actually be quite dangerous. Alcohol is often involved, which escalates the risk associated with this practice. Most schools and colleges ban hazing, but such regulations are difficult to enforce as there is often a "code of silence" whereby no one tells authorities what happened.

A study by researchers at Alfred University found that 48% of high school students who belonged to some group had been hazed. Of these individuals, 43% found the practice to be terribly humiliating. Most were hazed starting at age 15, and those in multiple groups endured multiple incidents of hazing. Although males tended to both haze and be hazed more frequently than females, females also reported such behavior. Those with lower grade-point averages were more likely to be hazed. Although hazing was most common among athletic groups, 24% of those involved with church-related clubs also reported being hazed.

Participants and the general public often defend hazing, saying it is not harmful and is an important tradition to increase group identity and unity. Experts counter that there are other, better ways to create unity among teammates or members in a group.

Although hazing is not often covered in the media, it has gained national attention when the results are particularly disturbing. Such was the case in 1988, when one sophomore was allegedly forced to insert his finger into the anus of another sophomore in front of 20 to 30 onlookers at a football camp for players at Lyndhurst High School in New Jersey. In 1992, teammates held a 15-year-old boy wrestler down while some sodomized him with a mop. He suffered internal bleeding and had to be hospitalized for a week. In 1996, team captain Travis Hawk pleaded no contest to a misdemeanor hazing charge after sodomizing several freshman football players with shampoo bottles at Alexander High School in Ohio. In 1999, one basketball player was expelled and six others suspended from North Branch High School in Michigan after they hit a freshman player in the genitals with a wire hanger, sprayed another with urine from a shampoo bottle, and forced another's face into the buttocks of an older player. Also in 1999, a football player from McAlester High School in Oklahoma suffered a head injury when he was jumped by a group of team members in the locker room.

Mepham High School in Long Island, New York, drew unwanted national attention when a group of football players sodomized freshman with broomsticks, pine cones, and golf balls. They also sprayed the young players with shaving cream, put powderpuff and gel in their eyes and hair, and ripped the hair from their legs and buttocks with duct tape. The older players had planned the assaults in advance of heading to the team camp where it occurred, bringing all the items they used with them as well as stereos to cover up the noise. The school board eventually cancelled the season and the assailants were charged with aggravated assault, kidnapping, and unlawful restraint.

Not long after the Long Island events, media attention was again drawn to a hazing incident. This time, the event involved females playing in an off-campus "powder football" game. Thirty-one senior girls were expelled after they kicked, punched, and beat junior girls. Some younger players were doused with urine, paint, fish guts, trash, pig intestines, and feces. In 2008, varsity cheerleaders at Morton Ranch High School in Texas bound and blindfolded junior varsity cheerleaders and then threw them into a swimming pool.

Laura L. Finley

Further Reading

Atkinson, M. (ed.). (2009). *Battleground sports, volume 1.* Westport, CT: Praeger.
Eriksen, H., Rogers, B., & Turner, A. (2008, November 20). Morton Ranch cheerleaders indicted in hazing. Retrieved May 2, 2010, from http://www.chron.com/disp/story.mpl/nb/katy/news/6120825.html

Finley, P., & Finley, L. (2006). *The sports industry's war on athletes.* Westport, CT: Praeger.

High school hazing. (n.d.). Alfred University Hazing Site: www.alfred.edu/hs_hazing

Nuwer, H. (2000). *High school hazing: When rites become wrongs.* New York: Franklin Watts.

Nuwer, H. (Ed.). (2004). *The hazing reader.* Bloomington, IN: Indiana University Press.

Stop Hazing: www.stophazing.org

Hazing Laws

Hazing can be defined as a rite of passage wherein new members of a particular group are taken through traditional practices by more senior members so as to initiate them into the next stage of their involvement in the group. The term "hazing" can also be referred to as initiations, initiation rites, and initiation rituals.

In the United States, 43 states have statutes against hazing. Each of these states has its own statutes, and collectively they use variable definitions of hazing and apply different penalties for engaging in activities associated with hazing. Despite these statutes, hazing remains a common problem in the United States, with reports indicating that more than 80% of high school and university students experience some form of hazing. The actual rates of hazing are difficult to gauge, as this activity usually occurs in private with few official legal reports ever being made.

Most legal cases involving hazing fall under tort law. Tort law addresses personal injury claims where compensation is typically sought. Compensation for personal injury caused by hazing is often sought either from the individuals who committed the act of hazing or from the school or governing body where the act occurred. High schools and universities in the United States have been held liable in cases involving hazing for appearing negligent or breaching their duty of care for their students.

Legal cases involving hazing can also involve criminal law. Criminal charges are often pursued that relate to the specific acts occurring during a hazing incident, such as physical or sexual assault. In Canada, other charges are pursued in all criminal cases involving hazing, as no legal statutes exist specifically to address this form of abuse. Such statutes do exist throughout most of the United States, although seven states—Alaska, Hawaii, Michigan, Montana, New Mexico, South Dakota, and Wyoming—currently do not have legal statutes against hazing including. This does not mean that individuals who engage in hazing activities in these seven states are immune from civil and criminal liability; rather, it indicates that these states simply do not have laws that specifically address hazing.

In the states that have legal statues pertaining to hazing, the intent and scope of the statutes can vary widely. In Illinois, engaging in hazing that is not authorized by an educational institution and causes serious bodily harm can result in a Class 4 felony, which typically results in a two- to three-year period of incarceration. In California, individuals can be charged with a misdemeanor for committing acts of hazing or for conspiring to commit such acts. The fine for a hazing misdemeanor in California ranges from $100 to $5,000, and the sentence can include up to one year in prison. In Nevada, a person committing acts associated with hazing is guilty of a misdemeanor if no substantial bodily harm results or of a gross misdemeanor if serious bodily harm occurs; the latter offense may result in up to one year in prison or a $2,000 fine. In Vermont, a statute exists against the perpetration of hazing, attempting to participate in an act of hazing, or failing to prevent an act of hazing; however, no predetermined penalty for these offenses has been established. Despite the existence of these laws, reports indicate that the presence, type, and severity of hazing statutes have done little to curb the prevalence of hazing in the United States.

Curtis Fogel

Further Reading

Guynn, K. L., & Aquila, F. D. (2005). *Hazing in high schools: Causes and consequences.* Bloomington, IN: Phi Delta Kappa Educational Foundation.

Johnson, J., & Holman, M. (Eds.). (2004). *Making the team: the inside world of sport initiations and hazing.* Toronto: Canadian Scholar's Press.

Nuwer, H. (2001). *Wrongs of passage: Fraternities, sororities, hazing and binge drinking.* Bloomington, IN: Indiana University Press.

Nuwer, H. (2004). *The hazing reader.* Bloomington, IN: Indiana University Press.

Honor Codes

The first honor code in America was established in 1779 at The College of William and Mary. It was created at the request of then-Governor Thomas Jefferson, who had graduated from the university in 1762. The code was to be policed by students. Jefferson went on to recommend a similar honor code at the University of Virginia (UVA), but it was never established.

UVA had a tumultuous beginning, rife with conflicts between students and faculty. These battles reached a peak on November 12, 1840, when professor John Davis was shot while trying to disperse a conflict on campus. He refused to identify his assailant, calling on any honorable persons to identify themselves. Shortly thereafter, in 1842, Henry St. George Tucker, an alumnus of the College of William and Mary who had replaced Davis on the UVA faculty, recommended that students submit their examinations with a signed statement declaring their honor and stating that they had received no assistance on the assignment. Although the wording of the honor code has changed over time, it remains in place today. Today, honor offenses at UVA include lying, cheating, and stealing. UVA's system is also unusual in that it remains student run. Only Princeton University has maintained a student-run honor code since its code was created in 1893.

At most colleges and universities, honor codes address only academic issues. The U.S. federal military academies (the U.S. Naval Academy, the U.S. Military Academy, the U.S. Air Force Academy, the U.S. Merchant Marine Academy, and the U.S. Coast Guard Academy) have the strictest honor codes. They govern academics, but also the cadets' behavior at all times, both on and off campus. A cadet is considered to have violated the honor code when she or he even tolerates another student committing a violation. Cadets must turn in the violator at all of the military academies, with the exception of the U.S. Naval Academy, as its honor code allows observers to confront the accused without formally reporting the violation.

A few universities have established very stringent honor codes. Hampden-Sydney College, an all-male school, has an honor code that covers student behavior on and off campus, and off-campus behavior can be prosecuted. It also considers toleration of violation to be a violation itself, just as the military codes do. Brigham Young University (BYU) also has a very strict honor code, prohibiting drinking, smoking, and premarital sex. Men must be clean and shaven, and no revealing clothing is allowed. The strictness and specificity of BYU's code reflect the Mormon influence at the university.

How honor codes are enforced differs from campus to campus. In many cases, students vote to ratify the code each year and can suggest changes to it. Some have a specific group that enforces the code, such as Haverford College's Honor Council. Research suggests that honor codes are effective when they help create a peer culture that reinforces ethical behavior. A survey conducted by the Center for Academic Integrity found that 23% of students at colleges with honor codes reported cheating on a test or exam in the previous year, compared to 45% of students at colleges with no honor code.

Honor codes do not fix all of a school's problems, of course. In 1951, an academic cheating scandal erupted at West Point, a school with a well-known honor code. At the end, 90 cadets ended up resigning from the academy, including 37 football players. All were found to have violated the school's honor code when upper classmen "tutored" them.

Research and reports documenting high levels of cheating at colleges and universities have prompted renewed interest in honor codes. In a survey conducted in 2005, approximately half of the college students admitted to at least one serious incident of cheating in the previous academic year, and two-thirds admitted to questionable activity, such as working in a group on assignments when directions specified the work was to be done independently. At the high school level, almost two-thirds of students reported one or more explicit incident of cheating in the previous year. A 2002 study of 12,000 high school students found 74% admitted to cheating in the past year. Author David Callahan has called the United States "a culture of cheats," asserting that individualism and cut-throat, competitive environments lead many astray.

Laura L. Finley

Further Reading

Callaghan, D. (2004). *The cheating culture: Why more Americans are doing wrong to get ahead*. New York: Harcourt.

Finley, P., & Finley, L. (2006). *The sports industry's war on athletes*. Westport, CT: Praeger.

McCabe, D., & Pavela, G. (2005, March 11). New honor codes for a new generation. *Inside Higher Education*. Retrieved May 2, 2010, from http://www.insidehighered.com/views/2005/03/11/pavela1

Houston, Eric

On May 1, 1992, 20-year-old Eric Houston, a former student, entered Lindhurst High School in Olivehurst, California. There, he killed three students and one teacher and wounded nine others with a 12-gauge shotgun and sawed-off .22-caliber rifle, before surrendering to police.

The day before his attack, Houston had called the principal at Lindhurst High, threatening to shoot up the pep rally that was to be held on May 1. The principal cancelled the rally. Houston came to the school at the end of the day and, upon entering the building, first shot his former Civics teacher, Robert Brens. He went on to kill 17-year-old Judy Davis, a student in Brens' class. Houston then walked outside the classroom and shot and killed Jason Edward White. He pointed his gun at a female student, but a classmate pushed her aside and took the shotgun blast to his head. Houston next went to a classroom containing 25 to 30 students and commanded a student to recruit more hostages so that the room ended up housing more than 80 people. He kept those students hostage for more than eight hours before he surrendered to the police.

Houston told the police that he was angry that he had failed to graduate from high school and had recently lost his job. He said he targeted Robert Brens because he had failed his Civics class. Houston was found guilty of first-degree murder on September 21, 1994, and is housed at San Quentin State Prison awaiting execution.

Lindhurst staff say that the incident is still what the school is known for, and they generally dislike media coming to the school to interview them after every high-profile school shooting. A film was made in 1997 that loosely follows the case. *Detention: The Siege at Johnson High* stars Freddy Prinze, Jr., as a student in the school and Rick Schroeder as the gunman who takes the school hostage after having flunked out. Some students at Lindhurst High School complained that the film makes it look like Robert Brens purposely failed Houston so that he would not graduate. They also complained that the assailant in the movie was named Jason, and that one of Houston's victims was Jason White.

Laura L. Finley

Further Reading

Detention: The Siege at Johnson High: http://www.imdb.com/title/tt0118969/usercomments

Mann, K. (2007, April 16). School shooting turns unwanted attention to Lindhurst. *Appeal-Democrat.* Retrieved May 2, 2010, from http://www.appeal-democrat.com/news/school-47104-shooting-eckardt.html

The shootings and siege at Lindhurst High School as told by the survivors. (n.d.). Retrieved May 2, 2010, from http://www.columbine-angels.com/lindhurst_story.htm

Human Rights Education

Human rights education aims to teach students of all ages about universal human rights, the treaties that guarantee them, and the work still needed to ensure all people receive the rights they are guaranteed. The United Nations Educational, Scientific, and Cultural Organization (UNESCO) calls human rights education an essential component of the right to education. It is most often included in high school or college social studies courses, although it can be integrated into a number of content areas. Many resources are available to educators seeking to include human rights topics in their courses, and to persons working in their communities to help ensure universal human rights. For example, a variety of websites offer curricula, news reports, training, research and evaluation, and networking on humans rights education. Most programs are based on the Universal Declaration of Human

Eleanor Roosevelt holds a poster of the Universal Declaration of Human Rights, an international agreement that she played an important role in crafting in 1948. (Corel)

Rights (UDHR), which was enacted by the United Nations in 1948. The UDHR includes 30 articles that articulate the human rights guaranteed to all, regardless of national origin.

Human Rights Education Associates is an international nongovernmental organization (NGO) devoted to training professionals and activists and developing materials to teach others about human rights. It provides assistance in developing curricula and materials; training for professional groups; research and evaluation; a clearinghouse of education and training materials; and networking for human rights defenders and educators. This NGO's website (www.hrea.org) links to the Portal for Human Rights, which offers resources for schools and educators, policymakers, and individuals seeking to incorporate human rights education into their curricula. It provides best practices and facilitates the sharing of resources. Another link allows visitors to access human rights courses, where interested persons can register to take a variety of distance learning courses on topics such as refugee law, the right to education, and gender and peace building. The report "Human Rights Education in the School Systems of Europe, Central Asia, and North America: A Compendium of Good Practice" is also linked to the site.

Human rights defender Amnesty International also provides human rights education ideas, materials, and resources. This organization's aim is to convey information about human rights as well as to inculcate values and attitudes that support respect for, promotion of, and defense of the human rights of all people. Through its website (www.amnestyusa.org/educate), this group provides online training on poverty and human rights, as well as an orientation to the work of Amnesty International and leadership training for new volunteers. A specific leadership program is available for college students, called Activate. In addition, Amnesty International has created film curriculum guides that can be used by classroom teachers, college professors, and other groups to facilitate dialogue about critical human rights issues. Guides cover the films *Blood Diamond* (about the global trade in conflict diamonds), *The Kite Runner* (about life in Afghanistan), *War Dance* (focusing on resilience during civil war in Uganda), and *Hotel Rwanda* (covering the Rwandan genocide and activists efforts to help). Amnesty International has also created curricula to go with the documentary *Intended Consequences: Rwandan Children Born of Rape,* and for the book *Stolen Voices: Young People's War Diaries from World War I to Iraq.*

Additional resources are available the Human Rights Resource Center through its website (http://www1.umn.edu/humanrts/edumat/).

Laura L. Finley

Further Reading

Amnesty International Human Rights Education: http://www.amnestyusa.org/educate/page.do?id=1102117

Human rights education: http://www.unesco.org/new/index.php?id=18683&L=0

Human Rights Education Association: http://www.hrea.org/index.php

Human Rights Resource Center: http://www1.umn.edu/humanrts/edumat/

Human Rights Watch

Human Rights Watch (HRW) is an independent organization dedicated to protecting and defending human rights across the globe. HRW aims to give voice to the oppressed and hold oppressors accountable for their actions. This organization conducts investigations and engages in advocacy that builds pressure on lawmakers and on the general public to support human rights.

HRW has operated for more than 30 years and has received Charity Navigator's highest rating of four stars. It was founded in 1978 as part of Helsinki Watch, an organization designed to support the citizens groups formed throughout the Soviet bloc to monitor government compliance with the 1975 Helsinki Accords.

Its members began using the "naming and shaming" approach, publicly describing human rights abuses in the Soviet Union and Eastern Europe, as a way to foster change. In 1981, during the bloody civil wars in Central America, America's Watch was created for the same purpose. In the 1980s, Asia Watch, Africa Watch, and Middle East Watch were added, until they were merged and took the name Human Rights Watch in 1988. In 1997, HRW shared the Nobel Peace Prize for its work as a founding member of the International Campaign to Ban Landmines, which was a leader in pushing forward the 2008 treaty banning cluster munitions.

HRW publishes reports on human rights issues across the globe. Its website (www.hrw.org) offers a search feature so that interested persons can browse by region or topics. General topics include arms, business, children's rights, counter-terrorism, disability rights, health, international justice, economic, social and cultural rights, LGBT rights, migrants, press freedom, refugees, terrorism, torture, the United Nations, and women's rights. In addition to regular updates related to each of these topics, HRW has published many lengthier reports and multimedia exposes. Each year, the organization authors the "State of the World's Human Rights" report and sponsors a human rights film festival.

In regard to schools and education, HRW authored an important piece documenting and critiquing the use of corporal punishment in the United States. Its news reports regularly offer scathing criticism of harsh punishments and abuse in other countries. Reports also document students' inability to obtain education in countries such as Israel and Pakistan, where fighting prohibits them from attending school. In addition, HRW has documented sexual abuse in schools, terrorist attacks against schools, and discrimination against students.

Laura L. Finley

Further Reading

Human Rights Watch: www.hrw.org

I

In loco parentis

In loco parentis is a legal doctrine describing a relationship similar to a parent's relationship to a child. In general, *in loco parentis* refers to an individual's or an organization's assumption of the parental status for a child—that is, it is the legal doctrine by which an individual or organization assumes the rights, duties, and obligations of a parent.

The most common usage of the *in loco parentis* doctrine relates to teachers and students. This principle has its foundation in English common law, where it governed the rights and obligations of tutors and private schools. The English common-law concept, in turn, shaped the rights and responsibilities of public school teachers. Under this understanding, the legal authority these individuals exercised over students was as broad as that of the students' parents.

The concept of *in loco parentis* has been a fundamental part of the educational system in the United States. Teachers and schools have assumed the legal authority accruing to parents, and exercised that legal authority over the children in their care. The courts have also defined some aspects of *in loco parentis*. In *Tinker v. Des Moines Independent Community School District* (1969), the U.S. Supreme Court ruled that conduct, either in class or out of class, that materially disrupts class and causes substantial disorder is not protected by the constitutional guarantee of free speech. In *Hazelwood School District v. Kuhlmeier* (1988), the Court ruled that the First Amendment rights of students in public schools are not equivalent to the First Amendment rights enjoyed by adults in other settings; that is, students' First Amendment rights have to be viewed in the circumstances of a school setting. In *New Jersey v. T. L. O.* (1985), the Court upheld the search of lockers by school representatives, ruling that students are not afforded the same right to privacy in a school setting as they would be if they were at their homes. Parents have the right to search their children's room and school administrators, acting *in loco parentis*, have the same authority. In *Ingraham v. Wright* (1977), the Supreme Court ruled that disciplinary paddling of public school students was not cruel and unusual punishment as prohibited by the Eight Amendment. The First and Fourth Amendments also been interpreted as offering less protection for public school students. The Court ruled that public high schools could utilize random drug testing to safeguard their students in *Vernonia School District v. Acton* in 1995.

In many cases, the courts have deferred to the school's authority to make rules and to discipline students. In doing so, they have made several points very clear in applying the *in loco parentis* doctrine to schools. The first point is that under this principle, speech rules and other school rules are treated identically. The second point is the *in loco parentis* doctrine imposes almost no limits on the types of rules that a school can set while students are in school. The third point is schools and teachers have tremendous discretion in imposing punishment for violations of the rules, as established in *Morse v. Frederick* in 2007.

Dennis Bulen

Further Reading

Blackstone, W. (1765). *Commentaries on the laws of England.* Oxford, UK: Clarendon Press.

Hazelwood School District v. Kuhlmeier, 484 U.S. 260 (1988).

Ingraham v. Wright 430 U.S. 651 (1977).

Morse v. Frederick 551 U.S. (2007).

New Jersey v. T. L. O. 469 U.S. 325 (1985).

Nolan, J. R., & Connelly, M. J. (1983). *Black's law dictionary*, 5th ed. St. Paul, MN: West.

Tinker v. Des Moines Independent Community School District 393 U.S. 503 (1969).

Vernonia School District v. Acton 515 U.S. 646 (1995).

Integrated Theories

In recent years, criminologists have begun to develop theories that address why and how juvenile delinquents may become adult criminal offenders. Referred to as integrated or developmental theories, this school of thought tends to focus on risk and protective factors and generally utilizes longitudinal studies to develop explanations for why some young people desist from offending and others do not. Most integrated theories also synthesize elements from various other theories.

One of the earliest studies of this type was conducted by Sheldon and Eleanor Glueck of Harvard University. In the 1930s and 1940s, the Gluecks carried out a series of longitudinal studies with samples of known juvenile delinquents using interviews and analyzing secondary sources of data. Comparing 500 delinquents with 500 nondelinquents, the Gluecks found that the most significant factor related to persistent offending was early involvement. Additionally, the most important factor relevant to a youth's likelihood of offending was the family, with children raised in large families, single-parent families, and those with limited funds or limited educational access being most at risk.

Decades later, John Laub and Robert Sampson reanalyzed the Gluecks' data. In a book called *Crime in the Making: Pathways and Turning Points Through Life* that was published in 1993, Sampson and Laub generally affirmed the Gluecks' findings. They then added to the field by developing what they called age-graded theory, which proposes that there are two critical life-turning points that enable young delinquents to desist offending: career and marriage. Further, Sampson and Laub maintained that people with the most social capital, or positive community and individual connections, were least likely to be long-term offenders.

Criminologists suggest that a positive relationship with family can break the cycle of juvenile delinquents evolving into adult offenders. (Katseyephoto/Dreamstime.com)

The Cambridge Youth Study—longitudinal research involving 411 boys from London who were all born in 1953—utilized self-reports, interviews, and other methods to identify life-course offending. The study identified several factors that were most related to desistance. Specifically, individuals with nondeviant families, shy individuals, persons with fewer friends at age eight, and those with a positive relationship with their mothers were least likely to persist as offenders.

Using longitudinal data, Rolf Loeber and associates developed a theory that identified three specific pathways from juvenile to adult crime: the authority-conflict pathway, the covert pathway, and the overt pathway. According to these researchers, stubborn behavior among young children becomes defiance or disobedience as adults in the first pathway. In the second pathway, minor acts of deviance—lying and shoplifting, for instance—lead to more severe acts of property crime. The overt pathway is the one most associated with violent behavior. Bullying, for example, is seen as leading to other forms of physical altercations.

Delinquent trajectories, a theory proposed by Terrie Moffitt, proposes that two types of offenders may be distinguished. Adolescent limited (AL) offenders generally engage in minor acts of deviance, but age out of such behavior when their peer group no longer is the most influential in their lives. Moffitt asserts that violence among youth in inner cities serves several important functions for this group, as it helps with impression management and the achievement of status (for young males, in particular), it helps young people acquire power, and it allows them to defy authority and command respect. Life-course persistent (LP) offenders persist in their criminal behavior due to a combination of family dysfunction and neurological problems. They often start with a small, sometimes undiagnosed, neuropsychological deficit such as a learning disability or behavioral disorder that goes unaddressed. Many LP offenders also persist because they fall into "snares" such as drug use or lack of education.

In 1998, Samples and Aber identified the most critical developmental task related to violence prevention at each of four developmental stages. At each stage, numerous social variables affect a child's successes. In early childhood (ages 2–5), the most essential developmental task is the development of self-regulation. The quality of caretaking influence a child's ability to self-regulate, but research confirms that small classes in school also make a big difference in this regard. During middle childhood (ages 6–11), the critical developmental tasks are the development of normative beliefs about aggression and the development of interpersonal negotiation strategies. Young people are aided in developing these skills when they are involved in family-like settings in which the individual can be an active participant and receive the acceptance and attention he or she needs. In early adolescence (ages 12–14), the primary developmental task is the development of prosocial peer groups. Samples and Aber found that most school-based violence prevention programs are still focused on the earlier developmental need and, therefore, on changing attitudes, rather than assisting young people with developing peer groups.

Many integrated or developmental theories focus on identifying risk and protective factors for young people. Risk factors are those individual, family, community, and other factors that make offending more likely, whereas protective factors are those factors that increase the likelihood of prosocial outcomes. Schools can either enhance risk factors or create climates that are protective. Research in the mid-1990s identified several characteristics of schools that help protect against crime and violence—namely, these schools help students develop a sense of caring relationships, encourage involvement and experiential learning, hold students to high expectations, and assist with remedial or corrective programs when needed.

Similarly, research on effective violence-prevention programs has identified several critical elements. Good programs must offer real challenges and targeted programs. That is, they must present information and scenarios relevant to the specific community. Given that power and endurance are highly valued by inner-city males, for example, good programs must incorporate ways to develop and demonstrate status and accomplishments. Development of group identity and organizational traditions is also essential, as is the opportunity to develop autonomy within a set of clear rules. Good programs feature family-like environments in which individuals are honored and valued, and the adults involved clearly show their commitment and personal interest.

Laura L. Finley

Further Reading

Elliott, D., Hamburg, B., & Williams, K. (Eds.). (1998). *Violence in American schools: A new perspective.* New York: Cambridge University Press.

Finley, L. (Ed.). (2007). *Encyclopedia of juvenile violence.* Westport, CT: Greenwood.

Loeber, R., Farrington, D., Stouthamer-Loeber, M., Moffit, T., & Caspi, A. (1998). The development of male offending: Key findings from the Pittsburgh Youth Study. *Studies in Crime and Crime Prevention, 3,* 197–247.

Moffit, T. (1993). "Life-course persistent" and "adolescent limited" antisocial behavior: A developmental taxonomy. *Psychological Review, 100,* 674–701.

Sampson, R., & Loeb, J. (1983). *Crime in the making: Pathways and turning points through life.* Cambridge, MA: Harvard University Press.

Sexton-Radek, K. (Ed.). (2005). *Violence in schools: Issues, consequences, and expressions.* Westport, CT: Praeger.

J

Jeremy

Pearl Jam's popular song and video about a boy who shoots up his school after being picked on was said to have influenced some school shooters. The video features graphic depictions of the rampage. Barry Loukaitis, who shot three people at his school in Moses Lake, Washington, was said to have been a fan of the song. Jurors were shown the video. Some have dubbed the video one of the most controversial in history, and MTV actually banned it after the 1999 Columbine High School massacre. Members of Pearl Jam claimed they were certainly not promoting school shootings but instead were calling attention to what can happen when kids are bullied and isolated and when no one responds.

Popular culture was often identified as the culprit in school shootings in the later 1990s. Listening to *Jeremy,* violent and misogynistic rap, the angst-ridden music lyrics of artist Marilyn Manson; playing violent video games; and watching hyperviolent movies such as *Natural Born Killers* was said to have influenced many of the shooters. Others pointed out, however, that this type of popular culture was widely consumed by many students who never went on to perpetrate acts of violence in their schools.

Laura L. Finley

Further Reading

Coleman, L. (2004). *The copycat effect: How the media and popular culture trigger the mayhem in tomorrow's headlines*. New York: Paraview.

Egan, T. (1998). Where rampages begin: A special report. From adolescent angst to shooting up schools. *New York Times.* Retrieved May 2, 2010, from http://www.nytimes.com/1998/06/14/us/where-rampages-begin-special-report-adolescent-angst-shooting-up-schools.html?pagewanted=all

Ramsland, K. (n.d.). School killers. *Tru TV.* Retrieved May 2, 2010, from http://www.trutv.com/library/crime/serial_killers/weird/kids1/index_1.htm

Journals Devoted to School Crime and Violence

A number of academic journals publish research and reviews about topics related to school and campus crime and violence.

Journal of School Violence is a peer-reviewed academic journal that aims to publish the latest theory and research relevant to preventing and responding to violence in schools. It publishes original research on the causes and correlates of school crime and violence, analyses of school policy and relevant legislation, and descriptions and evaluations of interventions and prevention programs. Recent articles have focused on teachers' perceptions of bullying, cyberbullying, evaluations of dating violence and sexual assault prevention programs, and bullying and teasing in middle schools. This journal serves as an important resource for educators, academics, and other professionals working with youth in school settings.

International Journal on Violence and Schools is a peer-reviewed journal founded by the International Observatory of Violence in Schools in 2005. It publishes articles relevant to school and juvenile crime and violence around the globe, offering a comparative perspective. Recent issues have focused on school crime and violence in Spain, Luxembourg, and Africa.

Journal of Peace Education publishes peer-reviewed articles describing theory, research, and practices in peace education. It is multidisciplinary and intercultural. Articles discuss such topics as conflict resolution, gender equality, human rights, cultural diversity, teacher professional development, and service learning.

Many other academic journals occasionally feature articles relevant to school and campus crime and violence, including Adolescence, *Contemporary Justice Review, Critical Criminology, Journal of Criminal Justice and Popular Culture, Journal of Youth and Adolescence, Social Problems, Violence and Victims,* and *Youth and Society.*

Laura L. Finley

Further Reading

International Journal on Violence and Schools: http://www.ijvs.org/
Journal of Peace Education: http://www.tandf.co.uk/journals/cjpe
Journal of School Violence: http://web.me.com/michaelfurlong/JSV/Home.html

K

Kent State National Guard Shootings

Nationwide protests against U.S. involvement in military actions in Vietnam reached a climax on the campus of Kent State University on May 4, 1970, as members of the Ohio National Guards opened fire on student protesters, resulting in the death of four students and wounding of nine others. Kent State students Allison Krause, Jeffrey Miller, Sandra Scheuer, and William Schroeder were killed during the shooting. Those injured included Joseph Lewis, Thomas Grace, John Cleary, Alan Canfora, Dean Kahler, Douglas Wrentmore, James Russell, Robert Stamps, and Donald Mackenzie. The actual shooting lasted only 13 seconds. However, this event marked the culmination of escalating tensions between Kent State students, the surrounding community of Kent, Ohio, and members of the Ohio National Guard, who were dispatched to the area to assist local authorities after a state of emergency was declared on May 1, 1970. The events of these four days in Kent had national ramifications, and today are viewed historically as a watershed event reflecting widespread sociocultural discontent during the Vietnam era.

The events leading up to the Kent State shootings are located within the larger context of the national anti-war movement of the 1960s, which was initiated in protest of U.S. military operations across Southeast Asia, the federal military draft system, and post–World War II expansion of U.S. military presence around the globe. In the event that triggered the Kent State protests and subsequent shootings, President Richard Nixon ordered U.S. troops to invade Cambodia in April 1970, effectively expanding the Vietnam conflict. This action was viewed by many as a direct contradiction of Nixon's 1968 campaign promise to deescalate and eventually conclude U.S. involvement in Vietnam. On April 30, 1970, before a live television audience, President Nixon advised the American public of his decision to invade Cambodia. The president explained the action as necessary to attack the

National Guard soldiers move up a hill on the Kent State University campus just before firing on students staging a Vietnam War protest. (Bettmann/Corbis)

headquarters of the Viet Cong, which was then located across the Vietnamese–Cambodian border.

Across the United States, reaction to Nixon's speech was immediate, taking the form of anti-war protests and demonstrations on many college campuses. At Kent State, a rally was quickly organized by students for noon on Friday, May 1. That day, students gathered on the University Commons, located at the center of the Kent State campus, to proclaim dissatisfaction with the Nixon administration and the further escalation of an undeclared war. During this protest, the students buried a copy of the U.S. Constitution to symbolically memorialize their view that the Constitution had been "killed" along with tens of thousands of U.S. soldiers who lost their lives in what was described as a military police action. Another rally was scheduled for noon on Monday, May 4.

Friday nights in Kent characteristically found students leaving campus and gathering in downtown bars and restaurants. The weekend of May 1–3, 1970, began in typical fashion, but soon mounting tensions between students and local police erupted in violent encounters. Although many specific details of the evening remain in doubt, certain actions on the part of both students and law enforcement have been clearly documented. A crowd of students gathered in the downtown area and an impromptu demonstration ensued. A bonfire was built in the street, bottles were thrown at police cars, and many buildings in the downtown area had windows broken out. The crowd grew larger as more students left the bars along "the strip" in downtown Kent and joined the demonstration. As the crowd grew, the demonstration moved to the center of town. Shouting anti-war slogans, the students directed their aggression toward businesses and institutions viewed as representing the *sociopolitical establishment* (e.g., law enforcement, banks and other financial institutions, utility companies). The crowd blocked traffic in the area for more than an hour, and Kent Mayor Leroy Sartrom called for assistance from county and surrounding municipal law enforcement agencies. Mayor Sartrom contacted Ohio Governor James Rhodes' office asking for further assistance and declared a state of emergency. He ordered the immediate closing of all bars, which caused even more students to be turned out onto the streets of Kent. The police, led by Sartrom, then confronted the students and ordered them back to the Kent State campus. Law enforcement officials finally succeeded in forcing the crowd to return to the campus with the use of teargas and nightsticks. Before the night was over, representatives from the Ohio National Guard were on their way to Kent.

The next day, Saturday, May 2, Sartrom met with other city officials and a representative of the Ohio National Guard. It was decided that Sartrom would make an official request to Governor Rhodes and that members of the Ohio National Guard would be dispatched to Kent. A dusk-to-dawn curfew was put in place, and students were restricted to the Kent Sate campus. Tension continued to mount as city officials assessed damages from the Friday night demonstration. Rumors continued to swirl that radical activists on the Kent State campus were planning further hostile acts. Reserve Officer Training Corps (ROTC) programs on many college campuses had become prime targets for violence over the years during the Vietnam anti-war movement, and Kent officials feared the same on the campus of Kent State.

On Saturday evening, students again gathered on the University Commons. By 10 o'clock, the Ohio National Guard had arrived to confront the more than 1,000 students at the demonstration. At this time, the ROTC building, adjacent to the Commons, was engulfed in flames and would eventually burn to the ground. Confrontations between students and Guardsmen continued throughout the night. Students cheered the burning of the ROTC building as Guardsmen attempted to disperse the crowd with teargas. In the mayhem, fire fighters were unable to reach the burning building, numerous students were arrested, and the campus was rapidly turning into a war-zone-like atmosphere.

Sunday morning (May 3, 1970) dawned with the campus of Kent State University under full occupation by the Ohio National Guard. Although there were reports of instances between students and Guardsmen engaging in small pleasantries, the overall campus atmosphere was charged with hostility amid anxious tension. City and state officials took advantage of the quiet day to speak with media. Ohio Governor Rhodes, who was also campaigning for a U.S. Senate seat on a platform of "law and order," came to Kent. During a news conference, he stated that the violence experienced that weekend in Kent was the handiwork of radical, highly organized revolutionists who were determined to "destroy higher education in Ohio." Rhodes also called the campus protesters the "worst type of people in America" and warned that "whatever force necessary" would be used against them.

During this press conference, Rhodes stated that he would seek a court order declaring a state of emergency. This step was never taken. Nevertheless, Rhodes' statement provided the platform for city officials, along with University officials, to presume a state of martial law had been declared, so that the Ohio National Guard was in lawful control of the campus. Such martial control would prohibit further free assemblies on campus.

On Sunday evening, tensions escalated once again, with students gathering on the Commons near the Victory Bell. Guard officials announced an immediate curfew and demanded that the crowd disperse. Around nine o'clock, the Ohio Riot Act was read to the students as helicopters dropped teargas into the crowd. Throughout the night, helicopters equipped with searchlights monitored student movements as teargas filtered throughout the campus. Students not honoring the new curfew were arrested.

On the morning of Monday, May 4, students moved forward with plans to hold the previously announced anti-war rally, scheduled for noon on the Commons. University officials attempted to stop this demonstration by distributing 12,000 leaflets to students explaining that all rallies were banned as long as the Ohio National Guard was in control of the campus. In defiance of this order, students started to gather on the Commons as early as 11 A.M. By noon, an estimated 3,000 Kent State students filled the Commons, now mostly in protest of the Ohio National Guard occupation of their university. The landscape of the Kent State campus that morning is generally considered as follows: approximately 500 students gathered on the Commons near the Victory Bell, another 1,000 students gathered in support of the active demonstrators, 1,500 additional students gathered around the perimeter of the Commons, and across the Commons, at the burned-out ROTC building, approximately 100 Ohio National Guardsmen armed with M-1 rifles.

The Guardsmen were under the command of General Robert Canterbury, who made the decision shortly before noon to order the students to disperse. A Kent State police officer made the announcement to the crowd using a bullhorn while standing by the Guard. The announcement had no effect on the crowd. The Kent

State officer was then driven across the Commons, in a Jeep and under Guard escort, announcing the rally was illegal and demanding that the students leave immediately. The crowd grew openly angry and the military jeep retreated. General Canterbury ordered his men to lock and load their weapons, and teargas was fired into the crowd assembled closest to the Victory Bell. Guardsmen then began a march across the Commons to disperse the crowd. The crowd moved off the Commons and up the steep hill known as Blanket Hill and down the other side toward Prentice Hall. Prentice Hall is adjacent to the football practice field, which is surrounded by a fence. Soon, the Guardsmen following the students found themselves more or less trapped by the fence. Hostilities between students and Guard members (e.g., rock throwing, shouting, and name calling) continued to escalate. After approximately 10 minutes, the Guard began to retrace their forward movement back up Blanket Hill. As they reached the top, 28 Guardsmen turned and opened fire on the protestors. Some shot into the air, while others shot directly into the crowd of students: 61 to 67 shots were fired in 13 seconds. In the end, four Kent State students lay dead, with nine more students wounded.

In the aftermath of the Kent State shootings, the university was immediately ordered closed by Kent State President Robert White and classes did not resume until the summer of 1970. Students and faculty members worked together to fulfill the semester class requirements for those enrolled in the university during the spring of 1970. The legal aftermath did not conclude until 1979, when an out-of-court settlement was reached between 28 defendants and the families of the dead and wounded. Part of this settlement included a letter of regret signed by the defendants in the case.

The question remains today: Why did the Guardsmen fire live ammunition into the crowd of students? Two different and competing conclusions have been reached: (1) The Guardsmen fired in self-defense, and (2) the Guardsmen were not in immediate danger and, therefore, were unjustified in discharging their weapons. Numerous studies and analyses of the shootings have been conducted over the years, and many books, articles, and collections of personal accounts have been published. In retrospect, scholars of the Kent State tragedy have identified several main themes associated with this incident. First, Kent State has come to symbolize a great sociocultural divide within the United States throughout the time known as the Vietnam era. Second, the United States has not completely healed from the wounds created during this period in its history.

Ideally, we can learn from the past, including painful incidents such as the Kent State shootings. As we seek better resolutions for conflict in the future, the lessons learned from Kent State can lead to better outcomes. In this case, the lives lost by four Kent State students will not have been in vain.

Karen Lindsey

Further Reading

Bills, S. (1988). *Kent State/May 4: Echoes through a decade*. Kent, OH: Kent State University Press.

Federal Bureau of Investigation. (n.d.). The shootings at Kent State. Retrieved from http://foia.fbi.gov/foiaindex/kentstat.htm

The Kent State May 4th Center, Kent, OH: http://www.may4.org/

Lewis, J., & Hensley, T. (1998, Summer). The May 4 shootings at Kent State University: The search for historical accuracy. Also published in revised form by the Ohio Council for *Social Studies Review, 34*(1), 9–21.

The May 4th Collection: Kent State University Library: http://www.library.kent.edu/page/11247

The May 4th Collection: Oral History Project: Kent State University Library: http://speccoll.library.kent.edu/4may70/oralhistory/129.html

Report of the President's Commission of Campus Unrest. (1970). Washington, DC: U.S. Government Printing Office. Reprint Edition by Arno Press.

King, Lawrence

On February 12, 2008, 15-year-old Lawrence "Larry" King was shot dead at E. O. Green Junior High School in Oxnard, California. Fellow student Brandon McInerney, who was 14 years old at the time, shot King twice. King did not die immediately, but rather was kept on life support for two days before dying from the head injuries he sustained.

King was small, just 5 feet 1 inch tall. He also stood out because he would regularly dress in women's clothing and accessories. He often wore make-up and stilettos to school. King was considered a troubled child. His biological mother was a drug user and his father had no presence in his life. He was suffering from signs of neglect when Greg and Dawn King adopted him at age two. King suffered from a speech impediment and was required to repeat first grade due to reading troubles. Although he was generally known as a gentle child, he got in trouble when he was young for shoplifting. At that time, he was diagnosed with reactive attachment disorder. This rare condition afflicts children who never form needed attachments with their parents or caregivers. King was also prescribed medication for attention-deficit/hyperactivity disorder (ADHD).

By the time King entered third grade at Hathaway Elementary School, children had noticed his effeminate ways and began asking King if he was gay. King told them he was. Classmates bullied and harassed him. One girl started a "burn book"—a notebook of gossip and slander, as described in the film *Mean Girls* (2004)—that detailed a variety of allegations about King, many of them false.

At the end of the book, the girl wrote that she hated King and wished him dead. The Kings were alerted to this threat and decided to transfer Larry to another elementary school.

King's life seemed to improve when he entered E. O. Green Junior High School. He had a circle of friends (a group of girls) who liked him and did not judge him. He was still pushed around in gym class and in the locker room, however, and the situation worsened when he began showing up in women's clothes. King also continued to act out. He vandalized a tractor with a razor blade, and at age 12 was put on probation and required to enter counseling. Larry began telling people that Greg King was abusing him. Although Greg denied that he ever hit Larry, King was removed from the home in November 2007 and placed in a group home and treatment center five miles away, in Camarillo. He continued to attend E. O. Green Junior High.

Although things seemed to go well at first, King had some difficulties with other students at the school. King flaunted his cross-dressing in ways that made other students uncomfortable, but school officials knew they would face discrimination charges if they denied him the right to dress as he preferred. King told his mother he wanted a sex-change operation and told a teacher he wanted to be called Leticia. One of the school's three assistant principals, Joy Epstein, who was also gay, tried to assist King. Her colleagues saw Epstein as encouraging King, however, and Greg King believes Epstein made the situation worse as she encouraged Larry to be "out."

On the day of February 12, however, King wore baggy pants, a sweater, and tennis shoes to school. Students noticed that he seemed nervous that day, and he claimed he had not slept well. He kept looking over his shoulder as he entered his first-period English class. Teacher Dawn Boldrin asked the students to take their belongings with them to a computer lab, where King found a seat in the middle of the room. McInerney took a seat next to King. McInerney pretended to read a history book but kept looking over at King. A half hour into the class, McInerney pulled out a handgun and fired a shot into King's head. Boldrin screamed and asked McInerney what he was doing. McInerney fired a second shot, then threw the gun on the floor and walked out of the classroom. He was arrested within seven minutes, having walked out of the school building.

King seemed to really like McInerney and he even told others they had dated but broken up. McInerney denies the two had any relationship. Near Valentine's Day, King walked onto the basketball court where McInerney was playing and asked Brandon to be his valentine. McInerney's friends teased him mercilessly about the relationship. Allegedly McInerney told one of King's friends she should kiss him goodbye, because she would never see him again. She did not tell King about the threat, as she assumed that McInerney was kidding. On February 11, there were rumors about a fight between the two boys, but no one seems to have taken them seriously. Greg King has admitted he believes his son's behavior toward Brandon McInerney could be considered sexual harassment.

McInerney had also been in trouble before. When he was six, his parents split up after his mother, Kendra, alleged that her husband, Bill, shot her in the arm. The home was filled with domestic violence, and Kendra had a restraining order against Bill. Bill claimed that Kendra was a drug addict. Brandon eventually came to live with his father. His father worked in a town 60 minutes away, so Brandon was alone a lot. He began to hang out with other kids who did not fit in, and he lost interest in school.

The gay rights community has taken up King's case as a way to draw attention to the harassment and discrimination faced by lesbian, gay, bisexual, and transgendered (LGBT) students in schools. Greg King resents the gay rights community for using his son as a "poster child." The murder was labeled a hate crime by many in the general public, and the Gay, Lesbian and Straight Education Network (GLSEN) devoted the National Day of Silence on April 25, 2008, to King.

McInerney is being tried as an adult on first-degree-murder charges. If convicted, he could serve 53 years to life in prison. In late August 2010, a Ventura County Superior Court judge denied a change of venue for the trial. The judge did agree that publicity about the case jeopardized McInerney's right to a fair trial and agreed to bring in jurors from Santa Barbara.

Laura L. Finley

Further Reading

Cathcart, R. (2003, February 23). Boy's killing, labeled a hate crime, stuns town. *New York Times.* Retrieved May 3, 2010, from http://www.nytimes.com/2008/02/23/us/23oxnard.html

Cloud, J. (2008, February 18). Prosecuting the gay teen murder. *Time.* Retrieved May 3, 2010, from http://www.time.com/time/nation/article/0,8599,1714214,00.html

Harris, C. (2008, February 21). Lawrence King—student who was murdered for being gay—to be honored with National Day of Silence. *MTV.* Retrieved May 3, 2010, from http://www.mtv.com/news/articles/1582039/20080221/story.jhtml

Judge in gay classmate murder trial to bring in jurors from Santa Barbara. (2010, August 24). *KTLA News.* Retrieved November 7, 2010, from http://www.ktla.com/news/landing/ktla-brandon- mcinerney-king-trial,0,5454894.story

Setoodeh, R. (2008, July 19). Young, gay and murdered. *Newsweek.* Retrieved November 7, 2010, from http://www.newsweek.com/2008/07/18/young-gay-and-murdered.html

Kinkel, Kip

On May 20, 1998, Kip Kinkel, a 15-year-old high school student, murdered his parents, Bill and Faith Kinkel, in their house. Then, the next day, he killed two students and injured 25 others in a school shooting at Thurston High School in Springfield, Oregon. The murdered students were Ben Walker, age 16, and Mikael Nickolauson, age 17.

Kinkel's parents were found in their house the day after the murder. Also in the house was a confession written by Kinkel, explaining that voices in his head made him kill. He expressed regret for what he had done, but also said that he needed to kill people. The prosecutors argued that Kinkel was rational after killing his parents, as there was the next day's newspaper on the table, a freshly used bowl, evidence that Kinkel had cleaned blood from the house, and proof that he had talked to his friends on the phone. Also found was a journal that confessed the youth's thoughts of killing others and uncontrollable rage, and weapons including knives, chemicals, books on explosives, and "a sawed-off shotgun and a handgun." Police also found a picture of the football team with one player's head circled and the word "kill" next to it.

Some believe that Kinkel's early school years were a precursor to what happened later, as there were signs of frustration and trouble in school at an early age. During Kinkel's first year in school, he and his family were living in Spain, and his teacher spoke only Spanish. His sister Kristin has said that this situation was very difficult for Kip, who then had to be held back a grade when the family returned to the United States. He became very frustrated when he had trouble in school. Kinkel was tested for a learning disability in second grade, but was not diagnosed until third grade when he was retested.

In middle school, Kinkel and his friends started looking up how to make bombs on the Internet. His mother found out and became worried about the kind of friends he had. Kinkel also started shoplifting and bought a sawed-off shotgun from one of his friends in eighth grade, which his parents were unaware of. He was also arrested with a friend that year for throwing rocks from an overpass and hitting a car below. Kinkel was charged with this act and put under the control of the Eugene, Oregon, Department of Youth Services.

After these incidents, Kip's mother Faith put him in therapy with Dr. Jeffery Hicks, who later testified in court after the school shooting. Faith was concerned about Kip's behavior, about his aggression, and about his relationship with his father. During this time, Kinkel also went to Skipworth Juvenile Facility as a result of the rock-throwing arrest. The psychologist there felt the boy was different from most juveniles who came there, in that he was truthful and remorseful about what he had done. Dr. Hicks felt Kinkel was improving over time with their therapy, although he realized his patient was still interested in bombs and was continually depressed.

Around the same time, Kinkel was suspended for two days in school when he kicked another boy in the head after the boy pushed him. Later, he was suspended again for three days after he threw a pencil at a student. Faith Kinkel and Dr. Hicks felt the school had over-reacted with its punishments. Dr. Hicks ended up putting Kip on Prozac, which seemed to help. That same month, Kip's father bought a 9-mm gun for his son, with an agreement that Kip would not use the weapon without his father being there, and that Kip could not have full possession of it until turning 21 years old. Kip and his parents seemed to be getting along better at this time, and his father was making more of an effort to be with him. His ninth counseling session was his last, after all agreed he was doing well enough to stop going.

Soon after that, Kinkel bought another gun from a friend without his parents' knowledge, a .22-caliber pistol. The same year, he started high school at Thurston High. Kinkel seemed to be doing much better at school and in the rest of his life at this time. After just three months, he went off the Prozac after starting high school. His father bought him another gun, a semi-automatic rifle, with the same conditions as had applied to the other weapon. In speech class in school, Kip gave his speech on making a bomb, including detailed pictures on the process. Students later reported that this did not seem strange, as other students had discussed out-of-the-ordinary topics as well, including one on joining the Church of Satan. Soon after these events, the Pearl, Mississippi; West Paducah, Kentucky; and Jonesboro, Arkansas, school shootings all occurred. Kip's friend commented that Kinkel had said the Jonesboro shooting was cool, after seeing TV clips of it.

On May 20, 1998, Kinkel bought a semi-automatic pistol from a friend, which was stolen from another friend's father. It is not known whether Kinkel was aware of the gun's origin. The same day, the owner of the gun, Scott Keeney, called the school to tell officials there that the gun had been stolen and that he thought a student might have it. A detective was at the school on an unrelated matter, and talked to Kinkel about the gun. Kinkel confessed that he had it, and he and Korey Ewert, who had stolen the gun, were arrested and suspended from school.

Kinkel went home with his father Bill that same day. According to people who talked to Bill on the phone that day, Bill was very upset and unsure of how to handle his son. Right after Bill talked to Scott Keeney at 3 P.M., Kip shot his father in the back of the head with his rifle. He put his father's body in the bathroom and placed a sheet over it. At about 3:30 P.M., Kinkel's English teacher, Mr. Rowan, called the house. Kinkel spoke to him and told him he had made a mistake, although he did not say what, and he said his father was not there. At about 4 P.M., his friend called and asked where his father was; Kinkel told his friend that his father had gone to a store. At about 4:30 P.M., students from Bill's community college class called wondering why he was missing class. Kinkel told them he was not going to make it because of family issues. Right after that, he talked to his friends Tony McCown and Nick Hiaason in a conference call. Kinkel said in the call that he had not known the gun was Mr. Keeney's, that his father was at a bar, and that he was worried what others would think about what had happened at school that day. Tony and Nick said Kip kept saying he felt sick, that he was upset and angry, and he kept wondering when his mother would be home.

When his mother did come home at about 6:30 P.M., Kip joined her in the garage. After telling her he loved her, he shot her six times in the head, face, and chest. Then he covered her with a sheet, as he had his father.

On the next day (May 21, 1998,) even though he was suspended, Kinkel went to school. He brought with him three guns and a knife. He shot Ben Walker and Ryan Atteberry, and then shot his guns randomly in the cafeteria. Five students forced him to the ground after he had killed two students and injured 25. When police arrived, Kinkel told them he wanted to die. Kinkel then attacked Detective Al Warthen, the same detective who had arrested him the previous day, with the hunting knife he had strapped to his leg, shouting that he wanted them to kill him. When he calmed down, Kinkel confessed that he had killed his parents. The officers discovered Kinkel had two bullets taped to his chest, which he explained were meant to kill himself.

Kinkel was indicted with four counts of aggravated murder, for the two students and his parents, and 26 counts of aggravated attempted murder, which included the police detective he assaulted after the school shooting. During his trial, 50 victims of the shooting and their relatives gave statements, all saying they wanted Kinkel to have the maximum punishment available. On November 9, 1999, after six days in court, Kinkel was sentenced to 111 years in prison without the possibility of parole. The judge explained that the Oregon State Constitution had changed in 1996 to place the safety of society over the ability for one person to change, which is how he ruled. Kinkel is the first juvenile in the state of Oregon to serve a life sentence.

The defense tried to prove Kinkel was mentally ill, although they did not use an insanity defense, instead trying to obtain a plea bargain. More than one expert said Kinkel was mentally ill after he was in custody, diagnosing him with a learning disability, depression, low self-esteem, and early forms of schizophrenia. There was also a history of schizophrenia in Kinkel's family. Dr. Hicks, the only one who had helped Kinkel before the murders, said the youth was not psychotic, but angry and depressed.

Sharon Thiel

Further Reading

Fast, J. (2008). *Ceremonial violence: A psychological explanation of school shootings*. Woodstock, NY: Overlook Press.

Flowers, R., & Flowers, H. (2004). *Murders in the United States*. Jefferson, North Carolina: McFarland.

McBride, R. (2007). After shooting, Bethel works to prevent bullying, peer abuse. Retrieved January 2, 2009, from www.ktuu.com.

The killer at Thurston High. Frontline documentary. Related information can be found at www.pbs.org

Kretschmer, Tim

On March 11, 2009, 17-year-old Tim Kretschmer entered his former high school in Winnenden. Germany, at approximately 9:30 A.M. Dressed in black combat gear, Kretschmer began firing, killing nine students and three teachers. He fled to a nearby clinic, where he killed one other person. He then took a hostage and drove to Wendlingen, a town approximately 25 miles away. The massacre ended in a shootout with police in front of a postal center. Two passersby were killed and two officers sustained serious injuries. At the end of the gun battle, Kretschmer was dead, although it was not initially clear whether he had been shot by police or had taken his own life.

Chief of Police Erwin Hetger called the massacre a bloodbath, saying he had not seen anything worse in his 19 years working in the area. German Chancellor Angela Merkel expressed outrage and proclaimed a day of mourning for all Germans.

It was reported that during the attack, Kretschmer entered one specific classroom three times. Allegedly a student teacher threw herself in front of a student and was then killed. Students were terrified and confused. Some were told by police to leave the building and go out by the swimming pool. Students claimed the situation felt surreal, like a scene in a film, and that they had no idea how to react.

Kretschmer came from an affluent family. His father was a wealthy businessman. He was also a gun enthusiast and a member of a Schützenvereine, or local shooting club. Membership includes training with air guns and then firearms. After a year, new members are allowed to apply for a weapons permit, which entitles them to buy and keep guns at home, although not to carry them in public. Approximately 20 million guns are held legally in Germany, mostly in citizens' homes. Just a few weeks before his attack, Kretschmer's father had taught him how to use a Beretta pistol at a club range. Reportedly, the family had 18 weapons in the house. The *Die Zeit* newspaper reported that one of the guns was not found when police searched the house.

In school, Kretschmer earned average grades and did not really stand out. He had left the school in 2008 to begin an apprenticeship. Students reported that he had a group of friends and did not appear to be bullied or isolated.

Although Germany has stricter gun laws than the United States, this and other incidents of school shootings prompted calls for even stiffer controls. At the time of Kretschmer's attack, citizens seeking to have guns had to meet specific age criteria as well as demonstrate weapons expertise. Members of the shooting clubs argued these were isolated incidents and that no major overhaul in gun control laws was needed.

Several school shootings have shocked Germany in recent years. In 2006, Sebastian Bosse, wearing a mask and explosives and brandishing rifles, opened fire at a school in the western town of Emsdetten, wounding at least 11 people before killing himself. In April 2002, Germany saw its worst school shooting when Robert Steinhauser killed 16 people before turning the gun on himself at a high school in the eastern city of Erfurt. Steinhauser was also a member of a shooting club, and his attack prompted similar calls for gun control. Germany has the second highest number of deaths from school shootings, behind only the United States.

Laura L. Finley

Further Reading

Dougherty, C., (2009, March 11). Teenage gunman kills 15 at school in Germany. *New York Times.* Retrieved May 2, 2010, from http://www.nytimes.com/2009/03/12/world/europe/12germany.html

Paterson, T. (2009, March 15). In Europe's league of school shootings, Germany comes top. *The Independent (UK)*. Retrieved May 2, 2010, from http://www.independent.co.uk/news/world/europe/in-europes-league-of-school-shootings-germany-comes-top-1645387.html

Pidd, H. (2009, March 11). Students killed in German school shooting. *The Guardian* (UK). Retrieved May 2, 2010, from http://www.guardian.co.uk/world/2009/mar/11/germany-school-shooting

Labeling Theories

Labeling theories see crime and deviance as social constructions. Theorists stress that it is not the act per se that is problematic, but rather society's negative reaction to it. Labeling theory asserts that individuals acquire certain stigmatizing labels through social interactions, particularly through institutions such as schools and the juvenile justice system. These labels may be internalized, thereby leading to perpetuation of the criminal or deviant activity.

Labeling theory emerged in the 1950s and 1960s. Drawing on the work of sociologists Charles Horton Cooley and George Herbert Mead, early labeling theorists emphasized that crime and deviance, like most other human behavior, are socially constructed through interactions. These early theorists used a micro theoretical approach, emphasizing individual and small-group interactions, the use of social control in daily life, and the ways that individuals make sense of the labels they are assigned.

Edwin Lemert posited that most individuals engage in minor acts of deviance at some point in their lives, what he called "primary deviance." The application of a stigmatizing label at this time can beget additional labeling by other entities. Often, those persons who are assigned negative labels internalize the belief that they are indeed deviant, making their deviance become what sociologists call a master status. Lemert called this phenomenon "secondary deviance." The transition between primary and secondary deviance is often facilitated through "degradation ceremonies," or public rituals that are shaming and can have permanent impact—for example, court trials or expulsion from school. Given that individuals at this point find their opportunities for legitimate behavior are more limited, and that many have internalized the label, they may join others who have similar stigmas, creating a sort of deviant network.

Howard Becker expanded this perspective to address persons who were in the position to assign labels—most notably, teachers, police officers, and social workers. He called these people "moral entrepreneurs." Later theorists followed Becker's lead and placed greater emphasis on the larger social structures that create differential relationships of power and social control. Modern labeling theorists blend the symbolic interactionist perspective with a more critical view to address the ways that the attachment of labels mirrors larger social inequalities.

Although all labels can have some effect, labeling theorists focus on those with the potential for long-term negative impact. As such, they assert that labels assigned by individuals with whom a young person has a close relationship and those given by persons who make important decisions about the youth's future have the greatest potential to be damaging.

In 1978, William Chambliss authored *The Saints and the Roughnecks*, which would become a classic in the field of criminology and a seminal work of labeling theory. It details his study of juvenile delinquency and what he observed while "hanging out" in the school and community. The Saints were a group of boys from "good" families, while the Roughnecks were a similarly sized group from working-class families. Chambliss noted that although the boys' behavior was virtually the same, the Saints suffered far fewer consequences. Both groups regularly skipped school, cheated on exams, drank alcohol outside of school, and perpetrated acts of violence. Neither school officials nor police perceived the Saints as deviant, however; instead, they saw this group as good boys who committed occasional pranks. Chambliss determined that the bias against the working-class Roughnecks was significant. He noted, "The community responded to the Roughnecks as boys in trouble, and the boys agreed with that perception."

Many have invoked labeling theories to explain some of the school shooting incidents that started in the 1990s. Some have noted that Eric Harris and Dylan Klebold, the shooters in the 1999 Columbine High School massacre, had been labeled as deviants and were bullied by their peers, although there is some evidence that bullying was not the cause of the incident. A common thread among all of these school shooters was that they were considered odd or strange and thus may have been subjected to negative labeling.

Laura L. Finley

Further Reading

Becker, H. (1963). *Outsiders: Studies in the sociology of deviance*. New York: Macmillan.

Chambliss, W. (1978) The Saints and the Roughnecks. Retrieved May 2, 2010, from http://www2.fiu.edu/~cohne/Theory%20S09/Ch%209%20-%20The%20Saints%20and%20the%20Roughnecks.pdf

Lemert, E. (1951). *Social pathology*. New York: McGraw-Hill.

La Salle University Sex Scandal and Cover-up

In April 2003, a female student and member of the women's basketball team at La Salle University reported to the men's team coach, Billy Hahn, and to her own coach, John Miller, that she had awoken in her bedroom to find male player Dzaflo Larkai sexually assaulting her. She claimed that the coaches discouraged her from telling anyone else about the incident and did not report it to campus authorities or to police. Because she was discouraged from reporting the rape, the woman waited another 14 months before finally telling authorities about the attack. The coaches have claimed that it was the player who asked them to keep the matter private. The university's failure to alert the student body of a major criminal incident was a violation of the Clery Act.

In 2004, a counselor who was working with La Salle University's summer basketball camp reported to the coach that she had been sexually assaulted by La Salle superstar Gary Neale and another player, Michael Cleavers. The incident allegedly happened at a party. Coach Hahn spoke to the players and reported it to athletic director Tom Brennan. This time the university did inform the campus community, albeit four days later, and the students alleged to have been involved were suspended. When the victim from 2003 heard about the incident, she, too, came forward.

Cleaves and Neal were tried the following fall and were acquitted on all eight counts. The prosecution argued that the men assaulted the woman while she was very drunk, having consumed at least eight shots of high-proof alcohol. Neal and Cleaves claimed the sex was consensual, and the defense maintained she had made up the charges because she was embarrassed. In the other case, the 19-year-old victim decided she did not want to go forward with a trial of Larkai, and the charges were subsequently dropped. Both coaches resigned when the charges were filed.

The U.S Department of Education fined La Salle University for violating the Clery Act. It was the first time the Department had cited a college for failing to inform the student body about an acquaintance assault, and only the 15th time since the enactment of the Clery Act that a college was fined. The Act was passed after Lehigh University student Jeanne Clery was raped and murdered in 1986.

Laura L. Finley

Further Reading

Finley, P., Finley, L., & Fountain, J. (2008). *Sports scandals.* Westport, CT: Praeger.

La Salle faces sanctions for handling of alleged sexual assaults. (2006, December 20). *Associated Press.* Retrieved June 12, 2007, from LexisNexis Academic database.

La Salle University cited for mishandling two rape cases. (2006, December 26). *Campus Safety Magazine*. Retrieved May 3, 2010, from http://www.campussafetymagazine.com/News/?NewsID=790

Latin America and School Crime and Violence

Latin America is a region of the Americas in which the Romance languages, largely derived from Latin, are spoken. Violence, or "violencia," is a major social problem in this region. Every day, media attention focuses on gang and drug-related violence in Latin America. International homicides, or those involving citizens of other countries, increased 50% from the early 1980s to the mid-1990s, especially in Panama, Peru, and Colombia. In particular, drug-related violence in Mexico is deadly, with an estimated 13,600 people having been killed in such violence between the end of 2006 and September 2009. Globalization may cause crime and violence, in that persons seize new opportunities afforded by the interaction with other counties. A 2008 survey by Latinobarometro found citizens believed crime was the most significant problem in the region.

Additionally, rates of poverty are very high in most of Latin America. Scholars have noted that when persons are unable to afford basic necessities, they may resort to violence to meet their needs. UNICEF has reported that 39% of youth living in Latin America and the Caribbean reside in poverty. Youth unemployment, unwanted pregnancies, and substance abuse are other major issues in these areas. The region also has a long history of conquest, domination, and civil wars, which set the social stage for additional violence by citizens. UNICEF has stated that 6 million children and adolescents suffer from abuse and neglect each year, and approximately 220 children younger than the age of 18 die every day from domestic violence. In some countries in Latin American, 12% of homicide victims are younger than the age of 12, while that age group perpetrates only 1% of all homicides. Violence is the leading cause of death among males aged 15 to 24 in the Caribbean and in some countries of Latin America. Adolescents are often recruited into hazardous work or forced labor. Many young people get involved in drug trafficking, especially in Mexico.

Young girls face different barriers. Recent reports have documented that in Latin America and other regions, girls endure high rates of sexual harassment and assault while in school, often at the hands of educators. Girls may be offered good grades in exchange for sex acts and given poor grades if they refuse to submit.

A foreign-sponsored theater program teaches Colombian school children about leadership and the justice system. (Javier Said/USAID)

In Latin America, much remains to be done to adequately respond to violence and to begin prevention programs. In Colombia and Argentina, innovative programs involving conflict resolution have been implemented in a total of 236 schools. Young people are trained and led as mediators in these initiatives.

In 2001, the government of Trinidad and Tobago announced that it planned to install metal detectors in schools in response to a surge in violence and the number of students caught carrying weapons. The Centers for Disease Control and Prevention (CDC) has collaborated with a number of groups to better analyze and respond to violence in the region. The Inter-American Coalition for the Prevention of Violence is also working to tally and analyze various forms of violence as well as increase awareness and education. In June 2007, MTV premiered a UNICEF program on bullying and terror in schools that focused on Argentina and Mexico.

Patrice Delevante

Further Reading

Agren, D. (2010, April 7). Cash, status lure youths to drug trade in troubled parts of Mexico. *The Catholic Review.* Retrieved May 3, 2010, from http://www.catholicreview.org/subpages/storyworldnew-new.aspx?action=7948

Girls being "raped for grades." (2008, February 10). Association for Women's Rights in Development (AWID). Retrieved May 3, 2010, from http://www.awid.org/Issues-and-Analysis/Library/Girls-being-raped-for-grades

News note. (2007, June 26). MTV Latin America and UNICEF unite efforts to present a reality which many adolescents and young people live in Latin America. Retrieved May 3, 2010, from http://www.unicef.org/infobycountry/media_40147.html

UNICEF. (n.d.). Fast facts about adolescents and youth in Latin America and the Caribbean. Retrieved May 2, 2010, from www.unicef.org/media/files/Fast_facts_EN.doc

Violence prevention. (2008, February 12). Centers for Disease Control and Prevention. Retrieved May 3, 2010, from http://cdc.gov/ncipc/dvp/international.htm

Youth gangs in Latin America. (2006). *SAIS Review, 26*(2), 133–146.

Lépine, Marc

In the late afternoon of December 6, 1989, a lone gunman shot and killed 14 women and wounded 14 more at l'École Polytechnique, an engineering school in Montreal. The attacker was armed with a hunting knife and a Sturm Ruger Mini-14 semi-automatic rifle, which he legally owned. Born Gamil Gharbi (his father's last name) in 1964, he changed his name to Marc Lépine in 1982. He perpetrated the massacre at the age of 25.

The attack was not random. Lépine targeted women at l'École Polytechnique, a school he wanted to attend. Ultimately, he was turned away not only from l'École Polytechnique, but also from the Canadian Armed Forces. In his suicide note, he cited affirmative action policies that he believed gave women preferential treatment over men. Lépine especially hated feminists and blamed them for his losing out on opportunities that he, as a man, felt he should have had, one of which was a seat in l'École Polytechnique. "[T]he feminists always have a talent for enraging me," he said in his suicide note, according to *Toronto CityNews* (2006), adding that "They want to retain the advantages of being women (e.g., cheaper insurance, extended maternity leave preceded by a preventive leave) while trying to grab those of the men." In the unfolding of the massacre, Lépine told the men to leave the room and shot the remaining women, whom he had ordered to line up against a wall.

Much of the commentary after the massacre focused on whether Lépine was an insane monster or a social barometer. Was he just a seriously deluded man who acted out his hatred toward women, or was the massacre an extreme expression of more common forms of sexism and misogyny? In other words, did Lépine's actions and the motivation behind them reflect an ugly characteristic of men and of society?

Some might argue the former, that Lépine was mentally ill and thus was different from most men. Lépine himself predicted in his suicide note that the news media would brand him a "Mad Killer." From this perspective, it might be said that most men were not "like him" and that Lépine was a "monster" who acted on his own accord. A psychological perspective would focus on the abuse he experienced at the hands of his father, as reported by his mother Monique Lépine in her 2008 book *Aftermath*. They might also draw attention to his appetite for war movies and violent computer games, as his mother described in an interview in *MacLean's* magazine. As psychiatrist Susan Penfold (1990) pointed out, a person with particular mental illnesses can sometimes come to believe that outside agencies such as the devil or the CIA are conspiring against her or him. Penfold suggested that, in Lépine's case, the outside "agency" was feminists.

The abuse that Lépine endured at the hands of his father provides little explanation for his rampage. Many men have been abused as boys by their fathers, yet the overwhelming majority do not commit mass murder. However, consideration of Lépine's actions within the social and political climate provides a more compelling theory behind his actions. Lépine's hatred and decision to murder women was extraordinary and extreme, giving him a status that separated him from ordinary men. Yet, the massacre occurred during a backlash against feminism that was in high gear in the conservative 1980s. Among neoconservatives, feminists (and others such as gays and lesbians) were blamed for the perceived moral decay in society and for attacks on the nuclear family, thought to be the cornerstone of American civilization. In addition, feminist men point out that violence against women in various forms (e.g., beatings, rapes, murders) is perpetrated by "normal" men on a daily basis. Further, violence against women is routinely depicted in media such as TV programs, movies, and video games. Thus, for some, Lépine's rampage against women is merely an extreme version of the everyday sexism and misogyny to which boys and men need to subscribe to succeed in a male-dominated world. In a biblical context, perhaps the story of Eve may be seen as an early example of men blaming the ills of society on women. In his own suicide note, Lépine blamed feminism for all of his troubles, indicating that his rampage was a political act. The massacre was planned and executed to get even with women, especially those he disparaged as "feminists."

For Green (2005), the massacre cannot be reduced to the "anomalous act of a madman." Rather, this author points out that such reductionism denies "the reality that misogyny is a social problem, present in our political culture and perpetuated by our popular culture and our faith-based myths that denigrate women" (pp. 2–3). Prior to the Montreal massacre, Kaufman (1987) wrote that "violence is... the individual man acting out relations of sexual power; [and]... the violence of a society... being focused through an individual man onto an individual woman" (p. 1). Mass murderers in the modern age attempt to make political statements or magnify social tensions through their actions.

For many feminists and allies, however, the massacre prompted discussion of the wider issue of violence against women. Green (2005) points out that the "normativeness of misogynist attitudes toward women makes the emergence of Lépine... possible." Similarly, Kaufman argues that Lépine was not a "monster" but rather was "rational" in his response to the gains made by feminists for equality with men. In an open letter to Lépine published in the *Toronto Star*, Kaufman (1990) asks him:

> By the way, did you hear the great line from one of Arnold Schwarzenegger's latest films? Right before he blew away his wife he says, "Consider this a divorce." Thought you'd like that one. These days there's great stuff on TV and in the movies that I know you'd love to see; to make you realize that you weren't alone.

In his suicide note, Lépine himself observed that, "Even though the Mad Killer epithet will be attributed to me by the media, I consider myself a rational and erudite person..."

For Brickman (1992), the Montreal massacre was thus "neither a surprising nor an isolated event" (p. 136). She explains that most "[female] abuse victims expected to be killed if they did not conform to the demands, expectations, and fantasies, explicit and implied of their [male] abuser" (p. 136). Lépine learned from his abusive father that women were not equal with men. Further, the particular social script of masculinity to which Lépine was exposed was one of violent masculinity. It is significant that the overwhelming majority of school shooters are boys and men, and likewise the perpetrators of violent crime. For pro-feminist theorists and activists, school shootings, and especially anti-feminist massacres, are extreme examples of everyday violent masculinity as "a cultural norm." For feminists groups, the massacre galvanized many to speak out against violence against women that, unlike the sensation of the Montreal incident itself, tends not to capture media or public attention.

In 1991, the Parliament of Canada established December 6 as the *National Day of Remembrance and Action on Violence Against Women*. The Day of Remembrance calls for a minute of silence to honor all women who have been victims of violence at the hands of men. It was initiated as a response to the inescapable fact that women at l'École Polytechnique were targeted and brutally gunned down. Evidently, the data showing that many other women have been killed by their husbands and male partners were not sufficient to spark such a national spotlight on violence against women, even though "wives and romantic or sexual partners are the most common victims of murderous men" (Green, 2005).

The Day of Remembrance also calls for men to educate themselves and one another about male-perpetrated violence against women. In 1991, a small group of pro-feminist men in Canada launched the first White Ribbon campaign to address men's violence against women. According to the White Ribbon website, the campaign is now "the largest effort in the world of men working to end violence against women," involving people in more than 55 countries.

In addition to White Ribbon campaigns and the annual National Day of Remembrance, lobbying for tighter gun control laws ensued in the aftermath of the Montreal massacre. Such efforts resulted in the passing in 1995 of Bill C-68 (the Firearms Act), which established a gun registry in Canada. Critics have charged that this measure is ineffective and costs Canadians millions of dollars. Supporters have argued that such gun control policies are necessary to reduce the harm from, or even prevent, further shooting sprees. The debate continues in light of other school shootings that have occurred since the massacre, including another attack in Montreal—the Dawson College shooting in 2006 that resulted in one death and several injured.

Public memorials to honor the victims of the Montreal massacre have been erected in several Canadian cities, including Montreal, Ottawa, Hamilton, and Vancouver. These sites are among the many others that memorialize women killed by men in Canada. A memorial ceremony also marks the event on the l'École Polytechnique campus. Such memorials are controversial, however. Criticism of them tends to focus on the perception that Lépine was a lone madman rather than evidence of hatred in wider society. Supporters advocate addressing violence against women as a social problem rather than as an individual pathology, in part through public memorials as a visible and continual reminder. Rosenberg (2006) argues that such memorials are a form of public pedagogy, which "is tied broadly to cultural practices and to any public, cultural endeavour to shape political visions of the past, present, and/or future" (p. 27). These debates continue.

The Montreal massacre remains the worst case of mass killing in Canadian history.

Gerald Walton

Further Reading

Bradley, M. (2006). Report: Reframing the Montreal massacre: Strategies for feminist media activism. *Canadian Journal of Communication, 31,* 929–936.

Brickman, J. (1992). Feminist lives, feminist deaths: The relationship of the Montreal massacre to dissociation, incest, and violence against women. *Canadian Psychology, 33*(2), 128–143.

Burfoot, A., & Lord, S. (Eds.). (2006). *Killing women: The visual culture of gender and violence.* Waterloo, ON: Wilfrid Laurier University Press.

Cultural Memory Group. (2006). *Remembering women murdered by men: Memorials across Canada.* Toronto, ON: Sumach.

Eglin, P., & Hester, S. (2003). *The Montreal massacre: A story of membership categorization analysis.* Waterloo, ON: Wilfrid Laurier Press.

Fillion, K. (2008, Oct. 22). Maclean's Interview: Monique Lépine. *MacLean's.* Retrieved December 11, 2008, from http://www.macleans.ca/canada/national/article.jsp?content=20081022_87668_87668

Green, J. (2005). Commemorating the Montreal massacre for the 15th time. *Canadian Dimension, 39*(1), 2–3.

Jones, A. (Ed.). (2004). *Gendercide and genocide.* Nashville, TN: Vanderbilt University Press.

Katz, J. (2006). *The macho paradox: Why some men hurt women and how all men can help.* Naperville, IL: Sourcebooks.

Katz, J., & Jhally, S. (1999, May 2). The national conversation in the wake of Littleton is missing the mark. *Boston Globe,* p. E1. Retrieved from http://www.jacksonkatz.com/pub_missing.html

Kaufman, M. (1987). The construction of masculinity and the triad of men's violence. In M. Kaufman (Ed.), *Beyond patriarchy: Essays by men on pleasure, power, and change* (pp. 1–29). Toronto, ON: Oxford.

Kaufman, M. (1990, December 6). A letter to Marc Lépine. *Toronto Star,* p. A23.

Kilbourne, J. (2000). *Can't buy my love: How advertising changes the way we think and feel.* New York: Simon & Schuster.

Lépine, M., with Gagne, H. (2008). *Aftermath.* Toronto, ON: Penguin Group (Canada).

Levy, B. (2008). *Women and violence.* Berkeley, CA: Seal Press.

Leyton, E. (1986). *Hunting humans: The rise of the modern multiple murderer.* Toronto, ON: McLelland and Stewart.

Malette, L., & Chalouh, M. (1991). *The Montreal massacre.* Charlottetown, PE: Gynergy.

Penfold, S. (1990, December 8). Portrait of a misogynist. *Vancouver Sun,* p. C1.

Ramsland, K. (2005). *Inside the minds of mass murders: Why they kill.* Westport, CT: Praeger.

Rosenberg, S. (2006). Neither forgotten nor fully remembered: Tracing an ambivalent public memory on the tenth anniversary of the Montreal massacre. In A. Burfoot & S. Lord (Eds.), *Killing women: The visual culture of gender and violence* (pp. 21–45). Waterloo, ON: Wilfrid Laurier University Press.

Status of Women Canada. (2000). *December 6, 2000: National Day of Remembrance and Action on Violence Against Women information kit.* Ottawa, ON: Author.

Toronto CityNews. (2006). CityNews rewind: The Montreal massacre. Retrieved December 11, 2008, from http://www.citynews.ca/news/news_5897.aspx

White Ribbon campaign: Men working to end men's violence against women. (2008). Retrieved January 11, 2009, from http://www.whiteribbon.ca/about_us/#2

Lo, Wayne

On December 14, 1992, Wayne Lo killed one student and a professor at Simon's Rock College of Bard in Massachusetts. Lo wounded four others before surrendering to police. He is now serving two life sentences without the possibility of parole.

Wayne Lo was an A student and gifted violinist. He was known as being obedient and helpful, working at his family's restaurant and studying late into the night. Educators said he genuinely seemed to like school. Friends and acquaintances commented on his excellent manners and his respect for others. His father, C. W, and his mother, Lin-Lin, emigrated to the United States from Taiwan in 1986.

Life was far from perfect, however. Brian Skinner, an assistant manager at the family's restaurant, said Wayne would often comment about how harsh his father was and how much he hated him. C. W. was a strict disciplinarian who would beat Wayne and his brothers for any indiscretion. During the second semester of Lo's freshman year at Billings Central Catholic High School in Billings, Montana, his teachers noticed he seemed especially stressed. He was the only student of Asian origin in the school, which likely added to the stress he felt. Lo's parents, like many Asians and Asian Americans, had tremendously high expectations for their son and placed a lot of pressure on him to achieve. Lo's English teacher noticed his grades had slipped and that instead of the pride he formerly took in his work, Lo seemed to be proud of his sloppiness and mistakes. She and another teacher, Gary Gaudreau, discussed their concerns with the school counselor, but little was done.

During the Easter break, Lo stole his mother's car and went to Oregon to visit a girl there—behavior very out of character for him. He kept dropping hints that his parents should transfer him to a boarding school. Some experts have speculated Lo desired this arrangement so he could escape from the pressure at home. His parents gave in and sent him to Simon's Rock in Massachusetts, a highly acclaimed, rigorous school.

Wayne Lo started at Simon's Rock in September 1991. He was 17 years old, and had also just earned his U.S. citizenship. He seemed to thrive at Simon's Rock, exploring a variety of courses and joining the basketball team. Lo claimed, however, that he still felt like an outcast. He had a group of friends, all of whom also seemed to cling to outcast status and who were described as perpetually angry. He did, however, develop an interest in guns and weapons, When he returned home on a break, Lo showed his best friend his new brass knuckles and told another friend he needed a pistol for protection, In his second year at Simon's Rock, Lo repeatedly asked others about obtaining weapons. A few days before the shooting, he used his mother's credit card to order several 30 bullet clips, a folding plastic stock, and 200 pounds of copper-jacketed, steel-core bullets; he had the package delivered to him at the school. On December 13, Lo told a student he was planning to bring a gun to campus to shoot people. Later that evening, the same friend called Lo, who said he was busy copying the Book of Revelations into his notebook so everyone would think he was crazy. His friend assumed he was joking.

A receptionist received Lo's gun-related package and alerted various campus authorities. They were hesitant to invade Lo's privacy or commit mail fraud by opening the package, however. They agreed to watch Lo while he opened the package, but somewhere there was a miscommunication and Lo opened everything except the ammunition in his room before officials got there. In the end, despite this strange behavior, Lo was allowed to keep his weapons and ammunition because he said it was a Christmas gift from his father. Lo did meet with the dean, but it was generally to discuss his transfer to college. The dean concluded that Lo was not a threat and did not have any weapons. That same night, an anonymous caller phoned several school officials, saying Lo had weapons and planned to target his residence director's family. The college provost alerted the family, who went to stay elsewhere, but no other action was taken.

The next morning, Lo traveled by taxi to Pittsfield, Massachusetts, where he purchased a semi-automatic weapon at Steve's Sporting Goods Store. He began shooting on campus that evening, first wounding receptionist Teresa Beavers, then killing Spanish teacher Nacunan Saez. He proceeded to the library, where he killed student Galen Gibson and wounded another student. Lo then headed to a dormitory, where he shot and wounded two other students. His rifle had jammed and he dropped the weapon and entered the student union, where he called the police. He surrendered to them when they arrived at the scene.

Throughout his trial, Lo was portrayed as a quiet and unassuming student, but also as a racist who was obsessed with violent music. Lo continues to say these allegations are not true, and that the racism allegation stems solely from a paper he wrote for class calling for the exile of people with AIDS. He claims that the paper was written because he was simply trying to earn a good grade. At the time of the shooting, Lo was wearing a shirt featuring the name of a hard-core band called "Sick of It All," although he claims he loved all kinds of music. The band spoke out after the attack, denouncing Lo's crime.

Lo's assault rocked the small, prestigious college and the Asian American community. Attention on the latter was renewed after Seung Hui Cho's massacre at Virginia Tech. Prior to the attacks by Lo and Cho, University of Iowa exchange student Gang Lu had opened fire during a physics department meeting, killing five and leaving another person paralyzed before shooting himself in the head. Asian Americans denounced these shootings, asserting that theirs is not a violent culture. Many did, however, discuss the high pressure placed on Asian children and lack of forgiveness in the culture. Additionally, commentators noted that Asian cultures often dismiss mental illness and reject treatment for it. There was also concern about possible retaliatory attacks on Asian immigrants.

In 1999, Greg Gibson, father of Galen Gibson, one of Lo's victims, wrote *Gone Boy: A Walkabout*, his account of the shooting and its impact. This was the start of regular correspondence between Gibson and Lo.

Laura L. Finley

Further Reading

Gibson, G. (1999). *Gone boy: A walkabout.* New York: Anchor.

Glaberson, W. (2000, April 12). Man and his son's slayer unite to ask why. *New York Times.* Retrieved May 2, 2010, from http://partners.nytimes.com/library/national/041200rampage-killers.html

Yang, J. (2007, April 19). Killer reflection. *Salon.* Retrieved May 2, 2010, from http://www.salon.com/news/opinion/feature/2007/04/19/cho_shooting

Loukaitis, Barry

Fourteen-year-old honor student Barry Loukaitis entered Frontier High School in Moses Lake, Washington, on February 2, 1996, armed with a high-powered hunting rifle and two pistols. He immediately headed to his algebra class, where he took the class hostage. Loukaitis killed two students, Manual Vela, Jr., and Arnie Fritz, as well as his algebra teacher, Leona Caires. He seriously wounded several other students before being overpowered by physical education teacher Jon Lane, who had talked his way into the room.

Loukaitis had a disturbing home life. His parents were divorced, and his mother repeatedly told him that she planned to take his father and his father's girlfriend hostage, tie them up, and commit suicide in front of them on Valentine's Day. His parents reportedly fought a lot about his father's drinking and womanizing behavior. Both parents had a history of depression. Loukaitis's grandmother on his mother's side had made at least one suicide attempt.

Although he seemed to do well and enjoy elementary school, Loukaitis was picked on in middle school. One of his victims, Manuel Vela, Jr., had reportedly tormented Loukaitis, calling him a faggot, spitting on him, shoving him in the hallway, and kicking him until his legs were bruised all over. Allegedly, Loukaitis had a crush on Vela's girlfriend. Other students teased him as well. He allegedly told classmates that he hated everyone and wanted to go on a shooting spree. Classmates said Loukaitis was an easy target because he was very serious, he was gangly looking, and he wore cowboy boots and strange clothes to school. On the day of the shooting, he was decked out as the man with no name from the film *Fistful of Dollars*.

The case drew great attention to popular culture, as Loukaitis was reportedly obsessed with the film *Natural Born Killers*. He had seen it many times, and classmates said he could quote the entire film. He also loved the song and video *Jeremy* by Pearl Jam, which featured a young man shooting his classmates after enduring their abuse. Additionally, Loukaitis was a Stephen King fan, and particularly loved the horror author's book *Rage*. *Rage* tells the story of a high school student who is bullied until he goes insane. He takes his class hostage and kills a teacher for revenge, much as Loukaitis did. He allegedly quoted a line from the book when he was holding the class hostage. King has expressed regret for authoring the novel.

Frontier High School was closed temporarily after the shootings, and areas in the school where the incident occurred were renovated. The district has since implemented a dress code, increased security, and hired guards for schools. Many commentators have noted that Loukaitis's attack was the first of a series of multiple-victim homicides in schools and was the impetus for a number of copycat shooters.

Loukaitis was waived to adult criminal court after a hearing in which it was determined that he was competent and that the severity of the incident warranted more serious penalty. He pleaded not guilty by reason of insanity, with the defense arguing that he lived in a fantasy world. The prosecution prevailed, showing that Loukaitis planned the attack with great detail. He was convicted and sentenced to life without the possibility of parole. Later, questions arose about the quality of his defense, given that his primary attorney, Guillermo Romero, was being investigated by the Washington State Bar Association for providing inadequate counsel for several clients.

Laura L. Finley

Further Reading

Armstrong, K., Davis, F., & Mayo, J. (2004, April 4). For some, free counsel comes at a high cost. *Seattle Times*. Retrieved May 3, 2010, from http://seattletimes.nwsource.com/news/local/unequaldefense/stories/one/

Fast, J. (2009). *Ceremonial violence: A psychological explanation of school shootings*. Woodstock, NY: Overlook Press.

Finley, L. (Ed.). (2007). *Encyclopedia of juvenile violence*. Westport, CT: Greenwood.

Langman, P. (2009). *Why kids kill: Inside the minds of school shooters*. New York: Palgrave Macmillan.

Lu, Gang

On November 1, 1991, 28-year-old Gang Lu, who had received his doctoral degree in physics during the previous spring, killed four faculty members and one student before seriously wounding another at the University of Iowa. Lu then committed suicide. Allegedly Lu was angry that he did not receive the prestigious D. C. Spriestershach Dissertation Prize, which was accompanied by a monetary award of $2,500 and would have increased the likelihood that Lu would have been hired.

On the day of the shootings, Lu entered Van Allen Hall at the University of Iowa campus, armed with a .38-caliber revolver. Van Allen was home to the university's physics and astronomy programs. Lu first shot and killed Christopher Goertz, Dwight Nicholson, Robert Smith, and Linhua Shan. Shan, also a physics student from China, had won the dissertation prize Lu coveted. Next, Lu left Van Allen Hall and entered the main administration building, Jessup Hall. He asked to see T. Anne Cleary, assistant vice president for academic affairs. He shot her, and she died the next day. Students have said they first thought these gunshots were firecrackers or pranks. Lu then shot a student employee, Miya Rodlofo-Sioson, in the mouth. She did not die but was left paralyzed from the neck down when the bullet went through her spinal cord. When he learned that police had arrived at the campus, Lu shot himself in the head.

Lu clearly planned the attack for many months, purchasing his weapon around the same time he was awarded his doctoral degree. He purchased another gun during the summer and practiced shooting at targets. In the weeks prior to the murder, he emptied his bank account and sent the money to his sister in China, asking her to deposit it as quickly as possible. On the day of the attack, he wrote a letter describing his grievances. He made photocopies of this letter and mailed them to news media in Iowa as well as to the *Los Angeles Times* and *New York Times* newspapers. A copy of the letter was in his briefcase in a seminar room. Lu insisted that Goertz, Smith, and Nicholson—all professors—had favored Shan and snubbed him. He had complained to Cleary and felt she ignored him. Rodlofo-Sioson was the only random victim.

Lu's assault occurred in the context of an economic recession that had hit universities hard, and from which physics graduates were not excepted. Lu desperately wanted a job but did not have one. In better times, the university might have kept him on as a teaching or research assistant, but in the recession there was room for only one—and that was Shan.

There is no doubt that Lu was gifted. By junior high school, his skills in math and physics were clear, and he was selected to attend a special school. He won several awards and was admitted to Beijing University, China's most prestigious college. In 1985, when he graduated, Lu was selected for a government-sponsored program that placed China's most promising physics students at U.S. universities.

Two years after he arrived in the United States, Lu showed some signs of being tired of physics. He inquired about switching his major to business, but was unable to do so because he was receiving a stipend from the physics department and was not granted one when he applied to the business department. His request to transfer to electrical and computer engineering was denied as well.

Apparently Lu was also unlucky in love. He tried to date women but often ended up paying for sex rather than having a relationship.

Coach Hayden Fry led the University of Iowa Hawkeyes football team in a solemn acknowledgment of the victims at their game the next day. The team stripped their helmets of all markings.

In 2007, Chinese director Chen Shi-Zheng won the Alfred P. Sloan Prize at the Sundance Film Festival for his film *Dark Matter*, which told Gang Lu's story. In 2009, a documentary about survivor Miya Rodolfo-Sioson was released called *Miya of the Quiet Strength*.

Laura L. Finley

Further Reading

Mann, J. (1992, June 07). The physics of revenge. *Los Angeles Times.* Retrieved May 3, 2010, from http://articles.latimes.com/1992-06-07/magazine/tm-411_1_lu-gang

Marriot, M. (1991, November 4). Iowa gunman was torn by academic challenge. *New York Times.* Retrieved May 3, 2010, from http://www.nytimes.com/1991/11/04/us/iowa-gunman-was-torn-by-academic-challenge.html?sec=health

Overbye, D. (2007, March 27). A tale of power and intrigue in the lab, based on real life. *New York Times.* Retrieved May 3, 2010, from http://www.nytimes.com/2007/03/27/science/27dark.html?_r=1&ei=5087%0A&em=&en=60699d2d8b90a79f&ex=1175227200&pagewanted=all

M

Manson, Marilyn

The music of shock-rocker Marilyn Manson (real name Brian Warner) is definitely controversial. This musician was banned from performing in South Carolina and has been offered $10,000 not to play in Salt Lake City. His stage name was derived from combining the names of actress Marilyn Monroe and serial killer Charles Manson. His work was described by some as playing a large role in several school shootings. Angry parents pointed to Manson's violent and misogynistic lyrics after Michael Carneal's 1997 shooting and the 1999 Columbine High School massacre. Fourteen-year-old Asa Coon, who wounded four people at his school in Cleveland, Ohio, in 2007, was also said to have been a fan. On May 18, 2009, a 15-year-old middle school student in Lafourche Parish, Louisiana, fired a gun at a teacher, demanding that she say "Hail Marilyn Manson." He then shot himself in the head and was in critical condition. Out of sensitivity to the community, Manson canceled the last five dates of a concert tour fol-

Marilyn Manson poses in full costume during a live performance in Denver, Colorado, on June 22, 2001. (Shutterstock)

lowing the Columbine massacre, but at the same time denounced the media for unfairly scapegoating him.

In his 2002 documentary *Bowling for Columbine*, film-maker Michael Moore interviews Manson. Manson suggests that music, film, and video games are being wrongly targeted and that politicians have created a "campaign of fear and consumption" intended to distract the public from other societal ills. He ends the interview by telling Moore that, given the chance to talk to Eric Harris and Dylan Klebold, he would not say anything. Instead, he said he would listen to them, as often no one listens to young people.

Laura L. Finley

Further Reading

Baddely, G. (2008). *Dissecting Marilyn Manson*. New York: Plexus.

Bowling for Columbine: http://www.imdb.com/title/tt0310793/quotes

Chi, T. (2007). *Studying Marilyn Manson: Groupies, school violence and bullying: Marketing revelations, Christianity, antichrists and psychiatrists*. New York: BookSurge.

Foster, M. (2009, May 18). Louisiana school shooting: Student shoots himself in the head after firing at teacher. *Huffington Post*. Retrieved May 3, 2010, from http://www.huffingtonpost.com/2009/05/18/louisiana-school-shooting_n_204704.html

Manson, M. (1999). *The long, hard road out of hell*. New York: IT books.

Sterngold, J. (1999, April 29). Terror in Littleton: The culture; Rock concerts are cancelled. *New York Times*. Retrieved May 3, 2010, from http://www.nytimes.com/1999/04/29/us/terror-in-littleton-the-culture-rock-concerts-are-cancelled.html

Mental Illness and School Crime and Violence

Although speculation about the mental stability of school shooters has generally ensued after each major incident, there seems to be no clear answer regarding whether those who perpetrate crime and violence on school and campus property are prone to suffer from some type of mental illness. Many times perpetrators have not been officially diagnosed with a mental illness, although they may be suffering from an undiagnosed problem. In *Rampage: The Social Roots of School Shootings*, the authors of this book identify mental illness as one of the five main factors that result in rampage school shootings. Most attackers have shown some history of suicidal attempts or thoughts, or a history of feeling extreme depression or desperation. In its analysis of school shootings, the U.S. Secret Service found that in more than three-fourths of major attacks, the perpetrators were struggling to cope with a significant life change, such as a breakup with a girlfriend, some type of public humiliation, or a loss of status. Other research suggests that prescription drugs, although intended to address an individual's mental illness, may actually push some people to commit violence.

After a shooting incident, pundits and the general public often point to what seem to be obvious signs of mental illness. In a recent publication, journalist Dave Cullen sought to debunk a number of myths about the Columbine massacre of April 1999. In his book titled *Columbine*, Cullen highlighted the role of mental illness, asserting that it was not pressure from bullying that prompted Eric Harris and Dylan Klebold to shoot 14 of their classmates. Instead, Cullen wrote, Klebold suffered from depression and was suicidal; Harris, he said, was a cold, calculating, homicidal psychopath. Harris was taking the antidepressant Luvox at the time of the massacre.

Jeff Weise, who killed 10 people (including himself) and injured seven others at Red Lake High School on Red lake Indian Reservation in Montana, had spent time in a psychiatric facility the summer before the shooting and had been banned from Red Lake High School five weeks earlier due to his odd and threatening behavior. Weise had been taking the antidepressant Prozac.

In cases where a diagnosis of mental illness was made, many have questioned why this information was not more widely distributed or why preventive measures were not taken by school or campus authorities. For instance, when Seung-Hui Cho killed 27 students, five professors, and then himself at Virginia Tech University, it became clear almost immediately that he suffered from some type of mental illness that had been previously identified by university officials. One of his former professors, who was at the time co-chair of the English Department, recalls being told by a colleague about Cho's disturbing writing and odd behavior toward classmates. She began to tutor Cho privately, and her interaction with him reinforced the suspicion that he was dangerous. The professor reported her observations to both the university police and the campus counseling center, but neither offered Cho help because students could not be forced to receive counseling and he had not overtly threatened anyone or himself at the time. Shortly thereafter, Cho threatened to commit suicide and did receive some assistance from an off-campus counseling center, but he was released when he was considered no longer a threat. Later, Cho himself contacted the university's counseling center. In an odd turn of events, the records of Cho's visits to the counseling center were missing until July 2009, when they were found at the home of a former counseling center employee. It is unclear why the employee had the files, which showed Cho visited the center several times but never received a specific diagnosis. Because Cho was older than the age of 21, his records were considered private and not even his parents were alerted to the fact that he had sought help.

Privacy laws generally make it difficult to share information—including mental health information—about students that might be prejudicial. Information can be shared when students make threats to themselves or others, but in many cases no such overt threat was made prior to a school attack.

The number of school or campus shooters who had been taking high-potency prescription drugs is disturbing and suggestive of a link between these agents and violence. The examples here include only some of the most infamous shooters. In 1988, Laurie Dann had been taking Anafranil and lithium when she killed one child and injured six in a Winnetka, Illinois, elementary school. Later that same year, 19-year-old James Wilson shot and killed two eight-year-old girls and wounded seven others at an elementary school in Greenwood, South Carolina. Wilson had been taking Xanax, Valium, and five other drugs. Kip Kinkel, a 15-year-old youth in Springfield, Oregon, had been taking both Prozac and Ritalin when he murdered his parents and then killed two students and wounded 22 others at his high school in 1998. In 1989, 25-year-old Patrick Purdy killed five and wounded 30 at an elementary school in Stockton, California. He had been treated with thorazine and amitriptyline. Michael Carneal (age 14), Andrew Golden (age 11), and Mitchell Thompson (age 14) were all reportedly taking Ritalin when they killed students and teachers at their schools. Most recently, Duane Morrison, age 53, shot and killed a girl at Platte Canyon High School in Colorado in 2006; antidepressants were later found in his vehicle.

It is less likely that there is an association between other forms of school and campus crime and mental illness. No data support the contention that perpetrators of property crime, dating violence, sexual assault, or drug-related crimes are more likely than nonperpetrators to suffer from mental illness.

Laura L. Finley

Further Reading

Cullen, D. (2010). *Columbine.* New York: Twelve.

Newman, K., Fox, C., Roth, W., & Mehta, J. (2005). *Rampage: The Social Roots of School Shootings.* New York: Basic.

Vossekuil, B., Fein, R., Reddy, M., Borum, R., & Modzeleski, W. (2002). *The final report and findings of the Safe School Initiative: Implications for the prevention of school attacks in the United States.* Jessup, MD: Education Publications Center, U.S. Department of Education.

Mentoring

Since the surge in juvenile violence in the 1980s and the very visible school shootings of the 1990s, activists, juvenile justice advocates, educators, faith leaders, and policymakers have created a number of mentoring programs for at-risk youth.

Mentoring aims to provide youth with role models, educational programming, and empowerment activities that dissuade them from involvement in criminal or violent activity and encourage successful transition into adulthood. Such interactions can be conducted on a one-on-one basis or in small groups. The U.S. Department of Education funds some mentoring programs.

In a school setting, typically teachers and staff identify academically and/or socially and emotionally at-risk youth for participation in the mentoring program. Volunteer mentors then generally meet with the students during the school day. Programs vary regarding the amount of time spent on academic and social activities. School-based programs tend to cost less than community-based mentoring programs, as they have lower overhead and other costs. School-based mentoring tends to be less intensive than community-based programs, however, due to constraints attributable to the school calendar. An average school-based program runs approximately five to six months and includes an average of six hours of activity per month. Often school-based programs rely on high school or college-aged mentors who may connect well socially to their mentees but can be less well equipped to make the needed impact.

The most widely used type of mentoring program involves intergenerational and youth-based programs that offer leadership-development seminars as well as various other rites of passage for youth. These programs generally target the most marginalized youth, such as ex-offenders and gang members. Some notable examples of this type of mentoring program include the San Francisco Bay Area's Omega Boys Club, Boston's Ten Point Coalition, and the Ameri-I-Can organization in Lose Angeles.

Identity-based mentoring focuses on youth who may be victimized by violence and crime because of their racial or ethnic background, gender identity, sex, sexual orientation, immigrant status, or other factors. These programs are intended to reduce discrimination and to raise the consciousness of youth such that they become empowered and self-confident. Many mentoring programs have been established to assist lesbian, gay, bisexual, transgendered, and questioning (LGBTQ) youth, for example. LGBTQ youth are frequent targets of harassment and physical violence in schools. The Office of Juvenile Justice and Delinquency Prevention (OJJDP) has recognized this risk and developed a mentoring guide for working with sexual minority youth (available at http://www.ppv.org/ppv/publications/assets/33_publication.pdf). Other well-regarded programs reaching LGBTQ youth include the North Carolina Lambda Youth Network and the Audre Lord Project in New York City.

Mentoring programs have been established to assist the children of undocumented persons as well, given that they are often targeted in schools. Groups such as the Committee Against Anti-Asian Violence (CAAAV) in New York City, the ESPINO organization in California, and the Community Youth Organizing

Campaign in Philadelphia have all been created to address physical harassment and assault as well as the violence surrounding deportation, detainment, and unhealthy work conditions.

At-risk girls have benefited tremendously from mentoring programs. Programs focused on girls aim to address such issues as dating violence, body image, eating disorders, bullying, self-esteem, and self-mutilation. The Ophelia Project is a well-known girl's mentoring program. Women of Tomorrow (WOT) is a school-based program in South Florida that combines a successful female role model from the community with a school-based coordinator to offer education and support for at-risk girls. WOT also has a scholarship program for girls seeking to attend college.

Other mentoring programs involve large-scale organizing campaigns to improve the living environment of marginalized youth. An example of this type of mentoring is the Democracy Multiplied Zone (DMZ), which was developed in the 1990s by the Youth Force of the South Bronx. The DMZ focuses special attention on youth in a specific area of the South Bronx, offering them mentoring, developmental resources, and special attention.

Some mentoring programs are established through diversion systems that assist youth who have been involved in the juvenile justice system. Missouri, for example, has established best practices in developing its extensive diversionary mentoring program.

Evaluations of school-based mentoring programs have generally found them to be effective at reducing students' misbehavior and increasing their performance. One study of a school-based mentoring program for at-risk middle school students found statistically significant reductions in office referrals and statistically significant improvements in attitudes toward school. The quality of mentorship matters, however. Positive mentors meet more consistently with mentees and report more relaxed meetings. Other studies have found that school-based mentoring programs produce short-term effects in regard to academic performance, school attendance, and behavior in school, but that the results were not sustained into the following school year. Many evaluations of school-based mentoring program have found positive effects on students' self-esteem and ability to connect to their peers.

Laura L. Finley

Further Reading

Converse, N., & Lignugaris-Kraft, B. (2009). Evaluation of a school-based mentoring program for at-risk middle school youth. *Remedial and Special Education, 30*(1), 33–46.

Rappaport, C., Olsho, L., Hunt, D., Levin, M., Dyous, C., Klausner, M., et al. (2009, February). Impact evaluation of the U.S. Department of Education's

Student Mentoring Program. Institute of Education Sciences. Retrieved March 29, 2010, from http://ies.ed.gov/pubsearch/pubsinfo.asp?pubid =NCEE20094047

Metal Detectors

Although some urban districts have had metal detectors for decades, suburban schools had not really considered adding them until the mid- to late 1990s, after a spate of multiple-victim school shootings occurred. Scared parents and good-hearted educators often see metal detectors as a way to ensure that guns and other weapons do not make it into school buildings. Approximately 10% of all U.S schools now use metal detectors. In urban areas such as Chicago, the proportion of schools with metal detectors is much higher. Some schools use the door-frame-style detectors commonly found in courts and other sensitive public buildings, whereas others use the less expensive hand-held versions that are manned by school personnel or security guards. The United Kingdom has also considered wider use of metal detectors, in particular in areas in which knife fights are common. Authorities say youth ages 12 to 24 are responsible for three-fourths of all knife violence, and these weapons often make it onto school grounds.

Critics contend that metal detectors are not really effective, are too costly, and prevent school administration from considering other, more useful, interventions. Proponents maintain that metal detector searches are not invasive and are commonly used in courtrooms and airports. The argument is that they can be a powerful deterrent to students considering bringing weapons to school.

One concern related to their use is the cost of metal detectors. A walk-through detector costs a minimum of $5,000. For a building to be truly secure, all entrances would need to be equipped with a detector or otherwise inaccessible. Additionally, someone must be posted at the detector to further inspect persons who make it go off, so there might be an additional personnel-related cost. Hand-held detectors are far less expensive, costing approximately $100 each, but again must be staffed.

Another problem is that many districts have installed detectors based on the fear generated by school shootings elsewhere, not on a particular need in their own community. Research has shown that, while metal detectors may be helpful in urban areas with long histories of students bringing weapons to school, when they are installed in districts that have not had any specific weapons-related problems, the result may be just the opposite. That is, the installation of metal detectors serves to tell students, staff, and parents that there must actually be a problem and ends up increasing fear levels. When people are fearful of school violence, they are more guarded, more likely to accuse others of deviant activity, less likely

Metal detectors screen students at the entrance of a Philadelphia school. (AP/Wide World Photos)

to find the educational climate conducive to learning, and—exactly opposite to the intended effect—may be more likely to bring weapons for self defense.

To date, no case has reached the U.S. Supreme Court challenging the constitutionality of school-based metal detectors. Lower courts have, however, deemed metal detector searches to be administrative in nature; hence they are an exception to the probable cause warrant rule. Metal detector searches are blanket searches, in that students are subjected to them simply because they are students and not because there is any individualized suspicion that they have a weapon. Some civil libertarians see this logic as problematic.

Additionally, critics contend that metal detectors are intrusive, in that once they indicate someone has contraband, that person must endure another, more personal screening. Unfortunately, sometimes officials charged with this work abuse their power, and there have been many instances in which young females allege they were groped while being patted down.

Another problem is that metal detectors sometimes do not work. One issue specific to hand-held detectors is that there is no way school officials can use the wand on every incoming student before the start of the school day. As a result, they often end up saying they are randomly searching students, but actually engage in a regular pattern, such as searching every third student. This pattern is easy to detect, and students interested in smuggling weapons into a school building can simply line up so that they will avoid the detector. Further, students can smuggle items through entrances or windows not staffed with detectors, or others who have passed through can be handed items from those who have not via windows or other openings. Several high-profile cases have illustrated these inadequacies in search policies. In some locations, the detectors are not even operational.

Critics contend that schools are not and should not be considered the same as airports or courtrooms. First, students are required to attend school through compulsory education laws. Second, the time spent in a school is significantly greater than that spent in airports or courtrooms, for the most part. Third, schools have a different purpose than do these locations. Ideally, educators will develop quality relationships with students, rather than accusing them of wrongdoing, which is what a metal detector does. Instead of investing time, money, and resources on metal detectors, experts suggest that schools should focus on prevention programming and identifying struggling students so that they can stop weapons-related violence from occurring.

Laura L. Finley

Further Reading

Beger, R. (2002). Expansion of police power in public schools and the vanishing rights of students. *Social Justice, 29*(102), 119–130.

Dedman, B. (2006, October 3). Does every school need a metal detector? *MSNBC*. Retrieved May 3, 2010, from http://www.msnbc.msn.com/id/15111439/

Diguilio, R. (2001). *Educate, medicate, or litigate? What teachers, parents, and administrators must do about student behavior.* New York: Corwin.

Ferraracio, M. (1999). Metal detectors in the public schools: Fourth Amendment concerns. *Journal of Law and Education, 28*(2), 209–229.

Finley, L., & Finley, P. (2004). *Piss off! How drug testing and other privacy violations are alienating America's youth.* Monroe, ME: Common Courage.

Morris, N. (2008, January 21). Teachers back metal detectors for schools. *The Independent (UK)*. Retrieved May 3, 2010, from http://www.independent.co.uk/news/education/education-news/teachers-back-metal-detectors-for-schools-771385.html

Middle East and School Crime and Violence

Assessing school violence in the Middle East is difficult because there are so many potential compounding and contributing factors. First, defining what makes up the region known as the Middle East is a rather convoluted question. For the purpose of this discussion, the Middle East refers to any of several countries in southwest Asia, including the Persian Gulf states, northern Africa, and the nations of Pakistan and Afghanistan. This region has experienced near-constant political turmoil throughout the 20th century and now into the 21st century. Furthermore, it is a region of great cultural, religious, and linguistic diversity, all of which can contribute to division and violent conflict. Societies within this region are at various levels of economic development and modernization. With this diversity in mind, it is difficult to make any sweeping generalizations about the condition of school violence in the region. The aim of this article is to highlight incidents of school violence from the region, discuss some of the underlying factors, and address measures being taken to mitigate the incidence of school violence in the Middle East.

Violence in the Middle East can be broken down into three key categories: violence perpetrated by teachers, violence perpetrated by students, and gender-based violence. Violence perpetrated by teachers generally takes the form of corporal punishment, which is widely employed as a form of school discipline and includes physical violence, sexual violence, verbal assault, and public humiliation. In a study conducted by the United Nations Children's Fund (UNICEF) in Jordan that was released in 2007, researchers found that more than half of all students in Jordan are subjected to some form of physical abuse or aggressive behavior as a form of punishment in school.

This violence is not restricted to the classroom, but is commonplace within homes as well. Statistics show that more than two-thirds of Jordanian students experience verbal abuse in the home, while more than half experience physical abuse in the classroom. The social and political climate in Jordan is currently strained due to the ongoing conflict occurring within the Gaza strip. Many of the abusive disciplinary measures in Jordanian schools are directed toward children of refugees—children who witness violence around them every day in poverty-stricken refugee camps. Teachers attribute their application of harsh disciplinary methods to a need to create order in an already strained circumstance. Countering this argument, advocates for change in school violence suggest that the strained social and political circumstances make it all the more important that children have a place to learn where they feel safe.

In November 2008, the United Nations Agency for Palestinian Refugees led an initiative to reduce conflict and violent incidents within schools. This initiative is being implemented in UNRWA (United Nations Relief and Works Agency) schools throughout Jordan, Lebanon, Syria, the West Bank, and Gaza. Students have also been taking matters into their own hands. In Jordan, a group of students organized on Universal Children's Day (November 19) and called for a change to the statute that accorded leniency to perpetrators of child abuse.

The violence being perpetrated within classrooms is not entirely one sided, however. Incidents of student violence against teachers are on the rise in Saudi Arabia, despite the severe standards of corporal punishment for students. One teacher was photographed and recorded being beaten until black and blue and falling unconscious at the hands of a student whose grade the teacher refused to change. In another incident, a teacher was held at gunpoint while his car was torched after he reported on students who had been joyriding outside the school building.

Teachers in Saudi Arabia are naturally alarmed by these incidents, and are imploring the government to enforce a stricter penal system. Some believe, however, that the existing model of physical violence and severe punishments inflicted by teachers lies at the heart of the student violence. Muhammad Rajab, a 16-year-old student from a private high school in Jeddah, has noted that many students come from a privileged background and "they generally don't listen to teachers because of this. They don't like being told what to do." Said Rajab, "I remember a pupil who beat up a teacher because he told him not to cheat in exams." Rajab went on to say that he believed some of the responsibility lay with teachers and their behavior in the classroom: "Our supervisors would sometimes take off their Igals [the black ring worn by Saudi men over their headscarves] and beat pupils who don't go to class." Another student interviewed said of the violence against teachers, "To save face and to prove that they are stronger, pupils naturally react aggressively. What goes around comes around."

School violence against women is particularly worrisome in the Middle East. This violence, which is perpetrated both by fellow students and by teachers, is largely verbal, moral, and sexual in nature. Assertive behavior that is met with severe punishment when perpetrated by boys is even less tolerated when it is perpetrated by girls. In Saudi Arabia, one girl was sentenced to 90 lashes and two months in prison after she hit her teacher on the head with a cup. The courts insisted that the lashes be administered in the classroom in the presence of the girl's peers as a deterrent to bad behavior. While the global community has condemned the country's use of corporal punishment in its schools, the Saudi government insists that such measures are widely approved within the country and help to prevent crime.

While efforts to train teachers and students in practices of gender equity and nonviolent conflict resolution have been proposed by organizations such as UNICEF, much progress remains to be made. Greg Mortenson, an American humanitarian and author of *Three Cups of Tea*, has founded an organization called the Central Asia Institute that has built more than 130 schools throughout Pakistan and Afghanistan. Mortenson has made one of his primary objectives the education of girls in particular, and is currently educating 58,000 students through Central Asia Institute schools.

One initiative, spearheaded by UNICEF, has been working to address all three forms of school violence discussed in this article. "Stopping Violence, Starting in Schools" was the title given to a live chat forum in which students from Tunisia, Yemen, Palestine, and Morocco were asked to respond to a series of questions regarding their experiences with school violence and their recommendations for change. In the ensuing dialogue, students talked about what they saw as underlying the violence in their schools and what they thought would be the most effective means for change. A summary of the students' views follows:

Causes Underlying Violence in Middle Eastern Schools

- The style of corporal punishment, involving physical violence and public humiliation of student in front of peers, that is employed by teachers
- Lack of interest or ability on the part of the school administration to resolve the issues of school violence, as they seem to side with school personnel regardless of the circumstance
- Failure to enforce existing laws or rules in place regarding violence in school
- Lack of dialogue in schools about violence because the school has a tendency to downplay the existing violence
- Low socioeconomic status and family circumstances of students
- Violent environmental conditions, such as the presence of war
- According to the female students, being female, as they felt they were exposed to more violence than male students
- In schools where parents pay tuition, school personnel are more cautious in their use of violence against students

Student-Suggested Solutions to Violence in Middle Eastern Schools

- Punishment should not be employed as a form of discipline in schools, and there should be repercussions for teachers who employ violence in the classroom.
- The formation of participatory committees including parents, students and teachers would enable them to try to resolve the issue of violence in schools.

- Having trained teachers and psychologists to respond to conflicts and violence would be helpful.
- The formation of extracurricular clubs in sports or the arts would give students creative outlets as an alternative to violence.
- School structures should not be placed next to rivers and woods where gangs could be hiding.
- Rules regarding weapons, violence, and gang activity at the school must be consistently enforced.
- In countries with child parliaments, school violence could be addressed as an issue at a high political level.

Finally, students concluded that if children's rights are not acknowledged in the Middle East, then the conversation about violence in schools is useless.

This conference, which was hosted by UNICEF, was intended as a precursor to an International Colloquium titled "Towards a School of Dialogue and Respect" that was held in Tunis. Based on its results, it would seem that students, parents, teachers, and administrators will need to engage in open dialogue about the sources of school violence in the Middle East before transformation in school violence can be accomplished.

Megan Barnes

Further Reading

Clinton, C. (2002). *A stone in my hand*. Cambridge, MA: Candlewick Press

IRIN. (2008). Middle East: UNRWA moves to combat violence in its schools. Retrieved February 7, 2010, from http://www.IRINnews.org

Mortenson, G., & Relin, D. (2006). *Three cups of tea*. London: Penguin Books.

Reuters. (2010). Teenager faces lashing for school violence. Retrieved February 7, 2010, from http://www.iol.co.za/

Shaikh, H. (2007). Violence in Saudi Arabia schools on the rise. Retrieved February 7, 2010, from http://www.khaleejtimes.com.

UNICEF. (2005). Young people speak out against violence in schools. Retrieved February 7, 2010, from http://www.unicef.org/voy

Middle Schools and Crime and Violence

Serious violent victimization rates were lower at school than away from school from 1992 through 2004. An online edition is available with up-to-date information. During that same period, the violent crime rate at school dropped by 54%

and thefts at school declined by 65%. During this span, middle school students (those from 12 to 14 years old) were more likely than older students (15 to 18 years old) to be crime victims at school. Additionally, while overall gang offenses in public schools are down, studies show gang offenses rising in middle schools. Some police officials are concerned that middle schools are emerging as epicenters of gang activity and recruitment, with more and more students are forging their first gang ties at ever younger ages. In interviews with 50 current and former gang members and their associates, researchers found that 75% of gang members joined these organizations by age 14 and 25% joined by age 12.

While overall crime statistics and school-based crimes have decreased in recent years, specific concerns have arisen regarding crimes, violence, and bullying on middle school campuses. As a result of zero-tolerance school violence policies put into effect as a response to the incident at Columbine High School and out of concern for school safety, middle school campuses often employ harsh disciplinary consequences for behavioral infractions. One school in Chicago is reported to have had 25 of its students, aged 11 to 14, arrested for participating in a food fight in the school cafeteria. A Madison, Wisconsin, sixth-grader was suspended and told he would be expelled for a year when he brought a steak knife to school to dissect an onion for a class science project. An 11-year-old girl was suspended for drawing stick figures of her teachers with arrows through their heads. A 10-year-old Florida girl was suspended after she pointed an oak leaf she was pretending was a gun at classmate. Thirty states have also adopted laws to address bullying prevention in recent years. For example, one New Jersey program sends middle and high school students who demonstrate at-risk bullying behaviors to a five-day out-of-school educational and rehabilitation program.

Critics of the zero-tolerance policies agree that children involved in high-risk behaviors should face some discipline or punishment, but argue that subjecting children to mandatory suspensions for these minor types of infractions does more harm than good. Some recent data indicate racial disparities among those students who receive harsh discipline. The Ohio Department of Education found that, in 297 districts that divided their discipline data by race, 252 districts disciplined blacks more frequently than whites. Those figures reflect nationwide trends.

Most critics of zero-tolerance would prefer more school autonomy in choosing appropriate consequences for offenses committed by students. A wide array of promising interventions and strategies exist for addressing problem behaviors, including positive behavioral interventions and supports. Some use graduated sanctions, promote positive overall school environments, and provide wraparound services for students with more-extensive needs. Some focus on individual classroom rules and interventions, because bullying often takes place inside classrooms and within groups of students who know one another. Some recommend practices that push students to examine their actions and make amends to those whom they hurt.

Doreen Maller

Further Reading

NSSC review of school safety research. (2006, December). Retrieved March 1, 2010, from http://www.schoolsafety.us/pubfiles/school_crime_and_violence_statistics.pdf

Schabner, D. (2008, May 8). Schools suspend for doodles and dye jobs. Retrieved March 1, 2010, from http://abcnews.go.com/US/story?id=91666&page=1

Stop Bullying Now. (n.d.). Retrieved March 1, 2010, from http://www.stopbullyingnow.hrsa.gov/kids/default.aspx

Wald, J., & Lisa, T. (2010, February 22). Taking school safety too far. Retrieved February 28, 2010, from http://www.edweek.org/ew/articles/2010/02/24/22wald.h29.html?tkn=UMPFYKxBS5qhfDNuWUX98T7cQIGVJQlfEw6K&cmp=clp-edweek

Zapotosky, M. (2009, October 27). In N. Va., mixed news about gang activity. *The Washington Post*. Retrieved February 28, 2010, from http://www.washingtonpost.com/wp-dyn/content/article/2009/10/26/AR2009102603038.html

Monitoring the Future Survey

The Monitoring the Future (MTF) survey is administered every spring to approximately 50,000 total students randomly selected in grades 8, 10, and 12. Surveys are administered annually at approximately 420 public and private middle schools and high schools that are representative of the U.S. student population at each of the three grade levels. As many as 350 students from each school can be selected to fill out survey questionnaires, whenever possible, in a classroom and during a regular class period. At schools with fewer than that number of students, all students are invited to participate. In schools with more than 350 students, a subsample is selected. The survey is funded by the National Institute on Drug Abuse at the National Institute of Health (NIH) and administered by the Survey Research Center in the Institute for Social Research at the University of Michigan, Ann Arbor.

The MTF survey was first administered in 1975 to 12th graders, when it was known as the *National High School Senior Survey*. Since 1991, the survey has included respondents in the 8th and 10th grades. A random sample of each graduating class is determined, and every two years a questionnaire is mailed to the home address of each student selected, along with a self-addressed, stamped envelope for return of the survey and nominal monetary compensation for its completion.

Survey and follow-up questionnaire respondents are asked about legal and illicit drugs, crime, social and ethical views, environmental issues, the changing roles of women in society, and social institutions. The same set of questions is asked of each cohort over a period of years, when enables researchers to compare the answers to individual questions and determine if, and how, the behaviors and attitudes of young people in the United States are changing.

According to the Survey Research Center, the study's design allows researchers to examine four kinds of changes: (1) changes connected to environment (e.g., middle school, high school, college, workplace) or transitions in life (e.g., moving out of the parent's home, marriage, parenthood); (2) period effects, or changes across all the age groups surveyed during a particular year; (3) age effects, or developmental changes that show up consistently in survey panel after survey panel; and (4) cohort effects, or consistent differences observed between class cohorts over time. Government officials, policymakers, health officials, and researchers use the results and general trends of the MTF survey to monitor the behaviors and attitudes of adolescents and young adults throughout the United States.

Richard Mora

Further Reading

National Institute of Health, National Institute of Drug Abuse. (December 15, 2009). Monitoring the Future survey. Retrieved from http://www.drugabuse.gov/drugpages/MTF.HTML

Survey Research Center in the Institute for Social Research at the University of Michigan. (January 22, 2010). Monitoring the future. Retrieved from http://monitoringthefuture.org/

Moral Panics and Campus Crime and Violence

Reports often indicate fears that violence in society is on the rise, especially on high school and college campuses throughout the United States. While there might be some validity in these concerns, they are often the result of what sociologists, psychologists, and criminologists term a moral panic. A moral panic can be defined as the occurrence of widespread fear about a perceived threat to societal values and interests. It is important to highlight that the threat is perceived, and might have little bearing in reality. Moral panics can arise out of new developments, such as concern over cybercrime due to rapidly changing Internet technologies, or can be based on problems that have existed prior to the panic and will likely persist long after the panic fades away, such as youth violence and illicit drug use.

Moral panics have arisen throughout history. In the 17th-century America, for example, Puritans became hysterical about the presence of witches, giving rise to widespread witch-hunts. At the time, many women (and a few men) were arrested and killed because they were believed to be witches. From a modern-day vantage point, this panic seems absurd, but it was a real concern at the time. Even today, some religious denominations are concerned by witchcraft and perceived occult activities. In the 18th century through to contemporary times, the older and middle-aged members of most generations have voiced serious concerns about the moral decay of the youth of their time, especially in relation to adolescent violence. Specific concerns often go away over time or are indoctrinated into legislation to prohibit the activity, which usually has little success in curbing the issue.

Violence on campuses throughout North America is an important social concern. It is not a new issue, however, nor is it an issue that can be solely linked to crazed students on sprees of violence. For instance, in 1966, Charles Whitman killed 14 people and injured 32 more at the University of Texas. In 1976, a custodian at California State University in Fullerton shot nine people in the school library, killing seven of them. In 1989, Marc Lépine killed 14 people before killing himself at a university in Montreal in Canada. In 1991, a graduate student named Gang Lu at the University of Iowa killed five people. In 2007, Seung-Hui Cho killed 32 people at Virginia Tech. While the number of victims in the Virginia Tech shootings is alarming, so is the number of victims of shootings on college campuses over the last 40 years. These examples reveal that serious violence on college campus is not a new phenomenon in the United States and is not perpetrated strictly by students. Likewise, in the 1970s, many students were killed on U.S. college campuses during important political protests; their deaths occurred at the hands of law enforcement officials. At Kent State University in 1970, four protestors against the American invasion of Cambodia were killed and nine others were injured by the National Guard. Also in 1970, two students were killed and 12 others injured when police began firing on student protestors at Jackson State College.

In general, school shootings on college campuses in the United States are infrequent. When they do occur, they garner major media attention, inciting new fears about the moral degeneration of America's youth. While rooted in actual events, the subsequent fears that no campus in the United States is safe probably do not warrant the increased security measures and precautions taken in the wake of such incidents. After each school shooting, moral panics develop that youth are out of control, violence is rising, violent crime is becoming more commonplace, and students are no longer safe at their schools. While some of these concerns might be legitimate, they are not recent phenomena.

Various theories have been proposed to explain how and why moral panics develop. Some suggest that humans have an innate sense of panic, which serves as a survival instinct. Others contend that the creation of a culture of fear is in the interest of the capitalist elite or the ruling class, as it leads people to become mindless consumers of products and services that make more money for the already wealthy. Similarly, many individuals and groups are reliant on the construction of crime for their livelihood, such as police officers, government officials, researchers, and members of the media. When panics arise, individuals working in the area of the panic see a rise in the amount of funding that they are provided. It can also be argued that moral panics are developed by moral entrepreneurs, or people who have a specific interest in pushing a particular social issue. For example, groups whose operation centers on the promotion of gun control laws in the United States have a vested interested in believing and revealing that crimes on campus that are perpetrated by guns are on the rise. Others suggest that the rise and spread of new media are contributing to the development of moral panics, as new images of violence on campus are being instantaneously broadcast on television, radio, and the Internet, reaching more people, faster than ever before.

Curtis Fogel

Further Reading

Cohen, S. (2002). *Folk devils and moral panics*. London: Routledge.

Critcher, C. (2003). *Moral panics and the media*. Buckingham, UK: Open University Press.

Erickson, K. (2005). *Wayward Puritans: A study in the sociology of deviance*. Boston: Allyn and Bacon.

Pearson, G. (1984). *Hooligan: A history of respectable fears*. New York: Schocken Books.

Thompson, K. (1998). *Moral panics*. London: Routledge.

Moral Panics and High School Crime and Violence

A moral panic is an episode or period of community fear or hysteria generated by a perceived social crisis or emergency. The term *moral panic* was coined by sociologist Jock Young in the early 1970s and popularized by sociologist Stanley Cohen in a 1973 book, *Folk Devils and Moral Panics: The Creation of the Mods and Rockers*. It is used to designate a response to a condition, episode, person, or group of persons that society defines as a threat to societal values and interests. A moral panic is predicated on an exaggerated fear—that is, it occurs when a community becomes unnecessarily alarmed or, at least, reacts with more alarm than is warranted by a sober assessment of the evidence.

Examples of moral panics include the witch scares of Medieval Europe and 17th-century Salem, Massachusetts, the anti-Communist crusades of the 1920s and 1950s, and, to some extent, the fear of Muslim fundamentalism that has occurred in the wake of the September 11, 2001, terrorist attacks. The United States' "War on Drugs" has also been described as a moral panic. There have also been regional moral panics over claims that Satanic ritual abuse and child molestation were escalating in certain geographic areas.

In the context of school violence, the national response to widely publicized school shootings in the late 1990s can be described as a national moral panic. It seemed to many Americans of the period that an epidemic of mass school shootings had struck U.S. schools. Children seemed to be obtaining firearms and explosives and going to schools to kill their classmates and teachers in escalating numbers. The fear of school violence led many parents to make school safety a high priority, and some parents even took their children out of the public schools altogether.

Moral panics often lead to political movements and the passage of legislation and other reforms. The moral panic over school violence in the 1990s has been identified with increases in security measures and spending at many schools. The "zero tolerance" policies already in place in many schools in the early 1990s were bolstered and applied even more stringently by the late 1990s as a result of this trend. Today, more than 80% of U.S. schools have zero-tolerance policies in place requiring any violence or threats of violence to be punished by suspension or expulsion. Metal detectors and security guards are in place at many schools where they did not exist previously. Policies in most jurisdictions now require school staff and administrators to report all threats and suggestions of threats to law enforcement authorities.

In many cases, the response of school authorities has been overwhelming and exaggerated, out of proportion to the supposed threat. Concern over school violence has led many school districts to suspend and expel larger numbers of students during the first years of the 21stcentury. Under the zero-tolerance policies now in place in most schools, students have been expelled for shooting paper clips with rubber bands at other students and possessing manicure kits containing metal fingernail files. Shooting spitwads or throwing crumpled pieces of paper has gotten some students suspended. Some students have even been incarcerated for saying things like "I'm going to get you" or writing scary Halloween stories with discussions of school violence.

Growing numbers of students have also been arrested and processed through the criminal justice system over school-related incidents. Tremendous attention is now paid to preventing weapons and violence in schools, even though the most frequent disciplinary matters occurring in most schools continue to be tardiness, class absences, disrespect. and noncompliance. Social scientists have suggested that the unbalanced focus on preventing violence in schools is an exaggerated response to unrealistic fears regarding school shootings.

Researchers have also documented consistent over-representations of low-income and minority students among students expelled and suspended from school under zero-tolerance policies. Under the tough antiviolence policies imposed on most school districts in the wake of the Columbine High School, Pearl, Mississippi, and Paducah, Kentucky, episodes, African American and Latino students have borne the brunt of suspensions, expulsions, criminal prosecutions, and other punishments directed toward school-related threats of violence. This trend has persisted despite the fact that the perpetrators of the vast majority of multiple-victim school shootings have been white, middle-class students.

Panic regarding school violence has also been directed at various cultural influences on children and adolescents, such as Stephen King's novel *Rage*, the film *The Basketball Diaries*, and violent video games. In the wake of some school shootings, such as the killing of three girls at West Paducah, Kentucky, in 1997, bereaved family members sued video game makers and film producers for contributing to the violence. For the most part, such lawsuits have proved unsuccessful; however, the distributors of media with violent content have been forced to invest large amounts of money in legal representation and defense.

The overreaction of school administrators and policymakers to mass school violence episodes is highlighted by injury risk data covering many years. Statistics gathered by the Justice Policy Institute and the U.S. Department of Education indicate that crime has actually decreased substantially in U.S. public schools since 1990. Less than 1% of all violent incidents involving adolescents occur on school grounds. Statistically, a child is three times more likely to be struck by lightning than to die violently at a school. Schools are safer than all other places where children gather, including homes and cars.

Sociologist Donna Killingbeck has pointed out the astounding overemphasis on school violence that has typified crime coverage in recent years. Although school shootings represented only 0.4% of homicides in the 15- to 24-year-old age group during 1998, "Network evening news crime coverage [of school shootings] represented nine percent of ALL network evening news crime coverage in 1998" (Killingbeck, 2001, p. 191). Also, although accidents were by far the leading cause of death for 15- to 19-year-olds in 1998, such accidents were the topic of only 5% of national news reports.

The phenomenon of moral panics says something about human social psychology. Decades of research by social scientists has established that people tend to adhere to the political, ideological, and social views of the majority, even when such views are demonstrably false. For example, people in groups tend to repeat assessments of beauty and some geometric measurements given by their peers. With regard to social risks, people tend to respond to perceived risks that create immediate fear among others in their communities with more alarm than they do with regard to more real risks to their lives.

Roger I. Roots

Further Reading

Cohen, S. (1972). *Folk devils and moral panics: The creation of the Mods and Rockers*. London: MacGibbon and Kee.

Heaviside, S., Rowand, C., Williams, C., & Farris, E. (1998). *Violence and discipline problems in U.S. public schools: 1996–97* (NCES 98-030). Washington, DC: U.S. Department of Education, National Center for Education Statistics.

Killingbeck, D. (2001). The role of television news in the construction of school violence as a "moral panic." *Journal of Criminal Justice and Popular Culture*, 8(3), 186–202

Sunstein, C. (2002). The laws of fear. Review of *The Perception of Risk*, by Paul Slovic. *Harvard Law Review, 115*, 1119–168.

Movies and School Crime and Violence

What, if any, are the connections between media violence and violence in schools? Does media violence *cause* violence in schools? Does exposure to media violence desensitize media consumers? To use Freedman's (2002) analogy, is media a villain or a scapegoat? These questions underlie research on the effects of media violence in society, and public discussion about precipitating factors that are thought to *cause* youth violence.

Public concern about violence in movies (as well as video games and television) has been a continual theme in analyses of media violence, even while many people insist that movies are "just entertainment." For media analysts such as Leistyna and Alper (2007), such a perspective is naïve. Specifically referring to television, they argue that "[i]t is precisely because we believe television is merely entertainment that we need to take its power and influence seriously" (p. 55). Similarly, Tisdell (2008) argues that "media have the power both to educate, when people critically reflect on the messages they are getting through the media, and to 'miseducate,' when viewers are passive consumers who don't think much about the images and messages that they are receiving" (p. 49). Giroux (1999) makes a more emphatic claim, that media culture "has become a substantial, if not the primary, educational force in regulating the meanings, values, and tastes..." and that it "defines childhood" (pp. 2–3).

Media, then, including movies, constitute a "process of influence" (Potter, 2003, p. 53) in society. In his extensive review of the scientific research on the effects of media violence on youth, Freedman (2002) concludes that there is "fairly good evidence" (p. 194) that media violence is correlated with aggressiveness of youth. Highly aggressive boys tend to be drawn to violent media more strongly than are less aggressive boys. For many people, the link between violence in movies and television and violent youth crimes seems obvious. However, as Freedman points out, correlation is not the same as causation. Among other problems, correlation does not account for the influence of intervening variables. Additionally, Freedman notes that correlation coefficients among various studies are not consistent, and that the strength of the relationship has been found to be weak across numerous studies. Violent movies, then, do not *cause* violence in schools, even if they are an influence in society and upon youth.

Nevertheless, journalists, politicians, judges, and religious leaders (among others) often point an accusing finger at various forms of media to perpetuate the idea that violence depicted in films and other media *causes* violence in society, including schools. In the documentary film *Bowling for Columbine*, for instance, the aggressive music of so-called shock rocker Marilyn Manson was repeatedly cited by conservative politicians and religious leaders as one of the causes of the Columbine High School massacre that took place in 1999. This artist's music, they concluded, should be banned and his concerts canceled. More generally, the perception that rates of youth violence have increased because of youth's embrace of violent media is widespread. In reality, such rates have declined since the early 1990s, even though homicides resulting from violence in schools have increased.

As an influential but not causal factor in society, violence in movies—and particularly in action films—has been implicated in male-perpetrated violence against women, as well as against other men. As Kaufman (1990) observes, Arnold Schwarzenegger declaring, "Consider this a divorce," as he blows his wife away in *Total Recall* is presented as justifiable homicide, suggesting that the woman deserved what she got. In one screening of *The Shining* men in the audience cheered as Jack Nicholson attacked his wife Wendy, who had been depicted as whiny and irritating, with an ax. Media critic Katz makes a similar observation in Jhally (2002), noting that mainstream media culture typically portrays girls and women as deserving to be dominated and abused by men. In combination with television, video games, and music video media, such violence against women becomes a social narrative that normalizes misogyny and degradation of women, and perpetuates the notion that women should be sexually available, but entirely disposable, to men.

Movie violence has also been considered as a reflection of broader social and political contexts. Reynolds (2007), for example, notes that

> Much of the muscle men action movies of the 1980s served to bolster masculine spirits after the debacle of Vietnam ... and the consequent Vietnam syndrome. In fact, these muscular heroes helped to rewrite our memories of the politics of Vietnam and reconstruct a more "honorable" masculinity. (p. 343)

According to Giroux (1999), the *Rambo* franchise (beginning with *First Blood;*) and other Hollywood action movies epitomized larger-than-life violent masculinity that collectively restored American macho heroism and demonized the Vietnamese people. In the Hollywood rewrite of the Vietnam war during the Reagan era, "[c]hemical warfare, forced settlements, and the burning of villages on the part of the U.S. military were written out of history [and replaced by] a vision of masculinity that resonated with the conservative image of national identity and patriotism that informed the Reagan years" (pp. 151–152).

Depictions of explicit physical violence in movies are just one form of violence presented in these media; relational violence is also shown. Movies and other media provide the public with narratives that glorify and reward behaviors such as revenge, cruelty, ruthlessness, and dominance. For instance, films like *Mean Girls* may normalize relationships among girls and young women that are characterized by nonphysical forms of violence, such as spreading vicious rumors, developing exclusive cliques, and uttering verbal slurs. Similarly, the *American Pie* franchise provides a template for boys and young men where losing one's virginity at almost any cost is legitimate, acceptable, and even celebrated, even if it means that women are sexually objectified and boys are sexually predatory.

Alternatively, perhaps such films merely reflect attitudes and narratives that already exist in society. Either way, films that routinely depict nonphysical forms of relational violence might also be a contributing factor to, even if not a cause of, violence in schools. In their research on bullying in schools, Craig, Pepler, and Atlas (2000), for instance, focus on the ways in which bullying is mostly relational rather than physical. Chesney-Lind and Irwin's (2008) perspective suggests that violence of girls and young women is not on the rise, even if media suggest otherwise:

> it appears that while public fear of the "super-predator" male youth has waned, the public is still very concerned about its female version—the new bad girl, largely because of an unrelenting media hype showcasing images of mean, bad, and violent girls. (p. 31)

Media-driven hype about "bad girls," they add, has not resulted in increased rates of actual violent crime of girls, but "increased surveillance and policing of girlhood" (p. 31).

Overall, North Americans (among other people) consume vast amounts of violence-oriented media. Katz in Jhally (2002) argues that slasher films such as *Friday the 13th, Halloween,* and *I Know What You Did Last Summer* depict not just violence against women, but sexualized violence. Such depictions may be a factor in normalizing sexual assaults of girls and women and teen dating violence perpetrated by young men. Rates of rape in the United States have not declined in the past few years, unlike overall crime rates.

Recently, entertainment in the form of brutality, sadism, and cruelty has proliferated through so-called torture porn films such as the *Saw* and *Hostel* franchises, among others. Are such films merely harmless entertainment, or do they contribute to a generation whose members some believe to be increasingly sociopathic? As Steinberg argues, the power of the media is that appears to be benign. But she also adds that media "have become the oxygen of our existence ... [and that] media affect us all" (p. xiv).

Gerald Walton

Further Reading

Astor, R. A., Pitner, R. O., Benbenishy, R., & Meyer, H. A. (2002). Public concern and focus on school violence. In: L. A. Rapp-Paglicci, A. R. Roberts, & J. S. Wodarski (Eds.), *Handbook of violence* (pp. 262–302). New York: John Wiley & Sons.

Carpenter, J. (Director). (1978). *Halloween* [motion picture]. Las Angeles, CA: Compass International.

Chesney-Lind, M., & Irwin, K. (2008). *Beyond bad girls: Gender, violence, and hype.* New York: Routledge.

Craig, W. M., Pepler, D. J., & Atlas, R. (2000). Observations of bullying on the playground and in the classroom. *International Journal of School Psychology, 21,* 22–36.

Cuklanz, L. M., & Moorti, S. (2009). *Local violence, global media: Feminist analyses of gendered representations.* New York: Peter Lang.

Cunningham, S. (Director). *Friday the 13th* [motion picture]. Las Angeles, CA: Georgetown Productions.

Freedman, J. L. (2002). *Media violence and its effect on aggression: Assessing the scientific evidence.* Toronto, ON: University of Toronto.

Gillespie, J. (Director). (1997). *I know what you did last summer* [motion picture]. Las Angeles, CA: Columbia Pictures.

Giroux, H. (1999). *The mouse that roared: Disney and the end of innocence.* New York: Rowman and Littlefield.

Goldstein, J. (1998). *Why we watch: The attractions of violent entertainment.* New York: Oxford University Press.

Jhally, S. (Director). (2002). *Tough guise: Violence, media, and the crisis in masculinity* [motion picture]. Northampton, MA: Media Education Foundation.

Kaufman, M. (1990, December 6). A letter to Marc Lépine. *Toronto Star*, p. A23.

Kirsh, S. J. (2006). *Children, adolescents, and media violence: A critical look at the research.* Thousand Oaks, CA: Sage.

Kotcheff, T. (Director). (1982). *First blood* [motion picture]. Las Angeles, CA: Anabasis.

Kubrick, S. (Director). (1980). *The shining* [motion picture]. Las Angeles, CA: Warner Bros.

Leistyna, P., & Alper, L. (2007). Critical media literacy for the twenty-first century: Taking our media seriously. In D. Macedo & S. R. Steinberg (Eds.), *Media literacy: A reader* (pp. 54–78). New York: Peter Lang.

Moore, M. (Director). (2002). *Bowling for Columbine* [motion picture]. Las Angeles, CA: Alliance Atlantis Communications.

Nakaya, A. C. (2008). *Media violence.* San Diego, CA: Referencepoint Press.

Potter, W. J. (2003). *The 11 myths of media violence.* Thousand Oaks, CA: Sage.

Reynolds, W. (2007). Under siege and out of reach: Steven Seagal and the paradox and politics of new age masculinity. In D. Macedo & S. R. Steinberg (Eds.), *Media literacy: A reader* (pp. 340–352). New York: Peter Lang.

Roth, E. (Director). (2005). *Hostel* [motion picture]. Las Angeles, CA: Hostel.

Steinberg, S. R. (2007). *Media literacy: A reader.* New York: Peter Lang.

Steinberg, S. R. (2007). Reading media critically. In D. Macedo & S. R. Steinberg (Eds.), *Media literacy: A reader* (pp. xiii–xv). New York: Peter Lang.

Strasburger, V. C., & Wilson, B. J. (2002). *Children, adolescents, and the media.* Thousand Oaks, CA: Sage.

Tisdell, E. J. (2008). Critical media literacy and transformative learning: Drawing on pop culture and entertainment media in teaching for diversity in adult higher education. *Journal of Transformative Education, 6*(1), 48–67.

Verhoeven, P. (Director). (1990). *Total recall* [motion picture]. Las Angeles, CA: Carolco International.

Wan, J. (Director). (2004). *Saw* [motion picture]. Santa Monica, CA: Lions Gate Entertainment

Waters, M. (Director). (2004). *Mean girls* [motion picture]. Las Angeles, CA: Paramount Pictures.

Weitz, P. (Director). (1999). *American pie* [motion picture]. Las Angeles, CA: Universal Pictures.

Music and School Crime and Violence

For more than half a century, popular music has been widely criticized for contributing to a variety of problematic behaviors among adolescents, ranging from early sexual activity to suicide. Initially, social critics and commentators claimed that popular musicians and bands such as Elvis Presley and the Beatles were encouraging young people to engage in early sexual activity. For example, when Presley first appeared on the Ed Sullivan show in 1956, the home viewing audience was able to see the performer only from the waist up. The cameras focused on the upper portion of Presley's body rather than providing a comprehensive view, because Presley's trademark hip gyrations were considered to be too sexually suggestive for mainstream America, especially for the young viewers of the Ed Sullivan show. Twenty years later, in 1976 the Reverend Jesse Jackson led a campaign to ban "sexy songs" from being played on the radio, citing concerns that songs with sexual references were contributing to high rates of teen pregnancy.

Over the following decades, the criticism of popular music shifted its focus. Rather than highlighting the sexual content of popular music, critics began to condemn popular music for contributing to alcohol use, drug use, and violence among adolescents. For instance, in 1985 Tipper Gore (wife of then Tennessee Senator and later U.S. Vice President Albert Gore) helped found the Parents Music Resource Center, which claimed that some types of rock music such as punk rock and heavy metal were contributing to increased drug use and violence among young people. The Parents Music Resource Center lobbied federal lawmakers to place restrictions on adolescents' access to rock music; as a result of its campaign, parental advisory notices were eventually placed on the packages of music with explicit lyrics.

A little over a decade later, in response to growing concerns about an increase in youth violence—concerns generated by the school shootings in Jonesboro, Arkansas, Littleton, Colorado, Springfield, Oregon, and West Paducah, Kentucky in the late 1990s—President Bill Clinton commissioned the Federal Trade Commission to study the marketing of violent entertainment, inclusive of the marketing of music with violent lyrics. More recently, in 2005 the Reverend Al Sharpton asked the Federal Communications Commission to punish musicians who had become involved in violent activity by denying the musicians airplay on television and radio for a period of 90 days.

Critics of popular music such as Tipper Gore and Al Sharpton charge that it is not only the lyrics and message of the music that contribute to risky behaviors such as alcohol use and violence, but also the lifestyles of the musicians who may serve as role models for young people. Rap music and musicians, in particular, have been widely criticized for encouraging youth violence. In its earliest

U.S. musician Elvis Presley was only shown above the waist on *The Ed Sullivan Show* in 1956 because his hip-shaking dances were considered too suggestive for the home audience. (AP/Wide World Photos)

days, this genre included controversial songs such as "Cop Killer" by Ice-T and "Deep Cover" by Dr. Dre, which have explicitly violent messages. There have also been widely publicized incidents of violence involving rap musicians. For example, during his brief life the enormously popular rapper and actor Tupac Shakur (founder of the rap group Thug Life) was suspected of numerous criminal activities and convicted on several criminal charges, including sexually assaulting a woman in a hotel room and physically assaulting a former employee. In addition to engaging in violent behavior, Shakur was the victim of violence. In 1994, he was shot and robbed while in the lobby of a recording studio in New York City but survived the assault. Two years later, he was again shot, this time in a drive-by incident in Las Vegas. Shakur died in a hospital several days later owing to complications related to the shooting. The aforementioned incidents involving Shakur, plus numerous other incidents of violence involving rap musicians such as Dr. Dre, Snoop Dog, and 50 Cent, have fueled widespread criticism of rap music.

While many individuals and groups have condemned popular music and musicians for encouraging risky behaviors among youth, little empirical evidence exists to indicate that music affects risky behavior (e.g., drug use) or encourages violence. Whereas an abundance of research indicates that viewing violent actions (e.g., violent television programs, violent movies) encourages violent behavior among young people, few scholars have investigated how listening to music with violent lyrics may influence violent behavior among youths. There is a very limited body of research that suggests certain types of music can contribute to hostile attitudes, suicidal behaviors, and the acceptance of violence against women, but there are no empirical studies that indicate a specific genre of music such as heavy metal or rap has a direct impact on levels of youth violence, nor are there any scientific studies that indicate the availability of music with explicitly violent lyrics is correlated with levels of school violence.

Despite the paucity of evidence supporting the contention that music with violent lyrics contributes to violent behavior, a number of individuals and groups have continued to condemn popular musicians for contributing to risky and violent behaviors among youths. For example, in 2007 the police in Colorado Springs claimed that an increase in homicides in the city was linked to violent rap music and the growing number of hip-hop clubs in the city. As previously noted, however, little empirical data exists that proves music with violent lyrics causes violent behavior. Also, there is no empirical evidence to suggest that the availability or popularity of music with violent lyrics has any impact on rates of violent crime. In fact, even though music with violent lyrics remains widely available, the rates of violent crime (inclusive of violent crimes committed by youths and school-associated violent crimes) have decreased at a steady pace since the mid-1990s—a social trend that indicates the availability of music with violent lyrics has little or no affect on levels of youth violence.

Ben Brown

Further Reading

Anderson, C. A., Carnagey, N. L., & Eubanks, J. (2003). Exposure to violent media: The effects of songs with violent lyrics on aggressive thoughts and feelings. *Journal of Personality and Social Psychology, 84*, 960–971.

Associated Press. (2005, March 24). Sharpton complains to FCC about violence in rap, requests penalties. *USA Today* [online version]. Retrieved from http://usatoday.com

Federal Trade Commission. (2000, September). *Marketing violent entertainment to children: A review of self regulation and industry practices in the motion picture, music recording, and electronic game industries.* Washington, DC: Author.

Federal Trade Commission. (2001, December). *Marketing violent entertainment to children: A one-year follow-up review of self regulation and industry practices in the motion picture, music recording, and electronic game industries.* Washington, DC: Author.

Frosch, D. (2007, September 30). Colorado police link rise in violence to music. *New York Times* [online version]. Retrieved from http://www.newyorktimes.com

Lawrence, J. S., & Joyner, D. J. (1991). The effects of sexually violent rock music on males' acceptance of violence against women. *Psychology of Women Quarterly, 15*, 49–63.

Martin, L., & Segrave, K. (1993). *Anti-rock: The opposition to rock n' roll.* Jackson, TN: Da Capo Press.

Stack, S., & Gundlach, J. (1992). The effect of country music on suicide. *Social Forces, 71*, 211–218.

Muslims and School Crime and Violence

Although faith can bring people together, it is also the one of the primary reasons for violent conflict throughout human history. Despite the fact that the United States was founded on the principle that all should be free to practice their religious beliefs, people who are non-Christian in the United States have often suffered discrimination, harassment, and assault. This situation worsened after the terrorist attacks of September 11, 2001, as many in the nation began to associate Muslim people with terrorism. In the United Kingdom, Muslims suffered increased harassment after a series of terrorist bombings in London in 2005. Throughout both countries, Muslim people—or, in some cases, those who appeared to be Muslim (for instance, men with long beards, people with Arabic last names)—endured verbal and even physical harassment. Many have referred to this fear of Muslims as Islamophobia.

This harassment has also extended to Muslim students at schools and on college campuses. In England, students have reported being harassed and being forced to pray outside on the playground because they were denied access to a room in which to meet, despite a legal obligation schools have to allow for the observance of all religious practices. Most U.K. students report that such bullying and abuse goes unpunished.

France bans Muslim students from wearing head scarves—hijabs—in public schools. Students who wore the hijab were often tormented, yet critics contend a ban is not the best way to resolve bias or to create unity. In September 2010, the French Senate approved a ban on wearing the facial veil—the burqa—in public spaces.

In February 2010, an Arab American Muslim student in the eighth grade at Beckendorff Junior High School in Katy, Texas, was violently assaulted after enduring months of racial and ethnic slurs. His jaw was broken in two places. The boy's family reported that the bullies called their son a terrorist and told him to "go home." Although the school district claimed the victim never reported the bullying, the boy told the Council on American-Islamic Relations (CAIR) that he had reported the bullying at least three times to school authorities.

In October 2010, four teenagers from Staten Island, New York, were charged with hate crime offenses for bullying a Muslim classmate in the previous school year. The bullies frequently called the Muslim boy a "terrorist," spit in his face, and punched him in the groin.

In May 2010, the U.S. Department of Education began an investigation into anti-Muslim harassment in the Minnesota Public Schools in Owatonna and St. Cloud. The investigation into possible civil rights violations was prompted by allegations that students and teachers had harassed Muslim students. Students reportedly shoved bacon into the face of a Muslim student, and a teacher was said to have repeatedly given students a can of air freshener spray and asked them to spray it when Muslim students walked into the classroom. Racial slurs and disparaging comments about Islam were alleged to have been made by students as well as teachers.

In late October 2010, U.S. Education Secretary Arne Duncan cautioned that certain types of bullying—those related to sexual orientation and religion—may violate federal civil rights laws. He implored schools to take these matters seriously and to proactively address bullying.

Recognizing that bullying based on religion worsened during the Gulf War in 1991, the National Union of Teachers in the United Kingdom provided teachers with a booklet in 2003 that demonstrated how to teach about all sides of the war in Iraq and to recognize signs of bullying. CAIR has also developed *An Educator's Guide to Islamic Religious Practices* (available at http://www.cair.com/Portals/0/pdf/education_guide.pdf) to help educators become more sensitive to the needs of their Muslim students.

Campuses also saw an increase in anti-Muslim speech and harassment of Muslim students after the September 11, 2001, terrorist attacks and U.S. invasion of Iraq in 2003. A series of incidents were reported at Yale University directly following the invasion. "Muslim students have felt physical dangers in everyday situations...[been] labeled unpatriotic and therefore terrorists...[and been] ostracized based on their beliefs," says Sumeyya Ashraf, president of Yale's Muslim Student Association (Chitty, n.d., para 9). At the University of California–Los Angeles Medical Center in 2003, Muslim prayer rugs in the chapel, which is nondenominational, were found soaked in pig's blood.

Students are not the only targets of anti-Muslim sentiment. Cases of discrimination against Muslim employees are being investigated at colleges across the United States. CAIR civil rights consultant Hassan Mirza says a Muslim at an Oklahoma university was repeatedly harassed by coworkers, who hung pictures depicting him as a terrorist and labeling him an "al-Qaeda operative." A Muslim woman claims she was fired from her job at a Maryland university for having a copy of the Koran on her computer.

Laura L. Finley

Further Reading

Birkey, A. (2010, May 26). Feds to investigate anti-Muslim activity at Minnesota schools. *The Minnesota Independent.* Retrieved October 27, 2010, from http://minnesotaindependent.com/59348/feds-to-investigate-anti-muslim-activity-at-minnesota-schools

CAIR: Injured Texas Muslim student says he did report bullying. (n.d.). *PR Newswire.* Retrieved October 27, 2010, from http://www.prnewswire.com/news-releases/cair-injured-texas-muslim-student-says- he-did-report-bullying-83824427.html

Chitty, G. (2003, May 9). Anti-Muslim attacks penetrate U.S "hallowed halls of Ivy." *IPS.* Retrieved October 27, 2010, from http://ipsnews.net/interna.asp?idnews=18109

French burqa ban clears last legal obstacle. (2010, October 7). *CNN.* Retrieved October 27, 2010, from http://articles.cnn.com/2010-10-07/world/france.burqa.ban_1_french-burqa-ban-ban-last-year- full-face-veil?_s=PM:WORLD

Samuels, C. (2010, October 27). Bullying may violate civil rights, Duncan warns schools. *Education Week.* Retrieved October 27, 2010. from http://www.edweek.org/login.html?source=http://www.edweek.org/ew/articles/2010/10/27/10bully.h30.html&destination=http://www.edweek.org/ew/articles/2010/10/27/10bully.h30.html&levelId=2100

Schools warned about anti-Islamic bullying. (2003, March 12). *BBC News Roundup.* Retrieved October 27, 2010, from http://news.bbc.co.uk/cbbcnews/hi/uk/newsid_2842000/2842729.stm

Smolowe, J. (2010, October 18). I was bullied. *People,* 66–69.

Staten Island teens charged with anti-Muslim crime. (2010, October 11). *New York Post.* Retrieved October 26, 2010, from http://www.nypost.com/p/news/local/staten_island/staten_island_teens_charged_with_SrukrkbX LjSH4cUwCzuYeK

Tan, S. (2006, November 24). Since 9/11, students bullied for being Muslim in schools. *The Muslim News.* Retrieved October 27, 2010, from http://www.muslimnews.co.uk/paper/index.php?article=2717

N

National School Safety Center

The National School Safety Center (NSSC) was created by a presidential directive in 1984 under a noncompetitive two-year grant from the Department of Justice's Office of Juvenile Justice and Delinquency Prevention (OJJDP). The NSSC represents a partnership between the U.S. Department of Justice, the U.S. Department of Education, and Pepperdine University. It was established to help restore school safety and discipline through a comprehensive national program of training, technical assistance, and coordination. It was modeled after the California School Safety Center, which was established in 1981 in the California State Attorney General's office.

The NSSC's overall goal is to provide a national focus on school safety. Ten tasks originally defined the project:

1. Encourage effective interagency efforts to improve school safety
2. Gather nationwide information on school safety and crime prevention techniques
3. Analyze nationwide legal information regarding school discipline
4. Develop a distinguished national school safety information network
5. Participate in relevant conferences
6. Create a national awards program to recognize exemplary school safety programs
7. Publish a national school safety bulletin
8. Prepare school crime and safety materials for use by educators
9. Conduct a nationwide multimedia school safety campaign
10. Liaise with key officials to provide assistance in the prevention of school crime

Presently, the NSSC's national headquarters are in Westlake Village, California. According to its current mission statement, the NSSC serves as an advocate for safe and secure schools and as an agent for the prevention of school crime and violence. It provides schools with quality information, resources, consultation, and training, and it promotes strategies, practices, and programs that support safe schools. NSSC's communications section conducts a comprehensive national public relations program that includes public service announcements, films, publications, resource papers, articles, conferences, and other promotional activities. Its *School Safety News Service* is published nine times annually and is considered one of the United States' leading school crime prevention news journals. It features topical articles by prominent authors and draws attention to trends and exemplary programs for delinquency prevention and school safety. The NSSC also maintains a resource center with more than 50,000 articles, publications, and films on victim's rights, school security, student discipline, bullying, character development, law-related education, drug trafficking and abuse, school/law enforcement partnerships, public/community relations, and attendance issues. The NSSC's field services section coordinates a national network of educational, legal, business, and civil leaders who cooperate in an effort to maintain safe schools. The field services section provides online training and technical assistance programs.

The NSSC believes that schools have the ability and obligation to create and maintain secure and effective places of learning. It contends further that this work is best done with the help of school safety partners, and that today great opportunities exist to apply the best of school safety research and practices to the vision of safe schools for all students.

Wendell Johnson

Further Reading

National School Safety Center. (October 22, 2009). Retrieved from www.schoolsafety.us

United States General Accounting Office. (1985). *Information on the National School Safety Center: Report to the Honorable Arlen Specter, Chairman, Subcommittee on Juvenile Justice, Committee on the Judiciary, United States Senate.* Washington, DC: Author.

National Threat Assessment Center

The National Threat Assessment Center (NTAC) was established in the United States in 1998 by the U.S. Secret Service with the aim of identifying, assessing, and managing "persons who have the interest and ability to mount attacks against

Secret Service protectees." Its mission is to "provide guidance on threat assessment both within the Secret Service and to its law enforcement and public safety partners."

The NTAC has been involved in conducting studies into attacks that have taken place on public officials and figures, and also within schools. The latter studies followed a rash of school attacks that were viewed with much concern owing to the inability of the authorities to protect every school at all times from every potential threat. To minimize the risk, in 2002, the NTAC conducted a Safe School Initiative (SSI), whereby its investigators studied all of the school shootings and other attacks related to schools that occurred over the period December 1974 to May 2000. This effort involved reviewing police records, school records, court documents, and other material for 37 incidents involving 41 students and ex-students. Investigators were also able to interview a number of the shooters themselves.

Based on these data, the NTAC concluded that most of the shootings were not impulsive, and that some of the shooters had engaged in extensive planning of their attacks. NTAC investigators also found that although there was no single "profile" of a shooter, the overwhelming majority of the students who became shooters had engaged in behavior that worried at least one adult, and sometimes a number of teachers or other staff at the school—and in certain cases, at least some students knew that a shooting might take place but did not warn the school authorities. Some of the shooters had discussed the ideas with others, and a few kept diaries in which they planned the attacks. The NTAC report also found that most of the shooters had used weapons prior to the attack, and that most of the shooting incidents were "stopped by means other than law enforcement intervention."

In May 2002, the NTAC published its report, *The Final Report and Findings of the Safe School Initiative* by Bryan Vossekull and Dr. Robert A. Fein, Directors of the National Violence Prevention and Study Center; Dr. Marisa Reddy of the NTAC; Associate Professor Randy Borum of the University of South Florida; and William Modzeleski, Director of the Safe and Drug-Free Schools Program of the U.S. Department of Education. The organization also published another report, *Threat Assessment in Schools: A Guide to Managing Threatening Situations and Creating Safe School Climates*, and made both reports available for free online.

Justin Corfield

Further Reading

Dedman, B. (1999, June 21). Secret Service is seeking pattern for school killers; Gunmen's motives and behavior examined.*New York Times*, p. A10.
National Threat Assessment Center: http://www.ustreas.gov/usss/ntac.shtml.

National Youth Survey

Beginning in 1976, the National Youth Survey has been administered to adolescents ages 11 through 17, with the purpose of gauging attitudes and behaviors on a variety of topics. The survey, which was created by Delbert Elliott, is run out of the University of Colorado at Boulder's Institute of Behavioral Science and Institute for Behavioral Genetics. The original survey included 1,725 respondents. It is a longitudinal study, so respondents were aged 46 through 55 in 2011. In 1993, researchers began interviewing the partners and the children of the original respondents as well. Consequently, the name of the survey was changed to the National Youth Survey—Family Study in 2000.

The survey is administered in all 50 states and in the District of Columbia, and respondents to the survey were randomly chosen from across the United States. Trained researchers administer the National Youth Survey by interviewing respondents for approximately 90 minutes. Originally, interviews included the young person and his or her parent. Questions address attitudes, beliefs, and values related to both conventional and deviant behavior. They cover problems at home, in neighborhoods, and in schools, including but not limited to victimization, pregnancy, substance abuse, depression, dating violence, sexual activity, school grades, communication with adults and community involvement. The National Youth Survey—Family Study includes additional questions that cover the respondent's family, family relationships, educational attainment, and careers. In the year 2002, researchers began collecting DNA from the respondents.

The current sample has the following demographic characteristics:

- 79% are white
- 15% are African American
- 4.5% are Latino or Hispanic
- 1% are Asian American/Pacific Islander
- 0.5% are Native American
- 53% are male

Several major research articles have been published based on the National Youth Survey, some of which are listed in the "Further Reading" section. The National Youth Survey has also been used in a number of doctoral dissertations.

Laura L. Finley

Further Reading

National Youth Survey—Family Study: http://www.colorado.edu/IBS/NYSFS/index.html

Books

Elliott, D. S., Huizinga, D., & Ageton, S. S. (1985). *Explaining delinquency and drug use.* Beverly Hills, CA: Sage.

Elliott, D. S., Huizinga, D., & Menard, S. (1989) *Multiple problem youth: Delinquency, drugs and mental health problems.* New York: Springer.

Journal Articles

Elliott, D. S. (1994). Serious violent offenders: Onset, developmental course, and termination. *Criminology 32*, 1–22.

Mihalic, S. W., & Elliott, D. S. (1997). Short- and long-term consequences of adolescent work. *Youth and Society 28*(4), 464–498.

National Youth Violence Prevention Resource Center

In the fall of 1999 the White House (under the leadership of President Bill Clinton) created the Council on Youth Violence in response to the series of school shootings that took place the late 1990s, such as the 1997 shootings at Heath High School in West Paducah, Kentucky; the 1998 shootings at Thurston High School in Springfield, Oregon; and the 1999 shootings at Columbine High School in Littleton, Colorado. The initial objective of the Council on Youth Violence was to coordinate federal youth violence prevention activities. In cooperation with the Centers for Disease Control and Prevention and other federal agencies, the Council on Youth Violence developed the National Youth Violence Prevention Resource Center.

The National Youth Violence Prevention Resource Center was created to serve as a clearinghouse of information about youth violence and youth violence prevention strategies, with its overall goal being to make quality information on violence prevention easily available to the public. In addition, the National Youth Violence Prevention Resource Center sought to provide technical assistance in the creation of youth violence prevention programs. As computers and information technology advanced, the Center established a user-friendly website (www.safeyouth.org) through which anyone may readily access a variety of information about youth violence, factors associated with youth violence (e.g., gang activity), and the prevention of youth violence.

The website of the National Youth Violence Prevention Resource Center contains numerous publications about a variety of forms of youth violence, such as bullying, dating violence, and school violence. In addition, it provides information about funding opportunities such as grant announcements and links to directories of funding sources. The website also offers a variety of information about youth violence prevention programs and links to other government websites such as those of the Centers for Disease Control and Prevention and the U.S. Department of Justice, which contain even more publications about effective youth violence prevention programs and strategies.

The numerous links currently available on the website of the National Youth Violence Prevention Resource Center reflect the most recent evolutionary change of the agency. In 2007, the Center altered its mission to include the facilitation of comprehensive community youth violence prevention programs. The agency's new objectives are to provide an online forum that encourages collaboration among local government and community leaders who are trying to prevent youth violence and to provide such individuals with assistance in their efforts to develop and assess youth violence prevention programs and policies.

Ben Brown

Further Reading
National Youth Violence Prevention Resource Center: www.safeyouth.org
U.S. Department of Justice: www.usdoj.gov

Natural Born Killers

Natural Born Killers, a film released in 1994, drew a cult following for its unique cinematography and hyperviolence. The film tells the story of Mickey Knox and his wife Mallory, who go on a cross-country shooting spree. Through flashbacks, viewers learn that Mallory grew up with an abusive father and neglectful mother. Mickey rescues her from that situation, and the two begin their life of crime. When Mickey is arrested for grand theft auto for stealing his father's car, he escapes and gets Mallory; the two then kill her father by drowning him in a fish tank and burn her mother in her bed. Throughout the scene, a canned laugh track can be heard, making it both visually and auditorily disturbing.

The pair continue their killing spree, which includes 48 victims in New Mexico, Arizona, and Nevada. Authorities are pursuing them, as are media sources. Detective Jack Scagnetti seems obsessed with Mallory. Journalist Wayne Gale, host of a TV show *American Maniacs,* which profiles mass murderers, enjoys the ratings he gets when he covers Mickey and Mallory's exploits.

After a strange scene in a desert with a Navajo Indian, Mickey and Mallory are captured and beaten by police. The film jumps ahead to one year later, with the two in prison and set to be moved to a mental institution, having both been judged insane. Mickey agrees to do a live interview with Wayne Gale during the Super Bowl. In it, he declares himself a "natural born killer" and incites other inmates to break free. All hell breaks loose. Mallory ends up killing Detective Scagnetti, and Mickey and Mallory escape with Wayne Gale. They later kill him, with the entire incident being televised. The last scene shows the couple some years later. They are in an RV and Mallory, clearly pregnant, is watching their two children play.

Natural Born Killers was nominated for a Golden Globe Award in 1995 and two MTV movie awards in the same year. Juliette Lewis won the Best Actress award at the 1994 Venice Film Festival for her performance as Mallory, and director Oliver Stone won the Special Jury Prize. Some have called the film a brilliant satire and sociological commentary on media.

Critics contend that *Natural Born Killers* not only glorified violence, but also incited real-life violence among viewers. On March 5, 1995, Sarah Edmondson and Ben Darras, both age 18 at the time, spent the evening together in a cabin in Oklahoma, taking LSD and watching *Natural Born Killers*. Reportedly they viewed the film several times in a row. Early the following morning, they left in Edmondson's Nissan Maxima, armed with a .38-caliber revolver. On March 7, they arrived at a cotton mill in Hernando, Mississippi, where Darras killed William Savage, shooting him twice in the head. The pair then traveled to a convenience store in Ponchatoula, Louisiana, where Edmondson shot store cashier Patsy Byers. Byers survived but was left a paraplegic and eventually died of cancer. Her husband, Lonnie Byers, filed suit against Edmondson and Darras on July 26, 1995, and in March 2006, amended the suit to include Time Warner Entertainment, Oliver Stone, and others associated with the production of *Natural Born Killers*. That portion of the suit was dismissed on January 23, 1997.

Fourteen-year-old Barry Loukaitis, who shot several people in his Moses Lake, Washington, school in 1996, reportedly loved the film and tried to emulate the main character, Mickey. Similarly, 14-year-old Michael Carneal, who killed three students in a Paducah, Kentucky, high school in 1997, loved the film. Attorneys for the parents of Carneal's victims have blamed the media for the shooter's actions, filing a lawsuit in April 1999 against Internet pornography providers, motion picture studios, and computer game manufacturers. The suits were subsequently dismissed. Allegedly, Eric Harris and Dylan Klebold, the Columbine shooters, were fans of *Natural Born Killers* as well.

Laura L. Finley

Further Reading

Kunich, J. Natural born copycat killers and the law of shock torts. *Washington University Law Quarterly, 78,* 1157–1270. Retrieved May 4, 2010, from http://lawreview.wustl.edu/inprint/78-4/1157Kunich.pdf

Natural Born Killers: http://www.imdb.com/title/tt0110632/synopsis
Oliver Stone and *Natural Born Killers* timeline. (n.d.). Retrieved May 4, 2010, from http://www.freedomforum.org/templates/document.asp?documentID=3962

New Jersey v. T.L.O.

On March 7, 1980, a teacher at Piscataway High School in New Jersey happened upon two girls smoking tobacco cigarettes in a school restroom. One of the girls was 14-year-old T.L.O. (a pseudonym). The teacher brought both girls to the assistant vice principal, Theodore Choplick, who interrogated them about the smoking incident. While the other girl admitted to smoking in the bathroom, T.L.O. asserted that she had not.

Suspicious that T.L.O. was lying, Choplick proceeded to open T.L.O.'s purse, which contained a pack of cigarettes. Upon removing the pack of cigarettes, he noticed cigarette-rolling papers, which caused him to believe that the purse might contain marijuana. Choplick then removed all of the purse's contents to reveal a small amount of marijuana, a pipe, several empty plastic bags, an index card listing the names of students who owed T.L.O. money, two letters from students indicating that T.L.O. was supplying marijuana to other students, and a large sum of money in single-dollar denominations. Mr. Choplick then phoned T.L.O.'s mother and turned over all of the contents in the purse to the police. In a confession to police, T.L.O. admitted that she had been dealing marijuana at her high school.

The Juvenile and Domestic Relations Court of Middlesex County, New Jersey, filed delinquency charges against T.L.O. based on the evidence in her purse and her admission of drug dealing at school. T.L.O. moved to suppress the evidence found in her purse, charging that Choplick violated her Fourth Amendment rights by conducting an allegedly unlawful search. As part of the Bill of Rights, the Fourth Amendment protects U.S. citizens against unreasonable search and seizure. It requires judicially approved search warrants to be issued based on probable cause, or the reasonable belief that a person has committed a particular crime. The juvenile court denied T.L.O.'s motion to suppress the evidence, maintaining that a school official does not need a judicial warrant and may search a student if there is "reasonable suspicion" of a crime or "reasonable cause" to believe that the ability to search is necessary to maintain and enforce school discipline policies. On March 23, 1981, the court found T.L.O. to be delinquent and on January 8, 1982, sentenced her to one year's probation. T.L.O. then appealed her conviction. The Appellate Division found no Fourth Amendment violation.

T.L.O. persisted and appealed the Appellate Division's ruling to the Supreme Court of New Jersey. The New Jersey Supreme Court agreed with the lower court that warrantless searches by school officials do not violate the Fourth Amendment as long as the official "has reasonable grounds to believe that a student possesses evidence of illegal activity or activity that would interfere with school discipline and order." However, the majority opinion of the New Jersey Supreme Court held that Choplick did not have "reasonable grounds." Possession of cigarettes did not violate school rules and, therefore, did not necessitate emptying out T.L.O.'s purse. Additionally, the Fourth Amendment prohibits unreasonable searches and seizures by state officials, which includes teachers and administrators. Based on this line of reasoning, the New Jersey Supreme Court reversed the appellate division's ruling and ordered the evidence in T.L.O.'s purse suppressed. The state of New Jersey appealed to the Supreme Court of the United States in *New Jersey v. T.L.O.* (No. 83-712, 469 U.S. 325; argued: March 28, 1984; decided: January 15, 1985).

Justice Byron White delivered the Court opinion. In a 6-3 ruling, the U.S. Supreme Court ruled that the searches by school officials are constitutional without a warrant as long as they are reasonable. The court argued that while schoolchildren should have legitimate expectations of privacy, the school has an equally legitimate responsibility to maintain a positive and safe learning environment. School officials do not need judicial warrants. Instead, school officials are held to the standard of "reasonableness." A school official has the right to search if he or she has "reasonable grounds to believe that a student possesses evidence of illegal activity or activity that would interfere with school discipline and order." According to the Supreme Court, Choplick had reasonable grounds to believe that T.L.O. was engaged in illegal activity.

Mary Christianakis

Further Reading

Alexander, S. M. (2004). Too much protection and, at the same time, not enough: Inconsistent treatment of adolescents by the Supreme Court. *DePaul University Law Review, 53*(3), 1739–1774.

Handler, J.G. (1994). *Ballentine's law dictionary: Legal assistant edition.* Albany, NY: Delmar Publishers.

Mansukhani, S. H. (1995). School searches after *New Jersey v. T.L.O.*: Are there any limits? *Journal of Family Law, 34*(3), 345–385.

New Jersey v. T.L.O. (n.d.). Retrieved December 28, 2009, from http://www.law.cornell.edu/supct/html/historics/USSC_CR_0469_0325_ZS.html

Pinard, M. (2003). From the classroom to the courtroom: Reassessing Fourth Amendment standards in public school searches involving law enforcement authorities. *Arizona Law Review, 45*(1), 1067–1128.

Zane, D. E. (1986). School searches under the Fourth Amendment: *New Jersey v. T.L.O. Cornell Law Review, 72,* 368–390.

No Child Left Behind Act

The No Child Left Behind Act of 2001 (NCLB) had its origin in the July 1998 U.S Department of Education rule called the principles of effectiveness. This rule, which was passed in light of a spike in youth drug use in the 1990s, required school districts receiving state funding to plan and evaluate their drug prevention and response programs that had previously been enacted under the Safe and Drug-Free Schools program. Schools were called upon to conduct needs assessments, establish measurable goals and objectives, and implement and evaluate research-based prevention programs. NCLB expanded these principles to emphasize accountability in education. Schools were to achieve five specific goals: (1) achievement in reading and math; (2) English mastery for students with low proficiency; (3) recruitment and training of highly qualified teachers; (4) establishment of school environments that are drug and violence free; and (5) graduation of all students. School districts received a variety of grants to help them achieve these goals.

To assist school districts, a list of authorized activities was prepared and provided to all grantees. It included some programs that had previously been listed in the Safe and Drug-Free Schools and Communities Act, such as character education and peer mediation. The list did not include some programs that had previously been recommended, including Drug Abuse Resistance Education (D.A.R.E.). Added to the list of approved activities were school resource officers, drug testing, locker searches, and alternative education programs. The list did not identify specific curricula.

A review of schools' responses to NCLB found that only 33% had implemented evidence-based curricula. This number does include some very large districts, however; thus 45% of students had been reached by this effort. The biggest barrier was funding, as school districts insist NCLB is underfunded. During the presidential administration of George W. Bush, student drug testing was emphasized, but many school districts did not implement it because it was too costly. Under NCLB, students enrolled in a school labeled "persistently dangerous" had the right to transfer to a safer school in the district. Although this sounded like a good idea, it gave schools an additional incentive to underreport school crime and violence.

Part of the impetus behind NCLB, which was passed during President George W. Bush's administration and was generally considered a bipartisan effort, was the fear that the United States was lagging behind in international comparisons of student performance. Some civil libertarians even praised NCLB for its focus on poor students, students of color, and those with limited English proficiency. Critics contended that instead of ensuring accountability and high-quality education, the act should be renamed "No Child Left Untested," because it placed far too much emphasis on high-stakes testing. Given that the United States has the most inequitable education system in the industrialized world, where many students attempt to learn in crumbling classrooms with outdated textbooks, the focus on testing means resources cannot be allocated to other necessary areas. Instead, schools are "dumbing down" their curricula, teaching to the test and not for critical thinking, and reducing students' opportunities in the arts, physical education, and other areas of interest so that they can better prepare students to pass standardized tests. Schools that do not make adequately yearly progress (AYP) are labeled as failing and receive less funding.

President George W. Bush discusses the No Child Left Behind Act (2002) at Logan High School in La Crosse, Wisconsin, on May 8, 2002. (The White House)

This capitalist model might work well in other institutions, but in education critics contend it has resulted in the removal of funding from the schools that need it most. By spring 2006, more than 10,000 schools had been placed on the "needs improvement" list. Schools that miss AYP for four years are required to either replace all school staff related to the failure, put in place a new curriculum, decrease management authority of the school, appoint outside experts to advise them on the running of the school, extend either the school year or the school day, or restructure the internal organization of the school. After five years of failing to meet AYP, districts are required to either reopen as a charter school, replace all or most of their staff, contract with a private entity to run the school, institute other significant and approved governance and staffing changes, or turn over operation of the school to the state. Critics maintain that NCLB is simply a tool of conservatives in their effort to dismantle public education.

Additionally, the emphasis on test scores has created incentives for schools to rid themselves of students who are not performing well or are otherwise problematic. Suspensions and expulsions have risen dramatically since 1999, and critics contend NCLB is one of the reasons. Young men of color—in particular, African American males—have been disproportionately impacted. by these trends. A 2006 study by the Civil Rights Project at Harvard University found that NCLB had not improved reading or math achievement, nor had it narrowed the achievement gap.

While campaigning for the presidency, Barack Obama criticized NCLB and its emphasis on testing. Yet critics contend that his administration's plan is virtually the same. Obama and Secretary of Education Arne Duncan agreed to get rid of AYP, but will replace it with some other form of accountability program. The Obama plan sets a deadline of 2020 for all students to be on a path for college and career readiness. While supporters like the fact that the Obama plan includes some provisions for funding arts and other curricula, it includes the controversial notion that teacher pay should be tied to student performance.

Laura L. Finley

Further Reading

Darling-Hammond, L. (2007, May 21). Evaluating "No Child Left Behind." *The Nation*. Retrieved May 4, 2010, from http://www.thenation.com/article/evaluating-no-child-left-behind?page=0,0

Higpen, D. (2009, December 17). Rethinking school discipline. *The Huffington Post*. Retrieved May 4, 2010, from http://www.huffingtonpost.com/david-e-thigpen/rethinking-school-discipl_b_395715.html

Karp, S. (2006, Spring). Band-aids or bulldozers. *Rethinking Schools*. Retrieved May 4, 2010, from http://www.rethinkingschools.org/special_reports/bushplan/band203.shtml

Lee, J. (2006, June). Tracking achievement gaps and assessing the impact of NCLB on the gaps: An in-depth look into national and state reading and math outcome trends. The Civil Rights Project, Harvard University. Retrieved May 4, 2010, from http://www.civilrightsproject.ucla.edu/research/esea/nclb_naep_lee.pdf

Miner, B. (2006, Spring). Why the right hates public education. *Rethinking Schools*. Retrieved May 4, 2010, from http://www.rethinkingschools.org/special_reports/bushplan/righPRO.shtml

No Child Left Behind Act: http://ed.gov/policy/elsec/leg/esea02/index.html

Strauss, V. (2010, March 13). Obama and NCLB: The good—and very bad—news. *Washington Post*. Retrieved May 4, 2010, from http://voices.washingtonpost.com/answer-sheet/education-secretary-duncan/obama-and-nclb-the-good—and-v.html

U.S. Department of Education. (2003). No Child Left Behind: A parents' guide. Retrieved May 4, 2010, from http://ed.gov/parents/academic/involve/nclbguide/parentsguide.pdf

Northern Illinois University Shooting

On February 14, 2008, a lone gunman made his way into an oceanography class at Northern Illinois University (NIU) and began shooting. The killer, Steven Kazmierczak, had completed an undergraduate degree and taken graduate courses in sociology from NIU. On the day of the shooting, the 27-year-old killed five students and wounded 16 others before killing himself. The Valentine's Day tragedy at NIU is considered to be one of the deadliest university shootings in U.S. history, ranking behind only the Virginia Tech massacre, the University of Texas Clock Tower shooting, and the library massacre at California State University, Fullerton. As in other cases of mass murder, authorities soon learned that the perpetrator had a long history of mental illness.

According to many accounts, Steven Kazmierczak's mental problems began long before his involvement in the NIU shootings. In fact, these problems can be traced as far back as his days as a high school student. As a teenager, Steven's mental illness was so extreme that his parents placed him in a psychiatric treatment center. Years later, a former employee of the treatment center recalled that Kazmierczak refused to take his medication and engaged in self-mutilation while at the facility. Ironically, as a graduate student at NIU, Kazmierczak would one day coauthor an academic paper related to self-mutilation. In spite of having a history of mental problems that required hospitalization, he avoided identifying himself with being mentally ill. Some believe, in retrospect, that Kazmierczak's failure to acknowledge his mental illness may have been a significant part of the problem.

While it is true that Kazmierczak had been treated for various mental illnesses, he was successful and even "revered" by some faculty members during his time as a student at NIU. Many faculty members and fellow students found him to be very easy to converse with and affable. He even earned the prestigious Dean's award while pursuing his degree in sociology. Despite Kazmierczak's success at NIU, however, he did possess at least a few idiosyncrasies. In hindsight, these quirks may have been red flags that he had a dark side that was not displayed to his professors. According to one source, for example, Kazmierczak had an infatuation with notorious figures, such as Adolph Hitler and Jeffrey Dahmer. When he was not studying, Kazmierczak also spent much of his free time playing violent video games and watching horror films. Nevertheless, Kazmierczak was an exceptional student while at NIU. He excelled in his classes, tutored other students, and was even able to find a girlfriend.

One can only wonder why Kazmierczak decided to stage his attack at NIU. By many accounts, he was able to thrive during his time at the university, despite his severe psychological problems. In fact, it is widely believed that Kazmierczak was able to function without any type of psychiatric drugs while he was a student at NIU. It was only after he transferred to another school, the University of Illinois at Urbana–Champaign, that he began to unravel. Perhaps the stress of a new place was simply too much for him. Kazmierczak, after all, was described by many as being extremely anxious and obsessive–compulsive. Shortly after moving, he developed an obsession with guns and made frequent trips to the firing range. Also, in 2007, after the horrific Virginia Tech shootings, Kazmierczak is reported to have stated that he admired the manner in which the attack was conducted. He also spoke admiringly about the teenagers responsible for the Columbine High School shootings.

Kazmierczak had a brief stint as a correctional officer after leaving NIU, though it proved to be a very short-lived occupational endeavor. In less than three weeks, he simply quit reporting to work and effectively ended his employment with the prison agency. His personal life also began to suffer. Even though he was living with his on-and-off-again girlfriend, evidence indicates that Kazmierczak began having promiscuous sexual relationships with women he met off the Internet. To cope with his problems, Kazmierczak eventually sought out the services of a mental health professional and was prescribed Prozac. He later quit taking the drug because he was afraid it might make him overweight or give him acne. His discontinuation of his medication did little to help his bizarre behavior and may have exacerbated the problems. Kazmierczak began to act strangely toward his family members. For example, on the Christmas before the NIU shooting, Steven gave his older sister a box of coal as a gift.

In spite of the many warning signs, Kazmierczak's behavior went largely ignored. He was able to obtain a state police-issued firearms owner's card and purchased three pistols and one shotgun; he would later use these weapons during the NIU shootings. In a bizarre coincidence, Kazmierczak also bought handgun accessories from the same online gun dealer who sold a weapon to the Virginia Tech shooter, Seung-Hui Cho. Days before the attack, Kazmierczak began to act especially mysteriously. Although he did not leave behind a suicide note, he sent goodbye presents, including expensive jewelry, to his girlfriend. He also deleted his email accounts and removed both the SIM card from his cell phone and the hard drive from his computer. In retrospect, it was clear that the killer was making his final preparations before the attack.

At approximately three o'clock in the afternoon on Valentine's Day, Kazmierczak entered a large lecture hall at NIU. He is said to have paused briefly before opening fire with a sawed-off shotgun on students sitting in the first row. Kazmierczak emptied the chamber of his shotgun and then reloaded. In total, he fired six shots from his shotgun and 48 shots from three pistols. Many of the victims were killed at point-blank range. Kazmierczak's last bullet was for himself. He committed suicide immediately after his attack on the large group of students. In this respect, his behavior was not unusual, as some mass murderers kill themselves after completing their attacks. Also, Kazmierczak, like many mass murderers, had a severe mental disorder. While he may not have been legally insane, Kazmierczak nevertheless had a long history of anxiety and personality disorders.

Following the NIU attacks, students assembled six white crosses outside of the crime scene. Each of five crosses had the name of a student who had died in the NIU shootings. The final cross bore no name: Kazmierczak's.

Robert Worley

Further Reading

Davey, M. (2008, February 16). Campus shooting spree: Illinois college gunman was "revered" by faculty: Gunman stopped taking medication before rampage. *New York Times*, p. A1.

Heher, A., & C. Rousseau (2008, February 7). Disparate views emerge about killer: Some say student unstable, others recall him as timid. *Houston Chronicle*, p. 7A.

Holmes, R., & Holmes, S. (2001). *Mass murder in the United States.* Upper Saddle River, NJ: Prentice-Hall.

Holmes, R., & Holmes, S. (2009). *Profiling violent crimes: An investigative tool* (4th ed.). Thousand Oaks, CA: Sage.

Tanner, L. (2008, February 7). Role of drugs debated in killings: Experts can't agree what set off graduate student's murderous attack. *Houston Chronicle*, p. 7A.

Thomas, J., Leaf, M., Kazmierczak, S., & Stone, J. (2006). Self injury in correctional settings: "Pathology" of prisons or of prisoners? *Criminology and Public Policy*, 5(1), 193–202.

Vann, D. (2008, August). Portrait of the school shooter as a young man. *Esquire.* Retrieved from http://www.esquire.com/features/steven-kazmierczak-0808

Vu, N. (2008, April 6). Fate of shooting site divides campus. *South Florida Sun-Sentinel*, p. 6A.

Northwestern High School Sex Scandal

On September 16, 2006, Antwain Easterling, the 18-year-old star of Northwestern High's football team, had sex with a 14-year-old girl on the floor of a bathroom in the school. By all accounts, the girl—who was an honor student and band member—consented to the sexual intercourse. Nevertheless, given her age, the act was considered statutory rape. Two other males were arrested with Easterling for lewd and lascivious behavior. Another man, Vincent Shannon Jefferson, was also arrested for statutory rape. Jefferson was 24 years old, and the same girl had said she had sex with him off the school grounds.

The incident might have ended there, but it erupted into scandal when it became clear that school officials knew about the event but covered it up so that Easterling could play in the football state title game, which Northwestern won. Easterling, who had a baby daughter from a different relationship, had already received scholarship offers from Florida, Miami, Rutgers, Wisconsin, and Nebraska. School officials were told about the incident in October 2006. The girl's mother spoke to a guidance counselor and two teachers, and the guidance counselor told the school's principal and two assistant principals. The girl's mother said that Principal Dwight Bernard assured her that he would call the police, but he did not. She contacted the police herself on December 5, which prompted Easterling's arrest. He should have been suspended for 10 days, according to Miami-Dade School Board policy. He was not, nor did he ever receive any sanction from the school. Easterling actually played in the state championship game while out on $7,500 bond. In June 2006, a grand jury released a document showing that at least 17 school employees knew about the incident.

Given the scandal, Easterling had to settle for a lesser-known college. He began playing football for the University of Southern Mississippi in fall 2007. The girl involved in the incident twice attempted suicide and was institutionalized. Bernard was indicted on two charges of third-degree felony official misconduct stemming from a report he wrote about the incident that the grand jury called "riddled with lies." During the trial, Bernard claimed he did not contact police because he did not want to report a false allegation. When the trial concluded in April 2010, Bernard was acquitted on all charges.

Bernard had been fired from his position at Northwestern. A number of other teachers who knew about the incident were fired as well. Athletic Director Gregory Killings resigned from his position in July 2007, after 24 years at the school. Coach Roland Smith and his entire coaching staff were fired. A grand jury report also found that the school district had interfered with the police investigation of the incident and that then-Miami Dade Superintendent Rudy Crew was aware that Easterling had been arrested, yet approved of allowing him to play in the state championship game. In July 2007, Superintendent Crew was considering canceling the entire 2007 football season. The community, long known as tremendous supporters of the team, was outraged. As the season approached, Crew changed his mind, perhaps partly because the team had been ranked first in the nation by *Rise* magazine. They went on to an undefeated season and won another state title.

Laura L. Finley

Further Reading

Finley, P., Finley, L., & Fountain, J. (2008). *Sports scandals.* Westport, CT: Praeger.

Football team faces suspension over sex scandal. (2007, July 11). *NBC Sports.* Retrieved May 4, 2010, from http://nbcsports.msnbc.com/id/19709971/

Navarro, M. (2006, December 8). Easterling charged with sex crime. *Miami Herald.* Retrieved July 11, 2007, from LexisNexis Academic database.

Ovalle, D. (2010, April 30). Ex-Northwestern High principal Dwight Bernard not guilty in sex scandal. *Miami Herald.* Retrieved May 4, 2010, from http://www.miamiherald.com/2010/04/30/1607288/ex-northwestern-high-principal.html

Powell, R. (2007, September 14). Sex scandals, stadium sponsors, and national TV. *Slate.* Retrieved May 4, 2010, from http://www.slate.com/id/2173804